Child Refugee Asylum as a Basic Human Right

AF804628

Sonja C. Grover

Child Refugee Asylum as a Basic Human Right

Selected Case Law on State Resistance

Springer

Sonja C. Grover
Faculty of Education
Lakehead University
Thunder Bay, Ontario
Canada

ISBN 978-3-030-08599-5 ISBN 978-3-319-78013-9 (eBook)
https://doi.org/10.1007/978-3-319-78013-9

© Springer International Publishing AG, part of Springer Nature 2018
Softcover re-print of the Hardcover 1st edition 2018
This work is subject to copyright. All rights are reserved by the Publisher, whether the whole or part of the material is concerned, specifically the rights of translation, reprinting, reuse of illustrations, recitation, broadcasting, reproduction on microfilms or in any other physical way, and transmission or information storage and retrieval, electronic adaptation, computer software, or by similar or dissimilar methodology now known or hereafter developed.
The use of general descriptive names, registered names, trademarks, service marks, etc. in this publication does not imply, even in the absence of a specific statement, that such names are exempt from the relevant protective laws and regulations and therefore free for general use.
The publisher, the authors and the editors are safe to assume that the advice and information in this book are believed to be true and accurate at the date of publication. Neither the publisher nor the authors or the editors give a warranty, express or implied, with respect to the material contained herein or for any errors or omissions that may have been made. The publisher remains neutral with regard to jurisdictional claims in published maps and institutional affiliations.

Printed on acid-free paper

This Springer imprint is published by the registered company Springer International Publishing AG part of Springer Nature.
The registered company address is: Gewerbestrasse 11, 6330 Cham, Switzerland

*With love and in honour of my brother,
Albert Gazan, and in respect for the basic
human rights of all child asylum seekers*

Acknowledgements

I thank my husband Roshan and my daughter Angeline for their love and support without which nothing would seem feasible or as worthwhile struggling to accomplish. I also express my gratitude to Dr. Brigitte Reschke, Executive Editor in Law for Springer, for her support and guidance with the project.

Contents

Chapter 1
Introduction: Contesting Barriers to Child Refugee Asylum

> . . .one voice has not faltered during Europe's refugee crisis: Angela Merkel's. "We will cope," she insists. . .To the critics at home, as the number of asylum seekers swelled over the summer, she said Germany would continue to welcome refugees. Otherwise, she argued, it would "not be my country".[1]

> . . .driven to the limit, de facto statelessness assumes that refugees, at the end of the day, ought to be there, i.e., in their own country, not here, where they are out of place and do not belong. But . . . de facto statelessness, by virtue of its strict opposition to *de jure* statelessness, veils the refugee's displacement, which I take in the strong sense as the lack of an own place.[2]

The foregoing quotes reflect a central aspect of the refugee dilemma; namely 'where does the refugee asylum seeker[3] belong?' Many States and regional organizations of States such as the European Union are, given the current global refugee crisis, grappling with the urgent question of determining precisely what are the State obligations and for which State in respect of: (1) the process for consideration of particular refugee asylum claims of individuals and individuals who are members of an identifiable collective and (2) the possible grant, if any, of asylum; these obligations being set out in various international law instruments and in some cases domestic law but their interpretation yet vigorously debated. Often as not States

---

[1]Nardelli, Alberto. Angela Merkel's stance on refugees means she stands alone against catastrophe The Guardian November 8, 2015. https://www.theguardian.com/commentisfree/2015/nov/08/angela-merkel-refugee-crisis-europe Accessed 27 April, 2017.

[2]Oudejans, N Asylum: A Philosophical Inquiry into the International Protection of Refugees, PhD Dissertation, Tilburg University, p. 10.

[3]The term 'refugee asylum seeker' is used here to refer to (1) a person who, on the facts, is a *bona fide* refugee as per the Refugee Convention or based on other international law and (2) who is seeking asylum and may or may not yet have entered the country in which he/she hopes to be granted asylum and who may or may not have declared their presence to State authorities as a refugee wishing to obtain asylum. The term here then refers to refugees who may or may not have been yet formally recognized as such or granted legal status as a *prima facie* refugee within a prospective asylum State or transit State and who, in any case, have not yet officially received asylum through a fair and impartial legal process considering individual cases on their merits.

© Springer International Publishing AG, part of Springer Nature 2018
S. C. Grover, *Child Refugee Asylum as a Basic Human Right*,
https://doi.org/10.1007/978-3-319-78013-9_1

that might serve as places of refuge for particular groups of asylum seekers earnestly attempt to sidestep the issue of refugee asylum and at times engage also in refoulement in various masked forms.[4] An example of the effort to avoid State obligations under international refugee law includes the initiative to establish so-called 'safe zones'[5] in Syria *as an alternative* to sharing with other States such as Jordan the obligation of offering asylum to those fleeing the barbaric attacks on civilians carried out by ISIS as well as according to, for instance, international NGO's; the Assad regime[6] and also certain proxy armed groups in a conflict involving a dizzying array of armed actors. We will here consider in detail, for example, the Trump travel ban on refugees abroad seeking asylum (refugees who have been cleared medically and in terms of security issues by U.S. authorities and for whom a U.S. resettlement agency has agreed to provide basic services for a time period upon their arrival in the U.S.[7]) and its impact on refugees including child asylum seekers.

This current work addresses (1) the intersection of various domains of international law (refugee law, human rights law including child rights international law and humanitarian law) in terms of implications for State obligations to child refugee asylum seekers in particular; both as a collective and as individual persons and (2) how these obligations have been interpreted and translated into practice in different jurisdictions. As the global refugee crisis grows exponentially, States are ever more commonly handling refugee asylum claimants or prospective claimants in a manner that is substantially inconsistent with applicable international law norms

---

[4]On the view here; persons internally displaced who have been forcibly displaced due to persecution/oppressive circumstances linked to persecution/discrimination etc. should properly be the beneficiary of refugee international law protections. Indeed, for instance, the U.S. under its refugee admission resettlement program (prior to the Trump travel ban on refugees abroad who allegedly did not have a bona fide tie to the U.S.) allowed Iraqi-US affiliated persons (Iraqis who had served to support U.S. military efforts during the Iraq war in some capacity as translators and the like) to apply for refugee asylum to the U.S. whether they were still *inside* Iraq or in some transit country. It seems illogical and incoherent at best to maintain that internally displaced persons "while they may have fled for similar reasons [to those recognized as refugees], . . .stay within their own country and remain under the protection of its government, even if that government is the reason for their displacement" and hence that actual and potential victims of persecution cannot be considered refugees per a narrow reading of the Refugee Convention (UNHCR Internally Displaced People at http://www.unhcr.org/en-us/internally-displaced-people.html). This topic, however, is beyond the scope of this book.

[5]'Safe Zones" combined with closed borders in neighboring potential transit countries arguably serve to negate the right to flee as a refugee seeking asylum. Countries supporting such safe zones while not challenging closed borders in respect of any neighboring country that could absorb additional asylum seekers if given the proper support from wealthier States is, it is here argued, in effect violating international refugee and basic human rights law (i.e. international human rights law as pertains to the right to freedom of movement (European Convention on Human Rights: Article 2 (2): "Everyone shall be free to leave any country, including his own").

[6]Human Rights Watch (2017) Syria: Coordinated chemical attacks on Aleppo: UN Security Council should impose sanctions (13 February, 2017).

[7]See Supreme Court of the United States, Donald J. Trump, President of the United States et al v International Refugee Assistance Project et al 582 U. S. ____ (2017) which provides a history of the Trump travel ban executive orders at pp. 1–4.

including, in some cases, even in a manner incompatible with customary and *jus cogens* law standards.

Child refugees are considered in this work to include both (1) those fleeing persecution based on race, religion, nationality, membership of a particular social group or political opinion (the prohibited grounds of persecution stipulated in the 1951 Refugee Convention and its 1967 Protocol) and (2) those fleeing other oppressive circumstances (i.e. the risk of female genital mutilation) that may be recognized as a basis for asylum under domestic law in certain jurisdictions but not necessarily in all others. Note that oppressive circumstances, depending on the particular instant fact pattern, are recognized under international refugee case law as conferring potential eligibility for refugee asylum. Since the focus in this work is on child refugees; international human rights and humanitarian law relevant to children is addressed in some detail insofar as it applies to the child refugee asylum seeking population (including both accompanied and unaccompanied child asylum seekers).

Save the Children in a 2017 document "Stolen Childhoods" reports that:

> Worldwide, nearly 28 million children have been forcibly displaced. This number includes some 10 million child refugees, approximately 1 million asylum seeking children and an estimated 17 million children displaced within their own countries by violence and conflict. Conflict has forced nearly I child in 80 from their homes, and some even onto the front lines[8]

> Though many communities and people around the world have welcomed refugee and migrant children, xenophobia, discrimination and exclusion pose serious threats to their lives and futures. . . .In too many cases, children are subject to immigration detention while their status is being assessed and resolved. This has a devastating impact on their psychological, social and educational development. In addition, policies around family reunification and returns are becoming more restrictive with a potential negative impact on children.[9]

This book seeks in particular also to examine and highlight some of the threats to refugee children realizing their asylum rights (those rights being set out in part in the Refugee Convention[10] and in related directives from organs of the United Nations such as the Office of the UN High Commissioner on Refugees and independent NGOs such as the International Committee of the Red Cross). To that end; selected cases are examined which, on the respectful view here, involve unreasonable domestic legal barriers and/or erroneous interpretations of relevant international law which underpin denial of these child asylum rights. Special focus is given here to extraterritorial migration control measures such as reflected in (1) the 90 day Trump travel ban on persons from six designated Muslim majority countries in addition to now (in the third iteration of President Trump's travel ban) Venezuela and North Korea and (2) the 120 day halt on the U.S. refugee admission/resettlement program. In both instances the travel ban applies to those who did not have entry papers by the President's travel ban specified date. The travel ban does *not* in its

---

[8]Save the Children (2017) End of Childhood Report, 2017 "Stolen Childhood' at p. 20.

[9]Save the Children (2017) End of Childhood Report, 2017 "Stolen Childhood' at p. 20.

[10]Refugee Convention (1951) and 1967 Protocol http://www.unhcr.org/en-us/about-us/background/4ec262df9/1951-convention-relating-status-refugees-its-1967-protocol.html Accessed 16 September, 2017.

latest iteration (third version) apply to legal permanent residents of the U.S. (green card holders) or dual nationals travelling on a passport issued by a country that is not on the travel ban list of restricted countries. Per an initial Supreme Court of the United States (USSC) June 26, 2017 ruling; persons with a *bona fide* relationship to an approved person or entity in the U.S. were exempted.[11] A later USSC ruling of December 4, 2017, however, removes the *bona fide* relationship exemption and allows full implementation of the travel ban (in its third iteration) pending the final determination by the USSC pursuant to the case being heard on its merits.[12]

According to the Trump administration both measures are intended to operate for a limited time while certain internal reviews of the U.S. refugee/immigration system are conducted and other data collection efforts relating to U.S. national security concerns are underway. However, in the view of some legal scholars the measures are likely, if upheld on the merits by the U.S. Supreme Court, to be extended for an indefinite period. If the latter be the case this can be expected to have particularly adverse effects for unaccompanied child refugees and other highly vulnerable refugee populations. We will examine thus some of the devastating effects on child refugees of such extraterritorial migration controls and other measures intended to block the children's very possibility of seeking asylum and the inconsistency of such measures with State international obligations to refugees including in particular child refugees.

Arguably the refugee asylum seeker fleeing persecution[13] is rendered by his/her status in seeking refuge to some extent, in effect, a global citizen. This in that each State in honoring customary law (the principle of non-refoulement) and as a State

---

[11]Supreme Court of the United States, Donald J. Trump, President of the United States et al v International Refugee Assistance Project et al 582 U. S. ____ (2017) (Opinion of June 26, 2017).

[12]For the time being, the latest Supreme Court of the United States ruling (without reasons provided) has allowed the third iteration of the Trump travel ban to be implemented notwithstanding whether or not the person in question barred from entry has a *bona fide* relationship to a person or entity in the U.S. save for any case-by-case exemption the government provides. Donald J. Trump, President of the United States, et al., Applicants v. Hawaii, et al. (Opinion of December 4, 2017). The question of whether or not the latest President Trump travel ban meets the constitutional test will be decided at the Supreme Court of the United States once the latest appeals have wound their way through the lower courts and the case is heard on its merits by the USSC.

[13]As previously mentioned the focus in this work is on those recognized under international law as refugees as opposed to persons recognized as internally displaced. This is the focus though, on the view here, since (1) at least a certain segment of the IDP population is *in practice* also (as with *de jure* refugees) no longer under the protection of their home State but rather persecuted by the State government and/or by non-State groups and others acting as proxies for the government as in Syria; as a result (2) this IDP population is arguably no longer in law under the jurisdiction of their home State; this given that protection of its citizens and those habitually residing in the State is a prime obligation in the exercise of sovereign authority. Where the State directly or through proxies persecutes any segment of its civilian population causing those persons to be internally displaced; it has lost the moral and legal authority to exercise sovereign jurisdiction over that IDP population. To hold otherwise is to suggest that international law considers the State's power of sovereign jurisdiction to be absolute and unfettered. On the current analysis then IDP populations should be regarded as entitled to refugee protections as de facto refugees (this entitlement being the case, it is here contended, regardless whether or not the IDPs are being protected by non-State actors such as UNHRC (such protection in any case typically involving circumstances not particularly conducive,

Party to the Refugee Convention more generally, at a minimum, has a shared responsibility to ensure the *bona fide* refugee a safe place *somewhere* and genuine integration into some certain State where he or she may enjoy the pursuit of a normal life in as much peace as is feasible.[14] Arguably so-called 'safe zones' within the home country in which the population at risk has been persecuted often by their own government or refugee camps in such or other settings do not offer refuge/protection in any fully meaningful sense. In fact 'safe zones' and refugee camps represent often very perilous living circumstances in innumerable respects including often creating the significant likelihood of being victimized by violence and discrimination in such settings.[15] The living circumstances for refugees seeking asylum at various points in their journey are then varied and all too often grossly substandard. The refugee may, for instance, be deprived of liberty and held in detention facilities with substandard conditions for a significant period,[16] or be housed in refugee encampments (set up by the UNHCR or NGOs) for protracted periods in very difficult or even high risk circumstances or struggle to survive in makeshift camps[17] or even be left without the most basic necessities of life.[18]

---

if at all, to children reaching their full potential for good physical, cognitive, psychological and spiritual development).

[14]Grover (2015), pp. 1112–1128.

[15]Townsend. M Women and children 'endure rape, beatings and abuse' inside Dunkirk's refugee camp The Guardian 12 February, 2017 https://www.theguardian.com/world/2017/feb/12/dunkirk-child-refugees-risk-sexual-violence Accessed 16 September, 2017.

[16]Many child refugees, even very young children, as will be discussed here through selected case law, have been held in unsuitable government-run detention facilities in various countries sometimes with other family members or, even separated from family (i.e. with parents held in a separate detention centre); the latter in violation of provisions of international human rights treaties that stipulate the right of children to stay with their family unit where such is in the child's best interests rather than being arbitrarily deprived of association with parents and other family members (i.e. Article 22 (2) of the Convention on the Rights of the Child stresses the right of the refugee child to the family unit and the State's obligation to make every effort to reunite families separated through circumstances such as occurred on their refugee journey in search of safety). In addition unaccompanied refugee children have often been held in non-child friendly detention centers by the prospective asylum State which facilities have frequently proved to be living circumstances deleterious to the child refugee's mental health.

[17]The makeshift camp which existed near Calais has been described through first-hand accounts as providing inhumane living conditions.

[18]Deprivation of the basic necessities of life threatening survival of a refugee collective then could potentially rise to a crime against humanity or if the group met the criteria set out in the Genocide Convention potentially even rise to the level of an actual act of genocide i.e. the Burmese military is creating masses of Rohingya refugees and depriving them of a means of survival in part by burning down their villages Human Rights Watch (15 September, 2017) Burma: Military torches homes near border: New Satellite Images, Data Show 62 Destroyed Rohingya Villages https://www.hrw.org/news/2017/09/15/burma-military-torches-homes-near-border Accessed 17 September, 2017.

The obligation to provide refuge to the persecuted is part of the 'law of nations', it is here contended, part and parcel of what defines civilized conduct on the part of the international community and individual State members. Further; providing protection within its own State territory or arranging for refuge in other jurisdictions to the persecuted identifiable group would seem to be an obligation also arising since the various State members of the international community often contribute to the creation of refugees and their dire plight. This they do by their own State actions (armed conflict) and inaction (failure to intervene to protect civilians where the home State of the targeted civilians is unable or unwilling to do so or is in fact persecuting its own citizens).[19] Further, refugees and internally displaced persons fleeing mass atrocities in particular arguably are owed what might be termed 'a universal jurisdiction of protection' (that is; a positive duty to protect) which is the logical corollary of the universal jurisdiction to hold accountable the perpetrators most responsible for those mass atrocities (or other forms of persecution which may or may not rise to the level of international crimes) that so often are a major factor leading to the creation of masses of refugees and internally displaced persons in various contexts. It is a grave affront to the civility and conscience, such as it is, of the international community to allow persons to remain in a protracted situation of legal limbo without formal legal status as refugees entitled to asylum and with the grant of the same by a State offering integration into its community of peoples. In unstable living circumstances as an externally or internally displaced person or collective; the fundamental human rights of these vulnerable persons are often further grievously violated (as has occurred over the last number of years for massive numbers of the refugees, including children, in may global jurisdictions for instance, as in Syria).

The refugee situation sets up, on this author's view, the quintessential test of the rule of international law (human rights, refugee and humanitarian law in particular) and domestic democratic rule of law as well. This since no person or collective—whether *de jure* or *de facto* stateless—can properly be considered beyond the protection of the law if that international rule of law grounded on respect for human dignity and human rights is in fact to prevail. Yet the illusory (on the respectful view here) notion (reflected in the quote below) is tragically perpetuated that refugee asylum seekers are beyond the law in principle and in practice. Such a view by certain legal scholars of the refugee as beyond the law serves, on the view here, inadvertently to cast as inevitable the ongoing abuse of this population not just by the offending home State but to a large extent the broader international community:

> By virtue of having lost state protection, the refugee is forced to live outside the pale of law and is therefore, Arendt argues, driven outside the common world. In a legal sense, the refugee is, strictly speaking, nowhere in this world. The claim that the refugee belongs nowhere in this world is not to be taken in a metaphorical sense. On the contrary, the argument derives from a basic insight into the spatiality of law.[20]

---

[19]Coen (2017), pp. 46–60.

[20]Oudejans, N Asylum: A Philosophical Inquiry into the International Protection of Refugees, PhD Dissertation, Tilburg University, p. 6.

Certain more contemporary scholars of the refugee situation such as N. Oudejans have cast the refugee issue in a similar fashion as does Arendt:

> Without a country of their own, both the refugee and the stateless person face the same fundamental and existential dilemma: where do they have a right to live? Casting the plight of the refugee as the loss of an own place, which signals, again, that the refugee is absolutely nowhere in this world, enables me to illuminate what the refugee is claiming in claiming asylum (emphasis added).[21]

The current author suggests, in contrast to Arendt's view, that international law applicable to the refugee plight transcends the so-called 'spatiality of law' assuming the latter exists in some legal contexts. This in that refugee law, for instance, has in large part become akin to a customary law norm founded on *jus cogens* principles relating to legal guarantees that serve to safeguard the basic human dignity and survival of these particular vulnerable individuals and collectives. The notion in law of asylum in some version for the foreign national in need of protection dates to antiquity.[22] On the current author's view then the fact that in contemporary times the all too familiar reality for innumerable refugees (often especially those caught in a protracted refugee situation) is to suffer gross human rights violations is not to be taken as evidence of their being in any legitimate technical and formal legal sense actually 'beyond the law' (to use Arendt's phrase). Yet as the case law we will examine illustrates, there is an increasing tendency in various jurisdictions to attempt to foster and perpetuate the fallacy that places the refugee asylum seeker outside the scope of the full legal protections owed under certain international and often domestic law as well. The latter is being accomplished through various means including but not limited to, for instance (1) extraterritorial migration controls formulated in such a way that they violate *in effect* the fundamental right of the refugee to *seek* asylum; and (2) legally insupportable (in a democratic context) domestic statutory schemes that are designed to penalize the asylum seeker in various ways including unduly through long detention periods often in inhumane conditions in order to: (a) dissuade the asylees[23] from pursuing their legal claim to asylum once at the border or in the country where they hope to gain asylum and to (b) simultaneously send the message to other potential asylum seekers to that State to

---

[21]Oudejans, N Asylum: A Philosophical Inquiry into the International Protection of Refugees, PhD Dissertation, Tilburg University, p. 7.

[22]Edwards (2005), p. 299: "The origins of the 'right to seek and to enjoy asylum from persecution in other countries' can be traced back to the 'right of sanctuary' in ancient Greece, imperial Rome and early Christian civilisation." Referencing Goldman and Martin (1983), p. 309.

[23]In the United States 'asylee' is the term applied most commonly to persons who have crossed into the United States without proper legal status and seek asylum either on their own initiative or pursuant to apprehension or who sought asylum at a port of entry to the U.S. In contrast, the U.S. uses the term refugee to refer to those who were outside of the U.S. when they were screened for admission and received status as a recognized *bona fide* refugee approved for resettlement in the U.S. See Zong, J. and Batalova, J Migration and Policy Institute: Spotlight: Refugees and Asylees in the United States (7 June, 2017) http://www.migrationpolicy.org/article/refugees-and-asylees-united-states Accessed 17 September, 2017.

abandon their effort or face harsh treatment and likely, if not certain, return to their place of origin or the last transit country they traversed.

The contention is here advanced then that the right to asylum for refugees[24] implicates *jus cogens* law and that there is often an intersection between two or more branches of international law applicable in the refugee context including but not limited to i.e. humanitarian law and/or refugee law, customary law, international human rights law and, where children are the victims of persecution, also child human rights law specifically. There has been furthermore, it should be understood, a longstanding pre-Refugee Convention recognition in international law that children, including unaccompanied or separated children, are entitled to special care and protection.[25] In more recent developments, the notion of the right of foreign national refugee children and non-refugee migrant minors (persons below age 18) to international protection by a State exercising jurisdiction both within and beyond its own borders has been articulated in soft law; for instance in Joint General Comments issued in collaboration between the respective monitoring bodies for the Convention on the Rights of the Child[26] and the Convention concerning migrant workers and their families:

> 11. States should ensure that children in the context of international migration are treated first and foremost as children. States parties to the Conventions have a duty to comply with their obligations set out therein to respect, protect and fulfil the rights of children in the context of international migration, regardless of their or their parents' or legal guardians' migration status.
>
> 12. *The obligations of States parties under the Conventions apply to each child within their jurisdictions,* ***including the jurisdiction arising from a State exercising effective control outside its borders.*** *Those obligations cannot be arbitrarily and unilaterally curtailed* either

---

[24]We will consider also children who had refugee status formally assigned i.e. by the UNHCR or would so qualify but have been unable to cross out of their home State or are unable to leave a third State that was to provide but temporary safe haven. This bar to movement being due to various factors such as extraterritorial migration controls being imposed (i.e. the Trump suspension of the U.S. refugee admission and resettlement program).

[25]For instance see the codification of this arguably customary law principle of a high duty of care and protection owed children in Article 78: Evacuation of Children: Additional Protocol I (1977) to the 1949 Geneva Conventions and Relating to the Protection of Victims of International Armed Conflicts regarding the evacuation from conflict zones (on ostensibly a temporary basis) including potentially to another country (with various restrictive stipulations applied in respect of implementing such an evacuation) also of children who are non-nationals where there are compelling reasons relating to the children's protection needs or for their health or to make possible their receiving urgent medical treatment.

[26]The Convention on the Rights of the Child (CRC), entry into force 2 September 1990, at Article 22 guarantees refugee children, whether accompanied or unaccompanied, "appropriate protection and humanitarian assistance in the enjoyment of applicable rights set forth in the present Convention [the CRC] and in other international human rights or humanitarian instruments to which the said States are Parties." Hence refugee children are entitled under the CRC to non-discriminatory treatment, as are all children, in realizing their protection and participation rights under the CRC and under other relevant international treaty law to which the CRC State Parties have agreed to be bound. In addition, on the analysis here, CRC Article 22 also implicates State Party obligations to children under *jus cogens* and customary law.

> by excluding zones or areas from the territory of a State or by defining particular zones or areas as not or only partly under the jurisdiction of the State, including in international waters or other transit zones where States put in place migration control mechanisms. The obligations apply within the borders of the State, including with respect to those children who come under its jurisdiction while attempting to enter its territory (emphasis added).[27]

We will explore through selected case law to what degree the collective and individual human rights of child refugee asylum seekers were considered and respected in the various contexts represented by these cases. This jurisprudence highlights, for instance (1) legal and NGO advocacy work yet to be done to change commonly promulgated erroneous conceptions of the child refugee asylum seeker as non -entitled to due process and special care and protection and (2) the need to eliminate unjustified systemic barriers in meritorious refugee cases which barriers serve to block realization of the right of child refugees to seek asylum and, at a minimum, be afforded genuine safe haven and, where at all feasible and reasonable, asylum with a path to citizenship in the asylum State. The systemic barriers for accompanied and unaccompanied child refugees seeking asylum have become more and more onerous and pervasive. These barriers often reflect the reflexive and unlawful response of many States to the burgeoning numbers of refugee asylum seekers globally including children. Also discussed are selected NGO reports concerning the child refugee crisis and the insights provided into the realities and challenges of ensuring that child asylum seeker human rights are protected and the possibility of grant of asylum not routinely discounted without due consideration on a case by case basis.

Considered also in this work are the fundamental human rights of the child refugee as an individual and as part of an identifiable refugee collective (i.e. identifiable refugee collectives include, for instance, unaccompanied child refugees, child refugees of a certain national origin such as Syrian, ex child soldier refugees[28] etc.). The view advanced here is that the rights of the individual refugee are ever more commonly being effectively negated using as the mechanism the denial at the outset of the collective human rights of the particular identifiable group of refugees of which the individual is a member (here the particular child refugee group or larger refugee collective in question) as will be illustrated through selected cases. For instance, the possibility of *prima facie* recognition of a small group of

[27]Joint General Comment No. 3 (2017) of the Committee on the Protection of the Rights of All Migrant Workers and Members of Their Families and No. 22 (2017) of the Committee on the Rights of the Child on the general principles regarding the human rights of children in the context of international migration. (See also Joint General Comment No. 4 (2017) of the Committee on the Protection of the Rights of All Migrant Workers and Members of Their Families and No. 23 (2017) of the Committee on the Rights of the Child on State obligations regarding the human rights of children in the context of international migration in countries of origin, transit, destination and return) The latter General Comment holds there must be a guarantee of access to the territory for a child who may be in need of international protection (regardless whether the child has proper entry documentation etc.) in order that their proper migration status can be determined with due regard to the child's best interests (Article 17 (a)) and other relevant factors.

[28]Grover (2012).

refugees as refugees based on credible overwhelming evidence may be ruled out for political rather than justifiable legal reasons, there may be a refusal to consider the merits of the refugee case for each member of the refugee collective and an opting instead for a ban on entry and asylum processing for the collective as a whole etc. In part due to the current massive numbers of asylum seeking refugees involved; many States have reneged on their obligation to recognize and respect the *collective rights* of particular groups of refugees and devised blanket bars to their entry. For instance; the Trump 120 day suspension of the U.S. refugee admission and resettlement program is a bar on entry for those refugees who did not have a visa or other entry papers to the United States by the date specified in the President's Executive Order (the bar being in place save for exceptional cases and not automatically exempting currently even those who have a *bona fide* family tie to a reasonably close family member with legal status in the U.S. or to a legal entity in the U.S.). This then amounts largely to a blanket bar and undermining of collective refugee rights. Infants and children *may* be exempted from the Trump temporary ban on refugee entry on a case-by-case basis but the onus is on the children and/or their representatives to make the convincing argument for an exemption. The case, in such instances, has to be made out that the Trump travel ban causes 'undue hardship' for the child or infant refugee asylum seeker and that the child or infant does not pose a security threat to the U.S.[29] with in that event yet no guarantee of the State exercise of discretionary compassion in any particular case. It seems ironic and beyond cynical to require of child refugees that they prove 'undue hardship' should they be barred from entry to the United States in search of asylum given the current refugee crisis, the dire situation of these refugees and the especially vulnerable position of child refugees. For example in regards to Syrian refugees:

> Roughly half of Syria's pre-war population of 23 million has been uprooted since the conflict began in 2011 – some six-and-half million within Syria's borders, and five million to other countries.[30]

> The countries affected by the Order include some of the most disordered areas in the world, areas where it is particularly dangerous to be a child. Syria, the world's largest producer of refugees, is now in the sixth year of continuous conflict. According to the United Nations Children's Fund, more than 6 million Syrian children are in "immediate" need of humanitarian aid. Millions of children witness unrelenting and brutal violence. 1.75 million children in Syria are no longer in school. At least 652 children were killed last year (a 20% increase from the prior year); 255 died in or near a school. As families get more desperate, more children are being pushed into child marriage and child labor.[31]

---

[29]Brief for Amicus Curiae American Professional Society on the Abuse of Children in Support of the Plaintiffs-Appellees In the United States Court of Appeals for the Ninth Circuit State of Hawaii; Ismail Elshikh v Donal J. Trump in his official capacity as President of the United States and others No. 17-15589.

[30]Power, S Remarks on "The Global Refugee Crisis: Overcoming Fears and Spurring Action," (June 29, 2016).

[31]In the Supreme Court of the United States Donald J. Trump et al v State of Hawaii et al Brief of Amicus Curiae American Professional Society on the Abuse of Children in Support of the Respondent (12 June, 2017), p. 6.

We will explore then (1) how through legally insupportable domestic statutory schemes, erroneous interpretations of UNHCR guidelines and other devices, legitimate refugee claims to asylum are being blocked[32] and (2) how child refugees, especially those unaccompanied, are highly vulnerable to such State strategies for denial of the children's legal rights as refugee asylum seekers notwithstanding the relevant State obligations under international law in various domains.

The focus in this work is thus on child refugees where the high duty of care in regards to protection owed by the international community to children in such vulnerable situations is well established in customary law, as well as in international human rights[33] and humanitarian law.[34] When considering unaccompanied younger child refugees, as we will do, furthermore, the central humanitarian and human rights issues are not as likely to be overshadowed and clouded by the overstated security concerns of a prospective asylum State.

It is to be noted that children are particularly hard hit by the current refugee crisis stemming as it does in large part from armed conflict and associated mass atrocity:

> At the end of 2015, more than 65 million people were displaced worldwide, over half of them children. That is the highest number on record since the UN's Refugee Agency started collecting statistics[35]

Indeed children are often the particularized targets of the mass atrocities[36] that so often create the displacement of child and other civilians. Consider then the December 13, 2016 following excerpts from the remarks of Samantha Powers, U.S. Ambassador to the United Nations, to those Member States gathered for the UN Security Council Emergency Briefing on Syria:

> . . .Here is what is happening now in eastern Aleppo. . . Terrorists. Clearly-young children-they must be terrorists because everybody being executed, everybody being barrel bombed, everybody who's been chlorine attacked, you're going to be told are all terrorists-every last one of them, even the infants. . .we keep insisting on answering the UN call for access, for safe and orderly evacuation, because we are not willing to accept that innocent men, women, and children can be butchered simply because they happen to live in a conflict areas . . .To the Assad regime, Russia and Iran, . . . Is there no act of barbarism against civilians, no execution of a child that gets under your skin, that just creeps you out a little bit? To the Members of this Council and all Member States of the United Nations: Know that the . . .starve-and-surrender-and -slaughter tactics. . .will be their model for attempting to retake

[32]Though the focus is on child refugees in this work, it is here suggested that similar legally insupportable bars are employed by States in respect of blocking adult refugee asylum seekers as are employed against child refugee asylum seekers i.e. domestic statutory schemes and extraterritorial migration measures arguably inconsistent with democratic constitutional values and designed *in effect* to deny the right to seek asylum and to prohibit entry.

[33]Convention on the Rights of the Child, entry into force 2 September 1990 (i.e. Article 3 on best interests of the child as a primary consideration).

[34]See for instance Additional Protocol 1 (Article 77) and II (Article 4(3) to the 1948 Geneva Conventions which set out the child's right to special protection consideration, care and respect in times of armed conflict.

[35]Power, S Remarks on "The Global Refugee Crisis: Overcoming Fears and Spurring Action," (June 29, 2016).

[36]Grover (2014).

cities and towns across Syria. It will not end with Aleppo. And it will not focus on terrorists. It never has, and there is no evidence that it will... Appeal to Moscow, to Damascus, to Tehran, that they have to stop. The lives of tens of thousands of Syrians still in Eastern Aleppo -between 30,000-60,000 people -and hundreds of thousands more across the country who are besieged depend on it...[37]

Respectfully, insofar as the child victims of the assault on Aleppo are concerned and the issue of the incredulity of the West at the lack of perpetrator shame for involvement in the torture, degradation and inhumanity shown in particular to children by the perpetrator States, their proxies and individuals most responsible this author comments as follows: The suffering of the child victims of Aleppo as witnessed by first responders, NGOs and relayed in small bits often in real time through social and other media to the world is precisely what the perpetrators see as beneficial to their ruthless efforts. The message from the perpetrators in brutalizing children and creating millions of child refugees is that: 'the regime is ferocious in its quest for supreme power and future generations of Syrian civilians will be wiped out until and unless any intervention or prospect of intervention becomes and remains a non-starter.'[38]

Refugees today are more likely than not, if they survive their treacherous flight, and find themselves in refugee encampments to be there for an indeterminate period:

..conflicts are lasting longer, meaning people have to wait longer before it is safe to return home. Roughly one in three refugees today is caught in what is called a "protracted refugee situation." In 1993, the typical protracted refugee situation lasted nine years; today, the median duration is 26 years and counting.[39]

The conditions in these camps are often highly insecure with camps run by the UNCHR for instance being vulnerable to "armed attacks, arbitrary killings, torture, and exploitation and military recruitments"[40] In this regard; it is held by some experts that to a large extent the UNHCR has relinquished its responsibility to protect the physical security and many other fundamental human rights of refugees in camps which UNHCR oversees along with partners. Instead the focus is increasingly limited to providing for the bare material needs of the refugees such as food and shelter.

Given this protracted refugee situation, the refugee fleeing persecution in his/her homeland is in practical terms too often rendered *de facto* stateless with no realistic hope of return. Indeed when it comes for example to Syria, the political opposition to the Assad regime has no hope of return for the foreseeable future and those civilians caught in the cross fire who were not actively engaged in the fight are nonetheless falsely portrayed by the regime as part of the agitator 'opposition'. At the same time

---

[37]Power, S. Remarks at a UN Security Council Emergency Briefing on Syria (December 13, 2016).

[38]See Grover, S on the targeting of children in particular for mass atrocities as a propaganda tool: Grover (2014).

[39]Power, S "The Global Refugee Crisis: Overcoming Fears and Spurring Action," (June 29, 2016).

[40]Janmyr M (2013) UNHCR-A Humanitarian Organization with a Mandate to Protect Civilians in Refugee Camps, Norwegian Centre for Humanitarian Studies.

however, as Oudejans explains, given the fact that large masses of refugees are not in fact *de jure* stateless; the distinction between *de facto* and *de jure* statelessness perpetuates what is in many cases an illusory presumption that return will one day be possible for the currently *de facto* stateless, As a result this contributes to unfounded justifications for the denial of asylum by prospective asylum States which could in practical terms accommodate a meaningful segment of the refugee population:

> Indeed, the refugee problem came to be identified as a problem of *de facto* statelessness, sharply delineated from the problem of *de jure* statelessness which expresses that the lack of protection a stateless person is suffering is a matter of law, as no single state on earth can be attributed a responsibility to protect the person concerned.[41]
>
> I am able to argue that the distinction between *de facto* and *de jure* statelessness is not as clear-cut as is commonly believed. Without a country of their own, both the refugee and the stateless person face the same fundamental and existential dilemma: where do they have a right to live?[42]

Finally, we will in considering the plight of the *de facto* and *de jure* stateless refugee, examine the concept of the responsibility to protect (R2P)[43] as an international norm[44]; part of the UN Member State obligations under the UN Charter[45] and its relevance to addressing the refugee crisis.

Literature, Materials and Cases

Literature

Coen A (2017) R2P, global governance, and the Syrian refugee crisis. In: Grover S (ed) The responsibility to protect: perspectives on the concept's meaning, proper application and value. Routledge, New York, pp 46–60

Edwards A (2005) Human rights, refugees and the 'right to enjoy Asylum. Int J Refug Law 17 (2):293–330

Goldman RK, Martin SM (1983) International legal standards relating to the rights of aliens and refugees and United States immigration law. Hum Rights Q 5(3):309–310

Grover S (2012) Child soldier victims of genocidal forcible transfer: exonerating child soldiers charged with grave conflict-related international crimes. Springer, Berlin

Grover S (2014) The Torture of children during armed conflicts: the ICC failure to prosecute and the negation of children's human dignity. Springer, Berlin

---

[41]Oudejans, N Asylum: A Philosophical Inquiry into the International Protection of Refugees, PhD Dissertation, Tilburg University p. 6.

[42]Oudejans, N A Philosophical Inquiry into the International Protection of Refugees, PhD Dissertation, Tilburg University pp. 6–7.

[43]Grover (2017).

[44]R2P refers, as most commonly understood, to the notion that the international community has a legal responsibility to protect civilians against the potential or ongoing occurrence of the mass atrocity crimes of genocide, large scale war crimes, ethnic cleansing and crimes against humanity.

[45]Grover (2015), pp. 1112–1128.

Grover S (2015) R2P and the Syrian crisis: when semantics becomes a matter of life or death. Int J Hum Rights 19(8):1112–1128

Grover S (ed) (2017) R2P: perspectives on the concept's meaning, proper application and value. Routledge Special Issues in Books Program. Routledge, New York

Materials

African Union Convention for the Protection and Assistance of Internally Displaced Persons in Africa (the Kampala Convention) entered into force 2012 Internal Displacement Monitoring website http://www.internal-displacement.org/sub-saharan-africa/kampala-convention/ Accessed 27 April, 2017

Brief for Amicus Curiae American Professional Society on the Abuse of Children in Support of the Plaintiffs-Appellees In the United States Court of Appeals for the Ninth Circuit State of Hawaii; Ismail Elshikh v Donal J. Trump in his official capacity as President of the United States; Department of Homeland Security; Department of State; John F. Kelly in his official capacity as Secretary of Homeland Security; Rex W. Tillerson in his official capacity as Secretary of State, United States of America No. 17-15589

Convention on the Rights of the Child, entry into force 2 September 1990. http://www.ohchr.org/en/professionalinterest/pages/crc.aspx Accessed 27 April, 2017

European Convention on Human Rights as amended by the provisions of Protocol No. 14 (CETS no. 194) as from its entry into force on 1 June 2010. http://www.echr.coe.int/Documents/Convention_ENG.pdf Accessed 21 August, 2017

Geneva Convention relative to the Protection of Civilian Persons in Time of War ('Fourth Geneva Convention') entry into force 21 October, 1950. http://www.wipo.int/wipolex/en/other_treaties/details.jsp?treaty_id=280 Accessed 27 April, 2017

Human Rights Watch (2017) Syria: Coordinated chemical attacks on Aleppo: UN Security Council should impose sanctions (13 February, 2017) https://www.hrw.org/news/2017/02/13/syria-coordinated-chemical-attacks-aleppo Accessed 30 January, 2018

International Covenant on Civil and Political Rights entered into force 23 March, 1976. http://www.ohchr.org/EN/ProfessionalInterest/Pages/CCPR.aspx Accessed 27 April, 2017

Janmyr M (2013) UNHCR-A Humanitarian Organization with a Mandate to Protect Civilians in Refugee Camps, Norwegian Centre for Humanitarian Studies http://www.humanitarianstudies.no/2013/10/15 unhcr-a-humanitarian-organization-with-a-mandate-to-protect-civilians0in-refugee-camps/ Accessed 27 April, 2017

Joint General Comment No. 3 (2017) of the Committee on the Protection of the Rights of All Migrant Workers and Members of Their Families and No. 22 (2017) of the Committee on the Rights of the Child on the general principles regarding the human rights of children in the context of international migration http://www.refworld.org/publisher/CMW.html Accessed 25 January, 2018

Joint General Comment No. 4 (2017) of the Committee on the Protection of the Rights of All Migrant Workers and Members of Their Families and No. 23 (2017) of the Committee on the Rights of the Child on State obligations regarding the human rights of children in the context of international migration in countries of origin, transit, destination and return http://www.refworld.org/publisher/CMW.html Accessed 25 January, 2018

Nardelli, Alberto. Angela Merkel's stance on refugees means she stands alone against catastrophe *The Guardian* November 8, 2015. https://www.theguardian.com/commentisfree/2015/nov/08/angela-merkel-refugee-crisis-europe Accessed 27 April, 2017

Ní Ghráinne, Bríd Oxford Public International Law (Max Planck Encyclopedia of Public International Law) Internally displaced persons (IDPs) February, 2015. http://opil.ouplaw.com/view/10.1093/law:epil/9780199231690/law-9780199231690-e833 Accessed 27 April, 2017

Oudejans, N. (2011). Asylum: A philosophical inquiry into the international protection of refugees Oisterwijk:BOXPress BV (PhD Dissertation, Tilburg University)

Pact on Security, Stability and Development of the Great Lakes Region (entered into force 2008) downloadable from https://www.icglr.org/index.php/en/the-pact Accessed 27 April, 2017

Power, S. (2016) Remarks at a UN Security Council Emergency Briefing on Syria (December 13, 2016, New York City) by Samantha Powers, US Ambassador to the UN, U.S. Mission to the United Nations https://usun.state.gov/remarks/7607 (Accessed 18 December 2016)

Powers, S (2016) "The Global Refugee Crisis: Overcoming Fears and Spurring Action," at the U.S. Institute of Peace, U.S. Mission to the United Nations, Washington D.C. June 29, 2016 https://geneva.usmission.gov/2016/06/30/samantha-powers-remarks-on-the-global-refugee-crisis-overcoming-fears-and-spurring-action-at-the-u-s-institute-of-peace/ (Accessed 18 December 2016)

Protocols I and II Additional to the 1949 Geneva Conventions Adopted 8 June, 1977 https://www.icrc.org/eng/resources/documents/misc/additional-protocols-1977.htm (Accessed 27 April, 2017)

Refugee Convention (1951) and 1967 Protocol http://www.unhcr.org/en-us/about-us/background/4ec262df9/1951-convention-relating-status-refugees-its-1967-protocol.html (Accessed 16 September, 2017)

Save the Children (2017). End of Childhood Report, 2017 "Stolen Childhood' Available for download at http://www.who.int/pmnch/media/events/2017/stolen_childhoods/en/ Accessed 21 August, 2017

Townsend. M Women and children 'endure rape, beatings and abuse' inside Dunkirk's refugee camp The Guardian 12 February, 2017. https://www.theguardian.com/world/2017/feb/12/dunkirk-child-refugees-risk-sexual-violence Accessed 16 September, 2017

UNHCR Internally Displaced People at http://www.unhcr.org/en-us/internally-displaced-people.html (Accessed 21 August, 2017)

Zong, J. and Batalova, J Migration and Policy Institute: Spotlight: Refugees and Asylees in the United States (7 June, 2017) http://www.migrationpolicy.org/article/refugees-and-asylees-united-states Accessed 17 September, 2017

Cases

Donald J. Trump, President of the United States, et al., Applicants v. Hawaii, et al. (Opinion of December 4, 2017) https://www.supremecourt.gov/search.aspx?filename=/docket/docketfiles/html/public/17a550.html

Supreme Court of the United States, Donald J. Trump, President of the United States et al v International Refugee Assistance Project et al 582 U. S. ____ (2017)(Opinion of June 26, 2017)

United States Court of Appeals for the Ninth Circuit State of Hawaii; Ismail Elshikh v Donal J. Trump in his official capacity as President of the United States; Department of Homeland Security; Department of State; John F. Kelly in his official capacity as Secretary of Homeland Security; Rex W. Tillerson in his official capacity as Secretary of State, United States of America

Chapter 2
The Intersection of Collective and Individual Child Refugee Asylum Seeker Rights

2.1 An Overview: Individual Refugee Rights Predicated on Collective Refugee and Human Rights

It is here contended that respect for individual human rights is in large part predicated on, at the outset, recognition and honouring of collective human rights. Often, however, individual basic human rights are violated on a blanket basis due to the actual or perceived membership of the individuals in an identifiable collective such as a refugee collective with a defined ethnic, religious, socio-political or other group characteristic. In such cases the State focus is then on the collective and not on the individual. In fact when the State adopts such an approach, from the State perspective, the individuals in the collective, in practice, for most if not all human rights related intents and purposes, no longer exist legally. Consideration of and regard for collective fundamental human rights is, however, as will be illustrated via the refugee cases here discussed, essential in regards to refugees if the individual refugee is to be fairly treated according to international customary and *jus cogens* norms and relevant international treaty and convention obligations. For instance, collectives of highly vulnerable people in many cases are entitled in the first instance, and are sometimes granted, in effect if not formally, *prima facie* recognition as refugees in terms of entitlement to protection. This occurring then even before individual cases are assessed on their merits. Thus, for example, Bangladesh has accepted a flood of Rohingya persons (400,000 as of September, 2017),[1] belonging to an ethnic Muslim minority group in their homeland of Burma. Thus Bangladesh has, in the first instance, regarded these Rohingya as a *prima facie* refugee collective comprised of individuals fleeing what has been described by the current U.N. High Commissioner

[1]Aljezeera News (17 September, 2017) Bangladesh restricts movement of Rohingya refugees: Police issue order prohibiting more than 400,000 Rohingya refugees from leaving areas designated by the government http://www.aljazeera.com/news/2017/09/bangladesh-restricts-movement-rohingya-refugees-170917004640300.html Accessed 20 September, 2017.

© Springer International Publishing AG, part of Springer Nature 2018

S. C. Grover, *Child Refugee Asylum as a Basic Human Right*,
https://doi.org/10.1007/978-3-319-78013-9_2

for Human Rights as ethnic cleaning[2] (by the Burmese military and certain non-State groups of different ethnicity):

> Burmese military forces have carried out mass arson, killing, and looting, destroying hundreds of villages and forcing nearly half a million Rohingya to flee to neighboring Bangladesh.[3]

At the same time; Bangladesh has ordered that the Rohingya refugees along its borders and within Bangladeshi territory are not to leave the camps set up at the border. Checkpoints and other monitoring has been set up by Bangladesh to ensure that this is the case. The situation is dire with many of the Rohingya living in overcrowded unsafe and inhumane conditions in these Bangladeshi border refugee encampments or even trying to survive at the border but outside the encampment without shelter or the basic necessities of life.[4] As yet there is no adequately effective relief organization on the ground to provide the full extent of the needed humanitarian aid to the hundreds of thousands of Rohingya refugees along the Bangladeshi -Burmese border.[5] The refugee camps are at capacity as more Burmese Rohingya refugees come into Bangladesh and humanitarian supplies are limited. Yet Bangladesh, itself an impoverished nation with highly constrained resources, is attempting to meet the refugee challenge posed by the influx of Rohingya, half of whom, according to the U.N., are children (it is estimated by the U.N. that by the end of 2017; 600,000 Rohingya child refugees will have crossed the border[6] from Burma into Bangladesh). This effort to improve the human rights/humanitarian situation, at least in some respects, for the Rohingya refugees in Bangladesh is illustrated for instance in Bangladeshi attempts to address certain of the Rohingya child refugee population *collective* health needs. This by providing immunization for measles, rubella and polio for child Rohingya refugees under age 15:

[2]"[T]he UN high commissioner for human rights has referred to [the Burmese military operation against Rohingya civilians]as a "textbook example of ethnic cleansing." See Human Rights Watch: Burma: Targeted Sanctions, Arms Embargo Needed: Ethnic Cleansing Demands Swift International Response https://www.hrw.org/news/2017/09/17/burma-targeted-sanctions-arms-embargo-needed Accessed 20 September, 2017.

[3]Human Rights Watch: Burma: Targeted Sanctions, Arms Embargo Needed: Ethnic Cleansing Demands Swift International Response https://www.hrw.org/news/2017/09/17/burma-targeted-sanctions-arms-embargo-needed Accessed 20 September, 2017.

[4]Alam, U. (17 September, 2017) Associated Press Bangladesh restricts Rohingya refugees, starts immunization http://abcnews.go.com/International/wireStory/bangladesh-restricts-rohingya-refugees-starts-immunization-49905267 Accessed 20 September, 2017.

[5]Alam, U. (17 September, 2017) Associated Press Bangladesh restricts Rohingya refugees, starts immunization http://abcnews.go.com/International/wireStory/bangladesh-restricts-rohingya-refugees-starts-immunization-49905267 Accessed 20 September, 2017.

[6]Child Rights International Network (CRINmail 1549, 20 September, 2017): Refugees and Migrants.

> With the U.N. saying there are some 240,000 children among the refugees living in dire conditions, *Bangladeshi authorities have kicked off a massive immunization drive*. Abdus Salam, the top government administrator in the Cox's Bazar district hospital, said that some 150,000 children would be immunized over seven days for measles, rubella and polio.
>
> "There are a lot of weak and malnourished children among the new arrivals," UNICEF's representative in Bangladesh, Edouard Beigbeder, said in an email. "If proper preventive measures are not taken, highly infectious diseases, especially measles, could even cause an outbreak"(emphasis added).[7]

Child refugees thus as a collective and as individuals have certain human rights entitlements both as children and as refugees as is clear in the aforementioned example and will be discussed in the legal cases here presented.

The acceptance by Bangladesh of the Rohingya refugees and new initiatives by Bangladesh to improve the refugee humanitarian and human rights situation in the border Rohingya refugee camps represent a move towards better compliance with international obligations. However often rights are compromised due to actual or perceived national security or other concerns and infringed on a legally insupportable collective basis with no determinations that are well—founded on a case-by-case basis that would potentially rationalize any particular rights violation. Thus, for instance, the restriction of movement by Bangladesh of the Rohingya refugees such that the Rohingya refugees *as a collective* are barred from movement beyond the refugee camps is a violation of refugee and human rights law (i.e. Article 26 of the Refugee Convention). This, it is here contended, since the Rohingya refugee group is, in practice, recognized by Bangladesh as a *prima facie* refugee collective and hence the newly arrived Rohingya refugees are lawfully within the territory of Bangladesh. Article 26 of the Refugee Convention sets out the right to movement for refugees as follows:

> **Article 26**
> Freedom of movement
>
> Each Contracting State shall accord to refugees lawfully in its territory the right to choose their place of residence to move freely within its territory, subject to any regulations applicable to aliens generally in the same circumstances.[8]

There is more recently the alarming spectre looming of a risk of refoulement by Bangladesh of most if not all of the 600,000 Rohingya refugees. This in that on November 23, 2017 Myanmar and Bangladesh signed an agreement that on a *purported* voluntary basis Rohingya refugees (escaped from Myanmar's Rakhine state in the midst of what independent NGO's have characterized as crimes against

---

[7]Alam, U. (17 September, 2017) Associated Press Bangladesh restricts Rohingya refugees, starts immunization http://abcnews.go.com/International/wireStory/bangladesh-restricts-rohingya-refugees-starts-immunization-49905267 Accessed 20 September, 2017.

[8]Convention and Protocol Relating to the Status of Refugees (1951 Refugee Convention and 1967 Protocol) Accessed 20 September, 2017.

humanity perpetrated by Myanmar's forces)[9] would be returned to Myanmar to an alleged safe situation.[10] Furthermore, at the time of writing, it should be noted that UNICEF has been largely blocked from accessing 60,000 Rohingya children still in Myanmmar Rakhine State thus preventing humanitarian assistance to these children (some trying to survive without adult caretakers) living in dire IDP camp conditions that threaten their health and often their very survival.[11] These Rohingya children are persecuted through inhumane camp conditions among other means. They are trapped in Myanmmar without legal status or citizenship or meaningful protection in that country and unable to leave without Myanmmar government permission and but for the latter fact would be considered Convention refugees.

Consider, as another example, the situation described by Human Rights Watch in a report of 20 September, 2017 detailing that 1400 women (some pregnant) and children (with none of the children being over 12) who surrendered with ISIS in late August, 2017 were being detained without charge and without having had an appearance before a judge:

> Hundreds of foreign children risk being abandoned in a hellish twilight zone, with no legal identity and no country willing to take them," said Bill Van Esveld, children's rights researcher at Human Rights Watch. "Iraq, foreign countries, and international organizations should not let these children fall into statelessness, or consign them and their mothers to detention without charge.". . .. Most of the children, particularly young children born in Iraq, had no birth certificates or ID documents.[12]

An Iraqi military officer informed Human Rights Watch that the women and children were being held "for their own protection" but, as Human Rights Watch points out, there is no such legal rationale for detention under Iraqi law.[13] This is an example of the violation of individual human rights to due process with the infringement arising consequent to the individuals being members of a collective such that the claim to substantive or procedural legal rights is denied on a blanket basis:

> On September 16, Prime Minister Haider al-Abadi of Iraq stated in an interview that most of the women and children were not guilty of a crime, and that his government was "in full communication" with their home countries to "find a way to hand them over." Human Rights

[9]Amnesty International. Myanmar: Military attempts to whitewash crimes against humanity targeting Rohingya (13 November, 2017).

[10]Azeem Ibrahim Why the Rohingya cannot yet return to Myanmar *New York Times*, 6 December, 2017.

[11]United Nations News Centre (9 January, 2018) Rohingya children trapped in 'appalling' conditions in Myanmmar's Rakhine state.

[12]Human Rights Watch (Beirut, 20 September, 2017) Iraq/KRG: 1400 Women, Children From ISIS Areas Detained: Investigate Killings, Abductions of Foreign Men https://www.hrw.org/news/2017/09/19/iraq/krg-1400-women-children-isis-areas-detained Accessed 20 September, 2017.

[13]Human Rights Watch (Beirut, 20 September, 2017) Iraq/KRG: 1400 Women, Children From ISIS Areas Detained: Investigate Killings, Abductions of Foreign Men https://www.hrw.org/news/2017/09/19/iraq/krg-1400-women-children-isis-areas-detained Accessed 20 September, 2017.

> Watch confirmed with humanitarian sources on September 18 that none of the women and children detained since late August at the Hammam al-Alil site had been repatriated.[14]

Essentially these children are now refugees who have an individual right to have their best interests as children considered as well as their individual refugee rights taken into account. Instead; these young children under 12, being members through family affiliations of a certain collective, have had their individual rights so far largely disregarded. The Human Rights Watch child rights researcher had the following to say in regards to these children in detention at the Hammam al-Alil site:

> The Iraqi government should ensure the women's safe repatriation, asylum or resettlement if they release them, or fair trials if it charges them with violating Iraqi laws," Van Esveld said. "*It would be a terrible irony if children, who were notoriously victimized by ISIS, were forced to pay with their future for ISIS's crimes* (emphasis added)."[15]

No more poignant an example of the denial of collective rights as a vehicle to denial of individual human rights then is to be found than in the plight of today's asylum seeking refugees fleeing mass atrocities and other forms of persecution perpetrated by State and/or non-State groups.[16] These refugees are *in practice* often no longer viewed by many of the States in which they seek asylum as individuals but rather are categorized and stigmatized as part of an alien larger entity (collective) to be guarded against. Consider, for example, the asylum seeking refugees fleeing the attacks by State and non-State actors on civilians and their treatment by border agents in certain Western Balkan countries. These groups of persecuted asylum seeking refugee civilians have not uncommonly suffered repeated violation of their collective refugee rights as well as infringement of their individual refugee and human rights by the border agents of particular Western Balkan States that could offer asylum.[17] Some of these prospective refugee asylum States have doled out abuse at times rising to the level of inhuman treatment and denial of the basic necessities of life:

> Rather than being places of safety, countries on the Western Balkan route have failed to offer protection or due process to many new arrivals and instead have pushed them back to their previous country of transit or even another country, without giving them a chance to claim asylum. Pushbacks are happening in different ways. Hungary and Croatia – both EU

[14]Human Rights Watch (Beirut, 20 September, 2017) Iraq/KRG: 1,400 Women, Children From ISIS Areas Detained Investigate Killings, Abductions of Foreign Men https://www.hrw.org/news/2017/09/19/iraq/krg-1400-women-children-isis-areas-detained Accessed 20 September, 2017.

[15]Human Rights Watch (Beirut, 20 September, 2017) Iraq/KRG: 1400 Women, Children From ISIS Areas Detained Investigate Killings, Abductions of Foreign Men https://www.hrw.org/news/2017/09/19/iraq/krg-1400-women-children-isis-areas-detained Accessed 20 September, 2017.

[16]It is to be noted that not all asylum seekers are refugees: "Asylum is different from refugee status, as the former constitutes the institution for protection while the latter refers to one of the categories of individuals –among others-who benefit from such protection" (Gil-Bazo 2015, p. 4).

[17]Independent News (2017) European border forces "frequently abuse ' refugees and migrants report finds (Independent News, Rachael Roberts, 6 April, 2017) http://www.independent.co.uk/news/world/western-border-forces-abuse-migrants-refugee-crisis-serbia-macedonia-hungary-asylum-seekers-a7671201.html Accessed 22 September, 2017.

member states – have used brutal tactics, such as attack dogs and forcing people to strip naked in freezing temperatures. The Serbian authorities have generated a climate of fear and uncertainty amongst migrants by expelling groups of people who have been legally registered and were expecting to receive their right to an individual hearing. This practice meant that in mid-winter, in freezing temperatures of -20°C, people were afraid to stay in government centres for fear of being pushed back to Macedonia or Bulgaria. Interviewees also accused Bulgarian authorities of treating people in such a brutal manner that they are afraid to return.[18]

Refoulement then under various guises is prevalent as will also be discussed in the context of certain cases. However, non-refoulement in itself is of insufficient spiritual or other comfort to these asylum seeking refugees when all too often they are significantly maltreated psychologically and/or physically *in situ* in the jurisdiction in which they have gained irregular entry or at some border entry point thereof. Oxfam comments in the conclusion of its April, 2017 report: *A dangerous 'game': the pushback of migrants, including refugees, at Europe's borders* that:

It is clear that authorities are determined to illegally push people back… However, it is equally clear that people are determined to continue their journeys in search of safety and dignity.[19]

While the Oxfam report concerned certain European States in the Western Balkans, the same aforementioned comment could be applied to any situation where a State is using 'pushback' strategies against refugees; strategies that are inconsistent with their own State constitutional democratic principles and with international norms concerning the proper treatment of refugees (regardless whether these strategies are non-violent in themselves or involve also extra- territorial measures as we will consider in Chapter five concerning U.S. President Trump's pushback strategies against refugees).

Refugees once having crossed into a territory outside of their homeland are not uncommonly victims collectively once more then of 'forced migration'; at that time in the form of 'collective expulsion' by certain States, including Western European States, that should and could be offering asylum but do not despite the availability of State resources to do so. For instance, in *Conka v Belgium*[20] the European Court of Human Rights made a finding of collective expulsion by Belgium of refugee asylum seekers from Slovakia:

The applicants, Slovakian nationals of Romany origin, said that they had fled from Slovakia where they had been subjected to racist assaults with the police refusing to intervene. They had been arrested with a view to their expulsion after they had been summoned to complete

[18]Oxfam report (April, 2017): A dangerous 'game': the pushback of migrants, including refugees, at Europe's borders at p. 2 Available at https://www.oxfam.org/en/research/dangerous-game-pushback-migrants-including-refugees-europes-borders Accessed 22 September, 2017.

[19]Oxfam report (April, 2017): A dangerous 'game': the pushback of migrants, including refugees, at Europe's borders at p. 15 Available at https://www.oxfam.org/en/research/dangerous-game-pushback-migrants-including-refugees-europes-borders Accessed 22 September, 2017.

[20]Conka v Belgium [2002], Chamber Judgment (no. 51564/99) https://hudoc.echr.coe.int/eng#{%22itemid%22:[%22003-491603-492872%22]} Accessed 21 September, 2017.

their asylum requests. The applicants complained, in particular, about the circumstances of their arrest and expulsion to Slovakia. The Court held that there had been a violation of Article 4 of Protocol No. 4 to the Convention,[21] noting in particular that the expulsion procedure had not afforded sufficient guarantees demonstrating that the personal circumstances of each of those concerned had been genuinely and individually taken into account.[22]

There are thus violations of the collective human rights of refugee asylum seekers often, to various degrees and in many forms,[23] by certain States reluctant to share the burden of meeting international law obligations to refugees or determined not to do so. On the view here collective refugee rights exist whether or not the individual State acknowledges them. For instance a State may decide only to consider those collectives of refugees in UNHCR camps for the possibility of refugee entry and resettlement pursuant to individual assessment and vetting of members of the collective. This then, it is here argued, represents a denial *on a collective basis* of the rights of groups of refugees travelling together on their journey of escape not having reached a UNHCR camp to be considered for asylum through individual assessments. Collective refugee rights thus are part and parcel of the necessary preconditions for acknowledgement of the individual refugee claimant's case. Collective expulsion measures or other collective measures including the failure to recognize the collective human rights of refugees are then, on this analysis, fundamentally both a denial of collective and individual refugee rights. The current author is thus disagreed with the view in the latter half of the following quote discounting the need to acknowledge refugee collective rights:

> All members of . . .refugee groups should have rights *as individuals*, just like other citizens. ***We should not ask for more***, but we cannot do with less (emphasis added).[24]

---

[21]"Article 4 (prohibition of collective expulsion of aliens) of Protocol No. 4 to the European Convention on Human Rights: "Collective expulsion of aliens is prohibited".

"Collective expulsion" = any measure compelling aliens, as a group, to leave a country, except where such a measure is taken on the basis of a reasonable and objective examination of the particular case of each individual alien of the group."(See European Court of Human Rights Collective Expulsions of Aliens http://www.echr.coe.int/Documents/FS_Collective_expulsions_ENG.pdf Accessed 21 September, 2017.

[22]European Court of Human Rights Collective Expulsions of Aliens http://www.echr.coe.int/Documents/FS_Collective_expulsions_ENG.pdf Accessed 21 September, 2017.

[23]For instance in 2016 expressions of grave concern were issued by the Office of the UN High Commissioner for Refugees . . . and the UN Children's Fund . . .concerning "the use of detention for *all* new arrivals in the Greek islands, *including children and other vulnerable persons*" (emphasis added). This detention approach by Greece in essence constituted a harsh tactic of deterrence directed to actual or prospective refugee asylum seekers and was imposed *collectively* by the State without due process for each individual and in violation of i.e. the Convention on the Rights of the Child and refugee law. See UN News Centre (24 March, 2016) UN rights chief concerned over 'collective expulsion' of migrants after EU-Turkey deal http://www.un.org/apps/news/story.asp?NewsID=53539#.WcSDhcZrzIU Accessed 21 September, 2017.

[24]Galenkamp (1998), p. 516.

It is generally accepted as a truism-here challenged- that the international law covering refugees concerns individual rights *exclusively* as opposed to, in addition, refugee collective rights. Further it is not necessarily a settled dispute as to whether the grant of the right to asylum to the individual is a discretionary expression of the powers associated with State sovereignty or a right of the individual to be granted, wherever feasible by a particular State, when an individual meets the international law requirements for asylum as set out by treaty and/or as a principle of international law. That asylum is an individual right is expressed in the following:

> *The rights of an asylum seeker are linked to the individual rather than the State* as the right to asylum under Article 18 of the CFREU [Charter of Fundamental Rights of the European Union] is to be construed as a subjective and enforceable right of individuals to be granted asylum under the Union's law. *The beneficiaries of this provision are all individuals*, who may be eligible for international protection on grounds established under any instrument of international human rights law, including the 1951 Refugee Convention and the European Convention on Human Rights, and EU law. Since asylum is a shared competence between the Union and its Member States, the protection of Article 18 CFREU applies in all areas of activity of the Union and its Member States that fall within the scope of application of the Union's law(emphasis added).[25]

It is here contended, however, that the Charter of Fundamental Rights of the European Union also *implicitly* acknowledges collective refugee rights. For instance; the right not to be expelled as a refugee collective is by definition a right of the collective though it simultaneously involves the right of each member of the collective to have their refugee claims assessed individually on its merits.

> **Article 19**
> Protection in the event of removal, expulsion or extradition
>
> 1. *Collective expulsions are prohibited.*
>
> 2. *No one* may be removed, expelled or extradited to a State where there is a serious risk that he or she would be subjected to the death penalty, torture or other inhuman or degrading treatment or punishment (emphasis added).[26]

The refugee collective, on the view here, has an identity in and of itself which is more than just the sum of the individual members' past unique histories. That collective refugee identity of a particular refugee group encompasses, for instance, the shared current very specific situation and story of suffering of particular refugee collectives at specific border crossings or in detention or caught up in other protracted refugee situations denied asylum and humane treatment *as a collective* (i.e. the refugees at the makeshift refugee camp near Calais (now removed by French authorities) constituted a refugee collective that resisted attempts to destroy the

---

[25]Blerim Greka, Agnesa Greka and Resul Greka v Police of the Czech Republic, Regional Directorate of the Police of the South Moravian Region, Amicus Curiae, European Council on Refugees and Exiles (ECRE) February, 2015, point 3.2 at p. 3.

[26]Charter of Fundamental Rights of the European Union (2000).

camp). The refugee collective also has identity in its efforts as a collective to resist inhumane treatment, and to struggle for respect of refugee entitlements under international law. The suggestion here is thus that persons belonging to any particular refugee collective may or may not have disparate ethnic, religious, cultural backgrounds and may often come from different homelands. However, these refugees who may or may not have a shared history in a same homeland, are most often thrust together at a certain location all seeking asylum as refugees (i.e. in following the same perilous journey often on the same route to the same State seeking asylum (whether the State of first arrival is the final asylum State sought or envisioned as a step along the way, the individuals in the specific collective are frequently corralled together in detention, or at a border crossing etc). On the analysis here then such a grouping of individual refugees meets the definition of a refugee collective as per the UNHCR criteria for a refugee collective; considered such on a presumptive/prima facie basis as set out in Guidelines for International Protection No. 11:

> A prima facie approach means the recognition by a State or UNHCR of refugee status on the basis of readily apparent, objective circumstances in the country of origin or, in the case of stateless asylum seekers, their country of former habitual residence. A prima facie approach acknowledges that those fleeing these circumstances are at risk of harm that brings them within the applicable refugee definition.[27]
>
> A prima facie approach operates only to recognize refugee status. *Decisions to reject require an individual assessment* (emphasis added).[28]

The contention here is that for all intents and purposes, the UNHCR guidelines on *prima facie* refugee status have been largely ignored by States to which refugee collectives have attempted to gain entry in the hopes of being granted asylum. This in that such *prima facie* refugee status confers on the individual all the benefits of refugee status under the 1951 Refugee Convention and its 1967 Protocol as well as under any relevant domestic and/or regional instrument concerning refugee rights:

> Prima facie recognition of refugee status is not to be confused with an interim or provisional status, pending subsequent confirmation. Rather, once refugee status has been determined on a prima facie basis, it remains valid in that country unless the conditions for cessation are met, or their status is otherwise cancelled or revoked.[29]

This reluctance and sometimes refusal to grant asylum based on *prima facie* recognition of the collective as a refugee group extends also to the most vulnerable i.e. unaccompanied refugee children (i.e. unaccompanied children from the makeshift camp at Calais were allowed asylum in the UK without having family members

[27]United Nations High Commissioner on Refugees (2015) Guidelines for International Protection No. 11 Prima Facie Recognition of Refugee Status HCR/GIP/15/11 (24 June, 2015) at p. 2.

[28]United Nations High Commissioner on Refugees (2015) Guidelines for International Protection No. 11 Prima Facie Recognition of Refugee Status HCR/GIP/15/11 (24 June, 2015) at p. 3.

[29]United Nations High Commissioner on Refugees (2015) Guidelines for International Protection No. 11 Prima Facie Recognition of Refugee Status HCR/GIP/15/11 (24 June, 2015) at p. 3.

there only after Lord Dubbs managed to have a legislative amendment allowing for the same passed and then only with certain statutory limitations as to when the children in question were to have arrived in Europe).

The UNHCR explains that *prima facie* recognition of refugee status is particularly useful in dealing with a large scale influx of vulnerable refugee groups from particular places of origin where the State and/or non-State agents working independently or as a proxy for the State are known to be engaging in persecution of targeted groups. However, it is precisely that situation (a large scale influx of vulnerable refugee groups) that has instead led, for instance, certain European States to sidestep the UNHCR Guidelines on *prima facie* recognition of refugee status for certain refugee collectives i.e. such as those refugee asylum seekers from Syria, Afghanistan and certain other places of origin where such prima facie recognition as refugees would seem warranted.

> A prima facie approach is particularly suited to situations of large-scale arrivals of refugees. Large-scale situations are characterised by the arrival across an international border of persons in need of international protection in such numbers and at such a rate as to render individual determination of their claims impracticable.[30]

Security concerns may arise with the *prima facie* recognition of refugee collectives:

> A prima facie approach may not be appropriate in all of the aforementioned situations, taking into account security, legal or operational factors. Alternative protection responses may be more suited to the situation at hand, such as screening or other procedures (e.g. temporary protection) *and, in some circumstances, individual status determination* (emphasis added)[31]

Arguably security concerns are less likely to be a legitimate key consideration with regard to unaccompanied children especially those of younger age seeking refugee asylum. However, in many instances, as will be revealed through certain of the cases presented in this work, there is no *prima facie* refugee recognition forthcoming for vulnerable child *bona fide* refugees. The latter being the case for even unaccompanied such children whether the denial of *prima facie* refugee status is on an individual or group (collective) basis. This is the situation not uncommonly though such *prima facie* refugee recognition is provided for under international law and often represents a more humane approach especially in the treatment of the very vulnerable such as children. UNHCR Guideline No. 11 describes such *prima facie* refugee recognition as potentially appropriate also in consideration of the age of the asylum seeker which then would include also young age:

---

[30]United Nations High Commissioner on Refugees (2015) Guidelines for International Protection No. 11 Prima Facie Recognition of Refugee Status HCR/GIP/15/11 (24 June, 2015) at p. 3.

[31]United Nations High Commissioner on Refugees (2015) Guidelines for International Protection No. 11 Prima Facie Recognition of Refugee Status HCR/GIP/15/11 (24 June, 2015) at p. 3.

> A prima facie approach may also be appropriate in relation to groups of similarly situated individuals whose arrival is not on a large-scale, but who share a readily apparent common risk of harm. *The characteristics shared by the similarly situated individuals may be, for example*, their ethnicity, place of former habitual residence, religion, gender, political background or ***age***, *or a combination thereof, which exposes them to risk* (emphasis added).[32]

Instead the child refugee collective has too often been arbitrarily denied refugee status as a collective either on a *prima facie* or temporary interim basis with rejection of the individual asylum claims following suit as will be discussed here through various case examples. Let us turn now to the topic of *prima facie* consideration of individual asylum claims under UNHCR Guideline No. 11.

> *In the context of individual procedures, a prima facie approach* may also be part of simplified or accelerated processes based on the manifestly founded nature of a class of claims or on a presumption of inclusion. Adopting a prima facie approach in individual procedures operates to provide an "evidentiary benefit" to the applicant in the form of accepting certain objective facts. Refugee status would be provided to those who can establish that they belong to the pre-established "beneficiary class", unless there is evidence to the contrary.[33]

The aforementioned statement by the UNHCR sets out then the relationship between a *prima facie* basis for recognizing *the individual's* refugee status as being linked to "the manifestly founded nature of a *class of claims* or on a presumption of inclusion of the individual in a "pre-established "beneficiary class" (a designated collective recognized as a refugee group on a *prima facie* basis)**.** The individual's *prima facie* refugee status thus on that analysis can be considered a derivative to some degree of the *prima facie* recognition of the refugee status (and rights) of the collective. Were the authorities to deny the substantive basis for the collective's *prima facie* refugee rights; the chances of any individual member of that collective receiving *prima facie* refugee status would be much less likely at best. Where *prima facie* refugee status is given to the collective, the individual members will in all likelihood, barring any adverse considerations, enjoy the same. Given the latter; let us digress for a moment and consider a perspective on the relationship between collective rights and individual rights (rights of the individual members of those collectives) relevant to the present discussion regarding the right to refugee status for a collective of persons and the rights of the group's individual members (though the original discussion by the author concerned was advanced in another context re multicultural/minority rights).

The individual rights of refugees fleeing armed conflict or those who are members of a political opposition that is being targeted for grievous harms in their homeland or those who are members of a social or other group persecuted in the homeland by State and/or non-State actors are cognizable via reference to the larger collective of which these individuals are a part. The collective in this instance is a *prima facie*

---

[32]United Nations High Commissioner on Refugees (2015) Guidelines for International Protection No. 11 Prima Facie Recognition of Refugee Status HCR/GIP/15/11 (24 June, 2015) at p. 3.

[33]Protection No. 11 Prima Facie Recognition of Refugee Status HCR/GIP/15/11 (24 June, 2015) at p. 8.

refugee group and as a refugee group a marginalized minority in the State in which they have entered without legal status or hope to enter on their path to asylum as refugees:

> *...some rights that are attributable to and exercised by individuals can be better seen as group rights because their recognition cannot be explained without reference to the group.* ...consider, for instance, the right to the official use of a minority language. The right of francophone Canadian representatives to use French in the federal institutions could be interpreted as an individual right, since it is, in fact, exercised individually. However, it would not exist were it not for reasons related to their membership to a cultural group, and its legitimate interest in using a minority language in the public sphere...(emphasis added).[34]

> Suppose, for instance, that in a country where the Catholic tradition is dominant like Spain, where Sunday is the official holiday, a minority of Jewish citizens claim their right to rest on Saturday, their Sabbath. If this right is indeed justifiable ... it could perfectly take the standard form of an individual right designed to make the religious freedom of Jews effective. *However, individuals would possess this right only by virtue of their belonging to a* minority *group*, and this is fundamental. In fact, only members of this religion could legitimately claim the right in question. *In such cases, using the vocabulary of collective or group rights helps to emphasise this trait* (emphasis added).[35]

> [I]t is the reference to the group or community that is essential, as it captures the central reason for the recognition of the [individual] right[36]

In the case of refugees the situation factually can be more complex. An individual may be a refugee in his or her own right and that may or may not be readily apparent without reference to a larger refugee group to which he or she may or may not belong which aggrieved group is being persecuted in the homeland or land of habitual residence. The vast majority of refugees globally are today fleeing armed conflict situations and, in many situations, belong to targeted groups of civilians as in Syria (i.e. perceived political opposition groups; namely civilians who had been living in rebel held territory in Aleppo). In situations where small or large groups of people seeking asylum arrive from points of origin where it is known these persons *as members of certain defined* actual or perceived groups are being persecuted by State and/or non-state agencies (the latter acting independently or as proxies for the State); a refusal to acknowledge the legitimate refugee status of the *group* is an unjust barrier to the individual group member's chances for refugee status and asylum (based on the individual merits of their case should the matter proceed to individual assessment).

In the case where *prima facie* recognition of refugee group rights ought, according to UNHCR guidelines, have been afforded as per international law; this author would argue that the group in and of itself has a right to, in some degree, self-determination and has what has been referred to by some in reference to group rights

[34]Torbisco Casals (2006) Group Rights as Human Rights: A Liberal Approach to Multiculturalism: Chapter 2 Towards an Alternative Notion of Group Rights at p. 58.

[35]Neo Torbisco Casals (2006) Group Rights as Human Rights: A Liberal Approach to Multiculturalism: Chapter 2 Towards an Alternative Notion of Group Rights at p. 57.

[36]Neo Torbisco Casals (2006) Group Rights as Human Rights: A Liberal Approach to Multiculturalism: Chapter 2 Towards an Alternative Notion of Group Rights at p. 56.

in other contexts as a claim to 'moral agency'.[37] This moral agency of the *refugee collective* might be expressed, for instance, in resisting the inhumane living conditions in a refugee detention centre or in protesting, as a group, the protracted nature of the detention situation and the failure to process individual refugee claims in a timely and fair manner. Thus, it is here argued that the factually *prima facie* bona fide refugee collective has a legitimate claim to moral agency under international law in its own right:

> ...there are other rights, such as the right to self-determination, that cannot sensibly be individually attributed and exercised, not because they are based on any collectivistic theory, but because the production and value of the good protected through them depends on the existence of shared individual interests ...[38]

In considering both the group that should be recognized *prima facie* as a particular refugee collective (as per UNHCR guidelines where the criteria are fulfilled) and the refugee status of the individual of that group; one can refer meaningfully both to the right of self-determination of the group and of the individual member in pursuing refugee legal rights under international law. The moral agency grounded in law of such self-determination is derived from respect for the human dignity of the individual person and of identifiable groups of persons under the UN Charter and other international legal instruments. The right of self-determination of the individual is part and parcel of his/her right to recognition as a person before and under the law. When it comes to children; such a right of self-determination (with due consideration to the child's age and maturity and the particular circumstances as well as the best interests of the child) is implicit in the child's right to participation and to be heard in decisions affecting him or her directly under Article 12 of the Convention on the Rights of the Child. This author is of the view that in part at least "collective rights derive their value...from ...shared individual interests."[39] In the case of refugees, including child refugees, the interests and legal rights of *refugee collectives* when acknowledged and respected are a pathway to increasing the likelihood of acknowledgement and fair assessment of the legal rights of the individual members of the particular refugee group at issue including that of individual asylum seeking refugee children (recall the aforementioned example discussed here regarding Bangladeshi attempts to address certain of the health needs of the Burmese Rohingya refugee children which coincides with acknowledgement that the rights of the Rohingya asylum seeking refugee collective as a whole must be better safeguarded by Bangladesh).

---

[37]See Neo Torbisco Casals (2006) Group Rights as Human Rights: A Liberal Approach to Multiculturalism: Chapter 2 Towards an Alternative Notion of Group Rights for a discussion of the possibility of moral agency of a collective.

[38]Neo Torbisco Casals (2006) Group Rights as Human Rights: A Liberal Approach to Multiculturalism: Chapter 2 Towards an Alternative Notion of Group Rights at p. 58.

[39]Neo Torbisco Casals (2006) Group Rights as Human Rights: A Liberal Approach to Multiculturalism: Chapter 2 Towards an Alternative Notion of Group Rights at p. 59.

2.2 Media Efforts to 'Humanize' the Refugee Asylum Seeking Collective Through Profiling of Individual Suffering

The international media has often attempted to "humanize" (as it is often so offensively phrased) the plight of the refugee collective by profiling individual stories and presenting graphic and even shocking photos of individual refugee suffering; often involving child refugee pain and even avoidable foreseeable death.[40] However, there has been continued resistance from many States to offer meaningful assistance to help ease the suffering of refugee asylum seeking particular collectives such as in the case of Syrian refugees and other groups. It is as if the denial of collective refugee rights *in practice* is held by the State to somehow legitimatize callous superficial legislative and policy edicts that negate the individual humanity of the members of that collective and their right to respect for their human dignity and the proper regard and consideration by the prospective Asylum State that such entails. Consider this reality and recall at the same time the preamble of the Charter of Fundamental Rights of the European Union which refers to State responsibilities to future generations:

> Enjoyment of these rights entails responsibilities and duties with regard to other persons, *to the human community* and *to future generations (emphasis added).*[41]

The Charter of Fundamental Rights of the European Union (CFREU) sets out the rights of the child at Article 24(1) which must be read in context with, for instance, the right to asylum as articulated at Charter Article 18. This in that if individual rights (as articulated in a human rights instrument) are to be meaningful they must correlate to State obligations to honour those rights to the best of the State's ability given the available resources and the high priority assigned to respect for human rights by the State in every respect. Thus CFREU Article 24(1), set out below, can be held to also refer implicitly to *the State obligation* to ensure children "such protection and care as is necessary for their well-being." This view is consistent with Article 24(2) which explicitly refers to the responsibility of public authorities to make children's best interest a primary consideration in decision making. Article 24 of the Charter arguably refers *both* to (1) the rights of children as a collective *qua* children and *qua* child refugees and (2) the rights of the individual child refugee member of a particular child refugee asylum seeking collective in a determination of what would be in his or her (their) particular best interests:

[40]The ethics of such media efforts which often involve filming of asylum seekers where there may not always be subject knowledge and informed truly voluntary consent are complex. This is so especially where children are profiled and filmed but that contentious matter is beyond the scope of this work.

[41]Charter of Fundamental Rights of the European Union (2000).

Article 24
The rights of the child

1. Children shall have the right to such protection and care as is necessary for their well-being. They may express their views freely. Such views shall be taken into consideration on matters which concern them in accordance with their age and maturity.

2. In all actions relating to children, whether taken by public authorities or private institutions, the child's best interests must be a primary consideration.[42]

Article 18
Right to asylum

The right to asylum shall be guaranteed with due respect for the rules of the Geneva Convention of 28 July 1951 and the Protocol of 31 January 1967 relating to the status of refugees and in accordance with the Treaty establishing the European Community.[43]

Thus, for example, we know that a particular child refugee asylum seeking *group* held in detention[44] with the members having committed no crime in the territory in which they are detained are in a situation where their *collective rights* as asylum seekers (as well as their individual rights) are being violated:

> As emphasised in the UNHCR Guidelines *seeking asylum is not an unlawful act* and therefore, detention of asylum seekers must never be automatic...(emphasis added)[45]
>
> Every person has the right to seek and enjoy in other countries asylum from persecution, serious human rights violations and other serious harm. Seeking asylum is not, therefore, an unlawful act. Furthermore, the 1951 Convention provides that *asylum-seekers shall not be penalised for their illegal entry or stay, provided they present themselves to the authorities without delay and show good cause for their illegal entry or presence.*[46] In exercising the right to seek asylum, asylum-seekers are often forced to arrive at, or enter, a territory without prior authorisation. *The position of asylum-seekers may thus differ fundamentally from that*

[42]Charter of Fundamental Rights of the European Union (2000).

[43]Charter of Fundamental Rights of the European Union (2000).

[44]This may occur in practice, at least for a time, even where less coercive options are available such as transfer to another EU country willing to provide proper service and support while the child refugee's asylum application is processed.

[45]Blerim Greka, Agnesa Greka and Resul Greka v Police of the Czech Republic, Regional Directorate of the Police of the South Moravian Region, Amicus Curiae, European Council on Refugees and Exiles (ECRE) February, 2015, point 4.3 and 4.4 at p. 4.

[46]On the current author's view; it would be legally supportable to consider that children, especially young children and those traumatized and/or unfamiliar with the requirements of asylum seeking, can properly be excused for not presenting themselves to authorities as refugee asylum seekers or doing so only after a long delay and for often not being able to articulate on their own a good reason for the grant of asylum though they may in fact be *bona fide* refugees meeting the criteria for a grant of asylum under relevant domestic and international law.

> *of ordinary migrants in that they may not be in a position to comply with the legal formalities for entry*. They may, for example, be unable to obtain the necessary documentation in advance of their flight because of their fear of persecution and/or the urgency of their departure. These factors, as well as the fact that asylum-seekers have often experienced traumatic events, need to be taken into account in determining any restrictions on freedom of movement based on irregular entry or presence (emphasis added).[47]

On the UNHRC perspective then, by implication, it is incorrect to conflate, as so often *in practice* occurs with State authorities, perhaps for strategic political effect, the notion of 'refugee asylum seeker' as a category of persons with the category of 'illegal immigrant[s].' Having entered the country on an irregular basis in the first instance for the purpose of openly seeking asylum does not render one or the larger asylum collective of which one may be a part "illegal immigrants." For instance illegal immigrants unlike refugees may not fit the 1951 Refugee definition of refugees entitled to seek asylum,[48] and the humanitarian considerations that are taken into account when asylum is granted may or may not apply to an illegal immigrant individual or collective depending on the scope of those considerations allowable under domestic and international law. The grant of amnesty for some period and possibly a pathway to citizenship for groups of illegal immigrants is grounded on a different basis than are the grants of asylum to refugees. The latter is inspired in large part by (1) the State duty to extend humanitarian assistance and human rights protections where refugees have no viable alternative and are persecuted in their homeland[49] and (2) by a concern for meeting State obligations to foster international peace and security which includes the responsibility to protect refugees and attempt to prevent those situations that give rise to mass forced migration (whether that forced migration was ordered directly by the offending State or *de facto* ensued due to the human rights abuses inflicted by that offending State on segments of its civilian population).[50] Though asylum seeking is not an unlawful act; in today's refugee crisis, in various locales globally, the asylum seeker is commonly, by various forms of maltreatment *in effect* punished—both as an individual and as member of a particular asylum seeking collective—for the very act of asylum seeking. For instance; unaccompanied and accompanied child refugee asylum

[47]United Nations High Commissioner on Refugees (2012): Detention Guidelines (Guidelines on the Applicable Criteria and Standards relating to the Detention of Asylum-Seekers and Alternatives to Detention).

[48]There are cases where persons generally regarded as illegal undocumented immigrants may also fit under a broader definition of refugee than that set out in the Refugee Convention; namely as 'persons of concern' such as children at high risk of victimization by gang violence and gang recruitment in their country of origin.

[49]The refugee in practice may be someone who fits the Refugee Convention limited categorical criteria or the State may apply a broader set of eligibility criteria and include as refugees also persons facing various coercive circumstances in their home country due to personal or other characteristics not listed in the Convention but considered to properly ground the request for and possible grant of asylum.

[50]Cohen (2017).

seekers have been and are detained as a matter of course for significant periods in many jurisdictions.

> Double vulnerability of asylum seeking children along with the principle of best interest of the child must always be a primary consideration when taking a decision to detain and it is impossible to conceive of a situation in which detention could be in the best interest of the child.[51]

> The detention of asylum seeking children together with their parents when the latter are found to be in an irregular situation, justified on the basis of maintaining family unity, may not only violate the principle of the best interests of the child and the right of the child to be detained only as a measure of last resort, but it may also violate their right not to be punished for the acts of their parents.[52]

This routine detention of child refugee asylum seekers in detention facilities, even for extended periods, rather than sheltering the children in family or child friendly facilities if they are accompanied by parents or guardians is in violation of international standards for the treatment of a child refugee as expressed, for instance, in the Convention on the Rights of the Child[53] (1) 'best interests of the child' principle (Article 3), (2) the right to non-discrimination on any basis in the State's according of the basic human rights articulated in the Convention (Article 2) and (3) the right to protection and humanitarian assistance for refugee children (Article 22) among other of the Convention provisions. These children as a group, whether accompanied children or children separated from parents or other guardian and unaccompanied, then should be entitled to file a collective human rights complaint or individual such complaints against the State when subjected to such collective maltreatment as is constituted by automatic detention.[54] Recognition of the collective rights of refugee asylum seeking children *both as children and as refugees*, and accountability where those collective rights of a particular such group are infringed by the State, are essential given the special vulnerability of child refugee asylum seeking groups. That vulnerability has been noted, for instance, in the European case law:

---

[51]Blerim Greka, Agnesa Greka and Resul Greka v Police of the Czech Republic, Regional Directorate of the Police of the South Moravian Region, Amicus Curiae, European Council of Refugees and Exiles (ECRE) February, 2015, 2(C) p. 2.

[52]Blerim Greka, Agnesa Greka and Resul Greka v Police of the Czech Republic, Regional Directorate of the Police of the South Moravian Region, Amicus Curiae, European Council of Refugees and Exiles (ECRE) February, 2015, 2(D) p. 2.

[53]Convention on the Rights of the Child entered into force 2 September, 1990 http://www.ohchr.org/en/professionalinterest/pages/crc.aspx Accessed 22 September, 2017.

[54]The African Charter on the Rights and Welfare of the Child allows for collective complaints. The complaint procedure under the Convention on the Rights of the Child while it allows for group complaints (where each child member has been identified and consent to be included in the complaint is normally provided by the minor or their guardian with some exceptions allowed) does not provide for collective complaints (See Grover (2015).

> The specific vulnerability of asylum seeking children, including within families has been affirmed consistently in the jurisprudence of the ECtHR.[55]

Let us consider for a moment another aspect of what is exactly meant by 'collective refugee rights' as the term is used in this work.

> The first category [of collective rights] consists of those rights that are conferred materially on individual group members, but may be looked after procedurally by the collectivity. In some instances, collectivities may act in law to represent their members' interests.[56] [i.e. a representative few individuals as a group may act on behalf of a larger refugee collective to advance the rights of the collective and its individual members as with *Conka v Belgium*[57] where the ruling of the European Court of Human Rights found against the State for its collective expulsion of Romany refugees]
>
> The second category of collective rights goes beyond the 'class-action' concept. Here, the rights are not only procedurally looked after by collectivities, but are also materially ascribed to them to protect their collective interests.[58] [i.e. *prima facie* recognition of a collective as a refugee group hence conferring *prima facie* refugee recognition/rights also on the individual members of the refugee collective]

When collective child refugee rights are not affirmed in respect of particular refugee asylum seeking child groups, individual children belonging to those collectives are forced often to re-litigate battles that may have been already won (or wrongfully lost) by other children who were similarly situated either within the same jurisdiction or in another jurisdiction governed by the same regional or other agreements and relevant treaty instruments.[59] This then in itself is violative of child refugee asylum seeker's individual and collective rights. Consider, for instance, the European Union refugee system's central objective which, as certain of the case law here discussed illustrates, is all to commonly not carried out in practice:

> The stated objective of the EU's Common European Asylum System (CEAS), is to establish a common area of protection and solidarity based on high standards of protection where, *regardless of the Member State in which an asylum application is lodged, similar cases result in the same outcome*, while Article 78 TFEU envisages the creation of a uniform status of asylum, valid throughout the Union . . .(emphasis added)[60]

The following three cases highlight and address the vulnerability of child refugee asylum seekers and some of the implications for State obligations in that regard. The

---

[55]Blerim Greka, Agnesa Greka and Resul Greka v Police of the Czech Republic, Regional Directorate of the Police of the South Moravian Region, Amicus Curiae, European Council of Refugees and Exiles (ECRE) February, 2015, point 4.9 at p. 5.

[56]Galenkamp (1998), p. 502.

[57]Conka v Belgium [2002], Chamber Judgment (no. 51564/99) https://hudoc.echr.coe.int/eng#{%22itemid%22:[%22003-491603-492872%22]} Accessed 21 September, 2017.

[58]Galenkamp (1998), p. 502.

[59]As will be evident in our examination of various cases to be discussed in this work.

[60]Blerim Greka, Agnesa Greka and Resul Greka v Police of the Czech Republic, Regional Directorate of the Police of the South Moravian Region, Amicus Curiae, European Council of Refugees and Exiles (ECRE) February, 2015, 3.4 at p. 3.

cases discussed in this chapter also highlight the need to consider the individual refugee child in terms of his/her membership in two intersecting collectives; that of "children" and, where applicable, 'refugee *asylum seekers*'. Both of these collectives are considered to constitute highly vulnerable groups entitled to special protection under international law. Thus individuals who belong to both such collectives are considered amongst the most vulnerable of persons globally. In addition, the three cases explicitly or implicitly raise the issue of the autonomous right of the child, separate from other family members, to consideration by the State of his/her refugee asylum claim on its independent merits.

2.3 Negation of Child Asylum Seekers' Collective Rights as 'Children' and as 'Refugees' as a Vehicle to Denial of Their Individual Human Rights

2.3.1 Case 1:Tarakhel, Mubilanzila Mayeka and Kaniki Mitunga v. Belgium (European Court of Human Rights)

Headnotes: Detention of an unaccompanied young child refugee, deportation of a 5 year old refugee unaccompanied by family or other, best interests of the child principle, the child's right to family reunification, the unaccompanied refugee child's right to adequate and appropriate protection as well as other humanitarian assistance and right to effective access to the courts, the child refugee's right to respect for her human dignity and special consideration.

2.3.1.1 The Facts

The Applicants in this case were Ms Pulchérie Mubilanzila Mayeka and her daughter Tabitha Kaniki Mitunga; both Congolese nationals. The child was born in 1997 and hence was nine at the time of the ECtHR decision but age five at the time of the occurrence of the relevant facts relating to the application to the ECtHR requesting redress for alleged violations of the European Convention on Human Rights. Ms. Mubilanzila Mayeka was successful in her refugee application to Canada in 2001 and in 2003 received the State's permission to lawfully stay in Canada indefinitely. The child's mother had asked her brother who resided in the Netherlands to bring her daughter Tabitha Kaniki Mitunga from the DRC to the Netherlands and look after her until the mother could arrange to bring the child to Canada to live with her. When Tabitha arrived at the Brussels airport en route to the Netherlands with her uncle on August 18, 2002 she was detained at the Brussels airport this, according to Belgium, for lack of the required entry documentation. Regarding the conditions of detention for this very young child (while she had been held at the Transit Centre in Belgium prior to her deportation); the alleged facts regarding those conditions are as follows:

> ... the director of Transit Centre no. 127 described the second applicant's [child's] living conditions at the centre in a letter of 23 November 2004. He explained that she had been looked after by two women who were themselves mothers, that she had played with other children, that her uncle and mother had telephoned her nearly every day and that she had been allowed to telephone them free of charge under the supervision of a team of social workers; he added that her lawyer had paid her a number of visits and had brought her telephone cards, confectionary.[61]

The child's uncle returned to the Netherlands and the 5 year old Tabitha was left unaccompanied in Belgian detention. Counsel was appointed by Belgium the same day as the detention to assist the child. The child's application for asylum was denied August 27, 2002 by the Belgian Aliens Office. That decision was then upheld by the Commissioner-General for Refugees and Stateless Persons on 25 September 2002. On September 26, 2002 Tabitha's lawyer filed a request with the Belgian Aliens Office that Tabitha be placed in foster care pending the outcome of further proceedings but that request received no reply.[62] On October 15, 2002 the child's Crown Counsel received the following notification from the Belgium Aliens Office:

> "... the enquiries have enabled the person concerned's family to be located in Kinshasa. In view of the positive results of the enquiries as a whole, a flight has already been arranged for Thursday 17 October 2002. The child will be met at Kinshasa by her family. A representative from our embassy will also be present. Lastly, we would note that the sole responsibility for the length of the applicant's detention lies with her uncle, who has been uncooperative and has studiously avoided giving the Aliens Office the family's address. Accordingly, in the child's own interest, she should remain in detention until Thursday 17 October 2002, when she can be returned to her own family in Kinshasa."[63]

On 16 October 2002 the Chambre de conseil of the Brussels Trial Court held that Tabitha's detention violated Article 3(1)(2) relating to the best interests of the child per the UN Convention on the Rights of the Child[64] and ordered her immediate

---

[61]ECtHR Judgment (2007) Tarakhel, Mubilanzila Mayeka and Kaniki Mitunga v. Belgium, point 37 (Decision Date 12/01/2007).

[62]The applicant argued before the ECt HR that there was no reason the child should not have been placed in foster care pending her appeals as it did not follow from the fact that she was not permitted by Belgian authorities to travel from Belgium to Holland that she instead should have been held in detention in a facility not intended for children.

[63]ECtHR Judgment (2007) Tarakhel, Mubilanzila Mayeka and Kaniki Mitunga v. Belgium point 29.

[64]Convention on the Rights of the Child (entered into force 2 September, 1990) ratified by Belgium 25 November, 1991.

> 1. In all actions concerning children, whether undertaken by public or private social welfare institutions, courts of law, administrative authorities or legislative bodies, the best interests of the child shall be a primary consideration.
>
> 2. States Parties undertake to ensure the child such protection and care as is necessary for his or her well-being, taking into account the rights and duties of his or her parents, legal

release. On the same day; the Office of the High Commissioner for Refugees requested of the Aliens Office that Tabitha be permitted to remain in Belgium while her application for a Canadian visa was being processed and informed that Office that the child's mother had obtained refugee status in Canada and that there was no adult in DRC related to Tabitha willing and able to care for her. Despite these efforts on 17 October 2002, Tabitha was deported to the Democratic Republic of Congo. The child went to the airport accompanied by a social worker but travelled alone back to the DRC though an air stewardess had been tasked by the executive of the airline to look after the child during the flight. There were three Congolese adults on the same flight who were also being deported. There was no family member to greet the child when she arrived at the airport in the DRC contrary to what the Belgium Alien Office had assured the child's Crown Counsel though the Belgian embassy in Kinshasa, DRC had sent a letter regarding the child's arrival to another of the child's uncles, a university student B and the only relative remaining in the DRC. He had promised to come to the airport to greet and take the child into his custody but reneged on his promise according to Belgium. The Belgian government had made no contingency plans in case the uncle did not show up at the airport in Kinshasa, DRC. In the end the child was left to be met by DRC authorities at the airport. The mother had not been informed in advance of Tabitha's deportation and on October 17, 2002 only discovered this after asking to speak with her daughter at the Belgian Transit Centre where the child had been detained.

As a result of the good offices of the Belgian and Canadian Prime Ministers and their effective intervention, the child was able to leave the DRC October 23, 2002 en route to Canada to be reunited with her mother. On 29 October 2002 the mother applied to the Canadian authorities for a visa permitting family reunification.

The case was brought forward to the European Court of Human Rights (ECtHR) which relied heavily on the *Convention on the Rights of the Child* (CRC) in rendering its decision in this case; specifically Articles 3, 10, 22 and 37 of the CRC[65]:

> **Article 3 [Best Interests of the Child and Rights of the Child to Protection and Care]**
> 1. In all actions concerning children, whether undertaken by public or private social welfare institutions, courts of law, administrative authorities or legislative bodies, the best interests of the child shall be a primary consideration.
>
> 2. States Parties undertake to ensure the child such protection and care as is necessary for his or her well-being, taking into account the rights and duties of his or her parents, legal guardians, or other individuals legally responsible for him or

guardians, or other individuals legally responsible for him or her, and, to this end, shall take all appropriate legislative and administrative measures...

[65]Convention on the Rights of the Child (entered into force 2 September, 1990) ratified by Belgium 25 November, 1991.

her, and, to this end, shall take all appropriate legislative and administrative measures.

3. States Parties shall ensure that the institutions, services and facilities responsible for the care or protection of children shall conform with the standards established by competent authorities, particularly in the areas of safety, health, in the number and suitability of their staff, as well as competent supervision.

Article 10 [Family Reunification]

1. In accordance with the obligation of States Parties under article 9, paragraph 1, applications by a child or his or her parents to enter or leave a State Party for the purpose of family reunification shall be dealt with by States Parties in a positive, humane and expeditious manner. States Parties shall further ensure that the submission of such a request shall entail no adverse consequences for the applicants and for the members of their family.

2. A child whose parents reside in different States shall have the right to maintain on a regular basis, save in exceptional circumstances personal relations and direct contacts with both parents. Towards that end and in accordance with the obligation of States Parties under article 9, paragraph 1, States Parties shall respect the right of the child and his or her parents to leave any country, including their own, and to enter their own country. The right to leave any country shall be subject only to such restrictions as are prescribed by law and which are necessary to protect the national security, public order (ordre public), public health or morals or the rights and freedoms of others and are consistent with the other rights recognized in the present Convention.

Article 22 [Accompanied and Unaccompanied Child Refugees]

1. States Parties shall take appropriate measures to ensure that a child who is seeking refugee status or who is considered a refugee in accordance with applicable international or domestic law and procedures shall, whether unaccompanied or accompanied by his or her parents or by any other person, receive appropriate protection and humanitarian assistance in the enjoyment of applicable rights set forth in the present Convention and in other international human rights or humanitarian instruments to which the said States are Parties.

2. For this purpose, States Parties shall provide, as they consider appropriate, co-operation in any efforts by the United Nations and other competent intergovernmental organizations or nongovernmental organizations co-operating with the United Nations to protect and assist such a child and to trace the parents or other members of the family of any refugee child in order to obtain information necessary for reunification with his or her family. In cases where no parents or other members of the family can be found, the child shall be accorded the same protection as any other child permanently or temporarily deprived of his or her family environment for any reason, as set forth in the present Convention.

Article 37 [Torture or Other Cruel, Inhuman or Degrading Treatment or Punishment]
States Parties shall ensure that:

(a) No child shall be subjected to torture or other cruel, inhuman or degrading treatment or punishment. . .;

(b) No child shall be deprived of his or her liberty unlawfully or arbitrarily. The arrest, detention or imprisonment of a child shall be in conformity with the law and shall be used only as a measure of last resort and for the shortest appropriate period of time;

(c) Every child deprived of liberty shall be treated with humanity and respect for the inherent dignity of the human person, and in a manner which takes into account the needs of persons of his or her age. In particular, every child deprived of liberty shall be separated from adults unless it is considered in the child's best interest not to do so and shall have the right to maintain contact with his or her family through correspondence and visits, save in exceptional circumstances;

(d) Every child deprived of his or her liberty shall have the right to prompt access to legal and other appropriate assistance, as well as the right to challenge the legality of the deprivation of his or her liberty before a court or other competent, independent and impartial authority, and to a prompt decision on any such action.

The ECtHR found a violation of Article 3 of the European Convention on Human Rights in respect of both the mother and the child's right to be protected from inhuman or degrading treatment. This arising first out of the child's detention at the Transit Centre in Belgium unaccompanied and the suffering it caused both mother and child and second in relation to the child's deportation and the trauma this caused mother and child. The Court also held there had been a violation of Article 8 of the European Convention for both mother and child in respect of the right to respect for their private and family life. The violation of Article 8 rights of both mother and child, the Court held, resulted from both the child's detention and her deportation given the facts of the case. The Court noted that detention separated the child from a family member (her uncle) in whose care the mother had placed the child and that this rendered the child an 'unaccompanied foreign minor'; a member of amongst the most vulnerable of child groups. The child's reunification with the mother the ECtHR found had been significantly delayed due to the detention and deportation of the child causing suffering to both mother and child. The ECtHR also found a violation in respect of Article 5(1)(f) of the European Convention[66] in respect of the child in that she was held in a detention facility that was inappropriate

[66]European Convention on Human Rights Article 5(1): "Everyone has the right to liberty and security of person. No one shall be deprived of his liberty save in the following cases and in accordance with a procedure prescribed by law.

for meeting her needs as a very young child.[67] Thus the detention was held incompatible with Article 5 of the European Convention in the first instance notwithstanding that she had been detained for not having entry documents and pending a deportation proceeding.[68] Also her detention was held unlawful in a later period when it continued despite a domestic court ordering her release. The ECtHR in this case also held that the child's rights under European Convention on Human Rights Article 5(4)[69] were also infringed. The latter violation arose in that despite the Court of first instance holding that the child's detention was unlawful; the government had made the decision to deport the child before even receiving the Court's of first instance (*chambre du conseil*) decision regarding whether she should be released from detention and never reconsidered its decision to deport her. Further she was deported before the appeal by Crown counsel had expired.[70] In essence then the child was denied (as a result of the government's conduct) effective access to the courts:

> In these circumstances, the Court finds that the second applicant's [child's] appeal to the chambre du conseil appears, in the circumstances of the case, to have been ineffective There has therefore been a violation of Article 5 § 4 of the Convention[71]

Though the ECtHR in the case at bar ruled in favour of child and mother in regards to finding Article 3 and 8 European Convention violations on the particular facts of the case; the ECtHR affirmed a view in *Tarakhel, Mubilanzila Mayeka and Kaniki Mitunga v. Belgium* that the:

> The Convention does not guarantee, as such, any right for an alien to enter or stay on the territory of the State of which he or she is not a national[72]

At the same time the ECtHR held in the case at bar that:

[67]ECtHR Judgment (2007) Tarakhel, Mubilanzila Mayeka and Kaniki Mitunga v. Belgium, point 102: " the Court's case-law requires that there must be some relationship between the ground of permitted deprivation of liberty relied on and the place and conditions of detention."

[68]ECtHR Judgment (2007) Tarakhel, Mubilanzila Mayeka and Kaniki Mitunga v. Belgium, point 103: "The Court notes that the second applicant was detained in a closed centre intended for illegal immigrants in the same conditions as adults; these conditions were consequently not adapted to the position of extreme vulnerability in which she found herself as a result of her position as an unaccompanied foreign minor."

[69]European Convention on Human Rights Article 5(4): "Everyone who is deprived of his liberty by arrest or detention shall be entitled to take proceedings by which the lawfulness of his detention shall be decided speedily by a court and his release ordered if the detention is not lawful."

[70]ECtHR Judgment (2007) Tarakhel, Mubilanzila Mayeka and Kaniki Mitunga v. Belgium, point 113:"the Government have acknowledged that the Belgian authorities' conduct was not dictated by the *chambre du conseil's* decision to grant the application for release as her deportation had been arranged in advance". Thus the child was released not as a remedy for an unlawful detention or in compliance with the *chambre du conseil* order to release her but rather to allow for deportation.

[71]ECtHR Judgment (2007) Tarakhel, Mubilanzila Mayeka and Kaniki Mitunga v. Belgium, point 113–114.

[72]ECtHR Judgment (2007) Tarakhel, Mubilanzila Mayeka and Kaniki Mitunga v. Belgium, point 81.

> ...detention in centres used for aliens awaiting deportation will be acceptable only where it is intended to enable the States to combat illegal immigration while at the same time complying with their international obligations, including those arising under the European Convention on Human Rights and the Convention on the Rights of the Child (ratified by Belgium in 1991). Furthermore, the States' interest in foiling attempts to circumvent immigration rules must not deprive aliens of the protection afforded by these *conventions or deprive foreign minors, especially if unaccompanied, of the protection their status warrants*. The protection of fundamental rights and the constraints imposed by a State's immigration policy must therefore be reconciled (emphasis added).[73]

Indeed the Belgian government itself in the case at bar did not rule out the legal supportability of the proposition that unaccompanied foreign minors of very young age may be owed a high duty of care and special consideration (though such was not accorded to the 5 year old in the case at bar who had been rendered an unaccompanied minor, in the first instance, through the Belgian State's disproportionate actions in response to the child entering the country without proper documentation):

> Detention enabled the State to issue a deportation order that would be enforceable in practice in the event of the request for asylum being turned down. *The Government accepted that it was legitimate to enquire whether these principles ought to be moderated when the immigrant concerned was a young child* (emphasis added).[74]

The ECtHR in the instant case contemplated there could be a range of circumstances in which detention of a minor would comply with international human rights standards including those stipulated in the European Convention regarding deprivation of the liberty of a minor:

> The Court does not agree with the second applicant's submission that paragraph (d) of Article 5 § 1 of the Convention is the only provision which permits the detention of a minor. It in fact contains a specific, but not exhaustive, example of circumstances in which minors might be detained, namely for the purpose of their educational supervision or for the purpose of bringing them before the competent legal authority to decide.[75]

At the same time the ECtHR affirmed in the case that accompanied and unaccompanied child refugee asylum seekers are owed special care and protection under various international treaty and customary law. Automatic detention in non-child friendly facilities with a view to deportation and further inadequate consideration of the specific child's circumstances and of humanitarian issues at play in the case (as occurred in *Tarakhel, Mubilanzila Mayeka and Kaniki Mitunga v. Belgium*) does not at all meet the required international human rights standard for treatment of a child refugee asylum seeker.

---

[73]ECtHR Judgment (2007) Tarakhel, Mubilanzila Mayeka and Kaniki Mitunga v. Belgium, point 81.

[74]ECtHR Judgment (2007) Tarakhel, Mubilanzila Mayeka and Kaniki Mitunga v. Belgium, point 74.

[75]ECtHR Judgment (2007) Tarakhel, Mubilanzila Mayeka and Kaniki Mitunga v. Belgium, point 100.

2.3.1.2 Commentary on the Significance of *Tarakhel, Mubilanzila Mayeka and Kaniki Mitunga v. Belgium* (European Court of Human Rights) for Child Refugee Collective and Individual Rights

The ECtHR in the case at bar found that there had been a violation of the European Convention on Human Rights Article 3 right to be protected from torture or inhuman or degrading treatment for the child due to her detention and for the mother as the result of the suffering she (the mother) endured resultant from her child's detention unaccompanied by any family member. In regards the child's detention the Court found the following:

> The Court is in no doubt that the second applicant's (the child's) detention in the conditions described…caused her considerable distress. Nor could the authorities who ordered her detention have failed to be aware of the serious psychological effects it would have on her.[76]

The ECtHR reaffirmed in *Tarakhel, Mubilanzila Mayeka and Kaniki Mitunga v. Belgium* that the Article 3 European Convention on Human Rights guarantee that "No one shall be subjected to torture or to inhuman or degrading treatment or punishment"[77] allows for no derogation therefrom regardless the legal status of the individual or group alleging the violation: "Article 3 makes no provision for exceptions"[78] This then reaffirms and prioritizes certain fundamental human rights also for non-citizens where the respondent State in question has custody and/or control as in this case where the child was under the jurisdiction of Belgium.[79] Further the ECtHR articulated a positive proactive obligation in regards to preventing violations of Article 3 of the European Convention in particular in respect of children (and most especially in regards to vulnerable groups of children such as child refugees) and other vulnerable groups (collectivities). The latter then simultaneously, on the analysis here, affirms the refugee[80] individual and collective group right to be protected from gross ill-treatment and especially that rising to the level

[76]ECtHR Judgment (2007) Tarakhel, Mubilanzila Mayeka and Kaniki Mitunga v. Belgium, point 58.

[77]European Convention on Human Rights, first entered into force of the Convention 21 September 1970.

[78]ECtHR Judgment (2007) Tarakhel, Mubilanzila Mayeka and Kaniki Mitunga v. Belgium, point 48.

[79]"Article 3, requires States to take measures designed to ensure that individuals within their jurisdiction are not subjected to torture or inhuman or degrading treatment, including such ill-treatment administered by private individuals": ECtHR Judgment (2007) Tarakhel, Mubilanzila Mayeka and Kaniki Mitunga v. Belgium, point 53.

[80]It is noteworthy that the ECtHR in Tarakhel, Mubilanzila Mayeka and Kaniki Mitunga v. Belgium referred to the child as an 'illegal immigrant' rather than a refugee. While the child was not seeking asylum or any other continuing legal status in Belgium clearly she was a refugee in want of safe passage through Belgium. Her only primary caregiver, the mother, was recognized as a refugee in Canada and had been granted asylum in Canada and the child sought (through her counsel and senior political level interventions) to be re-united with her mother in Canada.

contemplated under Article 3 of the European Convention (that of torture, inhuman or degrading treatment or punishment). Indeed the ECtHR in this case held that Article 3 of the European Convention "takes precedence" over the child's status as what the Court termed "an illegal immigrant":

> Steps should be taken to enable effective protection to be provided, particularly to children and other vulnerable members of society, and should include reasonable measures to prevent ill-treatment of which the authorities have or ought to have knowledge.[81]

> The second applicant's [the child's] position was characterised by her very young age, the fact that she was an illegal immigrant[82] in a foreign land and the fact that she was unaccompanied by her family from whom she had become separated so that she was effectively left to her own devices. She was thus in an extremely vulnerable situation. In view of the absolute nature of the protection afforded by Article 3 of the Convention, it is important to bear in mind that this is the decisive factor and it takes precedence over considerations relating to the second applicant's status as an illegal immigrant. She therefore indisputably came within the *class* of highly vulnerable members of society to whom the Belgian State owed a duty to take adequate measures to provide care and protection as part of its positive obligations under Article 3 of the Convention (emphasis added).[83]

Note also that various other international legal instruments aside from the Convention on the Rights of the Child set out the special care and protection owed to children caught in vulnerable situations:

UN Declaration on the Protection of Women and Children in Emergency and Armed Conflict

Paragraphs 4 and 5 of the 1974 UN Declaration on the Protection of Women and Children in Emergency and Armed Conflict state:

4. All the necessary steps shall be taken to ensure the prohibition of measures such as persecution, torture, punitive measures, degrading treatment and violence, *particularly against that part of the civilian population that consists of... children.*

---

[81]ECtHR Judgment (2007) *Tarakhel, Mubilanzila Mayeka and Kaniki Mitunga v. Belgium*, point 53.

[82]In fact the child was a refugee without proper entry papers to Belgium, and was (prior to her detention unaccompanied in Belgium) planned to be in transit first to Holland with her uncle and then to Canada once her mother arrived in Holland to pick her up and travel with her to Canada where the mother had been granted refugee status and permission to lawfully reside in Canada indefinitely. On the analysis of the current author the then young child of five was entitled to be considered by Belgium a *prima facie* bona fide refugee asylum seeker fleeing the DRC with all the rights that that entails. The latter then rather than the child's status being (on the view here) miscategorized by the Court by use of the more generic term of "illegal immigrant" (which generally includes persons who are not refugees) though the ECtHR in the case did affirm the special care and protection that was owed by Belgium to the child as child.

[83]ECtHR Judgment (2007) Tarakhel, Mubilanzila Mayeka and Kaniki Mitunga v. Belgium, point 55.

> 5. All forms of repression and cruel and inhuman treatment *of . . . children*, including imprisonment, torture, shooting, mass arrests, collective punishment, destruction of dwellings and forcible eviction, committed by belligerents in the course of military operations or in occupied territories shall be considered criminal (emphasis added).[84]

At the time of the case, according to the ECtHR, there was no legal avenue in Belgium for arguing that the detention of the child was not appropriate, for instance, on grounds relating to the conditions to which the child was subjected via the detention such as being in an adult detention centre etc. This as the Belgian law at the time did not set out how foreign minors who were in the country on an irregular basis were to be handled. "In such cases, the question before the *chambre du conseil* was whether the detention was lawful, not whether it was appropriate."[85] The *chambre du conseil* (Court of First Instance) ruled that the detention of the 5 year old was unlawful under the Convention on the Rights of the Child while at the same time acknowledging that the Court of first instance was not empowered by legislation to consider whether detention *per se* was appropriate in the case, whether the conditions in detention to which the child had been exposed were humane nor was the Court authorized to order alterative arrangements. There has since this case been some progress in establishing as suggested by the Committee on the Rights of the Child[86] more appropriate reception arrangements and facilities designated for unaccompanied minors seeking entry or having entered Belgium without proper documents.[87] It is to be noted that rather than expediting reunification of the child with her mother, Belgium separated the child from the uncle who had travelled with her from the DRC to Belgium by placing the child in detention and then deporting her unaccompanied back to the DRC. Though an airline employee on the flight was designated to take care of the child's needs on the flight; it is unclear how the child's psychological/emotional needs could have been fully adequately addressed by that stranger even with the airline employee's best of intentions in caring for the child during the flight. Thus not only the detention period but the trip back to the DRC under the circumstances can reasonably be considered contributors to the child's traumatisation by the Belgian State.

The ECtHR notes in the case at bar that:

> the Belgian authorities stood by their decision to proceed with the second applicant's [child's] deportation on 17 October 2002 despite two new factual developments, these being the *chambre du conseil*'s decision of the previous day to order her immediate release

---

[84]International Committee of the Red Cross (2016) Customary Humanitarian Law relating to Rule 135: Children (Rule 135. Children affected by armed conflict are entitled to special respect and protection).

[85]ECtHR Judgment (2007) Tarakhel, Mubilanzila Mayeka and Kaniki Mitunga v. Belgium, point 56.

[86]ECtHR Judgment (2007) Tarakhel, Mubilanzila Mayeka and Kaniki Mitunga v. Belgium, point 57.

[87]European Migration Network (2014) Policies, Practices and Data on Unaccompanied Minors in Belgium: 2014 Update pp. 29–30.

> on the grounds that her detention was unlawful and the fact that the UNHCR had informed the authorities that the first applicant [the mother] had acquired refugee status in Canada.[88]

One can reasonably wonder what perceived benefit to the State Belgium contemplated (correctly or incorrectly) in its taking this tack in its handling of this case involving a 5-year-old refugee and what the State sought to achieve. On the analysis here that likely contemplated advantage was to send a message that children—no matter how young-would not receive special consideration nor would this be the case for a parent travelling with a child and entering the country on an irregular basis without proper entry documents. Thus in handling this individual child's case so harshly and in violation of the European Convention the attempt was, it is here suggested, to take a stand that denigrated at the outset the *collective rights* of similarly situated children as a group (unaccompanied children seeking safe passage through Belgium as refugees making their way to another country of destination or those seeking asylum in Belgium).[89] Furthermore this was a child who had refugee status in Canada through her mother yet she was deported from Belgium while en route to Holland via Belgium with her uncle where she was to be met by her mother who would take her back with her to Canada. The applicant argued to the ECtHR that "deporting the child of a person with recognised refugee status was contrary to the fundamental rule that asylum-seekers should not be expelled."[90] Indeed, it would appear that in this case Belgium was sending the erroneous message, in effect, that borders are to be 'protected' from those who would enter without entry documents regardless their actual or potential refugee status and particular individual circumstance and due consideration to their being a vulnerable minor. This through what *in effect* in this case, without the government taking proper account of all of the relevant and particular facts, amounted to virtual automatic detention and deportation procedures being implemented against the child:

> The Government submitted that in the absence of papers authorising the second applicant [the child] to travel and to enter the country, the Belgian authorities had had no reason not to deport her.[91]

> The Court further notes that, far from assisting her reunification with her mother, the authorities' actions in fact hindered it. Having been informed at the outset that the first applicant was in Canada, the Belgian authorities should have made detailed enquiries of their Canadian counterparts in order to clarify the position and bring about the reunification of

---

[88]ECtHR Judgment (2007) Tarakhel, Mubilanzila Mayeka and Kaniki Mitunga v. Belgium, point 66.

[89]It would seem that the applicants also make a credible argument that the child's deportation to the DRC created certain tangible risks to the child and mother: "There was. . .a danger in such cases that the authorities in the country of origin would use the child's presence there to compel the refugee to return or even that they would seek to exact revenge on the child." (ECtHR Judgment (2007) Tarakhel, Mubilanzila Mayeka and Kaniki Mitunga v. Belgium, point 64).

[90]ECtHR Judgment (2007) Tarakhel, Mubilanzila Mayeka and Kaniki Mitunga v. Belgium, point 64.

[91]ECtHR Judgment (2007) Tarakhel, Mubilanzila Mayeka and Kaniki Mitunga v. Belgium, point 65.

> mother and daughter. The Court considers that that duty became more pressing from 16 October 2002 onwards, that being the date when the Belgian authorities received the fax from the UNHCR contradicting the information they had previously held.[92]

Ironically the ECtHR held that by the State having rendered the child an unaccompanied minor (by separating her through detention from her uncle) this in fact heightened the State's obligation to facilitate family reunification of the 5-year-old with her mother:

> Ultimately, since the second applicant [the child] was an unaccompanied foreign minor, the Belgian State was under an obligation to facilitate the family's reunification[93]

This latter ECtHR point in the case at bar (on the analysis here),intentionally or unintentionally, highlights that the *individual* unaccompanied foreign minor seeking asylum does so also as an individual member of a particular highly vulnerable refugee *collective* (unaccompanied child refugee asylum seekers) with particular rights derived from membership in this group. These child rights are correlated with a pressing State obligation to respect those rights both for the individual such child and the group as a whole where family reunification is feasible and in the child's best interest.[94] It should be recalled also that even where the child's asylum claim is denied there is a compelling State obligation to reunify the child with family (where in the child's interest and practicable) which is arguably part of customary law.[95]

While the government submitted that the mother had not proven she was the child's mother; it is not clear that the government sought any documentation in that regard or for that matter adequate documentation that the uncle who was to meet the child at the DRC airport upon her arrival after deportation was in fact her uncle and someone willing to care for her. The ECtHR noted that in the case at bar in the first instance the "interruption of family life was solely a result of her [the mother's] decision to flee her country of origin out of a genuine fear of persecution within the meaning of the Geneva Convention Relating to the Status of Refugees of 28 July

[92]ECtHR Judgment (2007) Tarakhel, Mubilanzila Mayeka and Kaniki Mitunga v. Belgium, point 82.

[93]ECtHR Judgment (2007) Tarakhel, Mubilanzila Mayeka and Kaniki Mitunga v. Belgium, point 85.

[94]Thus for instance an unaccompanied foreign minor seeking asylum cannot properly under international refugee law be deported and as a result put in grave harms way on the pretence of family reunification in the home State (in many instances the parents will actually have sent their children out of the home territory in order to save them from persecution by a State or non-State armed group).

[95]See for instance International Committee of the Red Cross (2015) Basic Rules of the Geneva Conventions and their Additional Protocols regarding Geneva Convention IV Protection for children which includes the stipulations that "Unless there are imperative reasons for doing so, no Party to the conflict shall arrange for the evacuation of children other than its own nationals to a foreign country. When evacuation does occur, all necessary steps must be taken to facilitate the return of the children to their families and their country. [P.I, 78]" and All the Parties to the Conventions and the Protocol must facilitate the reunion of dispersed families and encourage the work of the humanitarian organizations engaged in this task. [P. I, 74]"

1951."[96] The mother, as mentioned, was already a recognized refugee in Canada and Belgium was aware of this fact at some point prior to the child's deportation but proceeded with the child's deportation nonetheless. The Belgian government did not dispute that the ties between mother and child constituted a foundational aspect of family life to be protected under Article 8 of the European Convention. The Belgian State further conceded that the child's detention and deportation interfered with the mother-child tie (family life) but held that interference justified in the State's necessary protection of its interests; and a proper exercise of its authority and discretion. The State maintained that holding the child in detention until the outcome of consideration of her case would allow for (ensure the possibility of) enforcement of deportation if the child was unsuccessful in seeking safe passage through Belgium as a refugee (recall the child was not seeking to have asylum in Belgium for the purpose of residing in Belgium but rather just transit through Belgium to Holland). Belgium thus relied on Article 8 (2) of the European Convention as an alleged appropriate and applicable rationale for its handling of the child in the particular circumstance and on facts of the case:

> 1. Everyone has the right to respect for his private and family life, his home and his correspondence.
>
> 2. There shall be no interference by a public authority with the exercise of this right except such as is in accordance with the law and is necessary in a democratic society in the interests of national security, public safety or the economic well-being of the country, for the prevention of disorder or crime, for the protection of health or morals, or for the protection of the rights and freedoms of others.[97]

Yet it is incredible at best to suggest (as Belgium appeared in effect through its actions and purported justifications to do) that this 5 year old (who was intending to ultimately be reunited with her mother in Holland and then taken by the mother to Canada where the child also would be recognized as a refugee) was any sort of threat to Belgium's "national security, public safety or the economic well-being of the country" or that barring her from passing through Belgium on her way to Holland interfered with Belgium's interest in "the prevention of disorder or crime,... the protection of health or morals, or ...the protection of the rights and freedoms of others" within its jurisdiction. Rather the government was motivated, according to its own admission at other points in its submission, by factors other than consideration of this individual child's fundamental human rights given her particular circumstance. Indeed the government wished through this example of detention and deportation of a 5-year-old child of a person with refugee status[98] to block various refugee asylum seeking collectives as a whole (i.e. including but not limited to child

[96]ECtHR Judgment (2007) Tarakhel, Mubilanzila Mayeka and Kaniki Mitunga v. Belgium, point 75.

[97]European Convention on Human Rights; original entry into force of the Convention 21 September 1970.

[98]In the case at bar the mother having refugee status in Canada was a fact known to the Belgium State prior to the child's deportation.

refugee asylum seekers without proper documentation wishing to enter and travel through Belgium with an accompanying third person who may not be the legal guardian but rather a delegate in whose care the legal guardian has placed the child). The latter tack being adopted regardless whether this approach might deny the rights under refugee law of the particular individual minor involved as occurred in this instance:

> it would be hazardous to work on the premise that if a child was very young, it could "as it were serve as a safe conduct for third parties", which was the situation that was in danger of arising if a rule was established prohibiting the detention of minors.[99]

It is here contended that deporting the 5-year-old child Tabitha Kaniki Mitunga knowing that the child's mother had refugee status in Canada communicates a clear message to the international community and to refugee asylum seekers. That message was (at the time) that there would be no protection to be had in Belgium as a transit territory based on the designation of refugee or child refugee asylum seeker since Belgium chooses to disregard the protections such a designation would normally confer (such protections as family reunification). Such acts by the State of Belgium as occurred in the case at bar thus serve, it is here argued, to undermine the collective rights of refugees and the international refugee law framework and its operation. In essence such State handling of the case serves to (1) weaken the rule of international law as it applies to persons who arrive at a border and seek asylum as refugees or who have entered into a territory on an irregular basis and then ask for refugee asylum and (2) undermines the right of family reunification and other rights accorded refugees (this child being the child of a refugee) and in a number of respects the protection fundamental human rights of unaccompanied children more generally. Indeed the Belgian government stance appears to hold the mother responsible for first seeking asylum and refugee status in Canada alone before arranging to be reunited with her daughter.

> The Government further questioned why between July 2001 and August 2002 the first applicant had not made an application to the Canadian authorities and/or to the Canadian embassy in Kinshasa with a view to arranging for her daughter's lawful immigration, preferring instead to use an illegal route with her brother's assistance[100]

This then, it is here suggested, amounts to a punitive measure against mother and child for the mother seeking asylum in Canada by steps she considered most prudent and in the best interests of her daughter. The mother it would seem would be in the best position to assess the safest steps to take in securing refugee asylum for herself and her daughter in Canada.

We do not know from the facts described in the ECtHR judgment in the case why the mother made this decision not to apply for asylum at the Canadian embassy in Kinshasa, DRC. She may have feared the information would become known to DRC

[99]ECtHR Judgment (2007) Tarakhel, Mubilanzila Mayeka and Kaniki Mitunga v. Belgium, point 94.
[100]ECtHR Judgment (2007) Tarakhel, Mubilanzila Mayeka and Kaniki Mitunga v. Belgium, point 74.

authorities and her child would be at risk in the DRC and not allowed to leave the DRC in an effort by the DRC to secure the return of the mother. The mother may have decided that the journey from DRC to Canada—given the threat of persecution the mother faced (which is here assumed to be verified given that Canada granted the mother refugee status)—put her daughter also at grave risk. The mother may thus have thought that the journey was too treacherous and burdensome and an unjustified risk to impose upon the 5 year old until the mother herself had succeeded in obtaining refugee status in Canada.[101] That refugee status obtained by the mother would and did allow for her child to be reunited with her in a family life in Canada where both were recognized by the Canadian government as refugees with asylum granted.

Setting aside the possibility that there may have been good reason for the mother not to flee the DRC with the child in the first instance (and to instead place the child in the care of an uncle who would travel with her out of the DRC's jurisdiction); whatever legal error if any thereafter ensued it is the responsibility of the adult (the mother) and not the child. The ECtHR in this instance articulated the important principle that the child is not to be held *ipso facto* responsible for the actions of his or her legal guardians or other caretaker and denied asylum or safe passage on that basis. To do otherwise is not to recognize the separable legal personality of the child and in effect to deny the human dignity of the child as human being in his or her own right and as, therefore, a legal person entitled to have her refugee asylum status (prima facie or otherwise) and request considered on its independent merits:

> The Court considers that, in view of her young age, the second applicant cannot bear any responsibility for her uncle's attempts to deceive the Belgian authorities by passing her off as his daughter. The same applies to the conduct of her mother and family. Further, although the first applicant's [the mother] conduct was questionable and does not appear to have been entirely fault-free, it was not such as to deprive her [the mother] of victim status in the instant case.[102]

There may furthermore be mitigating facts where a child does tell an untruth to State authorities which facts do not properly allow for disqualification of the asylum application.

[101]This fear of the child also being persecuted by the DRC authorities should she be intercepted en route to seeking asylum in Canada and deported to the DRC may be the reason why the maternal uncle with whom she had travelled to Belgium in the first instance had lied to authorities in Belgium and claimed to be the child's father. The mother had in fact raised before the ECtHR that she feared that the DRC authorities were a potential threat to her child should they discover that the mother and through her the child were seeking asylum.

[102]ECtHR Judgment (2007) Tarakhel, Mubilanzila Mayeka and Kaniki Mitunga v. Belgium, point 84.

2.3.2 *Case 2:AM (Afghanistan) v Secretary of State for the Home Department (and Lord Chancellor as Intervenor), UK Court of Appeal (Civil Division) Royal Courts of Justice, London*

Headnotes: Special Accommodations Owed the Child and Other Vulnerable Refugee Asylum Seekers to Achieve Meaningful Access to the Courts, Procedural Unfairness in the Assessment of a Child Refugee Asylum Claim Due to an Overemphasis on Credibility of Oral Testimony and Underemphasis on Available Objective Evidence, Lack of Special Consideration Regarding the Child's Age, Vulnerabilities and Mental/Cognitive Status in Violation of Existing Legal Guidelines.

2.3.2.1 The Facts

The appellant was a 15-year old citizen of Afghanistan (his age as assessed by the UK authorities). The child travelled with the help of agents across Europe to the U.K. arriving the 4th of July, 2012 and requested asylum 20 July, 2012. Hence there was no significant delay in his request for asylum to UK authorities. His history was described as follows according to his testimony:

> He grew up in Afghanistan. His father was a member of the Taliban. As a consequence, he was not normally allowed outside of the compound in which he lived. His family were fed and provided for by the Taliban. When he was about 13 years old, his father was killed by British forces. A few days later the appellant was assaulted by the Afghan police and he was hospitalised. After returning home, Taliban men came and took him away to a training camp with the intention of training him to be a suicide bomber. Eight to ten days later he managed to escape. His maternal uncle handed him over to agents who facilitated his removal from Afghanistan and his journey into Europe.[103]

The child appellant explained then that he had a well substantiated fear of persecution both by (1) the Taliban who would, should he be returned to Afghanistan, seek to punish him for fleeing their hold or use him as a fighter and likely as a suicide bomber and (2) of the police who sought revenge on him as they perceived him to be a member of the Taliban. The child was described in Court based on an expert psychological report as having psychological difficulties and deteriorating mental health. The Secretary of State had refused the child's request for asylum on 13 May, 2013 but had granted him discretionary leave to stay in the U.K. until the appellant reached 17 and one-half years of age. The denial of the asylum application was based on the following: purported inconsistencies in the child's evidence and that he had allegedly "not demonstrated a risk to his life", the government's

[103] AM (Afghanistan) v Secretary of State for the Home Department (and Lord Chancellor as Intervenor), Royal Courts of Justice, London 27 July, 2017 Case No: C5/2015/0626 [2017] EWCA Civ 1123 at para 6.

deduction that had he fled for his life from Afghanistan he would have asked for asylum in one of the safe EU countries through which he transited on his way to the U.K. and the presumption that he could obtain help from Afghani authorities should he be returned[104]

The Royal Court of Justice noted that the First-tier Tribunal (Immigration and Asylum Chamber) ['the FtT'] had paid scant attention to the psychological report that was put before it regarding the child's cognitive and mental status and held the ignoring of this evidence as unacceptable. That psychological report made reference to the child appellant's disability (a learning disability) and the difficulties it would pose for him in recalling information and answering questions orally. The psychologist suggested accommodations that could be made by the court to allow the child to be better able to provide his evidence. The Royal Court of Justice found that the FtT had effectively denied the child access to justice rather than providing any legally supportable basis for the approach taken by the FtT:

> The psychologist was giving appropriate advice about the ground rules to be adopted in the proceedings to ensure that the appellant's access to justice was effective i.e. that he had a voice in the proceedings concerning him. There were a number of options open to the judge in coming to a determination in that circumstance, including hearing from the expert or reasoning a contrary or different position, but effectively ignoring the psychologist's strong advice was not one of those options.[105]

The Royal Court of Justice found, in addition, that the Upper Tribunal (Immigration and Asylum Chamber) ['the UT'], which also dismissed the child's appeal regarding the denial of asylum, did not take proper account of the psychological report regarding the child's learning difficulties and mental status. The Royal Court of Justice put the matter as follows:

> ...I have come to the firm view that the UT judge took no sufficient steps to ensure that the appellant had obtained effective access to justice and in particular that his voice could be heard in proceedings that concerned him. Procedurally, the proceedings were neither fair nor just. That was a material error of law...[106]

Ultimately the Secretary of State and the appellant were agreed that the appeal should be allowed and the case remitted back to the First-tier Tribunal (Immigration and Asylum Chamber). This in that:

> the FtT failed properly to take into account the appellant's age, vulnerability and learning disability in making adverse credibility findings, in rejecting his account of past events because of alleged inconsistency and implausibility and in dismissing the asylum claim on

---

[104] AM (Afghanistan) v Secretary of State for the Home Department (and Lord Chancellor as Intervenor), Royal Courts of Justice, London 27 July, 2017 Case No: C5/2015/0626 [2017] EWCA Civ 1123 at para 8.

[105] AM (Afghanistan) v Secretary of State for the Home Department (and Lord Chancellor as Intervenor), Royal Courts of Justice, London 27 July, 2017 Case No: C5/2015/0626 [2017] EWCA Civ 1123 at para 13.

[106] AM (Afghanistan) v Secretary of State for the Home Department (and Lord Chancellor as Intervenor), Royal Courts of Justice, London 27 July, 2017 Case No: C5/2015/0626 [2017] EWCA Civ 1123 at para 16.

that basis; no consideration was given to whether or not oral evidence was necessary and on what issues so as to enable a fair hearing and any prejudicial consequences of oral evidence in accordance with Rule 14 of the FtT Rules[107]

2.3.2.2 Commentary on *AM (Afghanistan) v Secretary of State for the Home Department* (and Lord Chancellor as Intervenor), UK Court of Appeal (Civil Division) Royal Courts of Justice, London[108]

What is especially striking about the AM case is that the immigration rules set out, as the Royal Court of Justice pointed out, incorporated the special considerations to be taken into account by the Immigration and Asylum Tribunals in respect of a child appellant and especially one who, as here, had certain vulnerabilities (learning disabilities, trauma etc.) for example

> Rule 351 adds the following (so far as is relevant to children and young people):"...account should be taken of the applicant's maturity and in assessing the claim of a child more weight should be given to objective indications of risk than to the child's state of mind and understanding of their situation. ... Close attention should be given to the welfare of the child at all times."

Yet both Immigration and Asylum Tribunals in this case ignored those guidelines as incorporated in the immigration and court rules in addressing how the child could best give evidence and access the tribunals in a meaningful way to have his voice heard impartially and without undue prejudice arsing due to his young age and disabilities. This speaks to the issue of in essence unwitting foregone conclusions in child refugee asylum cases when the tribunals (as appears respectfully, on this author's view, to have occurred in this case with the FtT and UT) simply, in practice, for whatever reason, fail to provide the child refugee access to procedural and substantive justice in addressing the contested issues. Evidence of that pull to a foregone conclusion by the FtT and UT in this case is the fact that the FtT dismissed the child's asylum claim on the basis of alleged inconsistency and lack of credibility of his oral testimony *before* considering available objective evidence on the conditions in Afghanistan in the relevant time period. That approach the Royal Court of Justice found was an error in law:

---

[107]AM (Afghanistan) v Secretary of State for the Home Department (and Lord Chancellor as Intervenor), Royal Courts of Justice, London 27 July, 2017 Case No: C5/2015/0626 [2017] EWCA Civ 1123 at para 18.

[108]For further commentary on AM (Afghanistan) v Secretary of State for the Home Department (and Lord Chancellor as Intervenor), Royal Courts of Justice, London 27 July, 2017 See Garden Court Chambers (1 August, 2017) "A child is foremost a child before he or she is a refugee": Court of Appeal provides new guidance to tribunals to ensure children and vulnerable persons have their voices heard in asylum proceedings https://www.gardencourtchambers.co.uk/a-child-is-foremost-a-child-before-he-or-she-is-a-refugee-court-of-appeal-offers-new-guidance-to-tribunals-to-ensure-children-and-vulnerable-persons-can-have-their-voices-heard/ Accessed 24 September, 2017.

> ... it is an error of approach to come to a negative assessment of credibility and then ask whether that assessment is displaced by other material... the FtT failed to have regard to the obligation to give precedence and greater weight to objective evidence and indicators of risk rather than personal credibility in light of the appellant's age, vulnerability and learning disability.[109]

It would appear, on this author's analysis, that the Immigration and Asylum Tribunals (FtT and UT) in the case at bar were issuing rulings blocking the child's asylum that were more reflective of government attempts to implement policy that would effect denial of entry to unaccompanied child refugees as a group rather than of the actual Immigration and Asylum rules arising from and relating to incorporation in UK law of the 1951 Refugee Convention and its 1967 Protocol and guidelines for the handling of child refugee cases.

Arguably the Immigration and Asylum Tribunals in this particular case in effect sidestepped their most pressing obligation[110] to ensure non-refoulement where the child would be at risk of substantial harm such as deprivation of liberty on an arbitrary basis, exploitation or even loss of life (not an exhaustive list):

> ...it is agreed that the FtT erred in law in failing to consider the risk on return to Afghanistan at the date of the hearing on the erroneous basis that the appellant would not face actual removal from the UK if his family could not be traced, until he was 18 years of age ... This was relevant to the appellant's claim for humanitarian protection based upon the objective evidence ....of the risks to and conditions for an unaccompanied child with the appellant's additional vulnerabilities, if returned to Kabul, in particular the risk of destitution and exploitation.[111]

This case then, on the analysis here, is an example of the need, among other things, to be ever vigilant regarding refoulement masked as justified returns where there is little or no objective evidentiary basis to support the returns as legally supportable. This vigilance is especially, but not only, necessary in the consideration of cases involving unaccompanied child refugee asylum seekers and other highly vulnerable individual refugees who, in practice, may not have had, for a variety of reasons, effective access to the immigration and asylum tribunal or higher courts even if they were *pro forma* ostensibly 'heard'. The judge of the Royal Court of Justice in *AM (Afghanistan) v Secretary of State for the Home Department* in fact seemed to be alluding to the potential for system-wide failure if guidelines for handling of child refugee asylum seeker cases as set out in the case at bar are not adhered to:

---

[109] AM (Afghanistan) v Secretary of State for the Home Department (and Lord Chancellor as Intervenor), Royal Courts of Justice, London 27 July, 2017 Case No: C5/2015/0626 [2017] EWCA Civ 1123 at para 19 (a)(c).

[110] Most pressing obligation given the potential grave consequences of a denial of asylum for the child refugee asylum seeker in this case.

[111] AM (Afghanistan) v Secretary of State for the Home Department (and Lord Chancellor as Intervenor), Royal Courts of Justice, London 27 July, 2017 Case No: C5/2015/0626 [2017] EWCA Civ 1123 at para 20.

> I recognise that this marks a failure of the system to provide sufficient and adequate protection in the asylum process for the particular requirements, needs and interests arising out of the disadvantages that the appellant has as a highly vulnerable child. There is a consensus that the critical errors arose from the focus on the credibility of the appellant's account and the failure to properly have regard to the objective evidence and to give it priority over the ability of the appellant to provide oral testimony.[112]

The Senior President of Tribunals, Sir Ernest Ryder giving the lead opinion for the Royal Court of Justice made reference to the quote "a child is foremost a child before he or she is a refugee" (McAdam J, Complementary Protection in International Refugee Law, P196, OUP, 2007).[113] It is here argued, in contrast, that these are in fact, in many instances, intersecting group memberships that must be considered as such in that the individual child refugee asylum seeker (accompanied or unaccompanied) enjoys certain protections as an individual predicated on, in large part, membership in both of these collectives as well as on the merits of his/her individual case and its unique particulars.

2.3.3 *Case 3: JA (Child: Risk of Persecution-Nigeria) v UK Secretary of State for the Home Department, UK Upper Tribunal Immigration and Asylum Chamber (IAC)*

Between JA (Appellant mother as litigation guardian for "N") and The [UK] Secretary of State for the Home Department (Respondent)

Headnotes: autonomous asylum rights of a child, autonomous right of the child to family and to protection from unlawful State interference in the family inconsistent with democratic values, refugee status, membership in an identifiable social group (children with albinism), intersecting group memberships of child refugees (here 'child', 'refugee', 'person with albinism', 'person of African ethnicity), special vulnerabilities and rights of the child, Convention on the Rights of the Child, assessing the risk of persecution.

2.3.3.1 The Facts

In this case a mother of a 7 year old boy with albinism appealed to the U.K. Upper Tribunal of the Immigration and Asylum Chamber to quash the U.K. Secretary of

[112] AM (Afghanistan) v Secretary of State for the Home Department (and Lord Chancellor as Intervenor), Royal Courts of Justice, London 27 July, 2017 Case No: C5/2015/0626 [2017] EWCA Civ 1123 at para 22.

[113] AM (Afghanistan) v Secretary of State for the Home Department (and Lord Chancellor as Intervenor), Royal Courts of Justice, London 27 July, 2017 Case No: C5/2015/0626 [2017] EWCA Civ 1123 at para 35.

State's decision to deny the asylum claim she had made on behalf of her son who has albinism. The mother originally from Nigeria had been in the U.K. for several years and her child was born in the U.K and had lived only in the U.K.

2.3.3.2 Commentary on JA (Child: Risk of Persecution-Nigeria) v UK Secretary of State for the Home Department, UK Upper Tribunal Immigration and Asylum Chamber (IAC)

The U.K. Secretary of State had denied the asylum request made by the mother on behalf of her son and also ordered the mother deported to her native Nigeria hence effectively deporting the child as well. There was no consideration given to the autonomous asylum rights of a child.[114] The mother contended that should her son, through her legal circumstance, be forced to live in Nigeria with his mother; her son would suffer persecution on account of his albinism. The mother had overstayed in the U.K. and was, from the point of the overstay, unlawfully in the UK. Hence she was eligible for deportation at least considering only the overstay. Her son had been born in the U.K. and had lived only in the UK. but the U.K. does not have birthright citizenship.

The mother's plea not to be returned to Nigeria (along with her son), as advanced at an earlier hearing before a different justice of the Immigration and Asylum Chamber, was in part grounded on ECHR Article 8:

> **ARTICLE 8**
> Right to respect for private and family life
>
> 1. Everyone has the right to respect for his private and family life, his home and his correspondence.
>
> 2. There shall be no interference by a public authority with the exercise of this right except such as is in accordance with the law and is necessary in a democratic society in the interests of national security, public safety or the economic wellbeing of the country, for the prevention of disorder or crime, for the protection of health or morals, or for the protection of the rights and freedoms of others.[115]

The Immigration and Asylum Justice of the first instance tribunal had ruled in the mother's favor and granted a continued stay in the U.K. The latter given his finding that deporting the mother to Nigeria would, on his view, be a disproportionate

[114]For a discussion of a child's autonomous right to asylum in a highly contentious case see Gonzalez v Reno 86 F.Supp.2d 1167, 2000 U.S. Dist. LEXIS 325 discussed in Grover (2008), Chapter 5: The Immigration and Refugee Context at pp. 221–239.

[115]European Convention on Human Rights as amended by the provisions of Protocol No. 14 (CETS no. 194) entry into force on 1 June 2010.

interference in the woman's family life as she would of necessity have to bring her very young son with her who had known no other life than that in the U.K. However her claim for asylum for her son based on the alleged risk to her son, who had albinism, suffering persecution in Nigeria was rejected. The mother appealed that asylum decision to the UT and her plea was dismissed by the UT's Deputy Justice. She then appealed to the Court of Appeal which Court sent the case on the matter of asylum for the child back for reconsideration by the UT[116] and it is the latter judgment that we are examining here.

In previous hearings of the case on the issue of the need for her son to be granted asylum, testimony had been introduced that there is a very sizeable population in Nigeria of persons with albinism and that they are in fact significantly discriminated against:

> This is based upon a view formed by many that albinism is a curse bestowed upon a family as a result of some form of witchcraft which persists in the nature of albinos. There is a further difficulty, albeit perhaps not one which is particularly general, namely that in some cases albinos have been murdered because it is believed that their body parts will bring benefit to others and this, as we say, has undoubtedly resulted in some attacks.[117]

The number of attacks on and murders of persons with albinism in Nigeria was, the UT held in the case at bar, not widespread and therefore the Honourable Justice Collins put the question for the UT on remittance as follows:

> However, it cannot we think be said that this is something which is of general application and the question arises as to whether that which undoubtedly would amount to persecution or fall within Article 2 of the Convention on Human rights [right to life guarantee] is sufficiently of a real risk as to justify on that basis a finding that there will be persecution.[118]

The earlier decisions in the case included a finding that persons with albinism constitute a 'social group' and hence the social group ground as an element regarding consideration of the potential for or actual 'persecution' was held at all hearing levels satisfied.[119] The Upper Tribunal thus further opined that if there was to be a finding of persecution then there would be a basis for finding that the child (as with other persons with albinism from Nigeria seeking asylum) was a Convention

---

[116]The Home Secretary attempted to cross appeal the grant of continued stay in the UK based on Article 8 of the European Convention but was not given leave to cross-appeal and hence the government abandoned that particular issue.

[117]JA v UK Secretary of State for the Home Department [2016] UKUT 00560 (IAC) para 5 (Upper Tribunal (Immigration and Asylum Chamber) Judgment Issued 24 November, 2016) (Anonymity Direction Made).

[118]JA v UK Secretary of State for the Home Department [2016] UKUT 00560 (IAC) para 7(Upper Tribunal (Immigration and Asylum Chamber) Judgment Issued 24 November, 2016) (Anonymity Direction Made).

[119]JA v UK Secretary of State for the Home Department [2016] UKUT 00560 (IAC) para 8(Upper Tribunal (Immigration and Asylum Chamber) Judgment Issued 24 November, 2016) (Anonymity Direction Made).

refugee.[120] The Upper Tribunal further held that the test for persecution was the same as the test for a breach of Article 3 of the European Convention on Human Rights[121] ("No one shall be subjected to torture or to inhuman or degrading treatment or punishment").[122]

The Upper Tribunal in considering the case on remittance found that the child would suffer discrimination at school should he and his mother be deported to Nigeria and consequently the child would be having to attend school there.[123] The Upper Tribunal held that such discrimination would be a manifestation of the fact that some in Nigeria regard persons with albinism as "lesser beings' simply because they have albinism.[124] Facing such discrimination would be particularly difficult, the Upper Tribunal held, for a child who had not lived in Nigeria previously and had not faced such systemic discrimination relating to his albinism.[125] The Upper Tribunal also noted that the previous justices hearing this case had concluded that (1) the Nigerian authorities were unlikely to be able to provide mother and son the protection from harm they needed and deserved (protection from discrimination for both and potentially also from "ritualistic abuse" of the son which could even involve loss of life of the child and concluded also that (2) the mother and son had a significant subjective fear of the persecution they might well endure if forced to Nigeria given the child's albinism.[126]

The Upper Tribunal (the Honorable Justice Collins considering the case on remittance) found that the *Convention on the Rights of the Child* was relevant in determining the nature and scope of protections from persecution available to children seeking asylum:

---

[120]JA v UK Secretary of State for the Home Department [2016] UKUT 00560 (IAC) para 8:"...if there is persecution, then there is a proper basis for finding that they [Nigerian persons with albinism seeking asylum] are refugees" (Upper Tribunal (Immigration and Asylum Chamber) Judgment Issued 24 November, 2016) (Anonymity Direction Made).

[121]JA v UK Secretary of State for the Home Department [2016] UKUT 00560 (IAC) para 8 (Upper Tribunal (Immigration and Asylum Chamber) Judgment Issued 24 November, 2016) (Anonymity Direction Made).

[122]European Convention on Human Rights Convention as amended by the provisions of Protocol No. 14 (CETS no. 194) entry into force on 1 June 2010.

[123]JA v UK Secretary of State for the Home Department [2016] UKUT 00560 (IAC) para 9 (Upper Tribunal (Immigration and Asylum Chamber) Judgment Issued 24 November, 2016) (Anonymity Direction Made).

[124]JA v UK Secretary of State for the Home Department [2016] UKUT 00560 (IAC) para 9 (Upper Tribunal (Immigration and Asylum Chamber) Judgment Issued 24 November, 2016) (Anonymity Direction Made).

[125]JA v UK Secretary of State for the Home Department [2016] UKUT 00560 (IAC) para 13 (Upper Tribunal (Immigration and Asylum Chamber) Judgment Issued 24 November, 2016) (Anonymity Direction Made).

[126]JA v UK Secretary of State for the Home Department [2016] UKUT 00560 (IAC) para 11 (Upper Tribunal (Immigration and Asylum Chamber) Judgment Issued 24 November, 2016) (Anonymity Direction Made).

> The Convention on the Rights of the Child is clearly a relevant consideration that this Tribunal and indeed all who deal with asylum issues should take into account, and it is clear that a child could be at risk of persecutory harm contrary to the Convention in circumstances where a comparably placed adult would not be at such risk.[127]

Recall that the *Convention on the Rights of the Child* specifically addresses the rights of child refugees (where 'child' is generally understood to mean person under age 18 years):

> **Article 22**
> 1. States Parties shall take appropriate measures to ensure that a child who is seeking refugee status or who is considered a refugee in accordance with applicable international or domestic law and procedures shall, whether unaccompanied or accompanied by his or her parents or by any other person, receive appropriate protection and humanitarian assistance in the enjoyment of applicable rights set forth in the present Convention and in other international human rights or humanitarian instruments to which the said States are Parties.
>
> 2. For this purpose, States Parties shall provide, as they consider appropriate, co-operation in any efforts by the United Nations and other competent intergovernmental organizations or non-governmental organizations co-operating with the United Nations to protect and assist such a child and to trace the parents or other members of the family of any refugee child in order to obtain information necessary for reunification with his or her family. In cases where no parents or other members of the family can be found, the child shall be accorded the same protection as any other child permanently or temporarily deprived of his or her family environment for any reason, as set forth in the present Convention.[128]

The Upper Tribunal in the case at bar emphasized the U.K.'s obligation under the Convention on the Rights of the Child to consider (1) the special vulnerabilities of children and (2) how such vulnerabilities properly should enter into an assessment of whether the particular circumstances of the child constitute persecution or the threat of persecution of that child (i.e. though the same circumstances may or may not constitute persecution for an adult).[129]

In the case at bar; the government argued that the risk of kidnapping and murder in Nigeria faced by persons with albinism because they suffer from this condition was "not such as could properly be said to amount to a real risk as opposed to a

---

[127]JA v UK Secretary of State for the Home Department [2016] UKUT 00560 (IAC) para 15 (Upper Tribunal (Immigration and Asylum Chamber) Judgment Issued 24 November, 2016) (Anonymity Direction Made).

[128]Convention on the Rights of the Child entered into force 2 September, 1990.

[129]JA v UK Secretary of State for the Home Department [2016] UKUT 00560 (IAC) para 16-18 (Upper Tribunal (Immigration and Asylum Chamber) Judgment Issued 24 November, 2016) (Anonymity Direction Made).

remote possibility."[130] The previous justices had agreed with that assessment[131] presumably based on overall statistics of such occurrences in Nigeria. It appears then that the government in opposing U.K. asylum for this child with albinism and favouring his effective deportation to Nigeria was prepared for the child to play an involuntary game of Russian roulette sort-to-speak with his chances of freedom from persecution and even survival in Nigeria. The latter given the prevailing attitude toward persons with albinism in Nigeria and the risk of ritualistic kidnapping and murder of the child for his body parts however low but very indisputably real that risk. The Upper Tribunal did make note that expert testimony before the lower courts in the case suggested that the risk of ritualistic murder and dismemberment of persons with albinism in Nigeria was an *increasing* one as trade in such body parts proved to be a lucrative business.[132]

Notwithstanding the expert evidence heard previously in the case regarding the significant harms amounting to persecution that could come to the child (due to his albinism) if he were deported to Nigeria, the government persisted before the Upper Tribunal in arguing *against* the proposition that the child 'N' would be persecuted in Nigeria and that on that basis he was entitled to refugee asylum. The government took the position that:

> *we cannot go so far, and we should not go so far, as to recognise that discrimination in Nigeria could amount to persecution* because there are a very large number, running into certainly at least, 1,000,000 of albinos in that country who would be entitled [to asylum] if that were right to protection (emphasis added).[133]

The U.K. in the individual case at bar thus relied on the erroneous (on the respectful view here) premise that it was justifiable and lawful to deny refugee asylum to 'N' based on the spurious notion that he faced no 'real risk' of *persecution* in Nigeria. The rationale for this rejection by the government of the potential genuine risk for persecution of the child 'N' in Nigeria (even admitting he might face significant *discrimination* in his mother's homeland) had to do with the U.K. government's concerns regarding the *collective* of persons with albinism in Nigeria. That is the U.K. government was concerned about the potential for large numbers of that very sizeable collective of persons with albinism in Nigeria seeking refugee asylum in the U.K. Thus the U.K. government argument against granting refugee asylum to the child 'N' (in the individual case) was largely, if not completely, grounded on the alleged pressing need to, as a foregone conclusion,

---

[130] JA v UK Secretary of State for the Home Department [2016] UKUT 00560 (IAC) para 15.

[131] JA v UK Secretary of State for the Home Department [2016] UKUT 00560 (IAC) para 15 (Upper Tribunal (Immigration and Asylum Chamber) Judgment Issued 24 November, 2016) (Anonymity Direction Made).

[132] JA v UK Secretary of State for the Home Department [2016] UKUT 00560 (IAC) para 6 (Upper Tribunal (Immigration and Asylum Chamber) Judgment Issued 24 November, 2016) (Anonymity Direction Made).

[133] JA v UK Secretary of State for the Home Department [2016] UKUT 00560 (IAC) para 21 (Upper Tribunal (Immigration and Asylum Chamber) Judgment Issued 24 November, 2016) (Anonymity Direction Made).

deny *prima facie* recognition of the refugee status of the aforementioned collective of persecuted peoples. In summary then the government feared that a grant of asylum to the child 'N' in the case at bar (asylum on the basis of the risk of persecution in Nigeria) would stand as a precedent for the recognition of the *prima facie* refugee status of the collective (persons in Nigeria persecuted on account of their albinism and seeking asylum in the U.K.). N's success in receiving refugee asylum then, according to the government, would allegedly open a 'floodgate' in terms of the numbers of refugees (children and adults) that could be expected to come to the U.K. from Nigeria to seek asylum due to their risks in Nigeria as persons with albinism.

Respectfully, on the view here, the U.K. government intent to decline any positive duty to the 'collective' (asylum seekers from Nigeria with albinism seeking international protection through refuge in the U.K.) leads to a forgone outcome in the case at bar also; namely denial of individual refugee rights of 'N'. The latter involved, on the analysis here, rejection of an asylum request on behalf of 'N' without due consideration of the merits of the individual case and the proper weighting of evidence.

The notion of a grant of asylum as a form of protection from persecution for an identifiable social group or members thereof appears to be, in the view of many States, particularly problematic as a challenge to adequate refugee migration control. That concern is articulated in sanitized terms in what follows:

> ...[A] sensible interpretation of the term [social group] must be responsive to victims of persecution without so expanding the scope of the 1951 Convention as to impose upon States obligations to which they did not consent. In striking that delicate balance, it must be kept in mind that international refugee law bears a close relationship to international human rights law – that refugees are persons whose human rights have been violated and who merit international protection.[134]

The Upper Tribunal held, quite appropriately, that the decision-maker must first and foremost address the individual child before him/her and that child's particular circumstances. The latter concern then must be prioritized rather than considering, in the first instance, the collective social group 'persons with albinism in Nigeria' who potentially had members who might also apply for asylum in the UK based on a claim of persecution or threat of persecution in Nigeria relating to their albinism:

> ... We have to consider the facts relating to the individual who appears before us. We have here as we have said, a child born in this country, and brought up in this country, who has not faced any of the discrimination and the basis of that discrimination which he could be at real risk of suffering were he to be returned to Nigeria (emphasis added).[135]

However, on the respectful view here, certain of the Upper Tribunal's statements inappropriately minimize the collective refugee rights of children with albinism who

---

[134] Aleinikoff (2001), p. 265.

[135] JA v UK Secretary of State for the Home Department [2016] UKUT 00560 (IAC) para 22 (Upper Tribunal (Immigration and Asylum Chamber) Judgment Issued 24 November, 2016) (Anonymity Direction Made).

were born in and had lived in Nigeria for several years but then became asylum seekers. The Upper Tribunal essentially implies that children who were born in Nigeria and had spent some years growing up in Nigeria are used to discrimination relating to their albinism and hence there is no pressing need for such children as a collective or individually to receive international protection on the basis of *persecution* or threat of persecution of a social group (as opposed to a child like 'N', the appellant in the case, who was born in and to date has lived only in the UK):

> Nonetheless, it seems to us to be certainly within the realms of a real risk that he will suffer bullying and unpleasant actions whether or not they amount to physical violence from fellow pupils, and certainly a general adverse attitude from the public at large, something which we do not doubt, he will find difficult to follow and which will affect him far more deeply perhaps than a child brought up in Nigeria exposed to that sort of attitude and no doubt so far as possible protected by his family and not expecting anything else from where he grows up than that sort of attitude. It will for "N" be something entirely new.[136]

Respectfully, on the analysis here, there is clearly an insufficient basis for the UT to generalize and conclude that the harms and risk of harms that children with albinism face in Nigeria *for them* do not rise to the level of persecution based on (1) objective criteria (i.e. inhuman, degrading treatment or torture) and (2) also on the subjective experience of persecution simply because they may have been born in Nigeria and may have lived there for a time. Having lived in Nigeria does not at all necessarily substantially eradicate, if at all, children's inherent and situationally created vulnerabilities. Children's special vulnerabilities as children and as members of specific social and other groups, and given their unique circumstances and frailties, must be given a high degree of consideration. This as part of the 'best interests of the child' analysis that must be a primary consideration as stipulated in the Dublin III Regulations which in that regard incorporates certain of the Convention on the Rights of the Child principles.[137]

> In accordance with the 1989 United Nations Convention on the Rights of the Child and with the Charter of Fundamental Rights of the European Union, the best interests of the child should be a primary consideration of Member States when applying this Regulation. In assessing the best interests of the child, Member States should, in particular, take due account of the minor's well-being and social development, safety and security considerations and the views of the minor in accordance with his or her age and maturity, including his or her background. In addition, specific procedural guarantees for unaccompanied minors should be laid down on account of their particular vulnerability.[138]

---

[136] JA v UK Secretary of State for the Home Department [2016] UKUT 00560 (IAC) para 14 (Upper Tribunal (Immigration and Asylum Chamber) Judgment Issued 24 November, 2016) (Anonymity Direction Made).

[137] United Nations Committee on the Rights of the Child "General Comment Number 14 (2013) on the Right of the Child to have his or her best interests taken as a primary consideration" (art 3 para 1) May 2013 Para 6(3) http://www2.ohchr.org/English/bodies/crc/docs/GC/CRC_C_GC_14_ENG.pdf Accessed 1 October, 2017.

[138] Dublin III regulation: Regulation (EU) No 604/2013 of the European Parliament and of the Council of 26 June 2013 establishing the criteria and mechanisms for determining the Member State responsible for examining an application for international protection lodged in one of the Member States by a

It appears to this author, with respect, that the Upper Tribunal in the case at bar attempted to draw rather arbitrary distinctions between (1) the purported likely consequences for child "N" should he be deported to Nigeria versus (2) the experiences of other children in Nigeria with albinism facing real risks of harm or experiencing such harms in Nigeria from others relating to the victims' albinism. The attempt was to suggest that the harms would be greater for "N" to such an extent as to amount to persecution for "N" if sent to Nigeria (harms amounting to i.e. degrading treatment; a violation of Article 3 of the *European Convention on Human Rights*). The Upper Tribunal in this regard, in order to make the argument, appeared to presume that "N" had not suffered discrimination relating to his albinism in the U.K. and would therefore be less prepared to handle discrimination in Nigeria and would experience it consequently as persecution. In fact no evidence was advanced that "N" had not suffered significant bullying or other forms of discrimination in the U.K. at school and in the community due to his albinism. Nor is it at all evident that a child born and growing up in Nigeria would ever be less affected by such harms having been exposed to them. It is equally likely that chronic exposure to such harms for a child born and growing up in Nigeria may produce debilitating effects relating to chronic stress and even post traumatic stress symptoms. In addition, having been born in Nigeria and living in Nigeria, such a child would be aware of the risk of kidnapping and being the victim of a murder due to his/her albinism. No matter how uncertain and low such a risk it would still be a real risk and one that would most likely engender great fear on a continual basis as the risk would be a continuing one. Given the aforementioned it would seem thus that the Upper Tribunal intentionally or unintentionally fashioned its judgment in such a way that it could *not* be relied on as precedent in support of children (and others) from Nigeria in making an asylum claim to the UK based on the persecution they had suffered or were under threat of suffering in Nigeria due to their albinism (membership in a discriminated against social group). The Upper Tribunal thus, on the legal analysis here, attempts to dismiss the refugee asylum seeking rights of the collective social group of persons with albinism in Nigeria all at risk of persecution in Nigeria relating to their albinism:

> As the previous judges have decided there is not likely to be any protection from the authorities that he can expect from such [discriminatory/adverse] conduct against him and thus *the effect on him is that much more serious than would have been the effect had he lived all 'his life and been brought up in the society in Nigeria* (emphasis added).[139]

third-country national or a stateless person (recast) at para 13 http://eur-lex.europa.eu/LexUriServ/LexUriServ.do?uri=OJ:L:2013:180:0031:0059:EN:PDF (Accessed 1 December, 2016).

[139]JA v UK Secretary of State for the Home Department [2016] UKUT 00560 (IAC) para 23 (Upper Tribunal (Immigration and Asylum Chamber) Judgment Issued 24 November, 2016) (Anonymity Direction Made).

> *That in our judgment puts him in a different position from the general position of albinos in Nigeria and in our judgment the likely effect on him* even short of any real risk of being slaughtered or otherwise his body parts being taken, *is sufficient to indicate that there is a real risk of persecution* (emphasis added).[140]

In the paragraphs above it appears evident, on the respectful view here, that the endeavour to assess the individual asylum case of "N" on its merits has morphed into an effort to undercut potential asylum claims to the UK from children (and others) with albinism whose homeland is Nigeria and who have fled Nigeria and who seek protection from persecution in Nigeria relating to their albinism. In fact the Upper Tribunal in a later segment of its judgment goes on to articulate just this, on the respectful view here, legally insupportable objective:

> We must make it clear that we are approaching this on the basis that the position and the particular vulnerability of children must be the starting point. But this is a case which depends upon its facts and the circumstances of the child having been brought up in this country and not having faced the general approach to albinos that exists in Nigeria. *Thus we do not regard this as really being appropriate to be a test case for albinos who are due to be returned to Nigeria or who face the turning down of any application made to stay in this country.* Those will depend upon the circumstances of their individual positions, their age, no doubt and their background. *That is why we say that this is not a case that can be regarded as one which is of general application save for the approach....*(emphasis added).[141]

Notwithstanding the Upper Tribunal's contention of "approaching this [the issue of U.K. asylum] on the basis that the position and the particular vulnerability of children must be the starting point"; it would appear that the UT has taken a perspective at the outset in regards to children who have lived for a significant period in Nigeria that is in fact *not* consistent with consideration of those children's vulnerabilities. That pre-existing perspective (that children who have lived in Nigeria will be psychologically largely immune to discrimination and other harms suffered in relation to their albinism) harbingers against a finding of persecution relating to the children belonging to the social group albinos in Nigeria hence reducing the likelihood that asylum to the U.K. will be granted to members of this collective.

The Court ended its judgment with an admonition of sorts asserting that while the appellant and her son were granted the relief sought from the Upper Tribunal-a grant of protection for both under the Refugee Convention-such was not necessarily an indeterminate grant in terms of its longevity:

> This [protection] will persist only so long as there is a need for it and there can in future if the need arises be a reconsideration because the old approach which this country adopted that

[140] JA v UK Secretary of State for the Home Department [2016] UKUT 00560 (IAC) para 24 (Upper Tribunal (Immigration and Asylum Chamber) Judgment Issued 24 November, 2016) (Anonymity Direction Made).

[141] JA v UK Secretary of State for the Home Department [2016] UKUT 00560 (IAC) para 25(Upper Tribunal (Immigration and Asylum Chamber) Judgment Issued 24 November, 2016) (Anonymity Direction Made).

> once refugee status was accepted there was permanent right of residence has in accordance with the precise terms of the Convention being changed.[142]

The Upper Tribunal included then in its judgment the aforementioned somewhat ominous proviso-namely the cautionary note that a potential loss of refugee status for mother and son in the case at bar was still possible should such withdrawal of recognition of refugee status be permissible in domestic policy and law and be determined by the State to be necessary and consistent with its international human rights obligations. The inclusion of the proviso appears to be, in part at least, an additional effort to remove the possibility that the case could become a compelling precedent in the unlikely event of a flood of refugee asylum applications to the U.K. from Nigerians with albinism. If the latter calculation did figure into the Upper Tribunal's reasoning (in including the reference to possible loss in future of refugee status for the appellant and her son) this would be an instance then of setting further the groundwork for automatic denial of the collective refugee rights of persons with albinism from Nigeria in respect of asylum seeking (i.e. in terms of the right to due process in consideration of the members' individual asylum requests or the possibility of *prima facie* recognition of the collective as refugees in need of international protection in the form possibly of asylum in the U.K.). Since the appeal to the UT in the case at bar was granted on "asylum grounds/humanitarian protection grounds"[143] it is difficult to conceive of a legally supportable basis for loss of refugee status as long as the persecution of persons with albinism continues in Nigeria.

It appears that in the case at bar concern over the alleged implied potential of the case for stimulating an enormous influx of asylum seekers from Nigeria persecuted due to their albinism was a major consideration. The government put the number of persons with albinism in Nigeria at one million; a number that may have been an overestimate in any case. Hence the Upper Tribunal made efforts to make out a distinction between these potential asylum cases and the case at bar using the fact that the child applicant at the time of the case at bar was aged seven had been born and raised in the UK. While the latter factor involved in the case at bar was an additional proper particular circumstance properly given humanitarian consideration; it is not at all clear why this should in any way undermine the asylum claims of children born in Nigeria and fleeing Nigeria due to persecution relating to their albinism. The latter being, as discussed, on the analysis here, the implication of the Upper Tribunal's non-empirical assumption that children who were born in Nigeria and resided there for several years would somehow be less harmed by discrimination and other harms due to their albinism having, according to the Upper

---

[142]JA v UK Secretary of State for the Home Department [2016] UKUT 00560 (IAC) para 27 (Upper Tribunal (Immigration and Asylum Chamber) Judgment Issued 24 November, 2016) (Anonymity Direction Made).

[143]JA v UK Secretary of State for the Home Department [2016] UKUT 00560 (IAC) at p. 7 (Notice of Decision) (Upper Tribunal (Immigration and Asylum Chamber) Judgment Issued 24 November, 2016) (Anonymity Direction Made).

Tribunal, in all likelihood habituated to that treatment. The UT's reasoning also seems to imply that such harms would not rise to the level of persecution given such alleged habituation. Contrast now the Canadian case of a child from Somalia seeking asylum due to the certainty that she would suffer female genital mutilation if deported from Canada to Somalia. In the latter case the persecuted social group; namely young women and girls at risk of forced female genital mutilation in their homeland has a very large membership (not only in Somalia itself but globally if one considers the various countries in which forced FGM is practiced). The reason for including this case here is to make the point that the size of the relevant social group to which the individual asylum seeker belongs (the alleged persecuted group from which smaller groups thereof might seek asylum as *prima facie* refugee collectives or whose members might individually file separately from the group) is not a legitimate basis for fair or proper consideration of the merits of the individual asylum case.

2.3.4 Case 4: Khadra Hassan Farah, Mahad Dahir Buraleh, Hodan Dahir Buraleh[144] Immigration Refugee Board of Canada

Headnotes: child refugee of Somali ethnicity and nationality, FGM, social group, Convention refugee, persecution, collective refugee rights.

2.3.4.1 The Facts

This case involved three claimants; a mother aged 30 (Khadra Hassan Farah) and two of her three children: Hodan Dahir Buraleh, 10, and Mahad Dahir Buraleh, 7. The asylum applicants were all citizens of Somalia. The woman had travelled with her husband and their three children to the U.S. as visitors in 1989 and stayed there until 1991 when the mother left her husband and came to Canada to ask for asylum for herself and her two children as refugees (the oldest child aged 12 lives with the father in Somalia). The focus for our purposes in this discussion is on the asylum claim of the female child Hodan Dahir Buraleh, aged 10 which was based on the fear that she would be subjected to female genital mutilation if returned to Somalia. Before discussing the case further it should be recognized that Somalia, since the case at bar, included a ban on FGM in its Constitution-However while

[144] *Khadra Hassan Farah, Mahad Dahir Buraleh, Hodan Dahir Buraleh*, Canada: Immigration and Refugee Board of Canada, 10 May 1994 Available at http://www.refworld.org/cases,IRBC,3ae6b70618.html Accessed 4 October 2017.

> [t]he Constitution bars circumcision in general [it]. . . does not specify which type. Since the Constitution . . . in place is still provisional, the Sharia takes precedence. [Statement of deputy Minister of Women and Human Rights Ms. Mumina Sheikh Omar, July 2016][145]

The constitutional ban regarding FGM in Somalia, however, does not ensure in itself that FGM is not yet practiced especially amongst traditionalists who may or may not be aware of its physical and psychological risks. Further there was as of 2016 no enabling law to give proper effect to the constitutional ban:

> Somalia's Attorney General Attorney General Ahmed Ali Dahir supported the push for legislation to end FGM. "We need to specifically fight FGM. We need an enabling law."[146]

2.3.4.2 Commentary on Khadra Hassan Farah, Mahad Dahir Buraleh, Hodan Dahir Buraleh[147] Immigration Refugee Board of Canada

The Refugee Board accepted the evidence that female genital mutilation was a widespread practice in Somalia at the time of the case and held that this raised an issue of persecution relating to gender. The Board accepted also that "Practised in Somalia is infibulation the harshest form of FGM"; that "Young girls subjected to FGM vary in age from infancy to adolescence and in Somalia infibulation is practiced on all females, almost without exception" and "Typically, the procedure is performed without the benefit of anaesthetic" and is a procedure often carried out by "older women with no knowledge of anatomy."[148] The Refugee Board also took note and considered evidentiary the common short and long term frequent medical and psychological complications of FGM as practiced in Somalia at the time.

The Refugee Board relied on the Convention on the Rights of the Child as instructive in the case referencing Article 37 prohibiting torture, inhuman or degrading treatment; Article 19 prohibiting all forms of mental and physical violence against the child and Article 24 concerning the State obligation to "recognize the right of the child to the enjoyment of the highest attainable standards of health"[149] The Refugee Board found that:

> . . .the authorities in Somalia will not protect the minor female claimant from the physical and emotional ravages of FGM given the evidence of its widespread practice in that

---

[145]African Union Mission in Somalia Mogadishu, July 27, 2016 *Somali Government Reaffirms Its Commitment to Fighting Female Genital Mutilation* (forum on FGM and gender issues in Somalia).

[146]African Union Mission in Somalia Mogadishu, July 27, 2016 Somali Government Reaffirms Its Commitment to Fighting Female Genital Mutilation (forum on FGM and gender issues in Somalia).

[147]*Khadra Hassan Farah, Mahad Dahir Buraleh, Hodan Dahir Buraleh*, Canada: Immigration and Refugee Board of Canada, 10 May 1994 Available at http://www.refworld.org/cases, IRBC,3ae6b70618.html Accessed 4 October 2017.

[148]Khadra Hassan Farah, Mahad Dahir Buraleh, Hodan Dahir Buraleh: Immigration and Refugee Board of Canada, 10 May 1994: Minor Female Claimant.

[149]Convention on the Rights of the Child 2 September, 1990.

country...The panel notes that FGM was outlawed in Somalia in 1947 but, in spite of this fact, estimates are that 98 per cent of Somali women have undergone the procedure.[150]

Based in large part on the above evidence; the Refugee Board found that the female child in this case was a member of a persecuted social group as a female child and hence fit the criteria as a Convention refugee:

... It is by reason of the fact that she is a female and a minor that the claimant fears persecution in the form of female genital mutilation in Somalia today. Accordingly, we find that Hodan Dahir Buraleh is a Convention refugee.[151]

It is well understood that the numbers of female children in Somalia and the other States in which FGM was practiced at the time of the case represented an inordinately huge number. Yet that issue, the size of the persecuted child social group particularly in Somalia (female children at risk of FGM in Somalia), was a factor weighing *in favour* of the individual claimant in this case and not against. This in that the Canadian Refugee Board found that the child's fear of FGM if returned to Somalia was well -founded given the numbers of female children subjected to the practice in Somalia. This was an instance then where the decision-maker (here a Refugee Board) implicitly acknowledged (through its reasoning in the case at bar) that the *collective social group* of female children at risk of FGM (female children from States where the practice is widespread as in Somalia) would meet the criteria for *prima facie* refugee status were groups of such children able to flee and ask for asylum. Recognition of the *prima facie* refugee claim of the collective (the persecuted social group as a group) facilitates the possibility of a grant of asylum to the individual member. In *JA v [UK] Secretary of State for the Home Department [2016] UKUT 00560 (IAC)*, in contrast, the U.K. Upper Tribunal of the Immigration and Asylum Chamber undermined the potential for recognition of *prima facie* refugee status for a particular persecuted child social group (child refugee asylum seekers with albinism and of Nigerian nationality and/or who had lived in Nigeria for several years or more) implicated in a particular individual asylum case as previously here discussed. This while not disputing that such children are rejected largely in Nigeria and face certain risks of serious harms of various sorts in Nigeria including discrimination and much worse but maintaining that the probable harms generally did not rise to the level of persecution warranting possible refugee asylum in the U.K. The latter refusal to recognize in the first instance the *prima facie* refugee status of the collective (Nigerian born children persecuted in Nigeria due to their albinism) then would unfairly significantly reduce the possibility for an individual from that persecuted group receiving UK asylum.

---

[150]Khadra Hassan Farah, Mahad Dahir Buraleh, Hodan Dahir Buraleh: Immigration and Refugee Board of Canada, 10 May 1994: Minor Female Claimant.

[151]Khadra Hassan Farah, Mahad Dahir Buraleh, Hodan Dahir Buraleh: Immigration and Refugee Board of Canada, 10 May 1994: Minor Female Claimant.

Literature, Materials and Cases

Literature

Aleinikoff TA (2001) Protected characteristics and social perceptions: an analysis of the meaning of 'membership of a particular social group'. Paper presented for roundtable discussion, San Remo, Italy, on 6–8 September 2001, UNHCR's Global Consultations on International Protection. http://www.refworld.org/pdfid/470a33b30.pdf. Accessed 14 Jan 2017

Cohen A (2017) R2P, global governance, and the Syrian refugee crisis. In: Grover S (ed) R2P: perspectives on the concept's meaning, proper application and value. Routledge Special Issues in Books Program. Routledge, New York

Galenkamp M (1998) Do we need special, collective rights for immigrants and refugees in Western Europe? Citizenship Stud 2(3):501–517

Gil-Bazo M-T (2015) Asylum as a general principle of international law. Int J Refug Law 27 (1):3–28

Grover S (2008) The child's right to legal standing. Lexus Nexis, Markham

Grover S (2015) Children defending their human rights under the CRC communications procedure: on strengthening the convention on the rights of the child complaints mechanism. Springer, Berlin

Torbisco Casals N (ed) (2006) Group rights as human rights: a liberal approach to multiculturalism. Springer, Dordrecht

Materials

African Charter on the Rights and Welfare of the Child entered into force 29 November, 1999. http://pages.au.int/acerwc/documents/african-charter-rights-and-welfare-child-acrwc

African Union Mission in Somalia Mogadishu, July 27, 2016 *Somali Government Reaffirms Its Commitment to Fighting Female Genital Mutilation* (forum on FGM and gender issues in Somalia) http://amisom-au.org/2016/07/somali-government-reaffirms-its-commitment-to-fighting-female-genital-mutilation/ Accessed 24 January, 2017

Alam, U. (17 September, 2017) Associated Press. Bangladesh restricts Rohingya refugees, starts immunization http://abcnews.go.com/International/wireStory/bangladesh-restricts-rohingya-refugees-starts-immunization-49905267 Accessed 20 September, 2017

Aljezeera News (17 September, 2017) Bangladesh restricts movement of Rohingya refugees: Police issue order prohibiting more than 400,000 Rohingya refugees from leaving areas designated by the government http://www.aljazeera.com/news/2017/09/bangladesh-restricts-movement-rohingya-refugees-170917004640300.html Accessed 20 September, 2017

Amnesty International Myanmar: Military attempts to whitewash crimes against humanity targeting Rohingya (13 November, 2017) https://www.amnesty.org/en/latest/news/2017/11/myanmar-military-attempts-to-whitewash-crimes-against-humanity-targeting-rohingya/ Accessed 2 January, 2018

Azeem Ibrahim Why the Rohingya cannot yet return to Myanmar New York Time 6 December, 2017. https://www.nytimes.com/2017/12/06/opinion/rohingya-myanmar-bangladesh.html Accessed 2 January, 2018

Charter of Fundamental Rights of the European Union Nice, 7 December. 2000. http://www.europarl.europa.eu/charter/pdf/text_en.pdf (Accessed 5 October, 2016)

Convention and Protocol Relating to the Status of Refugees (1951 Refugee Convention and 1967 Protocol) http://www.unhcr.org/4ca34be29.pdf Accessed 21 September, 2017

Convention on the Rights of the Child entered into force 2 September, 1990. http://www.ohchr.org/en/professionalinterest/pages/crc.aspx (Accessed 13 October, 2016)
Dublin III regulation: Regulation (EU) No 604/2013 of the European Parliament and of the Council of 26 June 2013 establishing the criteria and mechanisms for determining the Member State responsible for examining an application for international protection lodged in one of the Member States by a third-country national or a stateless person (recast) http://eur-lex.europa.eu/LexUriServ/LexUriServ.do?uri=OJ:L:2013:180:0031:0059:EN:PDF (Accessed 1 December, 2016)
European Convention on Human Rights (as amended by the provisions of Protocol No. 14 (CETS no. 194) as from its entry into force on 1 June 2010.) original entry into force of the Convention 21 September 1970. http://www.echr.coe.int/Documents/Convention_ENG.pdf (Accessed 21 October, 2016)
European Migration Network (2014) Policies, Practices and Data on Unaccompanied Minors in Belgium: Focused Study of the Belgian National Contact Point of the European Migration Network (EMN) 2014 Update p. 29-30
Garden Court Chambers (1 August, 2017) "A child is foremost a child before he or she is a refugee": Court of Appeal provides new guidance to tribunals to ensure children and vulnerable persons have their voices heard in asylum proceedings https://www.gardencourtchambers.co.uk/a-child-is-foremost-a-child-before-he-or-she-is-a-refugee-court-of-appeal-offers-new-guidance-to-tribunals-to-ensure-children-and-vulnerable-persons-can-have-their-voices-heard/ Accessed 24 September, 2017
Human Rights Watch: Burma: Targeted Sanctions, Arms Embargo Needed: Ethnic Cleansing Demands Swift International Response. https://www.hrw.org/news/2017/09/17/burma-targeted-sanctions-arms-embargo-needed Accessed 20 September, 2017
Human Rights Watch (Beirut, 20 September, 2017) Iraq/KRG: 1,400 Women, Children from ISIS Areas Detained: Investigate Killings, Abductions of Foreign Men https://www.hrw.org/news/2017/09/19/iraq/krg-1400-women-children-isis-areas-detained Accessed 20 September, 2017
Independent News (2017) European border forces "frequently abuse ' refugees and migrants report finds (Independent News, Rachael Roberts, 6 April, 2017) http://www.independent.co.uk/news/world/western-border-forces-abuse-migrants-refugee-crisis-serbia-macedonia-hungary-asylum-seekers-a7671201.html Accessed 22 September, 2017
International Committee of the Red Cross (2016) Practice relating to Rule 135: Children https://ihl-databases.icrc.org/customary-ihl/eng/docs/v1_rul_rule135 (Accessed 30 October, 2016)
International Committee of the Red Cross (2015) Basic Rules of the Geneva Conventions and their Additional Protocols http://www.geneva-academy.ch/RULAC/pdf/ICRC-Basic-Rules-in-the-1949-Geneva-Conventions-and-1977-Additional-Protocols.pdf (Accessed 30 October, 2016)
Oxfam report (April, 2017): A dangerous 'game': the pushback of migrants, including refugees, at Europe's borders Available at https://www.oxfam.org/en/research/dangerous-game-pushback-migrants-including-refugees-europes-borders Accessed 22 September, 2017
Protocol No. 4 to the Convention for the Protection of Human Rights and Fundamental Freedoms, E.T.S. No. 46, entered into force May 2, 1968. University of Minnesota Human Rights Library. http://hrlibrary.umn.edu/euro/z23prot4.html (Accessed 26 September, 2016)
United Nations Committee on the Rights of the Child "General Comment Number 14 (2013) on the Right of the Child to have his or her best interests taken as a primary consideration" (art 3 para 1) May 2013 Para 6(3) http://www2.ohchr.org/English/bodies/crc/docs/GC/CRC_C_GC_14_ENG.pdf Accessed 1 October, 2017
United Nations High Commissioner on Refugees (2015) Guidelines for International Protection No. 11 Prima Facie Recognition of Refugee Status HCR/GIP/15/11 (24 June, 2015) http://www.refworld.org/docid/555c335a4.html Accessed 22 January, 2017
UNHCR Handbook and Guidelines on Procedures and Criteria for Deciding Refugee Status (2011 ed.) http://www.unhcr.org/en-us/publications/legal/3d58e13b4/handbook-procedures-criteria-determining-refugee-status-under-1951-convention.html Accessed 17 January, 2017

United Nations High Commissioner on Refugees (2012): Detention Guidelines (Guidelines on the Applicable Criteria and Standards relating to the Detention of Asylum-Seekers http://www.unhcr.org/505b10ee9.pdf (Accessed 5 November, 2016)

UN News Centre (24 March, 2016) UN rights chief concerned over 'collective expulsion' of migrants after EU-Turkey deal http://www.un.org/apps/news/story.asp?NewsID=53539#.WcSDhcZrzIU Accessed 21 September, 2017

United Nations News Centre (9 January, 2018) Rohingya children trapped in 'appalling' conditions in Myanmmar's Rakhine state http://www.un.org/apps/news/story.asp?NewsID=58397#.WmraInxG3IU Accessed 26 January, 2018

Cases

AM (Afghanistan) v Secretary of State for the Home Department (and Lord Chancellor as Intervenor), Royal Courts of Justice, London, 27 July, 2017 Case No: C5/2015/0626 [2017] EWCA Civ 1123

Applicant A. and Another v. Minister for Immigration and Ethnic Affairs and Another, High Court of Australia, (1997) 190 CLR 225; 142 ALR 331

Blerim Greka, Agnesa Greka and Resul Greka v Police of the Czech Republic, Regional Directorate of the Police of the South Moravian Region, Amicus Curiae, European Council o Refugees and Exiles (ECRE) Before the Constitutional Court of the Czech Republic, February, 2015

Conka v Belgium [2002], Chamber Judgment (no. 51564/99) https://hudoc.echr.coe.int/eng#{%22itemid%22:[%22003-491603-492872%22]} Accessed 21 September, 2017

Gonzalez v Reno 86 F.Supp.2d 1167, 2000 U.S. Dist. LEXIS 325

JA v UK Secretary of State for the Home Department [2016] UKUT 00560 (IAC)

Khadra Hassan Farah, Mahad Dahir Buraleh, Hodan Dahir Buraleh, Canada: Immigration and Refugee Board of Canada, 10 May 1994. Available at http://www.refworld.org/cases,IRBC,3ae6b70618.html Accessed 4 October 2017

Tarakhel, Mubilanzila Mayeka and Kaniki Mitunga v. Belgium, Application No. 13178/03, European Court of Human Rights (Decision Date 12/01/2007) http://www.asylumlawdatabase.eu/en/case-law/ecthr-mubilanzila-mayeka-and-kaniki-mitunga-v-belgium-application-no-1317803 (Accessed 22 October, 2016)

Chapter 3
'Pushback' and 'Extraterritorial Collective Migration Control Measures' Imposed on Child Refugee Asylum Seekers

3.1 Introduction: 'Refoulement' by Any Other Name Is Still 'Refoulement'

This author is in accord with the view of the International Committee of the Red Cross that:

> International humanitarian law, refugee law and human rights law are complementary bodies of law that share a common goal, the protection of the lives, health and dignity of persons. They form a complex network of complementary protections...[1]

What is evident, however, is that extraterritorial collective measures designed to block the movement of refugee asylum seekers, including child refugees (accompanied and unaccompanied), to particular State borders flout State obligations under international law in regards often to all three of the aforementioned codified systems of legal protections for these vulnerable peoples. The current author concurs with the view that such so-called extraterritorial 'migration' controls amount to "an exercise of jurisdiction"; that is "effective control over the individual or over another State's territory"[2] and that:

> The obligation of non-refoulement does not arise only when a refugee is within or at the borders of a state but also when a refugee is under its effective or de facto jurisdiction outside its territory - including in international waters as well as in the territorial waters and the territory of another state[3]

[1]International Committee of the Red Cross. Statement of 23 April, 2005: Humanitarian Law, Human Rights and Refugee Law – Three Pillars https://www.icrc.org/eng/resources/documents/statement/6t7g86.htm Accessed 24 September, 2017.

[2]Vandvik (2008), p. 28. Accessed 26 September 2017.

[3]Vandvik (2008), p. 29. Accessed 25 September 2017.

© Springer International Publishing AG, part of Springer Nature 2018
S. C. Grover, *Child Refugee Asylum as a Basic Human Right*,
https://doi.org/10.1007/978-3-319-78013-9_3

Furthermore, refoulement, it is here argued, may not always involve return to the original offending State that led the refugees to flee in the first instance but can involve, in some instances, return to a transit State or blocking of movement out of a transit State where there is also grievous persecution of the particular refugee collective or individuals at issue in that transit State (i.e. their being persecuted as 'children, 'refugee asylum seekers' and also in relation to other intersecting identities relating for instance to ethnicity, national origin and/or religion etc.).

The cases discussed in this chapter involve the use of a statutory scheme (here the Dublin III regulations) to, on the view here, attempt to erroneously legitimize as lawful the denial of safe haven in the form of asylum in a prospective asylum State where: (1) the urgent circumstances demanded under international human rights law such humanitarian assistance and (2) failure to accord the same, while exercising *de facto* jurisdiction over the child refugee asylum seekers concerned through extraterritorial measures to block their effective access to asylum procedures, amounting to complicity in inhuman and degrading treatment.[4] In such contexts, it is here contended, there is derogation by the State of the *jus cogens* prohibition against inhuman, degrading treatment and possibly torture (depending on the fact pattern in the specific situation the treatment may rise to the level of torture) in its (1) declining to give access, if any, to fair asylum procedures and (2) at a minimum accord temporary or *prima facie* refugee status along with interim asylum to the collective pending individual assessments where such are deemed necessary in respect of, for example, the public's interest in national security and public health.

> A key attribute of national sovereignty is the right of states to admit or exclude aliens from their territory. *Only if exclusion from the territory or from protection would involve a breach of some other provision of international law are states bound to admit aliens. The concept of asylum is the most important example of the latter principle* (emphasis added) [5]

Let us turn then to two selected case examples of reliance on a statutory scheme as a smokescreen in denial to child refugees of asylum (on any temporary, *prima facie* or other basis) where such involves, in the particular circumstance, the State not honoring its *jus cogens* obligations. The first case *SSHD [Secretary of State of the Home Department] v ZAT (Syria)*[6] discussed in this chapter concerns children whose *prima facie* status as refugees, objectively speaking, is not at issue. The latter European case involves a small collective of children unaccompanied and a severely psychologically disabled adult relative fleeing the armed conflict and persecution by the Assad regime and non-government elements including ISIS in Syria. It should be appreciated, however, that even if a collective does not meet the Convention criteria

---

[4]Some such cases may involve torture. Whether the anguish suffered by the child refugee asylum seekers blocked from UK asylum (in the cases discussed in this chapter) rose to the level of psychological torture is a question left unanswered here.

[5]Council of Europe Report (Prepared by Mole, N and Meredith, C) Asylum and the European Convention on Human Rights http://www.refworld.org/pdfid/4ee9b0972.pdf Accessed 25 September, 2017 at p. 10.

[6]SSHD [Secretary of State of the Home Department] v ZAT (Syria) [2016] EWCA Civ 810).

as refugees, they are still entitled to some form of protection and legal status for entry, often asylum, in such instances in which they may be or are certain to be exposed to inhuman, degrading treatment or torture if barred from the prospective asylum territory or expelled from it.[7]

3.2 The Right to Asylum Where the State Exercises 'Pushback' or 'Extraterritorial Control' and Denial of Asylum Amounts to Inhuman and/or Degrading Treatment and/or Torture

Headnotes: 'Pushback' Collective Migration Control Measures, Denial of Urgently Needed Humanitarian Assistance, State request for Bypass of the Initial Process of the Dublin III Regulations, Inhuman and Degrading Treatment by the Transit State, Barring of Access to Asylum as Inhuman and Degrading Treatment, unaccompanied child refugee asylum seekers, family reunion, best interests of the child, the right to family as a human right.

3.2.1 Case 1: SSHD (UK Secretary of State of the Home Department) v ZAT (Syria) Court of Appeal (Civil Division) UK Royal Courts of Justice, London

3.2.1.1 The Facts

This case involved an expedited appeal by the U.K. Secretary of State of the Home Department (hereafter SSHD) against the decision of the Upper Tribunal (UT) of the Immigration and Asylum Chamber (IAC) which ordered the Secretary of State to allow entry into the UK of four Syrians (three unaccompanied minors and a disabled adult brother of one of the children which adult suffered mental health issues). That Upper Tribunal (UTIAC) decision reversed the Secretary of State's initial refusal of entry of the four Syrians in question to the UK. The four had been living in what has been described as a "makeshift [refugee] camp"[8] near Calais, France for several months which camp was colloquially referred to as 'the jungle'(here referred to as the Calais camp for ease of reference). The inhabitants of the camp received almost no aid from the French government with instead humanitarian groups and volunteers

[7]The issue of subsidiary or complementary protection for persons who do not easily fit into one or more of the five grounds listed in the 1951 Refugee Convention (relating to persecution on account of the victim's race, religion, nationality, membership of a particular social group or political opinion) is beyond the scope of this work.

[8]SSHD v ZAT (Syria) Court of Appeal at para 1.

providing basic necessities as best they could.[9] The entry of the applicants into the UK was grounded on their legal representatives making the argument for their right to bypass the Dublin III Regulation given: (a) France's inability and/or unwillingness to respond adequately to their intolerable situation while in France stuck as they were in legal limbo in the deplorable and degrading living conditions of the Calais makeshift refugee camp and (b) a claim by the applicants (made through counsel) to a freestanding right to assert their right to family under the European Convention which would entail reunification with their family members who had legal status in the U.K. and resided in the U.K. Thus, from the perspective of the applicants, their entry into the UK. was not in fact irregular in any *substantive* sense since, on their view, there was a highly legally supportable basis for their bypassing the Dublin III regulations under the aforementioned particular circumstances.

3.2.1.2 Commentary on SSHD (UK Secretary of State of the Home Department) v ZAT (Syria) Court of Appeal (Civil Division) UK Royal Courts of Justice, London

The four applicants were, per the decision of the Upper Tribunal, to be allowed entry into the U.K. pending determination of their refugee status in the U.K. They entered the UK on January 21, 2016. The approach of the Upper Tribunal of the Immigration and Asylum Chamber in the case at bar would seem consistent with the view of the Council of Europe that States are required to allow entry where failure to do so would derogate from an international norm that must be upheld. The latter obligation to allow entry is especially pressing where such infringement of an international norm arising from denial would have grievous consequences for the persons denied protection in the form of asylum or in another form (i.e. as when a *jus cogens* norm is violated by the denial of entry and instead once entered irregularly the persons are removed and face high risk to their personal liberty and security).[10] Here, given the situation in the Calais makeshift refugee camp, and France's unwillingness and/or inability to meet the most basic needs of the refugees[11] in the Calais camp; a refusal of entry to the U.K. (pending U.K. determination of the refugee status of the applicants who had fled persecution in Syria) would, it is here contended, amount to violation of the *jus cogens* norm prohibiting inhuman and degrading treatment. This arguably would be the case on two accounts; first: denial of entry would *in itself* be inhuman and degrading treatment in the particular circumstance since (a) the

---

[9]Chicago Tribune (October 24, 2016) France moving 6500 migrants, destroying 'the jungle' camp in Calais.

[10]Council of Europe Report (Prepared by Mole, N and Meredith, C) Asylum and the European Convention on Human Rights http://www.refworld.org/pdfid/4ee9b0972.pdf Accessed 25 September, 2017 at p. 10.

[11]The persons in the Calais camp, it is here contended, met the criteria for a refugee collective on a *prima facie* basis given their history and the objective situation in their home countries and were entitled to proper and fair individual assessment of their asylum requests.

denial would deprive the refugee applicants of family reunification and this would be excessively harsh and punitive since these particular applicants were persons who would likely be highly reliant on family (three of the applicants were children and one a significantly disabled adult) and (b) the denial of entry would be with the UK's foreknowledge that the applicants would likely to return to the Calais camp only then to try irregular entry to the U.K. by their own devices which attempt(s) would in all likelihood jeopardize the safety and perhaps even the lives of the applicants. Second: the denial of entry to the U.K. here violated the norm prohibiting inhuman and degrading treatment as, *in effect*, the "pushback" of these refugee applicants (removing them from the U.K. notwithstanding the order issuing from the Upper Tribunal to allow entry) constituted, on the analysis here, a *refoulement* to a transit State. The denial of entry to the U.K. can here be considered refoulement to France (to the French Calais camp) in that France had in the past in practice afforded the applicants but inhuman and degrading treatment[12] by (1) failing to provide the applicants the basic necessities of life[13] and respect for their dignity and (2) disregarding the best interests of the refugee children as children and of the refugee disabled adult in the group. All of the refugee asylum applicants in the case at bar were especially vulnerable persons deserving, under international human rights law, of a special high duty of care and protection. The latter then constitutes, it is here argued, on the part of the U.K. Home Office, *in effect* at least, also a form of persecution. This on account of the applicants' membership in certain collectives comprised of highly vulnerable persons all of which collectives intersected simultaneously with the *de facto* group status of *prima facie* but not formally declared 'refugees' (three of the applicants had the social status 'children', the adult's social status was of 'disabled person', and all had the national origin Syrian and likely were regarded with suspicion as to political identity and ideology notwithstanding there had been no adequate individual assessment of their claims by the UK Home Office).

The Court of Appeal formulated the central question in the case as

> in what circumstances can the processes and procedures of the Dublin III Regulation for determining the Member State responsible for processing an application for asylum be bypassed because of rights under the ECHR, in particular the right to family life under Article 8? When, if at all, can an individual who is not in the United Kingdom decide not to apply for asylum in the first Member State he or she enters and ask another Member State directly that it "take charge" of his asylum application, and, either directly or through a family member, require that other Member State to consider an application, or to admit him or her.[14]

[12]There was, furthermore, no certainty that this pattern would not be repeated on the applicants' return to France.

[13]The applicants like all others in the Calais makeshift refugee camp had to rely on an insecure flow of support from NGO's in Calais if and when such aid came and if they could access it.

[14]SSHD v ZAT (Syria) Court of Appeal at para 4 In the Court of Appeal (Civil Division) on Appeal from the Upper Tribunal Immigration and Asylum Chamber (Neutral Citation Number: [2016] EWCA Civ 810), Royal Courts of Justice, Strand, London, WC2A 2LL, 02/08/2016.

There was no dispute between the parties that the Dublin procedures are "premised on the importance of children's rights"[15] and fundamental human rights more generally:

> In accordance with the 1989 United Nations Convention on the Rights of the Child and with the Charter of Fundamental Rights of the European Union, the best interests of the child should be a primary consideration of Member States when applying this Regulation. In assessing the best interests of the child, Member States should, in particular, take due account of the minor's well-being and social development, safety and security considerations and the views of the minor in accordance with his or her age and maturity, including his or her background. In addition, specific procedural guarantees for unaccompanied minors should be laid down on account of their particular vulnerability.[16]

Further the parties were in accord that where the member State in which the child first arrives "will not react to the [asylum] claim and cannot be expected to act in accordance with the Dublin processes, including their affirmation of the importance of family life"[17] the mechanism has failed and fundamental rights under the European Convention on Human Rights have not been respected:

> The respondents' position is that the Dublin process in France failed to vindicate and protect the rights under the ECHR of the three unaccompanied minors and the fourth respondent. They also maintain that, in any event, they have a freestanding right to assert the right to family life under ECHR Article 8 and to claim that as a result the United Kingdom was under a positive substantive obligation to admit the first four respondents to the United Kingdom[18]

Nor was there any dispute between the parties in the case at bar that respect for family life was a primary consideration in applying the Dublin III procedures:

> In accordance with the European Convention for the Protection of Human Rights and Fundamental Freedoms and with the Charter of Fundamental Rights of the European Union, respect for family life should be a primary consideration of Member States when applying this Regulation.[19]

Certainly respect for family life would enter into weighing what would be in the best interests of especially vulnerable persons such as were the unaccompanied children and the disabled adult asylum applicants in this case:

> When the applicant is an unaccompanied minor, the presence of a family member or relative on the territory of another Member State who can take care of him or her should also become *a binding responsibility criterion* (emphasis added).[20]

Importantly, the Dublin III Regulation, furthermore, is written to incorporate the flexibility that would allow for a compassionate and humane response to the situation of particular persons entitled to refugee protection and their unique circumstances:

---

[15]SSHD v ZAT (Syria) Court of Appeal at para 5.

[16]Dublin III regulation para 13.

[17]SSHD v ZAT (Syria) Court of Appeal at para 5.

[18]SSHD v ZAT (Syria) Court of Appeal at para 5.

[19]Dublin III Regulation at para 14.

[20]Dublin III Regulation at para 16.

> Any Member State should be able to derogate from the responsibility criteria, in particular on humanitarian and compassionate grounds, in order to bring together family members, relatives or any other family relations and examine an application for international protection lodged with it or with another Member State, even if such examination is not its responsibility under the binding criteria laid down in this Regulation.[21]

The UK Upper Tribunal of the Immigration and Asylum Chamber affirmed that such humanitarian concerns were paramount in the case at bar:

> This application for judicial review raises issues of the keenest difficulty for the determination of individual rights against the background of the rule of law and for the exercise of a jurisdiction that is at the same time humanitarian and alive to the national and international regulatory context.[22]

The Court of Appeal in *ZAT* acknowledged European Court of Human Rights case law affirming the high duty of care and the special considerations to be taken into account and weighted heavily when child refugee protection matters are at issue:

> The requirement of "special protection" of asylum seekers is particularly important when the persons concerned are children in view of their specific needs and vulnerability. This is so even when the children are accompanied by their parents as they were in that case [referring to *Tarakhel v Switzerland* (Application no. 29217/12) Grand Chamber Judgment of the ECHR I 4 November, 2014].[23]

Interestingly the U.K. Home Secretary did not seek the return to France of the four refugee asylum seekers (a disabled adult and three unaccompanied minors) and agreed that "the United Kingdom is the correct place for their asylum claims to be determined substantively."[24] Rather the Court of Appeal articulated the Secretary of State's position thus:

> The Secretary of State's case is that the Upper Tribunal erred in granting relief to individuals who had refused to claim asylum in France and to make use of the Dublin III mechanism and also had made no application in the United Kingdom for asylum or for leave to enter, and had, for example, provided no biometric data before their arrival. A decision by this court would clarify the position.[25]

The Court of Appeal in the case at bar (*ZAT*) held that the decision reached in *ZAT* on the particular facts and evidence presented to the Upper Tribunal (i.e. psychiatric condition of the asylum claimants and the fact that even had the claimants made

---

[21]Dublin III Regulation at para 17.

[22]R (on the application of ZAT and Others) v Secretary of State for the Home Department, IJR [2016] UKUT 00061 (IAC) (21 January, 2016) Para 2 at p. 2.

[23]SSHD v ZAT (Syria) Court of Appeal at para 75 In the Court of Appeal (Civil Division) on Appeal from the Upper Tribunal Immigration and Asylum Chamber (Neutral Citation Number: [2016] EWCA Civ 810), Royal Courts of Justice, Strand, London, WC2A 2LL, 02/08/2016.

[24]SSHD v ZAT (Syria) Court of Appeal at para 6. In the Court of Appeal (Civil Division) on Appeal from the Upper Tribunal Immigration and Asylum Chamber (Neutral Citation Number: [2016] EWCA Civ 810), Royal Courts of Justice, Strand, London, WC2A 2LL, 02/08/2016.

[25]SSHD v ZAT (Syria) Court of Appeal at para 6. In the Court of Appeal (Civil Division) on Appeal from the Upper Tribunal Immigration and Asylum Chamber (Neutral Citation Number: [2016] EWCA Civ 810), Royal Courts of Justice, Strand, London, WC2A 2LL, 02/08/2016.

asylum application in France it would have taken just under a year to process), may have been a different one had the Upper Tribunal applied what the Court of Appeal contended was the proper test (in deciding whether the Dublin III Regulation can be bypassed in favour of enforcing the right to family under Article 8 of the European Convention on Human Rights).[26] Despite that conclusion, the Court of Appeal made no order that the case be returned to the Upper Tribunal of the Immigration and Asylum Chamber. The Secretary of State had already granted asylum to two of the four claimants at the time of the Court of Appeal hearing with the other two cases having a pending decision on asylum. It would appear to this author, with respect, that the decision of the Court of Appeal was intended, in part at least, to send a message that pressing humanitarian concerns (such as existed here given the inhuman conditions in the Calais camp, the psychiatric state of the asylum seekers and the fact that the asylum seekers as unaccompanied children and a disabled adult were especially vulnerable) may allegedly not suffice in law to set up that compelling exception[27] in future cases required to allow for bypass of the Dublin III regulation regarding which member state is responsible for the case. This Court of Appeal decision, on the respectful view here, was thus intended then to act as a basis (leading case precedent) for likely denial of bypass of the Dublin III Regulation in future cases where that bypass is petitioned for based strictly on compelling humanitarian considerations.

The Court of Appeal held in the case at bar that the test for bypass of the Dublin III Regulation applied by the Upper Tribunal in *ZAT* may *not* have been correct. The Court of Appeal references, with approval, counsel for the UK Home Secretary's emphasis on the need for an orderly procedural process from the onset.[28] However this assumes that allowance for compelling exceptions is not part of an 'orderly process' which is disputable. The Court of Appeals reference to the need for an orderly process-translation: 'strict adherence to the Dublin III Regulation notwithstanding particular facts which raise compelling humanitarian concerns'—implies an overriding concern by the Court of Appeal that (a) exceptions justifying departure from strict adherence to the Dublin III Regulation will occur very often given the current refugee crisis in Europe and that (b) consequently there will be no orderly process. The Court of Appeal seemed to belie this concern as foundational to its position when it stated: "There will be a need for expedition in many cases involving

---

[26]SSHD v ZAT (Syria) Court of Appeal at para 8–9. In the Court of Appeal (Civil Division) on Appeal from the Upper Tribunal Immigration and Asylum Chamber (Neutral Citation Number: [2016] EWCA Civ 810), Royal Courts of Justice, Strand, London, WC2A 2LL, 02/08/2016.

[27]SSHD v ZAT (Syria) Court of Appeal at para 8: "An application for entry by an unaccompanied minor, without first invoking the appropriate Dublin III procedures in the relevant Member State, can only be justified in an especially compelling case." In the Court of Appeal (Civil Division) on Appeal from the Upper Tribunal Immigration and Asylum Chamber) (Neutral Citation Number: [2016] EWCA Civ 810), Royal Courts of Justice, Strand, London, WC2A 2LL, 02/08/2016.

[28]SSHD v ZAT (Syria) Court of Appeal at para 81. In the Court of Appeal (Civil Division) on Appeal from the Upper Tribunal Immigration and Asylum Chamber (Neutral Citation Number: [2016] EWCA Civ 810), Royal Courts of Justice, Strand, London, WC2A 2LL, 02/08/2016.

unaccompanied minors"[29] thus acknowledging, in effect, that the cases of unaccompanied minors may place a strain on the Dublin III Regulatory system in terms of the possibility for strict adherence. The Court of Appeal concurred that the situation of the four asylum applicants was urgent and that, at the time, France could not adequately address that urgency but also expressed the compelling need for an orderly process:

> The circumstances of the first four respondents' cases, especially the psychiatric evidence, suggested in their cases there was a particular need for urgency. But an orderly process is also important in cases of unaccompanied minors.[30]

Recall, however, that the Dublin III Regulations codify the principle that flexibility (i.e. in burden sharing allocations in practice) allowing a humanitarian and compassionate response suitable to a unique refugee asylum seeking situation is part of what is desirable, the obligation of the States involved and legally supportable.[31] Thus, according to the Dublin III regulatory scheme itself, strict adherence to routine forms of application of the Dublin III Regulations does not always equate to proper or orderly application. Yet the Court of Appeal in *ZAT* opined in a generalized manner, in essence, on the inherent value in strict adherence to the Dublin III Regulation. This notwithstanding the fact that France, as was not contested, would not have been able to process any application for the four Syrians in question for almost a year thus denying these highly traumatized and vulnerable individuals reunification with their family members in the UK in the interim-their last tenuous link to the possibility of moving on with life in a positive and hopeful direction.

In addition, the Court of Appeal in *ZAT* seems to suggest that though exceptions are technically allowable under the Dublin III Regulations; permitting bypass of the Dublin III Regulation for desperate persons who make out their case for such an exception in a manner that departs from the normal protocol may be denied on that basis (here for instance the asylum claimants made no asylum claim in France nor in the UK. Rather their siblings in the UK (adults who had refugee status in the UK) made the case for the unaccompanied children and the disabled adult by letters (dated 11 November and 4 December 2015) to the UK prior to claim. The four asylum seekers then arrived for entry to the UK January 21, 2016 based on the decision of the Upper Tribunal of the Immigration and Asylum Chamber which decision was in their favour.

The Court of Appeal seems to be formulating an expectation for future cases that, notwithstanding exceptional circumstances, the Dublin III procedures will be followed until and unless the Member States involved make an exception and

[29]SSHD v ZAT (Syria) Court of Appeal at para 87. In the Court of Appeal (Civil Division) on Appeal from the Upper Tribunal Immigration and Asylum Chamber (Neutral Citation Number: [2016] EWCA Civ 810), Royal Courts of Justice, Strand, London, WC2A 2LL, 02/08/2016.

[30]SSHD v ZAT (Syria) Court of Appeal at para 87 In the Court of Appeal (Civil Division) on Appeal from the Upper Tribunal Immigration and Asylum Chamber (Neutral Citation Number: [2016] EWCA Civ 810), Royal Courts of Justice, Strand, London, WC2A 2LL, 02/08/2016.

[31]Dublin III Regulation at para 17.

make that exception part of the Dublin Regulation Protocol procedural steps somewhere down the line of processing the case. In practice such an approach by the Court of Appeal (on the view here) appears *in effect* to block the right and ability of asylum seekers to seek asylum even when Member States are not fulfilling their obligations under the European Convention on Human Rights i.e. to protect persons in their jurisdiction from inhuman or degrading treatment (i.e. Article 3).[32]

In *ZAT* the three unaccompanied minors and the disabled adult, while in the Calais camp and living in inhumane and indecent conditions, were virtually completely abandoned by the French government and left to their own devices to attempt survival. The French government tolerated the living circumstances for these children (persons under age 18 years) and the disabled adult in their group in the Calais camp which conditions, under the European Convention, it had a positive obligation to remedy. Yet (on the view here respectfully) the Court of Appeal appears to 'victim blame' these children and the significantly disabled adult for their own suffering when it unabashedly states:

> In this case, moreover, the emergency largely arose because of the appalling conditions in which the first four respondents found themselves *as a result of their decision not to seek assistance from the French authorities.* Notwithstanding their difficult histories and trauma, I do not consider that their subjective fear about the French process can, in itself, justify bypassing the Dublin process and the French courts. I consider that Mr Fordham [counsel for the asylum seekers] puts the matter too high when he states ... that "human rights law meets children where they are; it does not condemn them for the so-called wisdom of how they have got there". In my judgment, what has to be demonstrated by those who seek to bypass the Dublin processes and the legal procedures of the first Member State are objective reasons which justify that decision.[33]

It was, on the view here, not the children and their disabled companion who created this emergency. This as France was well aware of the Calais makeshift refugee camp, the inhuman and degrading living conditions there and of the substantial number of persons, including children, in the camp suffering those conditions. The French government took insufficient positive steps, if any, to reach out to these persons and facilitate their making asylum claims and to provide them with a secure and humane living environment in the interim. It is not surprising that children from Syria, fleeing government and non-government persecution in the homeland, including grave threats to life, would be distrustful of government generally and most especially one that, in practice, would resign people (as did France) to a fate such as was the Calais camp. The Calais camp living situation most likely was perceived by the inhabitants as intended to be a symbol of France's intent to deter current and any future would-be asylum seekers. The children's "subjective fear about the French process" (as the Court of Appeal put it) had some very real

[32]European Convention on Human Rights as amended by Protocols Nos. 11 and 14, Done 3 May, 2002.

[33]SSHD v ZAT (Syria) Court of Appeal at para 82. In the Court of Appeal (Civil Division) on Appeal from the Upper Tribunal Immigration and Asylum Chamber (Neutral Citation Number: [2016] EWCA Civ 810), Royal Courts of Justice, Strand, London, WC2A 2LL, 02/08/2016.

objective rational underpinnings given the lack of protection based on humanitarian and human rights considerations the children received living openly in the Calais camp. One could argue, as does this author, that this failure on the part of the French government to protect the four asylum seekers' Article 3 Convention rights *in itself* provided "objective reasons" justifying the decision "to bypass the Dublin processes and the legal procedures of the first Member State"[34]

While acknowledging that exceptions may occur where the Dublin III Regulations can legitimately be bypassed, the Court of Appeal, at the same time, seems to require pleading for grant of that exception to the very system that failed the asylum seekers in the first instance by leaving them in a degrading, inhuman living circumstance in the Calais Camp:

> There is a loose analogy with the triage stage of a visit to a hospital's Accident and Emergency Department. Although there will be some cases where the patient arrives in such a serious state that it is obvious he or she must go to the front of the queue, it is not up to a patient or his or her family to decide on the priority to be given to him or her.[35]

It should be understood that the Upper Tribunal Immigration and Asylum Chamber concluded, on the basis of the witness and other evidence presented to it, that:

> [it was] highly probable that if the first four Applicants had pursued asylum claims under the Regulation No 604/2013/EU ("the Dublin Regulation") in France, they would have established an entitlement to a "take charge" request by the French authorities, directed to the United Kingdom and a consequential transfer to England.[36]

Further, given the urgent situation and the need to resolve it sooner rather than later on, at least an interim basis, the Upper Tribunal did agree to hear a great deal of factual evidence in support of the four asylum seekers which the Upper Tribunal found sufficient to issue the order to have the four admitted entry to the UK pending final determination of their refugee claims:

> *These proceedings have generated a substantial quantity of evidence.* The contributors include some of the Applicants, their legal representatives, lawyers practising in France, representatives of humanitarian organisations and others. This evidence has been provided mainly in the form of detailed witness statements and reports. *It is of notable pedigree and consistently satisfies the requirements of reliability and objectivity.* We have evaluated all of this evidence with care and have conducted the penetrating analysis required by the principle of heightened scrutiny. Having done so, *we are satisfied that the core elements of the Applicants' cases are established* (emphasis added).[37]

---

[34]See SSHD v ZAT (Syria) Court of Appeal at para 82. In the Court of Appeal (Civil Division) on Appeal from the Upper Tribunal Immigration and Asylum Chamber (Neutral Citation Number: [2016] EWCA Civ 810), Royal Courts of Justice, Strand, London, WC2A 2LL, 02/08/2016.

[35]SSHD v ZAT (Syria) Court of Appeal at para 81. In the Court of Appeal (Civil Division) on Appeal from the Upper Tribunal Immigration and Asylum Chamber (Neutral Citation Number: [2016] EWCA Civ 810), Royal Courts of Justice, Strand, London, WC2A 2LL, 02/08/2016.

[36]R (on the application of ZAT and Others) v Secretary of State for the Home Department, IJR [2016] UKUT 00061 (IAC) (21 January, 2016) para 12 p. 5.

[37]R (on the application of ZAT and Others) v Secretary of State for the Home Department, IJR [2016] UKUT 00061 (IAC) (21 January, 2016) para 10 at p. 4.

Thus it is *not* the case that the four Syrians had circumvented the Dublin III Regulations in an effort to obtain an exception beyond the jurisdiction of a Member State, without adequate substantive objective and other evidentiary basis or one that was unjustified or likely would not have been given had the Dublin III Regulation formal process (regarding which member State ought to 'take charge') been adhered to from the outset with regard to proper allowance for an exception.[38] Respectfully, however, on this author's view, the Court of Appeal's statement that (referring to its own imperfect hospital emergency room analogy) "it is not up to a patient or his or her family to decide on the priority to be given to him or her"[39] seems to erroneously imply at least the converse and to ignore the abundance of objective evidence that rendered an exception in this case legally supportable under the Dublin III regulatory scheme. The Court of Appeal aforementioned statement implies that desperate persons at the end of their ability to cope (including unaccompanied children and psychiatrically disabled adults, ill and/or perhaps even non-informed on the Dublin III Regulation), and situated in what was described before the Upper Tribunal as a 'living hell' are not to take the situation into their own hands regardless their inhumane living circumstance and the lack of basic protection extended by the State (here France). Refugees, however, as refugees, it is here contended, are entitled to agency and self-advocacy making the choices for survival that they feel are their only option in circumstances where, for instance, their European Convention right(s) are being grossly violated as was the case in *ZAT*. This is perhaps even more apparent where children are involved given the high duty of care owed to refugee children under The Convention on the Rights of the Child and as incorporated into the Dublin III Regulations in terms of, for instance, regard for the notion of best interests of the child as a primary consideration in determining what constitutes appropriate State treatment of the refugee asylum seeking child under the Dublin III Regulations.[40]

In a case such as *ZAT* becoming entangled in the Dublin formal procedures at a point of personal crisis may have been contrary to the asylum seekers chances for survival. The children had been living in inhumane conditions in France in the Calais makeshift refugee camp[41] from October 2015 and by 21 January 2016 the camp was

[38]Here referring to exceptions in application of the Dublin III Regulations regarding initial process in determining which Member State will 'take charge' of the case to consider asylum for the persons at issue.

[39]SSHD v ZAT (Syria) Court of Appeal at para 81. In the Court of Appeal (Civil Division) on Appeal from the Upper Tribunal Immigration and Asylum Chamber (Neutral Citation Number: [2016] EWCA Civ 810), Royal Courts of Justice, Strand, London, WC2A 2LL, 02/08/2016.

[40]See para 13 and Article 6 of the Dublin III Regulation.

[41]The Upper Tribunal had heard witness testimony that the degrading and inhuman conditions in the Calais camp (documented in various reports and referenced in administrative decisions such as that by *Tribunal Administratif de Lille* on 2 November 2015) persisted at least into January 2016 (See SSHD v ZAT (Syria) Court of Appeal at para 23).

occupied by some 6000 others.[42] The four applicants had attempted irregular entry to the UK several times without success apparently considering that tack their only option as a way out of the Calais camp situation with a view to reunification with family. Notwithstanding the serious human rights concerns to which these facts give rise; the Court of Appeal took the approach of considering the Dublin III Regulations as on par with the European Convention on Human Rights and to frame the issue as one of balancing two legal regimes:

> The fact that ECHR Article 8 can be engaged by delay and that the operation of a procedural rule may be disproportionate, together with the existence of Article 17, brings one back to the question of the balance between what Laws LJ in *CK's* case . . .referred to as the two competing legal imperatives and the height of the hurdle required to permit the Dublin process to be "trumped" by ECHR Article 8.[43]

In fact, however, on the view here, the ECHR rights obligations *do* trump the Dublin III Regulations. Those Regulations as implemented in each and every case are to be a way of providing an orderly process for immigration and asylum considerations which *in practice*, and not just in theory, honour the ECHR State obligations. To the degree that the Dublin III Regulatory process in the particular case does or is likely to undermine the State faithfully fulfilling its ECHR obligations (given for instance the treatment the refugee asylum seekers had experienced in the Member State to date and the nature of the Dublin Process as implemented in that State (France) including expected time frames), the Dublin Process is, it is here contended, neither effective, nor orderly nor binding in law.

This author is thus in accord with the view below of the AIRE Centre (that Centre made a submission in the case at bar) but would argue that the conditions in the camp were as relevant in terms of the need to prioritize the European Convention on Human Rights (Article 3)[44] as was the issue of family reunion and delay in that regard viewed as interference in the ECHR Article 8 right to family provision:

> It was argued by the AIRE Centre [Advice on Individual Rights in Europe] that all that has to be shown is a manifest deficiency in the protection of ECHR rights in the first Member State, because that will defeat the presumption that Member States will comply with their inter-

[42] SSHD v ZAT (Syria) Court of Appeal at para 20. In the Court of Appeal (Civil Division) on Appeal from the Upper Tribunal Immigration and Asylum Chamber (Neutral Citation Number: [2016] EWCA Civ 810), Royal Courts of Justice, Strand, London, WC2A 2LL, 02/08/2016.

[43] SSHD v ZAT (Syria) Court of Appeal at para 86. In the Court of Appeal (Civil Division) on Appeal from the Upper Tribunal Immigration and Asylum Chamber (Neutral Citation Number: [2016] EWCA Civ 810), Royal Courts of Justice, Strand, London, WC2A 2LL, 02/08/2016.

[44] Article 3: Prohibition of torture: "No one shall be subjected to torture or to inhuman or degrading treatment or punishment." European Convention on Human Rights as amended by Protocols Nos. 11 and 14, done 3 May, 2002 http://www.echr.coe.int/Documents/Convention_ENG.pdf (Accessed 1 December, 2016).

> national obligations, including those in the ECHR protecting rights under the ECHR and the EU Charter... The criticisms relate only to the specific circumstances of family reunion of unaccompanied minors.[45]

Indeed the Court of Appeal appeared to accept as factual that the Syrian refugee children and the disabled adult had no possibility of having their case expedited in France had they filed a claim in France and requested as per the Dublin III provisions another Member State (the UK) to take responsibility/charge of their case:

> The evidence of the French lawyers and the NGOs suggested that there would be a delay of just under one year in the French system and *there was no possibility of expedition*. The tribunal was very concerned because of the strength of the psychiatric evidence about the mental health of the first four respondents, the absence of any parent or parental figure, and the conditions in the camp (emphasis added).[46]

> It also appears that the Code for Entry and Stay of Foreigners and Asylum Rights introduced on 1 November 2015 providing for registration of asylum applications within three to ten days had not yet led to a change in the treatment of unaccompanied minors. In those circumstances, it is understandable that the Upper Tribunal concluded that to refuse to allow entry to the United Kingdom would be a disproportionate interference with the respondents' Article 8 rights.[47]

Yet the Court of Appeal still found the Upper Chamber allegedly applied the wrong test for ordering a bypass of the Dublin III Regulation in the case at bar:

> I consider that the tribunal set too low a hurdle for permitting that process [the Dublin III process] to be displaced by Article 8 considerations[48]

On the respectful view here the Court of Appeal advanced an erroneous characterization of the test applied by the Upper Tribunal as "too low a hurdle"[49] for bypass of the Dublin III Regulation process. This since arguably the wording of the test applied by the Upper Tribunal and that in the Dublin III Regulation is a distinction without a difference. The Upper Tribunal set the test as "a strong and persuasive case

---

[45]SSHD v ZAT (Syria) Court of Appeal at para 86. In the Court of Appeal (Civil Division) on Appeal from the Upper Tribunal Immigration and Asylum Chamber (Neutral Citation Number: [2016] EWCA Civ 810), Royal Courts of Justice, Strand, London, WC2A 2LL, 02/08/2016.

[46]SSHD v ZAT (Syria) Court of Appeal at para 90. In the Court of Appeal (Civil Division) on Appeal from the Upper Tribunal Immigration and Asylum Chamber (Neutral Citation Number: [2016] EWCA Civ 810), Royal Courts of Justice, Strand, London, WC2A 2LL, 02/08/2016.

[47]SSHD v ZAT (Syria) Court of Appeal at para 90. In the Court of Appeal (Civil Division) on Appeal from the Upper Tribunal Immigration and Asylum Chamber (Neutral Citation Number: [2016] EWCA Civ 810), Royal Courts of Justice, Strand, London, WC2A 2LL, 02/08/2016.

[48]SSHD v ZAT (Syria) Court of Appeal at para 92. In the Court of Appeal (Civil Division) on Appeal from the Upper Tribunal Immigration and Asylum Chamber (Neutral Citation Number: [2016] EWCA Civ 810), Royal Courts of Justice, Strand, London, WC2A 2LL, 02/08/2016.

[49]SSHD v ZAT (Syria) Court of Appeal at para 92. In the Court of Appeal (Civil Division) on Appeal from the Upper Tribunal Immigration and Asylum Chamber (Neutral Citation Number: [2016] EWCA Civ 810), Royal Courts of Justice, Strand, London, WC2A 2LL, 02/08/2016.

on its merits"[50] [for bypass of the Dublin III process] which the Court of Appeal held was a lower bar than the allegedly higher requirement of an "especially compelling case under Article 8."[51] Further when one considers the conditions in the Calais camp, it is implausible and legally insupportable, on the view here, to hold that refugees whose ECHR Article 3 rights were being violated (as this author holds was the case here for these four asylum seekers) must be required to adhere strictly to the Dublin III process in any case or to maintain that they would not meet the requirements for bypass of the relevant regulations. It is noteworthy that, notwithstanding the inhumane Calais camp conditions, an "especially compelling case" was, according to the Court of Appeal, not made out under Article 8 for reunion with the U.K. siblings and grant of asylum (respectfully, it is here contended, an erroneous view). Apparently Article 3 of the ECHR was not pleaded as a separate ground for transfer of the ZAT case from France to the UK. Nevertheless, at the very least, the need for ECHR Article 3 considerations was implied in any case given the context in which the four asylum seekers held their Article 8 claim should be urgently addressed; namely the Calais camp conditions the applicants had suffered through and were effectively, in practice, at risk of being returned to post their arrival in the U.K. should asylum not be granted.[52]

The Court of Appeal seemed to rely on and be especially concerned with the alleged possible disruption of operation of the 'mutual confidence' presumption between the States as a central pillar girding the Dublin III Regulations:

---

[50]SSHD v ZAT (Syria) Court of Appeal at para 91. In the Court of Appeal (Civil Division) on Appeal from the Upper Tribunal Immigration and Asylum Chamber (Neutral Citation Number: [2016] EWCA Civ 810), Royal Courts of Justice, Strand, London, WC2A 2LL, 02/08/2016.

[51]SSHD v ZAT (Syria) Court of Appeal at para 92. In the Court of Appeal (Civil Division) on Appeal from the Upper Tribunal Immigration and Asylum Chamber (Neutral Citation Number: [2016] EWCA Civ 810), Royal Courts of Justice, Strand, London, WC2A 2LL, 02/08/2016.

[52]The UK government in ZAT maintained that the four applicants would not have met the criteria for family reunion as set out under one particular Dublin regulation since the children here, for instance, sought entry to the UK to join their siblings in the UK who had refugee status rather than joining immediate relatives contemplated by that regulation i.e. the regulation referring to parents of the asylum seeking child being reunited with their children (as stipulated at paragraphs 352A – 352FJ of the regulations—Siblings, grandparents, aunts or uncles are not considered 'family' under UK law in respect of asylum applications based on family reunion (UNICEF UK A child's crisis: Why the refugee and migrant crisis should matter to us all (see Petition to Home Secretary Amber Rudd to change this aspect of the law and broaden who is considered 'family' https://www.unicef.org.uk/uprooted-a-childs-crisis/ Accessed 30 September, 2017) The government also pointed to a bureaucratic obstacle to reliance on another Dublin III Regulation which "allows a child to seek leave to join a relative with limited leave to remain as a refugee or a beneficiary of humanitarian protection where the relative is not the parent of the child and the child is under the age of 18". The latter regulation requires the applicant to "...make an application...online and the individual must attend a visa application centre to provide biometric data and pay a fee" SSHD v ZAT (Syria) Court of Appeal at para 49.

> The operation of the tribunal's approach [in *ZAT*] would in many cases also involve the intense examination of the claimed failings of another Member State which Lord Kerr stated ...would lead to disarray.[53]

That conclusion of the Court of Appeal (that the Upper Tribunal's approach in *ZAT* would inevitably lead to disarray) is premised on the rebuttable notion that each member State is to be presumed, *prima facie* at least, to be acting effectively and in good faith in fulfilling its ECHR obligations and in implementing the Dublin III regulatory process in the most effective and humane manner practicable in the circumstance. The problem is that unaccompanied minors and disabled adults and other highly vulnerable, most often traumatized persons, are not necessarily or realistically able to participate in the complex bureaucratic morass that often is the Dublin III regulatory process as implemented in various particular case contexts. The Court of Appeal in the case at bar appears to hold two mutually contradictory and mutually exclusive views on the propriety of its insistence on adherence to the Dublin III process -even in urgent cases-grounded on the presumption of 'mutual confidence'. On the one hand the Court of Appeal in *ZAT* acknowledges the urgent and dire situation of the asylum seekers in *ZAT* and the untoward delay that would have occurred had the claimants followed the steps of the Dublin III process

> ...together with delay in bringing about reunification, the conditions [in the makeshift camp] go to the severity of any breach which is a relevant factor *in considering the proportionality of an interference with the respondents' Article 8 rights* (emphasis added)[54]

On the other hand, the Court of Appeal states:

> I consider that the tribunal set too low a hurdle for permitting that process to be displaced by Article 8 considerations.[55]

This author, in contrast, holds that, in addition, (1) the "conditions [in the makeshift Calais refugee camp] go to the severity of the breach" of Article 3 of the ECHR at play in the case and that (2) as there appeared to be such a breach of Article 3; a *jus cogens* norm (given the testimony to this effect before the Asylum Tribunal which testimony by experts, counsel, NGOs, the claimants and others was accepted as credible by the Tribunal), the Upper Tribunal of the Immigration and Asylum Chamber in fact did *not* set "too low a hurdle" for displacement of the Dublin procedure in deciding which Member State should take carriage of the ZAT asylum/family reunification case (a case involving several child refugee asylum seekers and their severely psychiatrically disabled adult companion who was related to one of the three minors but apparently not in a position to care for the children in

[53]SSHD v ZAT (Syria) Court of Appeal at para 92. In the Court of Appeal (Civil Division) on Appeal from the Upper Tribunal Immigration and Asylum Chamber (Neutral Citation Number: [2016] EWCA Civ 810), Royal Courts of Justice, Strand, London, WC2A 2LL, 02/08/2016.

[54]SSHD v ZAT (Syria) Court of Appeal at para 93. In the Court of Appeal (Civil Division) on Appeal from the Upper Tribunal Immigration and Asylum Chamber (Neutral Citation Number: [2016] EWCA Civ 810), Royal Courts of Justice, Strand, London, WC2A 2LL, 02/08/2016.

[55]SSHD v ZAT (Syria) Court of Appeal at para 92. In the Court of Appeal (Civil Division) on Appeal from the Upper Tribunal Immigration and Asylum Chamber (Neutral Citation Number: [2016] EWCA Civ 810), Royal Courts of Justice, Strand, London, WC2A 2LL, 02/08/2016.

any way).[56] Such an infringement of Article 3, as will be recalled, sets out a substantive basis for legitimate departure from the Dublin III regulatory process insofar as doing so would effectively assist in remedying the *European Convention on Human Rights* Article 3 human rights abuse situation.

Whether or not the asylum seeker raises (as a separate ground for transfer of their case to another State as the 'responsible State') Article 3 of the *European Convention on Human Rights* (the *jus cogens* protection guarantee against cruel, degrading or inhuman treatment or punishment), it is here contended that (1) the first Member State and the prospective asylum State are both duty bound under international law to consider this *jus cogens* guarantee when it is implicated in the case and (2) factor this issue into the calculus in determining if the case is to be duly transferred to the second Member State. At one point the Court of Appeal in *ZAT* referenced the imperative derived from Article 3 of the ECHR in relation to the Dublin regulatory process but despite the claimants living in the intolerable inhuman Calais camp conditions disregarded the ECHR Article 3 considerations as relevant to the case at bar:

> The anterior procedural stage involves the process of determining which Member State is responsible. In cases concerned with the substantive aspect, a strict approach has been taken, and ...only the risk of ill-treatment in violation of Article 3 of the ECHR will suffice. Mr Eadie's submission was that, if anything, a stricter approach should be taken in a case such as this which... [involved] the anterior procedural stage and the role of Article 8 in it.[57]

The government counsel in *ZAT* argued, among other things, for collection of age assessment data (including biometric data) as part of an initial stage in an alleged 'orderly process' and the Court of Appeal concurred. However, age assessment through biometric data in many ways has been unreliable data offering up age ranges (a proportion of them wrong) rather than precise age estimates. The result has frequently been that this type of data has been sometimes used to unjustifiably block the grant of asylum to many minors on the erroneous conclusion that the individuals involved were actually not under age 18 years at the time of their asylum seeking actions and instead engaged in a misrepresentation on that issue when this may not have been the case:

> There is considerable force in Mr Eadie's [government counsel's] emphasis on the importance of an orderly process at what I described as the anterior procedural stage and the need for biometric data, verification of identity, and assessments of age and the family relationships claimed.[58] [recall that the Asylum Tribunal had heard evidence on the various central factual claims underpinning the claimants' request that the UK take charge of their case and

[56]Rather it appeared the children were caring for the psychiatrically disabled adult who had fled Syria with them.

[57]SSHD v ZAT (Syria) Court of Appeal at para 60. In the Court of Appeal (Civil Division) on Appeal from the Upper Tribunal Immigration and Asylum Chamber (Neutral Citation Number: [2016] EWCA Civ 810), Royal Courts of Justice, Strand, London, WC2A 2LL, 02/08/2016.

[58]SSHD v ZAT (Syria) Court of Appeal at para 81. In the Court of Appeal (Civil Division) on Appeal from the Upper Tribunal Immigration and Asylum Chamber (Neutral Citation Number: [2016] EWCA Civ 810), Royal Courts of Justice, Strand, London, WC2A 2LL, 02/08/2016.

found the evidence compelling enough to satisfy the test for the order allowing entry to the UK while the refugee asylum claims were considered by the UK]

The issue of age assessment of child refugee asylum seekers via medical tests (biometric data of various sorts) is contentious. Yet, since child refugee asylum seekers are to be accorded special protections and considerations (i.e. under international human rights law and Refugee Convention guidelines etc.) there is generally an effort to objectively verify the purported minor's self-report of age. Yet these biometric tests often prove to be highly unreliable and especially are so in respect of pinpointing a specific chronological age but nevertheless are frequently used to erroneously block meritorious child refugee asylum claims:

> ...the Royal College of Paediatricians, the British Medical Association and Great Ormond Street Institute of Child Health have all pointed out, the tests are not accurate. Prof Tim Cole, of Great Ormond Street, said: "If you test children around the age of 18, or three years either side, in this way, the results get one-third of the ages wrong. When people are much older, say 30 or 40, it can be a lot more accurate. But if you think of puberty and what different rates children develop at, you can see how wrong these tests can be."[59]

The use of dental x-rays in determining the age of someone claiming to be a child refugee asylum seeker has been regarded by medical professionals as unethical since there is no medical benefit to the children in exposing them to radiation for this purpose.[60] Furthermore "practical as well as ethical considerations show that the idea cannot work; children are not "date stamped"[61]

In *ZAT*, the Court of Appeal states:

> I consider that applications such as the ones made by these respondents should only be made in very exceptional circumstances where they can show that the system of the Member State that they do not wish to use, in this case the French system, is not capable of responding adequately to their needs. *It will, in my judgment, generally be necessary for minors to institute the process in the country in which they are in order to find out and be able to show that the system there is not working in their case.* This is subject to the point that, as I have stated, these cases are intensely fact-specific. There will be cases of such urgency or of such a compelling nature because of the situation of the unaccompanied minor that it can clearly be shown that the Dublin system in the other country does not work fast enough... consider that those representing persons in the position of the respondents should first seek recourse from the authorities and the courts of the Member State in which the minor is. *Only after it is*

[59]Travis, A (Home Affairs Editor) The Guardian (19 October, 2016) Children don't come date-stamped-and that includes refugees: Using medical information to try to pinpoint a young person's age is folly, for both practical and ethical reasons https://www.theGuardian.com/world/2016/oct/19/child-refugees-date-stamped-medical-age Accessed 29 September, 2017.

[60]Travis, A (Home Affairs Editor) The Guardian (19 October, 2016) Children don't come date-stamped-and that includes refugees: Using medical information to try to pinpoint a young person's age is folly, for both practical and ethical reasons https://www.theGuardian.com/world/2016/oct/19/child-refugees-date-stamped-medical-age Accessed 29 September, 2017.

[61]Travis, A (Home Affairs Editor) The Guardian (19 October, 2016) Children don't come date-stamped-and that includes refugees: Using medical information to try to pinpoint a young person's age is folly, for both practical and ethical reasons https://www.theGuardian.com/world/2016/oct/19/child-refugees-date-stamped-medical-age Accessed 29 September, 2017.

> *demonstrated that there is no effective way of proceeding in that jurisdiction should they to turn to the authorities and the courts in the United Kingdom* (emphasis added).[62]

It is here contended that if the ZAT case was not compelling enough to legitimize bypass of the Dublin III process (given that the children and their companion were, by all accounts, 'living in a hell' in the Calais makeshift camp with no possibility of expedited remedy through the Dublin III system), then a compelling case for bypass seems but a 'legal fiction'. Such a legal fiction (the ever elusive "compelling case" for an exception to the Dublin III Regulation allowing bypass of the requirement to apply first to the State in which the minor is for transfer of their case to another member State) would serve State interests in deterring child refugees and other highly vulnerable refugee groups from seeking asylum in the second Member State and caters to bureaucratic convenience and a credo of form over substance. Respectfully, on the view here, to expect that unaccompanied minors in particular would have the opportunity or resources, psychological and otherwise, to "institute the process in the country in which they are in order to find out and be able to show that the system [the Dublin III Regulatory system] there is not working in their case" is to place an unrealistic,[63] and unjust burden on these child refugee asylum seekers, ignore the reality of their urgent plight and erode the effective exercise of their right to seek asylum as refugees and escape their current intolerable circumstances.

The Court of Appeal in *ZAT* went on to say:

> There will be cases of such urgency or of such a compelling nature because of the situation of the unaccompanied minor that it can clearly be shown that the Dublin system in the other country does not work fast enough.[64]

The problem is that in a case such as *ZAT*, by the time those Dublin III processes would have played out (regarding a formal request put to France at the outset for a bypass with a take charge request to be proffered by France to the UK) the asylum seekers (i.e. unaccompanied children and a disabled adult) may well have been dead. This given the egregious ECHR Article 3 violations to which they were being subjected in the Calais refugee camp where their chances of potential victimization through violence in the unregulated camp were high. Further living in the makeshift

[62]SSHD v ZAT (Syria) Court of Appeal at para 95. In the Court of Appeal (Civil Division) on Appeal from the Upper Tribunal Immigration and Asylum Chamber (Neutral Citation Number: [2016] EWCA Civ 810), Royal Courts of Justice, Strand, London, WC2A 2LL, 02/08/2016.

[63]The process is fraught with complexities and unexpected barriers. For instance in ZAT the lawyers for the four asylum seekers were not informed until March 2016 of any procedure for requesting the Secretary of State consider 'the ECHR Article 8 compatibility of refusing prompt entry to the United Kingdom' SSHD v ZAT (Syria) Court of Appeal at para 96. In the Court of Appeal (Civil Division) on Appeal from the Upper Tribunal Immigration and Asylum Chamber (Neutral Citation Number: [2016] EWCA Civ 810), Royal Courts of Justice, Strand, London, WC2A 2LL, 02/08/2016.

[64]SSHD v ZAT (Syria) Court of Appeal at para 95. In the Court of Appeal (Civil Division) on Appeal from the Upper Tribunal Immigration and Asylum Chamber (Neutral Citation Number: [2016] EWCA Civ 810), Royal Courts of Justice, Strand, London, WC2A 2LL, 02/08/2016.

refugee camp with desperate, hungry suffering people and violence was causing a fast decline in mental health for all of the applicants in the case at bar:

> ZAT states that he has experienced physical violence in the camp. IAJ states that he was attacked by a group of older men, whom he believed were people traffickers, but with assistance he escaped. KAM has acted as AAM's carer in the camp. AAM's medical needs were unmet in the camp.[65]

Yet as to the situation in *ZAT*, the Court of Appeal concluded (erroneously on the respectful view here) that:

> . . .the tribunal failed to apply the correct test, and I am not entirely persuaded that if it had done so it must inevitably have reached the same conclusion.[66]

In the final analysis it would seem that the Court of Appeal decision in *ZAT* (if it is to stand unchallenged via any future case ruling) forecloses, in most cases involving child refugee asylum seekers, the realistic possibility of bypass of the Dublin III initial process (re process in deciding which State member should 'take charge' of the case). This by (1) placing the burden on the unaccompanied minor to rely on the Dublin III process itself to set out the case for a member State, one other than the State of first arrival, taking charge of the case. The latter notwithstanding mitigating circumstances hindering an unaccompanied child's ability to do so and by (2) holding that "bypassing the "initial procedural stage" of the Dublin process (i.e. on Article 8 grounds) in the way that occurred in these (the ZAT) proceedings is unlikely to meet the required threshold of 'an especially compelling case'".[67] The Court of Appeal in *ZAT* thus, on the view here, distracts in its ultimate holding from the issue of the Article 3 ECHR violations that can occur in the country of first arrival being inseparable from the factors to be properly considered in assessing the Article 8 claim for expedited family reunion and a request (by whatever means and process) to bypass of the Dublin III initial process.

Respectfully, it would seem that the Court of Appeal in *ZAT* did not properly acknowledge that the Dublin III process objective of being a humane system was not just an afterthought. Rather it was an integral aspect of making the Dublin III regulatory process orderly and one likely to keep chaos in check in the midst of a refugee crisis. To insist on strict adherence to the Dublin III initial process in a case such as *ZAT* under the conditions that existed in France at the time for

---

[65]SSHD v ZAT (Syria) Court of Appeal at para 22. In the Court of Appeal (Civil Division) on Appeal from the Upper Tribunal Immigration and Asylum Chamber (Neutral Citation Number: [2016] EWCA Civ 810), Royal Courts of Justice, Strand, London, WC2A 2LL, 02/08/2016.

[66]SSHD v ZAT (Syria) Court of Appeal at para 101. In the Court of Appeal (Civil Division) on Appeal from the Upper Tribunal Immigration and Asylum Chamber (Neutral Citation Number: [2016] EWCA Civ 810), Royal Courts of Justice, Strand, London, WC2A 2LL, 02/08/2016. The Appeal was allowed however rather than returned to the Asylum Tribunal for a rehearing in that the UK Secretary of State did not seek the return of the four asylum seekers in ZAT to France.

[67]SSHD v ZAT (Syria) Court of Appeal at para 100. In the Court of Appeal (Civil Division) on Appeal from the Upper Tribunal Immigration and Asylum Chamber (Neutral Citation Number: [2016] EWCA Civ 810), Royal Courts of Justice, Strand, London, WC2A 2LL, 02/08/2016.

unaccompanied child refugee asylum seekers is to foster more distrust of the State (i.e. the UK) amongst refugees including in particular also unaccompanied child refugees. Further, it is, on the view here, to fail to respect the spirit of the Dublin III Regulations system which prioritizes family reunification especially for unaccompanied children and allows for derogation of the State responsibility criteria (re which State is to take charge of the case) under the regulations on that basis.[68]

The refugee makeshift camp at Calais was destroyed by the French government in October 2016. The French government put the number of camp inhabitants at 6500 most of whom were evacuated and transported by the authorities to various reception centres across France where they could apply for asylum. Non-governmental aid agencies estimated there were 1200 unaccompanied minors amongst the camp inhabitants and put the overall number of camp inhabitants at closer to 8300.[69] Many of the unaccompanied minors were reluctant to get on the evacuation buses:

> "It was difficult to get children on to buses because they didn't have much faith in the system," said Dorothy Sang, a humanitarian adviser at Save the Children. "They didn't believe that their cases would be followed up if they were taken out of Calais."[70]

Some of those children were transported to heated containers as temporary shelter in another part of the city on the promise their asylum requests to the U.K. would be looked at and processed for a decision.[71] However access to those containers was restricted:

> Ms Sang [humanitarian adviser at Save the Children] said she had seen terrified, exhausted, ill, and injured teenagers forced to sleep alone in the ruined camp. Registering to enter the container area was difficult she said, with registration only possible for a short time...
>
> She [Ms. Sang] catalogued serious failings, from the "unclear registration" process, to "allowing the bulldozers to go in before accounting for where they would be placed", and the "endless evenings when the only people looking for accommodation for the children who hadn't been put in the container camp were humanitarian organisations and volunteers on the ground"[72]

[68]Dublin III Regulation at para 17.

[69]Chicago Tribune (October 24, 2016) France moving 6500 migrants, destroying 'the jungle' camp in Calais http://www.chicagotribune.com/news/nationworld/ct-france-migrant-camp-calais-20161024-story.html Accessed 8 January, 2017.

[70]England, C. Independent: Refugee children sleeping rough three days after Calais camp 'cleared' http://www.independent.co.uk/news/world/europe/calais-jungle-latest-refugee-children-unaccompanied-minors-camp-migrants-destroyed-relocated-moved-a7386551.html Accessed 29 September, 2017.

[71]England, C. Independent: Refugee children sleeping rough three days after Calais camp 'cleared' http://www.independent.co.uk/news/world/europe/calais-jungle-latest-refugee-children-unaccompanied-minors-camp-migrants-destroyed-relocated-moved-a7386551.html Accessed 29 September, 2017.

[72]England, C. Independent: Refugee children sleeping rough three days after Calais camp 'cleared'http://www.independent.co.uk/news/world/europe/calais-jungle-latest-refugee-children-unaccompanied-minors-camp-migrants-destroyed-relocated-moved-a7386551.html Accessed 29 September, 2017.

NGO's reported difficulty accessing the children in the container encampment with access very restricted and with limited aid workers distributing food to the children housed in the containers.[73] These NGOs and others were thus concerned that the children had no access to adult support via social work or other youth workers:

> Volunteers in Calais said they believed the children inside had not been provided with youth workers; the only adults working with them were thought to be security guards and police.[74]

Such a restriction of access to information, support and the possibility for self-advocacy for however long it lasted is, it is here contended, a clear violation of France's international legal obligations under the Convention on the Rights of the Child in regards to but not limited to: the Article 12 guarantee of the right to participate in decisions that affect the child, and Article 22 regarding the rights of the unaccompanied refugee child to "receive appropriate protection and humanitarian assistance in the enjoyment of applicable rights set forth in the ...Convention and in other international human rights or humanitarian instruments to which the said States are Parties."[75]

A small group of such children, around twelve, were unable or unwilling to get on the buses and were simply left behind to fend for themselves in the ruins of the camp looking for shelter (some may have been inadvertently overlooked but in any case these were persons who appeared to be children left without shelter provided by the authorities and there was no attempt made to ensure that no children were left behind in the destroyed Calais makeshift camp).[76] Many of these persons who presented themselves as unaccompanied minors requested family reunification with family members who had legal status in the U.K.[77]

Some of what occurred post the *ZAT* case in terms of the U.K. response to family reunification pleas by some of the former Calais camp inhabitants presenting as unaccompanied minors has not engendered much confidence in the possibility for

[73]England, C. Independent: Refugee children sleeping rough three days after Calais camp 'cleared' http://www.independent.co.uk/news/world/europe/calais-jungle-latest-refugee-children-unaccompanied-minors-camp-migrants-destroyed-relocated-moved-a7386551.html Accessed 29 September, 2017.

[74]England, C. Independent: Refugee children sleeping rough three days after Calais camp 'cleared' http://www.independent.co.uk/news/world/europe/calais-jungle-latest-refugee-children-unaccompanied-minors-camp-migrants-destroyed-relocated-moved-a7386551.html Accessed 29 September, 2017.

[75]Convention on the Rights of the Child entry into force 2 September, 1990 (France ratified the Convention 7 August, 1990).

[76]England, C. Independent: Refugee children sleeping rough three days after Calais camp 'cleared' http://www.independent.co.uk/news/world/europe/calais-jungle-latest-refugee-children-unaccompanied-minors-camp-migrants-destroyed-relocated-moved-a7386551.html Accessed 29 September, 2017.

[77]Chicago Tribune (October 24, 2016) France moving 6500 migrants, destroying 'the jungle' camp in Calais http://www.chicagotribune.com/news/nationworld/ct-france-migrant-camp-calais-20161024-story.html Accessed 8 January, 2017.

non-politicized, objective, fair and humane implementation of U.K. refugee policy and procedures in regards to unaccompanied minors. In December 2016, 36 youth (former inhabitants of the Calais camp) brought a legal action against the U.K. home secretary Ms. Amber Rudd alleging that she reneged on the U.K.'s promise to allow eligible unaccompanied children entry to Britain and that she unlawfully rejected their asylum applications. As of 31 October 2016, 28 of these children bringing the legal challenge had their applications for asylum rejected, and the remaining eight were awaiting the decision.[78] Further, the legal challenge alleges that the U.K. Home Secretary did not provide proper written decisions in that no reasons were provided for rejecting those Calais child asylum applications that were declined:

> The [UK] government has rendered these children, including some as young as 13, to effectively be without any legal remedy until well into the new year, which is the earliest that the relevant Home Office officials have agreed to give reasons for refusing some of these children.
>
> The way that this has all been handled by both the UK and French authorities is nothing short of shameful. It is morally reprehensible and, we argue, simply unlawful that these children have not been given written reasons as to why their applications were refused and that these children were told about the refusals in group meetings without a proper procedure in place.[79]

This author would argue that the U.K.'s refusal to give written reasons for the denial of asylum to these unaccompanied child refugees (at least for a time) was a denial of asylum rights that are both collective and individual. That is to say that none in this Calais child refugee group who had officially been denied U.K. asylum had received reasons and hence they were treated as a refugee collective in that respect and denied their collective rights as refugee asylum seekers to receive reasons. The denial may have been based on the applicants' collective identity as unaccompanied child refugee asylum seekers with the U.K. intending to send a hard line message intended to deter other refugee asylum seekers including unaccompanied children. Ultimately, of course, this collective denial of the child group's refugee rights also resulted in the denial, at least for a period, of the right of each child to individual reasons for rejection of his or her asylum application and consideration of his/her unique case circumstances. This has the impact of dehumanizing the children to some degree since their individual identity (manifest in their articulation of the merits of their individual asylum application) is lost in the denial of their refugee rights as a collective. It is very telling also, on the view here, that the refusals of asylum were communicated in a group setting. The latter approach (announcement to the group of rejection of most of the asylum claims

---

[78] Taylor, Diana The Guardian: Hundreds of Calais child refugees have UK asylum claims rejected http://www.theGuardian.com/world/2016/dec/28/calais-child-asylum-seekers-legal-action-agsint-uk-government Accessed 1 March, 2017.

[79] Toufique Hossain, Director of public law at Duncan Lewis Solicitors; the firm that is representing these children. Cited in Taylor, Diana. The Guardian: Hundreds of Calais child refugees have UK asylum claims rejected http://www.theGuardian.com/world/2016/dec/28/calais-child-asylum-seekers-legal-action-agsint-uk-government Accessed 1 March, 2017.

with a small number of additional decisions pending) symbolically denied openly and unabashedly the individual rights of each of these unaccompanied refugee children to consideration of the merits of their particular case independently from the consideration of the merits of another and arguably also violated the children's individual privacy rights.

The Calais child asylum seekers in the legal challenge referred to argue that they are *bono fide* refugees eligible for relocation to the U.K. and that the U.K. government in declining their applications is violating s. 67 of the UK Immigration Act commonly referred to as the Dubs Amendment.[80] The *Dubs amendment* was legislation put forward by Lord Dubs (a member of Britain's labour party under Cameron) which legislation passed promising asylum for some of the child refugees flooding Europe *even if the children had no family members in the UK*. This based on concern for the children's vulnerability and the continuing risk of grievous harm that was created for these *prima facie* (unaccompanied) child refugees should they not be offered asylum (Interestingly Lord Dubs himself was a former child refugee who had received asylum in the U.K. having arrived from Czechoslovakia in 1939).[81] The legislation (the Dubs Amendment) requires the unaccompanied children arrived in Europe by March 31, 2016 to be eligible for asylum in the UK:

> Even if the "Dubs" amendment were being actively implemented, children need to have arrived in Europe before 31 March to be eligible, a clause inserted to prevent more parents from sending their children on a perilous journey to come to Britain.[82]

Lily Caprani, Deputy Executive Director of UNICEF U.K. pointed out that:

> The [UK] Government agreed to the Dubs amendment on the basis that it would end dangerous journeys for children [unaccompanied child refugees] travelling across Europe. If the scheme were to finish before . . .children. . .have reached safety then it will have been a failure. If children do not have safe and legal routes to the UK they will continue to make perilous journeys and continue to fall into the hands of smugglers and traffickers.[83]

Clearly consideration of the humanitarian imperative and international obligations regarding refugees is being, to some extent, constrained by political expediency, lack of political will and difficulties, in practice, in efficiently implementing a

---

[80]Taylor, Diana The Guardian: Hundreds of Calais child refugees have UK asylum claims rejected http://www.theGuardian.com/world/2016/dec/28/calais-child-asylum-seekers-legal-action-agsint-uk-government Accessed 1 March, 2017.

[81]Gentleman, A. (5 September, 2016) The Guardian: Immigration and asylum: 'It's a disgrace to Europe': Former child refugee Lord Dubs on the Calais camp https://www.theGuardian.com/uk-news/2016/sep/05/disgrace-to-europe-former-child-refugee-lord-dubs-calais-camp Accessed 9 January, 2017.

[82]Gentleman, A. (5 September, 2016) The Guardian: Immigration and asylum: 'It's a disgrace to Europe': Former child refugee Lord Dubs on the Calais camphttps://www.the Guardian.com/uk-news/2016/sep/05/disgrace-to-europe-former-child-refugee-lord-dubs-calais-camp Accessed 9 January, 2017.

[83]UNICEF UK and Save the Children Briefing on the refugee crisis in Europe (15 December, 2016) What's Next for the child refugees in Europe? Available for download at https://www.unicef.org.uk/ Accessed 29 September, 2017.

shared responsibility amongst European countries in the grant of refugee asylum to those eligible, including the most vulnerable among them, such as are unaccompanied children. At the same time it must be acknowledged that according to UNICEF certain aid agencies estimated that, for instance, around 850 unaccompanied children had in fact been relocated from France to the U.K. in 2016 to be reunited with family members who had legal status in the U.K. compared to none in 2015 (mostly under the Dublin III regulation which in those cases would have set out that the U.K. was the proper State to take charge of the cases given the presence of the children's family members lawfully residing in the U.K.).[84]

In February 2017 it was reported that the U.K. Home Office would reconsider asylum applications from unaccompanied child refugees from France as it appeared some had returned to France to the general area near the location of the former makeshift Calais camp (then removed) and had tried again to make the crossing to the U.K. and enter irregularly into the U.K. The Home Office stated:

> We have agreed with the French authorities that we will review any new information from children formerly resident in the Calais camp to assess whether it would change our determination of their eligibility under the Dublin regulation, to encourage an application.[85]

It should be noted that the U.K. supported and committed to enormous expenditure for *extraterritorial* 'migration control' methods trying to prevent further refugees, including unaccompanied child refugees asylum seekers, from entering the U.K. through irregular means:

> The UK government spent £36m on helping to shut down the Calais camp and committed £80m to pay private security firms to patrol northern French ports for the next three years. The UK also agreed to pay £2m to fund a wall designed to bolster border security in the area.[86]

At the same time in response to a petition,[87] pressure from various faith groups and NGO's and the desperate acts of the children still trying to enter the U.K. by

---

[84]UNICEF UK and Save the Children Briefing on the refugee crisis in Europe (15 December, 2016) What's Next for the child refugees in Europe? Available for download at https://www.unicef.org.uk/ Accessed 29 September, 2017.

[85]Cited in The Guardian (Diane Taylor) Home Office agrees to review asylum claims of child refugees in France 19 February, 2017 https://www.theGuardian.com/uk-news/2017/feb/19/home-office-agrees-to-review-asylum-claims-of-child-refugees-in-france?CMP=Share_iOSApp_Other Accessed 1 March, 2017.

[86]The Guardian (Diane Taylor) Home Office agrees to review asylum claims of child refugees in France 19 February, 2017 https://www.theGuardian.com/uk-news/2017/feb/19/home-office-agrees-to-review-asylum-claims-of-child-refugees-in-france?CMP=Share_iOSApp_Other Accessed 1 March, 2017.

[87]The petition stated: "We demand that the Home Office swiftly process the remaining family reunification cases of Calais minors formally under the Dublin III regulations and grant them the full rights and protections it affords." Cited in The Guardian (Diane Taylor) Home Office agrees to review asylum claims of child refugees in France (19 February, 2017) https://www.theGuardian.com/uk-news/2017/feb/19/home-office-agrees-to-review-asylum-claims-of-child-refugees-in-france?CMP=Share_iOSApp_Other Accessed 1 March, 2017.

dangerous methods to be with their family, the U.K. Home Office agreed to reconsider the asylum applications, as previously mentioned, of at least some of the former Calais unaccompanied refugee children whose applications had been rejected (recall that many of these children had their requests for asylum rejected without being given the reasons for the rejection).[88]

The situation for refugees including unaccompanied refugee children in France seeking asylum was reported by Human Rights Watch to be quite dire even several months after destruction of the makeshift refugee camp at Calais:

> Nine months after French authorities closed the large migrant camp known as the Jungle," on the edge of Calais, between 400 and 500 asylum seekers and other migrants are living on the streets and in wooded areas in and around the northern French city.[89]

Human Rights Watch documented "police abuse of asylum seekers and migrants, police disruption of humanitarian assistance, and harassment of aid workers"[90] in Calais post removal of 'the jungle'. Human Rights Watch interpreted such police behaviour as designed to deter other asylum seekers and irregularly entered migrants[91]:

> In March 2017, local authorities barred humanitarian groups from distributing food, water, blankets, and clothing to asylum seekers and migrants. *A court suspended those orders on March 22, finding that they amounted to inhuman and degrading treatment.* The French ombudsman (Défenseur des droits) has also criticized these and other measures taken by local authorities, concluding that they contribute to "inhuman living conditions" for asylum seekers and migrants in Calais (emphasis added).[92]

Various forms of harassment of aid workers also continued in Calais in summer 2017 such as multiple identity document checks within a few hours of each other and "As of the end of June [2017], authorities were allowing a single two-hour

---

[88]"The Home Office spokeswoman said that in total the government had transferred more than 900 unaccompanied children to the UK from Europe in 2016, including more than 750 from France as part of the UK's support for the Calais camp clearance." Citation from The Guardian (Diane Taylor) Home Office agrees to review asylum claims of child refugees in France 19 February, 2017 https://www.theGuardian.com/uk-news/2017/feb/19/home-office-agrees-to-review-asylum-claims-of-child-refugees-in-france?CMP=Share_iOSApp_Other Accessed 1 March, 2017.

[89]Human Rights Watch (July 2017) Like living in hell: Police abuses against child and adult migrants in Calais at p. 1 https://www.hrw.org/report/2017/07/26/living-hell/police-abuses-against-child-and-adult-migrants-calais Accessed 29 September, 2017.

[90]Human Rights Watch (July 2017) Like living in hell: Police abuses against child and adult migrants in Calais at p. 1 https://www.hrw.org/report/2017/07/26/living-hell/police-abuses-against-child-and-adult-migrants-calais Accessed 29 September, 2017.

[91]Human Rights Watch (July 2017) Like living in hell: Police abuses against child and adult migrants in Calais at p. 1 https://www.hrw.org/report/2017/07/26/living-hell/police-abuses-against-child-and-adult-migrants-calais Accessed 29 September, 2017.

[92]Human Rights Watch (July 2017) Like living in hell: Police abuses against child and adult migrants in Calais at p. 1 https://www.hrw.org/report/2017/07/26/living-hell/police-abuses-against-child-and-adult-migrants-calais Accessed 29 September, 2017.

humanitarian distribution each day, in an industrial area near the former migrant camp."[93]Human Rights Watch made a number of recommendations regarding (1) increasing access to asylum procedures for the refugees of Calais and the need to provide emergency shelter for the asylum seekers as well as for undocumented migrants until their cases were determined and (2) providing protective services for unaccompanied children and appropriate shelters for these children.[94]

What is likely is that the tremendous numbers of desperate unaccompanied minors fleeing persecution in their homelands and arriving in Europe[95] will continue substantially unchanged no matter the various extraterritorial control measures aimed to stop the influx; this given the children's indomitable will to survive. What is unclear is the extent to which European Union State Members as well as the U.K. post Brexit will seek not to further the persecution of this group[96] through their own forms of inhuman and degrading treatment of this child refugee asylum seeking collective including unaccompanied child refugees (i.e. through effective denial of access to asylum procedures, unreliable age assessments, mandatory detention, abuse by agents of the State, collective expulsions, collective denials of asylum, extraterritorial control measures of various types etc.)

3.2.1.3 Concluding Remarks

It has been noted by OXFAM[97] that while the U.K. is part of the European Union (until end March, 2019), it has continuing obligations under the Dublin III Regulations. The U.K. thus, until the Brexit date must, under the Dublin III Regulations, continue to consider asylum applications of persons arrived in Europe based on the

[93]Human Rights Watch (July 2017) Like living in hell: Police abuses against child and adult migrants in Calais at p. 2 https://www.hrw.org/report/2017/07/26/living-hell/police-abuses-against-child-and-adult-migrants-calais Accessed 29 September, 2017.

[94]Human Rights Watch (July 2017) Like living in hell: Police abuses against child and adult migrants in Calais at p. 4 https://www.hrw.org/report/2017/07/26/living-hell/police-abuses-against-child-and-adult-migrants-calais Accessed 29 September, 2017.

[95]UNICEF(September, 2017) Harrowing journeys: Children and youth on the move across the Mediterranean Sea, at risk of trafficking and exploitation Available at https://www.unicef.org/publications/index_100621.html Accessed 29 September, 2017.

[96]House of Lords (26 July, 2016) Children in crisis: Unaccompanied migrant children in the EU at p. 3: "In 2015 88,245 unaccompanied children applied for asylum in the EU, including 3,045 in the UK. In May 2016 alone, 3,133 unaccompanied migrant children arrived in Italy. Many children do not even reach the EU's shores: at least 137 children have drowned in the Mediterranean since the start of 2016.... The implementation of existing EU measures to protect unaccompanied migrant children has been poor." https://publications.parliament.uk/pa/ld201617/ldselect/ldeucom/34/3402.htm Accessed 29 September, 2017.

[97]OXFAM (OXFAM Media Briefing 15 June, 2017) Brexit and the Refugee Crisis http://www.oxfam.org.uk/~/media/files/OGB/Media%20Centre/Press%20Releases/BrexitRefugeeCrisis.pdf Accessed 29 September, 2017.

desire of the asylum seekers to be reunited with family members who have legal status in the U.K.[98]

The new Conservative Party leader Theresa May became prime minister in July 2016. No doubt U.K. refugee law will be revised to take effect post Brexit and as OXFAM comments:

> ...the UK will have to decide whether it turns its back on some of the most vulnerable people in the world or finds other ways to help them. Sadly, some of the indications of the government's approach from before the election are not encouraging.[99]

OXFAM notes that the Conservative Party Manifesto prior to the election suggested a two tier system that favored those who applied for resettlement in the U.K. from abroad when compared to those who applied for U.K. asylum after having arrived in Europe. Oxfam holds that "It is a worrying development that could undermine the spirit of the 1951 Refugee Convention under which governments should offer refuge to those fleeing persecution, irrespective of how they have reached safety."[100] This two tier proposed system would seem to be but another dimension of extraterritorial control of asylum seekers as it is easier to control and reduce the flow of refugee asylum seekers, by setting caps for instance to admission through resettlement from abroad, when the asylum seekers are not yet arrived in Europe and their suffering is not tangibly on the U.K.'s doorstep embarrassingly left unaddressed. In addition the numbers of refugees who are considered for resettlement to any specific countries from UNHCR camps is already, as its stands, but an exceedingly small fraction of the overall refugee asylum seeker population. While the U.K. has made but a very modest contribution to burden sharing in terms of providing refuge to desperate Convention and other refugees,[101] it has spent enormous monies to help other countries cope with the influx of refugee asylum seekers:

[98]OXFAM reports "More than 65 million people around the world—half of them children—have been forced to flee their homes because of violence, disasters and persecution." OXFAM (OXFAM Media Briefing 15 June, 2017) Brexit and the Refugee Crisis at pp. 2 http://www.oxfam.org.uk/~/media/files/OGB/Media%20Centre/Press%20Releases/BrexitRefugeeCrisis.pdf Accessed 29 September, 2017.

[99]OXFAM (OXFAM Media Briefing 15 June, 2017) Brexit and the Refugee Crisis at p. 2 http://www.oxfam.org.uk/~/media/files/OGB/Media%20Centre/Press%20Releases/BrexitRefugeeCrisis.pdf Accessed 29 September, 2017.

[100]OXFAM (OXFAM Media Briefing 15 June, 2017) Brexit and the Refugee Crisis at p. 2 http://www.oxfam.org.uk/~/media/files/OGB/Media%20Centre/Press%20Releases/BrexitRefugeeCrisis.pdf Accessed 29 September, 2017.

[101]" ... the UK hosts less than one percent of the world's refugees – a figure dwarfed by the numbers being hosted in countries that are significantly poorer, such as Turkey (16.4 percent), Pakistan (10.1 percent), Lebanon (6.9 percent) and Uganda (3.1 percent) Developing countries still host the majority (86 percent) of refugees, while the six richest countries – the UK, Germany, US, France, China and Japan – host less than nine percent." OXFAM (OXFAM Media Briefing 15 June, 2017) Brexit and the Refugee Crisis at pp. 3–4.

> ...the UK has taken a leading role in providing aid to countries hosting large numbers of refugees. In April 2017, the UK increased funding pledges to support Syrian refugees living in Lebanon, Turkey and Jordan to £1bn. British aid has also helped large numbers of refugees in Serbia and Greece as well as displaced people in South Sudan and Nigeria, among other places[102]

While such U.K. aid to other countries in support of these other States' efforts to provide refuge to vulnerable persecuted peoples is necessary and welcomed, the U.K. as part of the international community has obligations of its own in respect of processing fairly asylum claims and burden sharing in offering asylum (obligations under the Refugee Convention and various international human rights treaties, including the Convention on the Rights of the Child, as well as obligations regarding *jus cogens* norms and other international standards that relate to the treatment of vulnerable persons). Arguably these obligations, given the intent and meaning of the aforementioned law, give rise to a *positive* duty to burden share to a reasonable level in consideration of the U.K.'s resources in terms also of granting asylum to larger numbers of *bona fide* refugees than is currently the case. For instance, in 2015–2016, overall, the U.K. Home Office rejected 40% of asylum applications relating to family reunion and discretion was rarely exercised in application of the Dublin III regulations.[103]

Insofar as unaccompanied child refugee asylum seekers are concerned, it is disheartening that the U.K. to date has not fully met its positive obligation to respect the high duty of care owed this group under international law including in terms of facilitating family reunification. In fact there are aspects of U.K. immigration and asylum law that work against family reunification even for unaccompanied child refugee asylum seekers:

> The UK is the only country in the EU that does not allow unaccompanied child refugees to bring even their closest family members to join them [thus eliminating the possibility of that adult supporting the child in the U.K. financially and psychologically]. Its highly restrictive definition of what constitutes a family – two parents and children – is forcing refugee families to live apart and more people [i.e. unaccompanied child refugee asylum seekers] to embark on dangerous journeys out of desperation].[104]

OXFAM and its partners made several recommendations regarding urgently needed changes to U.K. law to ensure a more humane approach to the family reunification matter. The approach suggested by OXFAM and its partners is, on the view of the current author, better consistent with the international refugee and

[102]OXFAM (OXFAM Media Briefing 15 June, 2017) Brexit and the Refugee Crisis at p. 3 http://www.oxfam.org.uk/~/media/files/OGB/Media%20Centre/Press%20Releases/BrexitRefugeeCrisis.pdf Accessed 29 September, 2017.

[103]OXFAM (OXFAM Media Briefing 15 June, 2017) Brexit and the Refugee Crisis at p. 5 http://www.oxfam.org.uk/~/media/files/OGB/Media%20Centre/Press%20Releases/BrexitRefugeeCrisis.pdf Accessed 29 September, 2017.

[104]OXFAM (OXFAM Media Briefing 15 June, 2017) Brexit and the Refugee Crisis at pp. 4–5 http://www.oxfam.org.uk/~/media/files/OGB/Media%20Centre/Press%20Releases/BrexitRefugeeCrisis.pdf Accessed 29 September, 2017.

human rights law obligation to respect human dignity and prevent inhuman, degrading treatment as well as torture than is the U.K. current approach. The recommendations put to the U.K. government by OXFAM and its partners are as follows:

- Amend the UK Immigration Rules by expanding which 'family members' qualify for claiming asylum in the UK through the family reunion policy to include: young adults who were dependent on the family unit prior to flight, parents, siblings, in-laws and any dependent relative.
- Allow an expanded group of extended family members, including adult siblings, aunts and uncles, and grandparents to sponsor child relatives to join them in the UK under refugee family reunion policies, where it is deemed in the child's best interests.
- Allow children found to be in need of international protection in the UK to bring family members to the country under the refugee family reunion policy.
- Reintroduce legal aid for refugee family reunion.
- Allow British citizens to sponsor family members who have been forcibly displaced or are at risk in their home country, under the same terms as set out in refugee family reunion policy.
- Ensure transfers under the Dublin III Regulation can proceed from Greece, France and Italy in a timely manner by providing UK expertise, including resourcing outreach teams to work with member states to identify children and adults that may be eligible for transfer to the UK. Unaccompanied children, pregnant women and other vulnerable adults should be prioritized.[105]

All of this, as OXFAM and its partners note, will help decrease the risk to child refugee asylum seekers (many of them unaccompanied) and others refugees desperate to reunite with family in the U.K. Hopefully the U.K. will work to reverse the trend of very low acceptance of asylum applications[106] in particular those from unaccompanied child refugees due to unjustifiable existing bureaucratic hurdles and unreasonably overly restrictive rules for family reunification and in other respects and not institute such barriers also post Brexit.[107]

The Commission to the European Parliament and the Council issued a report December 4, 2017, "The protection of children in migration." The report noted there had been a six fold increase in the number of total child asylum applicants over the

[105]OXFAM (OXFAM Media Briefing 15 June, 2017) Brexit and the Refugee Crisis at p. 6 http://www.oxfam.org.uk/~/media/files/OGB/Media%20Centre/Press%20Releases/BrexitRefugeeCrisis.pdf Accessed 29 September, 2017.

[106]Alan Travis (Home Affairs Editor) The Guardian: UK has not taken in any child refugees under Dubs scheme this year (19 July, 2017) https://www.theguardian.com/uk-news/2017/jul/19/uk-not-taken-any-child-refugees-dubs-scheme-this-year Accessed 30 September, 2017.

[107]UNHCR, UNICEF and IOM report (April 2017) Refugee and Migrant Children -Including Unaccompanied and Separated Children-in Europe: Overview of trends in 2016 https://www.unicef.org/eca/Factsheet_refugee_migrant.pdf Accessed 29 September, 2017.

last six years (applicants to an EU Member State).[108] The Commission advanced what should go without saying but, as we have discussed, most commonly is not the reality in practice:

> Protecting children is first and foremost about upholding European values of respect for human rights, dignity and solidarity. It is also about enforcing European Union law and respecting the Charter of Fundamental Rights of the European Union and international human rights law on the rights of the child. This is why protecting all children in migration, regardless of status and at all stages of migration, is a priority.[109]

The European Commission in the aforementioned report sets out a series of actions that are intended to better respect, in practice, the rights of refugee children and other migrant children. These include, but are not limited to, the following steps: working with partner countries re "mainstreaming child protection at the global, regional and bilateral level"[110] and addressing the root causes of child migration (re child refugees and child (most often undocumented) non-refugee migrants), providing better protection for child refugees and non-refugee child migrants along their migratory routes,[111] ensuring all child refugees and non-refugee child migrants receive education and health care, facilitating cross-border family tracing and reunification, addressing the problem of missing refugee and non-refugee migrant children with the same urgency as is the case for missing children who are nationals, providing adequate reception facilities for child asylum seekers and other

---

[108]European Commission (2017) Communication from the Commission to the European Parliament and the Council (4 December, 2017) COM(2017) 211 final 'The protection of children in migration' at p. 2.

[109]European Commission (2017) Communication from the Commission to the European Parliament and the Council (4 December, 2017) COM(2017) 211 final 'The protection of children in migration' at p. 2.

[110]European Commission (2017) Communication from the Commission to the European Parliament and the Council (4 December, 2017) COM(2017) 211 final 'The protection of children in migration' at p. 4.

[111]For an example of just some of the security of the person risks facing refugee and non-refugee children on their migratory route see, for instance, Digidiki, V and Bhabha, J: Report for the FXB (Francois-Xavier Bagnoud) Center for Health and Human Rights, Harvard University (17 April, 2017) ' Emergency within an emergency: The growing epidemic of sexual exploitation and abuse of migrant children in Greece' Available at https://fxb.harvard.edu/new-report-emergency-within-an-emergency-exploitation-of-migrant-children-in-greece/ Accessed 30 September, 2017 This Harvard study reports on (1) the sexual abuse and exploitation of migrant children (refugee and non-refugee) in migrant camps and in large cities within Greece and on (2) the State's practice and policy deficiencies in the State's protection services which deficiencies contribute significantly to the migrant children being sexually victimized. "Data collection was completed in late November 2016 in four sites in Greece—namely, the islands of Lesvos and Chios and the cities of Athens and Thessaloniki"(p. 3). Extensive recommendations to effectively address this sexual abuse and exploitation of child migrants in Greece are provided on pp. 37–41 of the report.

migrant children (accompanied or unaccompanied),[112] carrying out an individual assessment of special needs and vulnerabilities that must be addressed in providing for the proper care and protection of each child taking into account also gender and age related vulnerabilities, using "reliable multi-disciplinary age and non-invasive assessment procedures",[113] providing a guardian for all unaccompanied child refugee and non-refugee migrant arrivals as well as independent representation and prioritizing child refugee and non-refugee migrant status determinations. Only time will tell whether these aspirations as set out in the 2017 European Commission report to accord child refugees and other child migrants collectively and individually their fundamental human rights as children and as asylum seekers in fact materialize in any significant systematic way.[114] Further, it is an open question as to what degree the U.K. will honor fully and proactively its obligations to child refugee asylum seekers under international human rights and refugee law in the period pre and post Brexit.

3.2.2 Case 2: The Queen on the Application of MK, IK (a Child by His Litigation Friend MK) and HK (a Child by Her Litigation Friend MK) v UK SSHD, UK Upper Tribunal Immigration and Asylum Chamber, Judicial Review Decision

Headnotes: The positive duties under the Dublin III Regulations of the State requested to 'take charge', unaccompanied child refugee asylum seekers, family reunion, best interests of the child, the right to family as a human right, denial of urgently needed humanitarian assistance, degrading treatment by the State requested to take charge.

---

[112]European Commission (2017) Communication from the Commission to the European Parliament and the Council (4 December, 2017) COM(2017) 211 final 'The protection of children in migration' at p. 8: "Suitable options could include, for unaccompanied children in particular, placement with adult relatives or a foster family, accommodation centres with special provision for children or other suitable accommodation, such as closely supervised open reception centres designed to ensure the protection of children, or small scale independent living arrangements for older children. The United Nations Guidelines for the Alternative Care of Children constitute relevant standards... Given the negative impact of detention on children, administrative detention should be used, in line with EU law, exclusively in exceptional circumstances, where strictly necessary, only as a last resort, for the shortest time possible, and never in prison accommodation."

[113]European Commission (2017) Communication from the Commission to the European Parliament and the Council (4 December, 2017) COM(2017) 211 final 'The protection of children in migration' at p. 10.

[114]We will discuss in later chapters how the U.S. administration under President Trump is also being tested, as are the member States of the European Union, by the refugee crisis in terms of the State's willingness to uphold international legal norms requiring respect for human dignity and guarantee of fundamental human rights; the latter serving as the foundation ultimately that allows for democratic rule of law.

3.2.2.1 The Facts

This asylum case involves repeated requests from France under the Dublin III Regulations for the U.K. to take charge of the case in consideration of whether it could effect a family reunion of two teen refugee asylum seekers with their biological mother. The central contested issue of import in the case was whether or not the child asylum applicants, IK and HK, were in fact the biological children of the female applicant; MK.[115] The Upper Tribunal noted in the case summary that: "The Secretary of State is not persuaded by this assertion [that IK and HK are the biological children of MK]. This disbelief has formed the cornerstone of the decision making lying at the heart of these proceedings."[116] The take charge request had been denied by the U.K. Home Secretary three times and the applicants requested judicial review.

The applicants represented that they were all Iraqi nationals. IK and HK, the children, had lived in France in the makeshift Calais "jungle' for about two and one-half months whereafter they were living with a French foster family. MK had been lawfully residing in the U.K., with indefinite leave to remain, since being recognized by the U.K. as a refugee in 2010. MK lived in the U.K. with three of her children ranging in age from 6 to 16.

According to MK's initial UK asylum interview in 2010; her husband died around 2006. MK claimed that the marriage had been troubled and that after her husband's death her mother-in-law had taken HK and IK from her. MK reported in her asylum interview, further, that she had fled with her remaining children to Syria in November 2009. From there, with the help of people smugglers, she made her way with the remaining children to the U.K. on 23 December, 2009 and, according to her testimony, thought she would never be reunited with HK and IK again (her eldest child is missing and one daughter died according to her testimony in the asylum interview).

France requested that the UK 'take charge' of the case and consider/assess its merits as a family reunion based asylum petition. The UK Home Office, however, responded 12 February, 2016 to the first letter requesting that the UK take charge and declined to honor the request. The UK Home Office responded again 16 March, 2016 to a second letter from France that had requested the UK reconsider its refusal to take responsibility for the case and this time also the UK would not accede to taking charge of the case. The UK Home Office maintained that certain aspects of

[115]The issue then was whether IK aged 17, was in fact MK's second oldest biological child and HK, aged 15, in fact MK's fourth oldest biological child.

[116]UK—The Queen on the application of MK, IK (a child by his litigation friend MK) and HK (a child by her litigation friend MK) v Secretary of State for the Home Department, JR/2471/2016, 29 April 2016. Available at http://www.asylumlawdatabase.eu/en/case-law/uk-queen-application-mk-ik-child-his-litigation-friend-mk-and-hk-child-her-litigation Accessed 30 September, 2017.

MK's asylum interview in 2010,[117] certain alleged features of the children's witness testimony and particular other factors cast doubt on whether HK and IK were in fact MK's biological children or whether there was some other objective evidence of any verifiable family relationship of professed parent (mother) and children (IK and HK). The Home Secretary's response letter to France in part stated:

> Therefore, unless further evidence of the family relationship, such as a DNA match, is received, I regret to inform you that your request to take charge of the above named is respectfully denied."[118]

There was arguably no doubt, however, that the children (IK and HK) had suffered much over the last years and were highly traumatized and in need of family and a hopeful more certain future. According to HK and IK; after the separation from their mother they had spent two years living with their paternal grandmother in Iraq and then they and their grandmother fled the worsening conflict in Iraq and escaped to Turkey. According to IK and HK's testimony further:

> In early 2015 their paternal grandmother died. IK and HK then travelled to Izmir where they made contact with an aunt who, in turn, communicated with their mother. Subsequently, arrangements were made for IK and HK to travel to Europe, following which their sojourn in Calais began.[119]

The children IK and HK had had daily telephone communications with MK by November 2015 when they met with their UK solicitors.[120]

Expert psychiatric assessment provided in a detailed report available to the UK Home Secretary included, in part, the following and attested to the children's severely deteriorating mental health and trauma:

[117]During her 2010 asylum interview when asked if her children lived with her in Syria when she escaped there from Iraq, MK answered yes and stated she had five children and that three of her children were with her in the UK, and that one of her five children had died before the age of two and that her eldest child was missing (UK—The Queen on the application of MK, IK (a child by his litigation friend MK) and HK (a child by her litigation friend MK) v Secretary of State for the Home Department (SSHD), JR/2471/2016, 29 April 2016 at para 6. Available at http://www.asylumlawdatabase.eu/en/case-law/uk-queen-application-mk-ik-child-his-litigation-friend-mk-and-hk-child-her-litigation Accessed 30 September, 2017).

[118]UK—The Queen on the application of MK, IK (a child by his litigation friend MK) and HK (a child by her litigation friend MK) v Secretary of State for the Home Department, JR/2471/2016, 29 April 2016 at para 6. Available at http://www.asylumlawdatabase.eu/en/case-law/uk-queen-application-mk-ik-child-his-litigation-friend-mk-and-hk-child-her-litigation Accessed 30 September, 2017.

[119]UK—The Queen on the application of MK, IK (a child by his litigation friend MK) and HK (a child by her litigation friend MK) v Secretary of State for the Home Department, JR/2471/2016, 29 April 2016 at para 7. Available at http://www.asylumlawdatabase.eu/en/case-law/uk-queen-application-mk-ik-child-his-litigation-friend-mk-and-hk-child-her-litigation Accessed 30 September, 2017.

[120]UK—The Queen on the application of MK, IK (a child by his litigation friend MK) and HK (a child by her litigation friend MK) v Secretary of State for the Home Department, JR/2471/2016, 29 April 2016 at para 8. Available at http://www.asylumlawdatabase.eu/en/case-law/uk-queen-application-mk-ik-child-his-litigation-friend-mk-and-hk-child-her-litigation Accessed 30 September, 2017.

As regards IK, the expert states:

"['His] overwhelming need is for reunification with his family, to be relieved of the responsibility for the safety and well being of his sister, an end to the uncertainty and insecurity of being a refugee in Calais and to have a secure home."

With regard to HK, the expert states:

"She is extremely vulnerable and regressed and has an **urgent** need for reunification with her mother and a secure home." (emphasis in the original)[121]

The psychiatric report and other additional evidence led to a third decision of the UK Home Secretary dated 19 April, 2016; a decision once again declining to take charge of the case. Further, the U.K Home Secretary challenged the credibility of the applicants' witness statements in some respects and placed the onus of presenting DNA evidence proving family relationship completely on the applicants:

The asserted breaches of Article 8 ECHR, Article 7 of the Charter and the relevant provisions of the Dublin Regulation [were] . . .all resisted on the ground that there was insufficient evidence to establish a familial relationship among the three Applicants. [122]

"It is a matter for the Applicants should they wish to have DNA tests conducted. In any event, the Respondent does not require DNA evidence to be submitted in order to prove a familial relationship under the [Dublin Regulation] or in support of visa applications . . ..[123]

3.2.2.2 Judicial Review Decision of the UK Upper Tribunal Immigration and Asylum Chamber: The Queen on the Application of MK, IK (a Child by His Litigation Friend MK) and HK (a Child by Her Litigation Friend MK), v UK SSHD

The Upper Tribunal (UT) pointed out that the Dublin III regulatory scheme

[121]UK—The Queen on the application of MK, IK (a child by his litigation friend MK) and HK (a child by her litigation friend MK) v Secretary of State for the Home Department, JR/2471/2016, 29 April 2016 at para 9. Available at http://www.asylumlawdatabase.eu/en/case-law/uk-queen-application-mk-ik-child-his-litigation-friend-mk-and-hk-child-her-litigation Accessed 30 September, 2017.

[122]UK—The Queen on the application of MK, IK (a child by his litigation friend MK) and HK (a child by her litigation friend MK) v Secretary of State for the Home Department, JR/2471/2016, 29 April 2016 at paras 32–33. Available at http://www.asylumlawdatabase.eu/en/case-law/uk-queen-application-mk-ik-child-his-litigation-friend-mk-and-hk-child-her-litigation Accessed 30 September, 2017.

[123]The Queen on the application of MK, IK (a child by his litigation friend MK) and HK (a child by her litigation friend MK) v Secretary of State for the Home Department, JR/2471/2016, 29 April 2016 at para 33. Available at http://www.asylumlawdatabase.eu/en/case-law/uk-queen-application-mk-ik-child-his-litigation-friend-mk-and-hk-child-her-litigation Accessed 30 September, 2017.

establishes the criteria and mechanisms for determining which EU Member State is responsible for "*examining*" an asylum application lodged in one of the Member States by a national of a non-EU country (emphasis in the original)[124]

The UT further highlighted the special emphasis in the Dublin III Regulations as it existed at the time of the case in regards to the need to protect children by ensuring that the 'best interests of the child' be a primary consideration in assessing child asylum cases and ensuring the unaccompanied child has an independent, qualified representative in the asylum proceedings and in regards to take charge State requests.[125] Especially noteworthy given the nature of the case at bar is that, as the UT pointed out, Article 6 of the Dublin III Regulations includes a stipulation that essentially sets out a *positive duty*, upon receipt of a take charge request, to explore family reunion possibilities and "take appropriate action to identify the family members, siblings or relatives of the unaccompanied minor on the territory of Member States". This as an aspect of regard for the best interests of the child as a prime consideration in addressing asylum applications from unaccompanied children:

...In assessing the best interests of the child, Member States shall closely cooperate with each other and shall, in particular, take due account of the following factors:

(a) family reunification possibilities...

For the purpose of applying Article 8, the Member State where the unaccompanied minor lodged an application for international protection shall, as soon as possible, take appropriate action to identify the family members, siblings or relatives of the unaccompanied minor on the territory of Member States, whilst protecting the best interests of the child.[126]

The take charge responsibility under the Dublin III Regulations, furthermore, as set out in Article 8, as the UT made clear, states that

Where the applicant is an unaccompanied minor, the Member State responsible shall be that where a family member or a sibling of the unaccompanied minor is legally present, provided that it is in the best interests of the minor.[127]

[124]UK—The Queen on the application of MK, IK (a child by his litigation friend MK) and HK (a child by her litigation friend MK) v Secretary of State for the Home Department, JR/2471/2016, 29 April 2016 at para 14. Available at http://www.asylumlawdatabase.eu/en/case-law/uk-queen-application-mk-ik-child-his-litigation-friend-mk-and-hk-child-her-litigation Accessed 30 September, 2017.

[125]UK—The Queen on the application of MK, IK (a child by his litigation friend MK) and HK (a child by her litigation friend MK) v Secretary of State for the Home Department, JR/2471/2016, 29 April 2016 at para 15. Available at http://www.asylumlawdatabase.eu/en/case-law/uk-queen-application-mk-ik-child-his-litigation-friend-mk-and-hk-child-her-litigation Accessed 30 September, 2017.

[126]UK—The Queen on the application of MK, IK (a child by his litigation friend MK) and HK (a child by her litigation friend MK) v Secretary of State for the Home Department, JR/2471/2016, 29 April 2016 at para 15. Available at http://www.asylumlawdatabase.eu/en/case-law/uk-queen-application-mk-ik-child-his-litigation-friend-mk-and-hk-child-her-litigation Accessed 30 September, 2017.

[127]UK—The Queen on the application of MK, IK (a child by his litigation friend MK) and HK (a child by her litigation friend MK) v Secretary of State for the Home Department, JR/2471/2016, 29 April 2016 at para 16. Available at http://www.asylumlawdatabase.eu/en/case-law/uk-queen-application-mk-ik-child-his-litigation-friend-mk-and-hk-child-her-litigation.

The UT went on to point out that Article 8 of the Dublin III Regulations also makes reference to "individual examination" of the relative of the unaccompanied child asylum applicant (the relative in the territory of the Member State) as to relevant factors (i.e. whether the relative has the ability to take care of the child) with the implication that DNA testing could have been a relevant part of 'individual examination' on the particulars of the case at bar.[128]

The Upper Tribunal concluded that the U.K. Home Secretary's initial refusal to take charge of the case as well as the two 'on reconsideration' subsequent denials to take responsibility were all unlawful given that (1) there was no attempt by the U.K. Home Secretary's Office to investigate the "availability" or "viability" of DNA testing in France for the child applicants IK and HK; (2) there was no attempt to determine whether French law would permit such DNA testing of unaccompanied child refugees for the purposes of establishing a family relationship with the professed biological mother which could potentially provide grounds for grant of asylum based on family reunion considerations; and (3) the Home Secretary did not consider allowing IK and HK to enter the U.K. on a temporary basis for DNA testing that the Home Office would arrange to take place in the U.K. and pending final determination of the asylum request (which final determination would depend on the outcome of the DNA testing in combination with other evidence relating to any family relationship of IK and HK with MK).[129] The UT rejected the U.K. Home Secretary's contention that her office had no positive duty to investigate upon receipt of the take charge request from France and that the onus was completely on the applicants.[130] The UT held that "enquiry, investigation and evidence gathering" were at the core of the Dublin III regulations expressed explicitly at points and also implied at others.[131] The UT held further that since the Home Secretary had acknowledged that had DNA evidence proved the family relationship the 'take charge' request would have been accepted, there was a positive duty on that Office to arrange for gathering of the DNA evidence which was a reasonable step. The UT noted that:

---

[128] UK—The Queen on the application of MK, IK (a child by his litigation friend MK) and HK (a child by her litigation friend MK) v Secretary of State for the Home Department, JR/2471/2016, 29 April 2016 at para 16. Available at http://www.asylumlawdatabase.eu/en/case-law/uk-queen-application-mk-ik-child-his-litigation-friend-mk-and-hk-child-her-litigation Accessed 1 October, 2017.

[129] UK—The Queen on the application of MK, IK (a child by his litigation friend MK) and HK (a child by her litigation friend MK) v Secretary of State for the Home Department, JR/2471/2016, 29 April 2016 at para 36. Available at http://www.asylumlawdatabase.eu/en/case-law/uk-queen-application-mk-ik-child-his-litigation-friend-mk-and-hk-child-her-litigation Accessed 1 October, 2017.

[130] UK—The Queen on the application of MK, IK (a child by his litigation friend MK) and HK (a child by her litigation friend MK) v Secretary of State for the Home Department, JR/2471/2016, 29 April 2016 at para 38–39. Available at http://www.asylumlawdatabase.eu/en/case-law/uk-queen-application-mk-ik-child-his-litigation-friend-mk-and-hk-child-her-litigation Accessed 1 October, 2017.

[131] UK—The Queen on the application of MK, IK (a child by his litigation friend MK) and HK (a child by her litigation friend MK) v Secretary of State for the Home Department, JR/2471/2016, 29 April 2016 at para 38. Available at http://www.asylumlawdatabase.eu/en/case-law/uk-queen-application-mk-ik-child-his-litigation-friend-mk-and-hk-child-her-litigation Accessed 1 October, 2017.

> The key to breaking the logjam was DNA evidence: but none was available. The Applicants were unable to provide such evidence for a variety of reasons, including in particular lack of resources and uncertainties relating to French law. The Secretary of State was at all material times in a position to proactively take steps to at least attempt to overcome this *impasse*. However, the evidence establishes beyond peradventure that nothing was done.[132]

For these reasons, the UT found the UK Secretary of State Office had breached both the Dublin III Regulations and the procedural aspect of ECHR Article 8 right to family. The UT commented that there did not appear to be any insurmountable legal impediment to the DNA testing.[133] Ultimately the UT quashed all three of the denials of the take charge decisions of the UK Secretary of State and issued a mandatory order to the UK Secretary of State to take all reasonable steps to have the DNA testing of IK and HK conducted and to liaise with the French authorities in that regard. The UT issued strict reasonably short deadlines for the completion of the DNA testing and the new decision to be made by the U.K. Home Secretary on the take charge in light of the results of the DNA testing as new evidence.[134] Those short deadlines, the UT explained, were consistent with the:

> central themes of the Dublin Regulation, namely efficient and expeditious decision making, which applies with particular force in the case of children.[135]

3.2.2.3 Commentary on The Queen on the Application of MK, IK (a Child by His Litigation Friend MK) and HK (a Child by Her Litigation Friend MK), v UK SSHD, UK Upper Tribunal Immigration and Asylum Chamber, Judicial Review Decision

The passive approach in the case at bar of the UK Home Secretary in declining to assist in any way in order to have DNA testing conducted to address *the* central question in the case (whether IK and HK are the biological children of MK) reflects, on the analysis here, a strategy intended to facilitate 'pushback' from the UK frontier

[132]UK—The Queen on the application of MK, IK (a child by his litigation friend MK) and HK (a child by her litigation friend MK) v Secretary of State for the Home Department, JR/2471/2016, 29 April 2016 at para 45. Available at http://www.asylumlawdatabase.eu/en/case-law/uk-queen-application-mk-ik-child-his-litigation-friend-mk-and-hk-child-her-litigation Accessed 1 October, 2017.

[133]UK—The Queen on the application of MK, IK (a child by his litigation friend MK) and HK (a child by her litigation friend MK) v Secretary of State for the Home Department, JR/2471/2016, 29 April 2016 at para 46–48. Available at http://www.asylumlawdatabase.eu/en/case-law/uk-queen-application-mk-ik-child-his-litigation-friend-mk-and-hk-child-her-litigation Accessed 1 October, 2017.

[134]UK—The Queen on the application of MK, IK (a child by his litigation friend MK) and HK (a child by her litigation friend MK) v Secretary of State for the Home Department, JR/2471/2016, 29 April 2016 at para 52. Available at http://www.asylumlawdatabase.eu/en/case-law/uk-queen-application-mk-ik-child-his-litigation-friend-mk-and-hk-child-her-litigation Accessed 1 October, 2017.

[135]UK—The Queen on the application of MK, IK (a child by his litigation friend MK) and HK (a child by her litigation friend MK) v Secretary of State for the Home Department, JR/2471/2016, 29 April 2016 at para 53. Available at http://www.asylumlawdatabase.eu/en/case-law/uk-queen-application-mk-ik-child-his-litigation-friend-mk-and-hk-child-her-litigation Accessed 1 October, 2017.

of not just IK and HK but of a collective. It is here contended that the collective being pushed back[136] was constituted of unaccompanied child refugee asylum seekers already arrived in a European Union State (not only in France but any EU State) and seeking refugee asylum in the UK. This UK collective migration control measure then, in the final analysis, denied IK, HK and MK, among other things, their Article 8 individual rights under the Dublin III regulations, the European Charter and the European Convention on Human Rights (ECHR) Article 8 in regard to their "right to respect for . . .private and family life."[137]

Consistent with this collective control measures approach, the UK Home Secretary declined to take any positive steps to effect not only the individual assessment of most import in the case (DNA testing) but also any other investigative measures that might establish the family relationship between the three applicants. Hence the UK Home Office approach resulted in (1) the U.K. avoiding the possibility of garnering the proof from its own investigations and examinations that might establish the U.K.'s responsibility to take charge of the case and (2) obtaining the proof of its obligation to properly consider as well as grant the children's asylum request based on family reunification grounds should the family relationship be established according to the U.K. evidence gathered independently as well as the totality of evidence provided on the case by French NGOs, the children's counsel and other sources.[138]

It is interesting and relevant to note that in the case at bar (*The Queen on the application of MK, IK (a child by his litigation friend MK) and HK (a child by her litigation friend MK) v Secretary of State for the Home Department*)[139] the unaccompanied child applicants and MK followed the normal procedures per the Dublin

[136]That is, 'pushed back' by the UK Home Secretary via her three time refusal to take charge of this particular case (the IK, HK, MK case) though there was ample evidence of the urgency for family reunion and much circumstantial evidence of family relationship between the three applicants. The latter evidence could have been further strengthened with relatively definitive direct proof of biological ties between the three applicants as mother and children had the Home Secretary arranged for DNA testing. The attempt appeared to be to set somewhat of a case precedent that would be perceived as an indication of a high likelihood of refusal for future unaccompanied child refugees seeking asylum in the UK thus sounding a note that would be expected to discourage asylum applications for family reunion from this child population.

[137]European Convention on Human Rights (as amended by the provisions of Protocol No. 14 (CETS no. 194) as from its entry into force on 1 June 2010.) original entry into force of the Convention 21 September 1970. http://www.echr.coe.int/Documents/Convention_ENG.pdf Accessed 1 October, 2017.

[138]This is not to suggest that there may not have been other humanitarian grounds for admitting IK and HK (unaccompanied child refugees) to the United Kingdom to reside with MK even if she were not the biological mother but was willing and able to care for them and had a strong relationship with the children (i.e. returning the children to an uncertain future in France may have constituted inhuman and degrading treatment -a violation of a *jus cogens* norm-given the children's history and mental state at the time of their asylum application to the UK).

[139]UK—The Queen on the application of MK, IK (a child by his litigation friend MK) and HK (a child by her litigation friend MK) v Secretary of State for the Home Department, JR/2471/2016, 29 April 2016 at para 16. Available at http://www.asylumlawdatabase.eu/en/case-law/uk-queen-application-mk-ik-child-his-litigation-friend-mk-and-hk-child-her-litigation Accessed 1 October, 2017.

III regulations in contrast to the first case discussed in this chapter *R (on the application of ZAT and Others) v Secretary of State for the Home Department*, IJR [2016] UKUT 00061 (IAC) (21 January, 2016) where there was a request to bypass the Dublin III regulations as *to routine* initial process re 'take charge' requests (concerning which EU member State was responsible for handling the case)[140]

> In contrast with the situation prevailing in ZAT, the processes and procedures of the Dublin Regulation had been fully observed in the present case. In summary, IK and HK made their respective claims for asylum in France, these claims were examined by the French authorities, a "take charge" request ensued and the Secretary of State made her refusal decision accordingly and reaffirmed it subsequently. The contrast with ZAT, where no Dublin Regulation steps had been taken, is striking.[141]

Nonetheless in both *ZAT*[142] and *IK, HK, MK,*[143] the U.K. Home Secretary denied not only the particular children's requests for family reunion but, on the respectful view here, was directed *in effect at least*, to set a new legal standard allowing for 'pushback' of a collective (unaccompanied child refugee asylum seekers) out of the UK territory if already entered or back from the UK border or the near frontier (in a neighboring State) preventing entry to the U.K.. However, the U.K. Home Secretary refusals in both cases were ultimately found by the Upper Tribunal and in the other case by the Court of Appeal to be inconsistent with the Dublin III obligations and various international human rights law. In both of the cases, on the view of the current author, there was not sufficient concern for the best interests of the children as a primary consideration. Rather there appeared to be, on the respectful view here, an emphasis on sending a message aimed at deterring future unaccompanied child refugee asylum seekers to the U.K. through the often complicated and unnecessary barriers set by the U.K. Home office to asylum for these unaccompanied child refugee asylum applicants.

[140]It is to be recalled as discussed previously that derogation from routine process pertaining to take charge requests is permissible under the Dublin regulatory scheme where consistent with the humanitarian family reunion priority re unaccompanied child refugee asylum seekers and with reasonable well grounded application of the Dublin III Regulations (see Dublin III Regulation at para 17).

[141]UK—The Queen on the application of MK, IK (a child by his litigation friend MK) and HK (a child by her litigation friend MK) v Secretary of State for the Home Department, JR/2471/2016, 29 April 2016 at para 37. Available at http://www.asylumlawdatabase.eu/en/case-law/uk-queen-application-mk-ik-child-his-litigation-friend-mk-and-hk-child-her-litigation Accessed 1 October, 2017.

[142]SSHD [Secretary of State of the Home Department] v ZAT (Syria) In the Court of Appeal (Civil Division) on Appeal from the Upper Tribunal Immigration an Asylum Chamber (Neutral Citation Number: [2016] EWCA Civ 810, 02/08/2016.

[143]UK—The Queen on the application of MK, IK (a child by his litigation friend MK) and HK (a child by her litigation friend MK) v Secretary of State for the Home Department, JR/2471/2016, 29 April 2016. Available at http://www.asylumlawdatabase.eu/en/case-law/uk-queen-application-mk-ik-child-his-litigation-friend-mk-and-hk-child-her-litigation Accessed 1 October, 2017.

Contrary to what is required under the Dublin III Regulations and the U.K.'s Convention on the Rights of the Child treaty obligations, the U.K. Home Secretary in the *IK, HK, MK* case discounted the expert evidence on the then current highly troubled psychiatric state of the children. The U.K. Home Secretary Office held the psychiatric evidence to be allegedly completely irrelevant to decision-making re the matter at hand. This was the tack taken by the U.K. Home Secretary though the psychiatric evidence certainly went to the issue of the 'best interests of the children' and notwithstanding the priority that is to be assigned to the best interests of the child (children) as stipulated under the Dublin III Regulations. Instead of due regard to the 'best interests of the child' considerations the Home Secretary took the following position:

> The information provided about the difficult situation of the children in Calais and their psychiatric trauma does not address the central issue of 'proven family links' raised in the SSHD's reconsideration of the take charge request...
>
> The SSHD does not consider that the further material submitted above demonstrates 'proven family link'.[144]

Had the U.K. Home Secretary viewed the case through a human rights lens such disregard for the psychiatric evidence might have been avoided by consideration that such disregard could potentially be adjudged by the Upper Tribunal as a violation of Article 3 of the European Convention on Human Rights prohibiting inhuman and degrading treatment.

The Upper Tribunal in the case at bar noted that the 'best interests of the child' concept has "the status of a right, a principle and a rule of procedure" and cited the following excerpt from the CRC General Comment 14 on the best interests principle in respect of best interests of the child as a rule of procedure[145]:

> Whenever a decision is to be made *that will affect a specific child, an identified group of children or children in general, the decision making process must include an evaluation of the possible impact (positive or negative) of the decision on the child or children concerned.* Assessing and determining the best interests of the child require procedural guarantees (emphasis added)[146]

---

[144]UK—The Queen on the application of MK, IK (a child by his litigation friend MK) and HK (a child by her litigation friend MK) v Secretary of State for the Home Department, JR/2471/2016, 29 April 2016 at para 11. Available at http://www.asylumlawdatabase.eu/en/case-law/uk-queen-application-mk-ik-child-his-litigation-friend-mk-and-hk-child-her-litigation Accessed 30 September, 2017.

[145]The Queen on the application of MK, IK (a child by his litigation friend MK) and HK (a child by her litigation friend MK) v Secretary of State for the Home Department, JR/2471/2016, 29 April 2016 at para 22.

[146]United Nations Committee on the Rights of the Child "General Comment Number 14 (2013) on the Right of the Child to have his or her best interests taken as a primary consideration" (art 3 para 1) May 2013 Para 6(3) http://www2.ohchr.org/English/bodies/crc/docs/GC/CRC_C_GC_14_ENG.pdf Accessed 1 October, 2017.

The above excerpt from CRC General Comment 14 on 'best interests of the child'[147] thus calls on decision makers to consider the impact of State decisions on both children as individuals and any potential impact as well of the decision on child collectives of which the individual child or children at issue may or may not be a member (the collective being "children generally" or an "identifiable group" that might be affected by the decision as a case precedent or in some other fashion). In addition, the CRC General Comment 14 points out that considering 'best interest of the individual child' will in part require regard also for the child's group membership (s) and the implications of the child belonging to those particular collective(s). The latter further requires consideration of the wider context in which the child collective itself is situated i.e. socially, culturally and in terms of the degree to which the collective itself is having its protection needs met etc.:

> Assessing the child's best interests is a unique activity that should be undertaken in each individual case, in the light of the specific circumstances of each child . . .such as belonging to a minority group, . . . the social and cultural context in which the child or children find themselves, such as the presence or absence of parents, . . .the environment in relation to safety . . .etc.[148]

Thus the child's best interest as an individual child refugee must be assessed with due regard also to the collective(s) of which he/she is a member such as, for example, 'unaccompanied child refugee asylum seekers' and what it means to be part of that group i.e. the high likelihood of exploitation and abuse should protection not be offered by the State, return to the home country constituting refoulement in most cases given that unaccompanied child refugees are often targeted in conflict zones for child soldiering and other form of abuse etc.

The cases discussed in this current work (including those in this chapter) illustrate that decisions affecting particular individual child refugee asylum seekers who have filed applications (and related State take charge requests) are often decisions also implicitly or explicitly directed to impacting in various ways the larger collective of unaccompanied and accompanied child refugee asylum seekers (including those who have not yet entered the State in question and who may or may not yet have arrived in a neighbouring State). This all amounts; it is here contended, to insidious collective migration control measures. Those collective control measures used alone or in combination with other migration control strategies, especially when applied to child refugees generally, and, in particular, to unaccompanied child refugee asylum seekers, rarely if ever meet international human rights standards for humane treatment, and the requirement for individual case assessment let alone treatment based on 'best interests of the child' as at least one of several primary considerations.

---

[147] United Nations Committee on the Rights of the Child "General Comment Number 14 (2013) on the Right of the Child to have his or her best interests taken as a primary consideration" (art 3 para 1) May 2013 Para 6(3) http://www2.ohchr.org/English/bodies/crc/docs/GC/CRC_C_GC_14_ENG.pdf Accessed 1 October, 2017.

[148] United Nations Committee on the Rights of the Child "General Comment Number 14 (2013) on the Right of the Child to have his or her best interests taken as a primary consideration" (art 3 para 1) May 2013 Para 48 http://www2.ohchr.org/English/bodies/crc/docs/GC/CRC_C_GC_14_ENG.pdf Accessed 1 October, 2017.

Literature, Materials and Cases

Literature

Vandvik B (2008) Extraterritorial border controls and responsibility to protect: a view from ECRE (University of Amsterdam). Amst Law Forum 1(1). http://amsterdamlawforum.org/article/view/38. Accessed 23 Feb 2017

Materials

AIRE Centre [Advice on Individual Rights in Europe]. http://www.airecentre.org/ Accessed 30 September, 2017

Chicago Tribune (October 24, 2016) France moving 6,500 migrants, destroying 'the jungle' camp in Calais http://www.chicagotribune.com/news/nationworld/ct-france-migrant-camp-calais-20161024-story.html Accessed 8 January, 2017

Convention on the Rights of the Child entry into force 2 September, 1990 http://www.ohchr.org/en/professionalinterest/pages/crc.aspx Accessed 9 January, 2017

Council of Europe Report (Prepared by Mole, N and Meredith, C) Asylum and the European Convention on Human Rights http://www.refworld.org/pdfid/4ee9b0972.pdf Accessed 25 September, 2017 at p. 10

Digidiki, V and Bhabha, J: Report for the FXB (Francois-Xavier Bagnoud) Center for Health and Human Rights, Harvard University (17 April, 2017) 'Emergency within an emergency: The growing epidemic of sexual exploitation and abuse of migrant children in Greece'. Available at https://fxb.harvard.edu/new-report-emergency-within-an-emergency-exploitation-of-migrant-children-in-greece/ Accessed 30 September, 2017

Dublin III regulation: Regulation (EU) No 604/2013 of the European Parliament and of the Council of 26 June 2013 establishing the criteria and mechanisms for determining the Member State responsible for examining an application for international protection lodged in one of the Member States by a third-country national or a stateless person (recast) http://eur-lex.europa.eu/LexUriServ/LexUriServ.do?uri=OJ:L:2013:180:0031:0059:EN:PDF (Accessed 1 December, 2016)

European Commission (2017) Communication from the Commission to the European Parliament and the Council (4 December, 2017) COM(2017) 211 final 'The protection of children in migration'

European Convention on Human Rights as amended by Protocols Nos. 11 and 14, done 3 May, 2002. http://www.echr.coe.int/Documents/Convention_ENG.pdf (Accessed 1 December, 2016)

Gentleman, A. (5 September, 2016) The Guardian: Immigration and asylum: 'It's a disgrace to Europe': Former child refugee Lord Dubs on the Calais camp https://www.theguardian.com/uk-news/2016/sep/05/disgrace-to-europe-former-child-refugee-lord-dubs-calais-camp Accessed 9 January, 2017

House of Lords (26 July, 2016) Children in crisis: Unaccompanied migrant children in the EU https://publications.parliament.uk/pa/ld201617/ldselect/ldeucom/34/3402.htm Accessed 29 September, 2017

Human Rights Watch (July 2017) Like living in hell: Police abuses against child and adult migrants in Calais at p. 1 https://www.hrw.org/report/2017/07/26/living-hell/police-abuses-against-child-and-adult-migrants-calais Accessed 29 September, 2017

Independent (October 29, 2016): Refugee children sleeping rough three days after Calais camp 'cleared' http://www.independent.co.uk/news/world/europe/calais-jungle-latest-refugee-children-unaccompanied-minors-camp-migrants-destroyed-relocated-moved-a7386551.html Accessed 29 September, 2017

International Committee of the Red Cross. Statement of 23 April, 2005: Humanitarian Law, Human Rights and Refugee Law – Three Pillars https://www.icrc.org/eng/resources/documents/statement/6t7g86.htm Accessed 24 September, 2017

OXFAM (OXFAM Media Briefing 15 June, 2017) Brexit and the Refugee Crisis http://www.oxfam.org.uk/~/media/files/OGB/Media%20Centre/Press%20Releases/BrexitRefugeeCrisis.pdf Accessed 29 September, 2017

Taylor, Diane (2016) The Guardian: Hundreds of Calais child refugees have UK asylum claims rejected http://www.theguardian.com/world/2016/dec/28/calais-child-asylum-seekers-legal-action-agsint-uk-government (Accessed 1 March, 2017)

Taylor, D (2017) The Guardian: Home Office agrees to review asylum claims of child refugees in France 19 February, 2017 https://www.theguardian.com/uk-news/2017/feb/19/home-office-agrees-to-review-asylum-claims-of-child-refugees-in-france?CMP=Share_iOSApp_Other (Accessed 1 March, 2017)

Travis, A (Home Affairs Editor) (19 July, 2017) The Guardian: UK has not taken in any child refugees under Dubs scheme this year https://www.theguardian.com/uk-news/2017/jul/19/uk-not-taken-any-child-refugees-dubs-scheme-this-year Accessed 30 September, 2017

Travis, A (Home Affairs Editor) The Guardian (19 October, 2016) Children don't come date-stamped-and that includes refugees: Using medical information to try to pinpoint a young person's age is folly, for both practical and ethical reasons https://www.theguardian.com/world/2016/oct/19/child-refugees-date-stamped-medical-age Accessed 29 September, 2017

UNHCR, UNICEF and IOM report (April 2017) Refugee and Migrant Children -Including Unaccompanied and Separated Children-in Europe: Overview of trends in 2016 https://www.unicef.org/eca/Factsheet_refugee_migrant.pdf Accessed 29 September, 2017

UNICEF (September, 2017) Harrowing journeys: Children and youth on the move across the Mediterranean Sea, at risk of trafficking and exploitation Available at https://www.unicef.org/publications/index_100621.html Accessed 29 September, 2017

UNICEF UK and Save the Children Briefing on the refugee crisis in Europe (15 December, 2016) What's Next for the child refugees in Europe? Available for download at https://www.unicef.org.uk/ Accessed 29 September, 2017

UNICEF UK A child's crisis: Why the refugee and migrant crisis should matter to us all (see Petition to Home Secretary Amber Rudd) https://www.unicef.org.uk/uprooted-a-childs-crisis/ Accessed 29 September, 2017

United Nations Committee on the Rights of the Child "General Comment Number 14 (2013) on the Right of the Child to have his or her best interests taken as a primary consideration" (art 3 para 1) May 2013 Para 6(3) http://www2.ohchr.org/English/bodies/crc/docs/GC/CRC_C_GC_14_ENG.pdf Accessed 1 October, 2017

Cases

SSHD [Secretary of State of the Home Department] v ZAT (Syria) In the Court of Appeal (Civil Division) on Appeal from the Upper Tribunal Immigration an Asylum Chamber (Neutral Citation Number: [2016] EWCA Civ 810, 02/08/2016

R (on the application of ZAT and Others) v Secretary of State for the Home Department, IJR [2016] UKUT 00061 (IAC) (21 January, 2016)

The Queen on the application of MK, IK (a child by his litigation friend MK) and HK (a child by her litigation friend MK), v UK SSHD JR/2471/2016, 29 April 2016 UK Upper Tribunal Immigration and Asylum Chamber, Judicial Review Decision Available at http://www.asylumlawdatabase.eu/en/case-law/uk-queen-application-mk-ik-child-his-litigation-friend-mk-and-hk-child-her-litigation Accessed 24 October, 2017

Chapter 4
'Unaccompanied Child Refugee Asylum Seekers' as a Persecuted 'Social Group'

Refugee children are children first and foremost, and as children, they need special attention.[1]

4.1 A Cycle of Persecution for 'Child Refugee Asylum Seekers' Relating to Their Social Group Status

We begin here with the understanding that under refugee law as the UNHCR (United Nations High Commissioner on Refugees) has pointed out: (1) one category of refugee asylum seekers is constituted of those who are persecuted on the basis of their membership in a 'particular social group'; (2) there is no definitive exhaustive list of groups qualifying as (persecuted) 'social groups' in Refugee Convention terms and (3) for the latter reason and others "the term 'membership of a particular social group' should be read in an evolutionary manner".[2] As we will discuss; 'child refugee asylum seekers'[3] and especially 'unaccompanied child refugee asylum seekers', are members of a 'social group' that is a particular social group *in and of itself* as well as being, at the same time, a subcategory of the larger persecuted

[1]Refugee Children: Guidelines on Protection and Care (preface) (1988) http://www.unhcr.org/protect/PROTECTION/3b84c6c67.pdf (Accessed 4 October, 2017).

[2]UNHCR Handbook and Guidelines on Procedures and Criteria for Determining Refugee Status under the 1951 Convention and the 1967 Protocol Relating to the Status of Refugees (re-issued December, 2011 ed.) HCR/IP/4/ENG/REV.3 at p. 92 http://www.refworld.org/docid/4f33c8d92.html (Accessed 4 October, 2017).

[3]Recall that not all asylum seekers are refugees. The term refugee asylum seeker is used here thus to describe persons who seek asylum and State recognized refugee legal status per the Refugee Convention grounds or under complimentary legal schemes relating to international protection of persecuted persons. The term refugee for the purposes of this discussion does not include persons who are *solely* in search of a better economic situation rather than fleeing persecution or also fleeing persecution.

© Springer International Publishing AG, part of Springer Nature 2018

S. C. Grover, *Child Refugee Asylum as a Basic Human Right*,
https://doi.org/10.1007/978-3-319-78013-9_4

collective (i.e. refugee asylum seekers more generally). These children are specifically targeted for rights violations given (1) their special vulnerabilities as children[4] and (2) the symbolic messages sent to the larger society via maltreatment rising to the level, in some instances, of inhuman or degrading treatment or even torture of children.

It is important to understand then that under Refugee Convention law:

> There is no "closed list" of what groups may constitute a "particular social group" within the meaning of Article 1A(2). The [Refugee] Convention includes no specific list of social groups, nor does the ratifying history reflect a view that there is a set of identified groups that might qualify under this ground. *Rather, the term membership of a particular social group should be read in an evolutionary manner, open to the diverse and changing nature of groups in various societies and* ***evolving international human rights norms*** (emphasis added).[5]

According to the UNHCR:

> Children's claims to refugee status most often have been analysed in the context of the Convention ground of "membership of a particular social group", although any of the Convention grounds may be applicable.[6]
>
> Being a child is directly relevant to one's identity, both in the eyes of society and from the perspective of the individual child. Many government policies are age-driven or age-related...[7] *Where children are singled out as a target group*[8] [for instance] for

---

[4]Grover (2014).

[5]UNHCR Handbook and Guidelines on Procedures and Criteria for Determining Refugee Status under the 1951 Convention and the 1967 Protocol Relating to the Status of Refugees (re-issued December, 2011 ed.) HCR/IP/4/ENG/REV.3 at p. 92 http://www.refworld.org/docid/4f33c8d92.html (Accessed 4 October, 2017).

[6]UNHCR (22 December, 2009) Guidelines on international protection: Child Asylum Claims under Articles 1(A)2 and 1(F) of the 1951 Convention and/or 1967 Protocol relating to the Status of Refugees at para 48 http://www.unhcr.org/afr/publications/legal/50ae46309/guidelines-international-protection-8-child-asylum-c Accessed 7 October, 2017.

[7]UNHCR (22 December, 2009) Guidelines on international protection: Child Asylum Claims under Articles 1(A)2 and 1(F) of the 1951 Convention and/or 1967 Protocol relating to the Status of Refugees at para 49 http://www.unhcr.org/afr/publications/legal/50ae46309/guidelines-international-protection-8-child-asylum-c Accessed 7 October, 2017.

[8]"In situations of armed conflict and violence, an applicant may be at risk of being singled out or targeted for persecution. Equally, in such situations, entire groups or populations may be at risk of persecution, leaving each member of the group at risk. The fact that many or all members of particular communities are at risk does not undermine the validity of any particular individual's claim. The test is whether an individual's fear of being persecuted is well-founded. At times, the impact of a situation of armed conflict and violence on an entire community, or on civilians more generally, strengthens rather than weakens the well-founded nature of the fear of being persecuted of a particular individual" Cited from UNHCR Handbook and Guidelines on International protection No. 12 HCR/GIP/16/12/02 (Issued 2 December, 2016) at p. 4 Available at https://reliefweb.int/report/world/guidelines-international-protection-no-12 Accessed 4 October, 2017.

> recruitment or use by an armed force or group[9], *they may form a particular social group due to . . . age as well as the fact that they are perceived as a group by the society in which they live*[10]
>
> *A range of child groupings, thus, can be the basis of a claim to refugee status under the "membership of a particular social group" ground.* Just as "women" have been recognized as a particular social group in several jurisdictions, *"children" or a smaller subset of children may also constitute a particular social group* (emphasis added).[11]

It is argued in this chapter that 'unaccompanied child refugee asylum seekers' are a 'particular social group' in and of themselves in Refugee Convention terms. The members of the aforementioned persecuted child social group, it is contended, have endured or were at real risk of persecution in their home country (or country of habitual residence) and commonly face persecution *as unaccompanied children* and as *refugee asylum seekers* also by State and non-State agents of many other countries in their asylum seeking journey. In the latter case of persecution of the social group "child refugee asylum seekers' and especially 'unaccompanied child refugee asylum seekers' outside their homeland or country of habitual residence; the persecution is often directed to an attempt to effectively interfere, in the first instance, with the child refugees' legitimate right under international law to *seek* asylum[12] (i.e. as presumptive refugees whose individual refugee claims the State of first arrival generally speaking (barring other considerations) is obligated to fairly process as to eligibility and the merits under the Refugee Convention and/or any other relevant international protection schemes).

The objective and/or effect of *State interference in child refugee group/collective rights* is also to prevent these children from realizing their individual human rights as refugees and as 'accompanied or unaccompanied child refugee asylum seekers' in particular. The latter often occurs with little or no compassionate regard or humanitarian concern about the costs to the child refugee victims of such interference in child asylum rights. That interference may in itself, depending on the specifics, rise to the level of persecution tantamount to inhuman and degrading treatment or worse. Hence children belonging to an identifiable social groups(s)[13] may have been the

[9]The current author holds this would apply to targeting of children for persecution of any form.

[10]UNHCR (22 December, 2009) Guidelines on international protection: Child Asylum Claims under Articles 1(A)2 and 1(F) of the 1951 Convention and/or 1967 Protocol relating to the Status of Refugees at para 52 http://www.unhcr.org/afr/publications/legal/50ae46309/guidelines-international-protection-8-child-asylum-c Accessed 7 October, 2017.

[11]UNHCR (22 December, 2009) Guidelines on international protection: Child Asylum Claims under Articles 1(A)2 and 1(F) of the 1951 Convention and/or 1967 Protocol relating to the Status of Refugees at para 50 http://www.unhcr.org/afr/publications/legal/50ae46309/guidelines-international-protection-8-child-asylum-c Accessed 7 October, 2017.

[12]There are of course also instances where the home State attempts to prevent the refugee from leaving in search of asylum (The German Democratic Republic building the Berlin Wall in 1961 and preventing for an extended period escapes to West Germany on pain of death).

[13]The unaccompanied child refugee asylum seeker may be a member of several intersecting social groups such as, for instance, children orphaned by war targeted for recruitment by a State or non-State armed force, children whose parents belong to or are perceived by the State to belong to a

targeted victims in their homeland or place of habitual residence of persecution and attain the status of Convention Refugees and *further then tragically become the victims of persecution on the very basis of their new identity as, for instance, "unaccompanied child refugee asylum seekers'*. This then creates for a large segment of this child refugee population an endless cycle of misery and human rights violations.

Supreme Court of Canada Justices La Forest, L'Heureux-Dube and Gothier in a dissenting opinion in *Chan*, a refugee case, have commented on the meaning of 'social group' in the Refugee Convention context as follows:

> A refugee alleging membership in a social group does not have to be in voluntary association with other persons similar to him-or herself. Rather he or she must be voluntarily associated with a particular status for reasons so fundamental to that person's human dignity that he or she should not be forced to forsake that association.[14] *The association or group exists by virtue of a common attempt made by its members to exercise a fundamental human right* (emphasis added)[15]

On the view of the current author; the 'particular social group' 'unaccompanied child refugee asylum seekers' exists *in part* by virtue of the unifying element of the common attempt by the members to enjoy their entitlement to the fundamental right to security of the person (which States have an especially high duty under international law to honour in the case of children) and to exercise their right (under international human rights and refugee law) to seek asylum. Various collectives of 'unaccompanied child refugee asylum seekers' arrive each day at State borders/ports of entry and frequently enter irregularly into the territory by an array of means in search of asylum. Recognition of such child collectives as constituting subgroups of the larger 'particular social group' (in Refugee Convention terms) 'unaccompanied child refugee asylum seekers' is fundamental to the children's human dignity in that therein lies an avenue to potential international protection and preservation of their fundamental human rights. As the cases here to be discussed illustrate, however, in practice 'unaccompanied child refugee asylum seekers' are commonly maltreated by agents of the prospective asylum State and/or transit State(s) even to the level of inhuman or degrading treatment.

---

certain political group which group the State has targeted for persecution, children persecuted by the State due to their non-mainstream sexual orientation, children previously internally displaced due to fleeing persecution in the place of origin who then crossed out of the homeland territory in search of permanent refuge etc.

[14]Aleinikoff (2003), p. 293 explains that Justice LaForest of the Supreme Court of Canada poses the relevant question as "whether the persecutor treats people with a shared attribute as comprising a social group -not whether the members of the group voluntarily associate with each other." Aleinikoff, TA commentary Available at http://www.refworld.org/docid/470a33b30.html Accessed 7 October, 2017.

[15]Chan v Canada (Minister of Employment and Immigration) [1995] 3 S.C.R. (Dissenting Opinion La Forest, L'Heureux-Dube and Gothier, JJ at p. 597.

Often acknowledgement of the ground supporting asylum (membership in a particular persecuted social group) is not forthcoming; this using the vehicle of erroneous denial of the asylum seeker's child status. This in that being recognized as a member of this 'particular social group' and as therefore an '*unaccompanied child* asylum seeker' would set in motion special requirements which are preconditions for proper treatment of such children by agents of the State (i.e. immigration authorities) and by the Courts. That is, for example, UNHCR guidelines set out the requirements for due consideration to be given to the standards set by the Convention on the Rights of the Child and other relevant instruments in the treatment of child refugees and in particular additional considerations in respect of *unaccompanied* child refugee asylum seekers.[16] The UNHCR Guidelines, for instance, stipulate as to the obligation for proper regard to the 'best interests of the child' as *a* primary consideration.[17] Recognition of the child's membership in the particular social group 'unaccompanied child refugee asylum seeker', furthermore, entitles the child to special protections and considerations under international human rights (including child rights law) and UNHCR guidelines (i.e. exemptions from immigration detention, provision of child targeted and child friendly services, placement in a non-custodial setting pending the outcome of asylum application processing, the right to education etc.).

Members of this collective/special category of refugee asylum seekers are thus attempting to pursue their basic right as 'unaccompanied persecuted children' to special protection of their security of the person and realization of their developmental rights (i.e. right to education etc.) threatened by the circumstances of persecution in their homeland or place of habitual residence, proper regard for their best interests *as children* and as child refugees etc. Note that where the victim is a vulnerable child; the threshold for treatment rising to the level of persecution may be lower than in the case of most adults and that therefore the prospective asylum State properly must take this into account if the child is to receive a fair asylum process. Likewise there is a need for recognition of 'child-specific' forms of persecution in the processing of asylum requests from child refugee asylum seekers i.e. forced FGM performed on very young girls etc. In addition; fair and impartial asylum processing in the case of accompanied or unaccompanied child asylum applicants requires recognition of the child's independent right to claim asylum.[18] Further where possible, legally supportable and in the child's 'best interest', the

---

[16] UNHCR Refugee (1997) Guidelines on Policies and Procedures in dealing with Unaccompanied Children Seeking Asylum Available at http://www.unhcr.org/3d4f91cf4.pdf Accessed 7 October, 2017.

[17] UNHCR (2008) Guidelines on Determining the Best Interests of the Child http://www.unhcr.org/4566b16b2.pdf Accessed 7 October, 2017.

[18] UNHCR (22 December, 2009) Guidelines on international protection: Child Asylum Claims under Articles 1(A)2 and 1(F) of the 1951 Convention and/or 1967 Protocol relating to the Status of Refugees: "Each child has the right to make an independent refugee claim, regardless of whether s/he is accompanied or unaccompanied" at para 6.

potential avenues for family reunification (perhaps in a place of refuge; the country of asylum) need to be explored.[19]

The 1951 Refugee Convention makes "no distinction ... between children and adults in social welfare and legal rights"[20] and "the same definition of refugee applies regardless of age."[21] However, in this regard, it is important to note that in order for children to, in practice, receive equitable access to social welfare and their legal rights under the Refugee Convention they require special care and protection given their unique age -related vulnerabilities (differential treatment in some respects then to achieve equal protection).[22] The same applies, it is here argued, at every stage of the asylum process from initial request to final outcome and post asylum process; that is children require special considerations and certain differential treatment in order to have an equitable asylum process. For this reason, the UNHCR has adopted, among other instruments, the *Convention on the Rights of the Child* in articulating standards for the proper handling of cases pertaining to (accompanied and unaccompanied) child refugee asylum seekers pre affirmation of their legal status as refugees and of cases involving children who have obtained official recognition of their legal status as refugees with all of its correlated benefits.

The contention is advanced here that both in respect of accompanied[23] and 'unaccompanied child refugee asylum seekers'; it has often been the case that the

[19]"The circumstances of the parents and other family members, including their situation in the minor's country of origin, will have to be taken into account. If there is reason to believe that the parents wish their child to be outside the country of origin on grounds of a well-founded fear of persecution, the child himself may be presumed to have such fear" (Cited from UNHCR Handbook and Guidelines on Procedures and Criteria for Determining Refugee Status under the 1951 Convention and the 1967 Protocol Relating to the Status of Refugees (re-issued December, 2011 ed.) HCR/IP/4/ENG/REV.3 at p. 41 para 218 http://www.refworld.org/docid/4f33c8d92.html (Accessed 4 October, 2017).

[20]Refugee Children: Guidelines on Protection and Care (preface) (1988) http://www.unhcr.org/protect/PROTECTION/3b84c6c67.pdf (Accessed 4 October, 2017).

[21]UNHCR Handbook and Guidelines on Procedures and Criteria for Determining Refugee Status under the 1951 Convention and the 1967 Protocol Relating to the Status of Refugees (re-issued December, 2011 ed.) HCR/IP/4/ENG/REV.3 at p. 41 para 213. http://www.refworld.org/docid/4f33c8d92.html (Accessed 4 October, 2017.

[22]See the Supreme Court of Canada judgment of *Andrews* v. *Law Society of British Columbia* [1989] 1 SCR 143 which articulates that sometimes differential treatment is required to achieve equal rights. That differential treatment then is lawful where it supports and promotes human rights rather than constituting discriminatory treatment that violates basic human rights of an identifiable group and its members.

[23]Note that *except where it would not be consistent with the legal status of a particular child* "If a minor is accompanied by one (or both) of his parents, or another family member on whom he is dependent, who requests refugee status, the minor's own refugee status will be determined according to the principle of family unity." [the dependent minor child will also be granted refugee status if the head of the family is so recognized] Para 213, see also para 181–188 in UNHCR Handbook and Guidelines on Procedures and Criteria for Determining Refugee Status under the 1951 Convention and the 1967 Protocol Relating to the Status of Refugees (re-issued December, 2011 ed.) HCR/IP/4/ENG/REV.3 http://www.refworld.org/docid/4f33c8d92.html (Accessed 4 October, 2017.

children's *jus cogens* right to protection from torture, degrading or inhuman treatment or punishment *as forms also of 'persecution'* targeting their identifiable Refugee Convention 'social group' has been disregarded (i.e. certain of the selected cases in this work in fact illustrate such targeting of these child groups). The latter is not uncommon and has occurred both in various transit States and in a number of States in which the children sought temporary or permanent refugee asylum. The children are often being targeted for persecution then based on *the children's very membership in the social groups 'accompanied or unaccompanied child refugee asylum seekers'* as well as, in some instances, based on the children's intersecting other group statuses (relating to national origin, 'race' etc). Further, the denial of the child refugee asylum seekers' *jus cogens right to non-refoulement*[24] (violated either directly or indirectly by whatever means notwithstanding that the collective meets the criteria as a *prima facie* child refugee group and the members are mostly if not all *bona fide* child refugees) has often itself been a mechanism or vehicle for 'persecution' as that term is understood in the Refugee Convention. The latter is in violation of the *Convention on the Rights of the Child* (CRC)[25] guarantee of protection against persecution collectively or individually for (1) child refugees and children seeking refugee status; (2) for unaccompanied (or accompanied) child refugees or child refugee asylum seekers (the latter being further distinct social groups under CRC Article 22). Maltreatment often rising to the level of persecution of child refugees and children seeking refugee status is an infringement also of other CRC Articles including but not limited to Articles 19 and 37; the latter guaranteeing all children protection against violence of all forms and also in regard to particular inhuman or degrading treatment:

> **Article 19**
> 1. States Parties shall take all appropriate legislative, administrative, social and educational measures to protect the child from all forms of physical or mental violence, injury or abuse, neglect or negligent treatment, maltreatment or exploitation, including sexual abuse, while in the care of parent(s), legal guardian(s) or any other person who has the care of the child.
>
> **Article 22**
> (1).States Parties shall take appropriate measures to ensure ***that a child who is seeking refugee status or who is considered a refugee*** in accordance with applicable international or domestic law and procedures shall, ***whether unaccompanied or accompanied*** by his or her parents or by any other person, ***receive appropriate protection and humanitarian assistance in the enjoyment of applicable rights set forth in the present Convention and in other international***

[24]Allain (2001), pp. 533–558, "...the principle of *non-refoulement* has acquired the status of *jus cogens*, that is, a peremptory norm of international law from which no derogation is permitted."(Abstract).

[25]Convention on the Rights of the Child entered into force 2 September, 1990.

human rights or humanitarian instruments to which the said States are Parties....(emphasis added)...

Article 37
States Parties shall ensure that:

(a) No child shall be subjected to torture or other cruel, inhuman or degrading treatment or punishment...[26]

Let us consider further the contentious term 'social group' and its meaning under the Refugee Convention and how it is that 'child refugees' generally and 'unaccompanied child refugee asylum seekers' in particular may each be considered a 'social group' as that term is used in the Refugee Convention.

4.2 More on the Contentious Notion of Persecution Relating to 'Membership of a Particular Social Group'

Social group is a term, set out at Article 1A(2) of the 1951 Convention:

> A. For the purposes of the present Convention, the term "refugee" shall apply to any person who:
>
> ...
>
> (2) ... owing to wellfounded fear of being persecuted for reasons of race, religion, nationality, *membership of a particular social group* or political opinion, is outside the country of his nationality and is unable or, owing to such fear, is unwilling to avail himself of the protection of that country; or who, not having a nationality and being outside the country of his former habitual residence as a result of such events, is unable or, owing to such fear, is unwilling to return to it. ... (emphasis added).[27]

It has been noted by scholars of refugee law that the term 'social group' in the *Convention and 1967 Protocol Relating to the Status of Refugees* is *not defined* and is open to conflicting interpretation:

> Invocation of the particular social group ground is not surprising. Its potential breadth makes it a plausible vehicle for refugee claims that do not easily fall under the other grounds set out in Article 1A(2) of the 1951 Convention.[28]

---

[26]Convention on the Rights of the Child entered into force 2 September, 1990.

[27]Convention and 1967 Protocol Relating to the Status of Refugees, Original Convention entered into force 22 April, 1954, 1967 expanding in certain respects the scope of who could be classed as a refugee.

[28]Aleinikoff (2003), p. 264.

> Courts and jurists have taken widely differing views as to what constitutes 'membership of a particular social group' for the purposes of the Convention. This is not surprising. The phrase is indeterminate and lacks a detailed legislative history and debate. Not only is it impossible to define the phrase exhaustively, it is pointless to attempt to do so.[29]

TA Aleinikoff makes the point that attempts to delimit the meaning of 'particular social group' under the Refugee Convention by linking it to other grounds under the Convention and the elements of those grounds such as the immutability of 'race'[30] is misguided[31] in part since:

> This strategy ... is not compelled by the Convention or other authoritative sources; it is possible that the term was adopted to cover an assortment of groups whose need for protection was based on circumstances distinct from those that provide the justification for inclusion under the other grounds.[32]

In considering whether (1) child refugee asylum seekers and (2) 'unaccompanied child refugee asylum seekers' in particular constitute 'particular social groups' under the Refugee Convention consider that the UNHCR stipulates that:

> Mere membership of a particular social group will *not normally* be enough to substantiate a claim to refugee status. ***There may, however, be special circumstances where mere membership can be a sufficient ground to fear of persecution*** (emphasis added).[33]

It is here argued that mere membership in the social group 'child refugee asylum seeker' and, in particular, in the social group 'unaccompanied child refugee asylum seeker' is sufficient ground for these children to realistically fear persecution as the cases discussed in this work so graphically attest.[34] Recall the UNHCR statement re what constitutes persecution:

> Persecution
>
> There is no universally accepted definition of "persecution", and various attempts to formulate such a definition have met with little success. From Article 33 of the 1951 Convention, it may be inferred that *a threat to life or freedom on account of* race, religion, nationality, political opinion *or membership of a particular social group is always*

[29]Applicant A. and Another v. Minister for Immigration and Ethnic Affairs and Another, High Court of Australia, (1997) 190 CLR 225; 142 ALR 331.

[30]The term 'race' appears in the Refugee Convention.

[31]Aleinikoff (2003), p. 266.

[32]Aleinikoff (2003), p. 266.

[33]UNHCR Handbook and Guidelines on Procedures and Criteria for Deciding Refugee Status para 79 at p. 17.

[34]Note that the 'social group' 'unaccompanied child refugee asylum seeker' is defined in terms of common characteristics such as age below 18 years, being an asylum seeker and most commonly some or all of the following factors, amongst others: traumatic history, displacement, age -related vulnerabilities, being targeted for persecution as children in the homeland, and also commonly the experience of violation of his/her refugee rights.

> *persecution. Other serious violations of human rights – for the same reasons – would also constitute persecution* (emphasis added).[35]

Xenophobia may be a useful political tool for the State leadership at various times, at least in the short-term, and 'child refugee asylum seekers', being amongst the most vulnerable of all refugees, especially if unaccompanied, are an easy target for persecution by transit States and States in which the children seek asylum. The very existence of this social group irregularly within the State territory in which the child refugees seek asylum or at or near its frontier may be antithetical to the government's isolationist policies. The child refugee and child refugee asylum seeker groups may, for some States, serve as a useful symbol reinforcing politically fuelled paranoia, racism, 'extreme right-wing takes' on nationalism and a multitude of other dark, and destructive societal impulses. In addition consider that unaccompanied refugee children seeking asylum generally may be *perceived* to have broken, in a sense at least, from the social norms by *in effect* self-advocating by seeking asylum as persons in their own right (setting aside here the actual circumstances that led to their being unaccompanied in their quest for refugee asylum i.e. the parents may have sent them on this asylum seeking journey for any number of reasons including that it was in the children's best interests given the situation in the homeland or the children may have made the decision on their own, the children may be orphaned etc). The 'unaccompanied child refugee asylum seeker' is in this way, for many prospective asylum States, an unwitting symbol also of the 'unruly child' and a perceived threat to traditional family power structures.

Governments have too often resisted applying the Refugee Convention label of 'particular (persecuted) social group' to various refugee distinctive groups due primarily or even exclusively to political expediency and State self-interest inconsistent with international human rights legal obligations and those under the Refugee Convention and certain other instruments. This occurs not uncommonly then when in fact the refugee asylum claim relating to persecution of a certain identifiable 'social group' is well grounded and meritorious. Denying 'particular social group' status to certain persecuted groups that may or may not fit other Refugee Convention identifiers (i.e. in terms of persecuted groups defined by race, religion, political opinion or nationality or a combination of these etc.) is *in effect* to set up the 'rules of the game' in such a way that they unfairly disadvantage also the individual asylum claimant member of that Refugee Convention persecuted 'social group' the State declines to recognize. Thus where the very existence of the Convention 'particular social group' is unjustly denied-for instance denying that a certain 'unaccompanied child refugee asylum seeker' collective fits the definition of the Refugee Convention 'particular social group' - there is at the outset a denial of the *collective asylum rights* of the particular refugee identifiable persecuted 'social group'. The latter then may also serve as the basis for rejection of the individual members' meritorious refugee

---

[35]UNHCR Handbook and Guidelines on Procedures and Criteria for Deciding Refugee Status para 51 at p. 13.

asylum claims where no other Convention ground is available and the children are held not to be entitled to international protection under any other scheme.

The very existence of the persecuted identifiable 'social group' as a discrete social group (*in Refugee Convention terms*) thus may be erroneously denied by the State. Further, even if the existence of the particular social group for the purposes of establishing a Convention ground for refugee status is acknowledged by the State; the particular individual refugee asylum seeker's truthful claim to membership in that persecuted particular social group may be rejected without proper basis by that same State (i.e. the State may falsely deny that the individual is biologically and chronologically a child (person under 18 years of age) thus denying his/her membership in the particular Convention persecuted social group 'unaccompanied child refugee asylum seekers'). Thus the child refugee asylum seeker is frequently persecuted outside the homeland or place of habitual residence precisely due to his/her membership in that identifiable persecuted social group through maltreatment and violation of his/her rights under international refugee and human rights law.

That the particular (persecuted) social group 'unaccompanied child refugee asylum seekers' is in large part, though not exclusively, defined by the common attempt of the group members to exercise their fundamental right under international human rights and refugee law to seek asylum importantly contributes to the status of the group as a 'particular social group' in Refugee Convention terms. Further the fact that certain States respond to the 'unaccompanied child refugee asylum seeker' group *in effect* as a 'particular social group' to be unduly delayed or blocked in attaining asylum in as many cases as possible (lest the wells of compassion for unaccompanied child refugee asylum seekers or child refugee asylum seekers in general not be contained and State priorities be undermined) also affirms the Refugee Convention 'particular social group' status of the collective 'unaccompanied child refugee asylum seekers':

> It may be observed that it is the very nature of a human right, especially... a "fundamental" one, that it is common to all humanity. The wish of a number of persons to exercise a right which all persons share and are entitled to exercise at any time can hardly be enough to unite those persons into a particular social group. Something more would be required.. ***.A fundamental human right could ... constitute a unifying characteristic if persons associated with each other on the basis of the right or, it may be added, if society regarded those persons as a group because of their common wish to exercise the right. And in that situation, it would be the unifying aspect of that element, and not its character as a fundamental human right, which allowed it to delineate a particular social group*** (emphasis added).[36]

Next we consider two cases that illustrate violation of refugee rights of individual child asylum seekers through strategies that essentially, in the first instance, targeted the collective "unaccompanied child refugee asylum seekers" and were not in truth fashioned to properly weigh the merits of the individual case and its unique fact pattern. In the first case the U.K. argued that an immigration officer's judgment or belief alone was in the first instance dispositive of whether an individual was an unaccompanied *child* refugee asylum seeker (person under 18 in which instance that

[36]Applicant A. and Another v. Minister for Immigration and Ethnic Affairs and Another, High Court of Australia, (1997) HCA 4, 190 CLR 225 at p. 15.

person would be protected in certain respects by a specific domestic immigration/asylum statute that stipulates that a child asylum seeker arrived at the border or irregularly entered cannot be held in a detention facility longer than 24 h). That is the U.K. argued that the term 'child' (person under 18) in the particular U.K. immigration/asylum statute relating to detention of an asylum seeker was *not* to be interpreted as a status that had to be determined from the outset based on objective factual evidence (i.e. professional age assessments with some reasonable degree of reliability and validity, valid relevant documents as to chronological age of the asylum seeker or other factual sources that might be available). Here the U.K. government attempted to greatly delay what should have been treated as high priority child asylum applications; those most often involving older children namely teenage refugee asylum seekers. This was accomplished by denying these especially vulnerable children, for a significant period, recognition of their membership in the relevant 'particular social group' (that social group being 'unaccompanied *child* refugee asylum seekers' including in respect of those who were *prima facie* child refugees but not acknowledged as such). [37] The latter is a form of denial of the collective asylum seeking and certain other rights that the individual holds and shares with other members of the particular social group in question (denial of the group rights of unaccompanied child refugee asylum seekers). Thus there is occurring in parallel a violation of collective child refugee rights and also of the basic human rights of the individual child refugee asylum seeker members. The effect hoped to be achieved by the U.K. government in adopting this approach, it would seem, was to deter other unaccompanied child refugee asylum seekers from entering the U.K. in search of refuge even where they were, on available credible evidence, *prima facie* unaccompanied children and refugees. The assumption by the U.K. government likely was then that news would filter out to other unaccompanied child refugee asylum seekers in the European Union outside the U.K., and perhaps also even at the point of origin in some cases, that the U.K. would not be a reasonable possibility as an asylum country (i.e. the latter given the anticipated low rate of success for members of the social group 'unaccompanied child refugees asylum seekers' in obtaining asylum in the UK). The second case concerns greatly delayed professional age assessments and failure to treat the child complainants as members of the group 'unaccompanied child refugee asylum seekers' before the results of the age assessments were available and for a considerable period even after those assessments confirmed their child status (i.e. the children were detained for a lengthy period even after the confirmation of their child status though this violated domestic immigration law, child rights law etc.).

[37]This initial *prima facie* child status (pending the detailed age assessment outcome) could be assigned, for instance, based on the individual's physical appearance in terms of developmental aspects consistent with childhood (height and weight etc.). However, even in borderline cases in terms of what to deduce based on the superficial aspects of physical appearance re chronological age; an older child's status as 'child' might be apparent on other indicators such as level of emotional maturity, demeanour, language style and level of educational/knowledge sophistication etc all consistent with age under 18 years.

4.3 Case 1: AA v [UK] SSHD and Wolverhampton City Council (Interested Party) UK High Court of Justice, Queens Bench (Administrative Court)

Headnotes: State endorsed unreliable age assessments based on immigration officer *belief* and not on reliable objective documentary or scientific evidence, 'pushback' collective refugee migration control measure, unlawful detention of an unaccompanied child refugee asylum seeker, erroneous denial of the child refugee asylum seeker's membership in a persecuted 'social group' namely 'unaccompanied child refugee asylum seekers'.

4.3.1 The Facts

The claimant AA in the case at bar was a child from Sudan who arrived in the U.K. on 19 July 2014 and sought asylum whilst also reporting to authorities that he was 17 years old. He was detained by the U.K. Secretary of State from 17 February 2015 until 1 March 2015 when he was released. The clamant sought (1) a declaration that he had been unlawfully detained for the aforementioned period and (ii) damages in tort for the alleged false imprisonment. It was not disputed that the claimant had been unlawfully detained from 27 February, 2015 to 1 March, 2015. The matter in dispute was whether the detention was unlawful between 17 February, 2015 to 27 February, 2015. It was on 23 February, 2015 that the U.K. Secretary of State received a written age assessment report from Wolverhampton City Council. The accuracy of that age assessment received from Wolverhampton City Council was *not* disputed by the parties. The aforementioned report confirmed that AA was a child and placed his chronological age at somewhere in the range of 16–17 years. It was not disputed by the parties in the case at bar that AA was, objectively speaking as a factual matter, a child throughout the period of his detention in the U.K.

Note that a key relevant statutory provision in the case was the 1971 Immigration Act clause that set out that an unaccompanied child could only be held in a short-term detention facility and that for 24 h. In this case, however, the child had been detained for 13 days rather than the 24 h allowable by the relevant statutory provision (The statute defined 'child' as a person under 18 and 'unaccompanied' as child "who is not accompanied (whilst in detention) by his or her parent or another individual who has care of him or her").[38]

The child AA had first arrived in Italy before having made his way to the U.K. by way of a lorry. On 25 July, 2014 Italy had accepted that under the Dublin Regulations Italy was the State responsible to handle the alleged child's asylum claim as

[38] AA vs. [UK] SSHD (Secretary of State for the Home Department) [2016] EWHC 1453 (Admin) para 10.

Italy had been the "initial entry point to the European Union."[39] On 6 August, 2014 the U.K. Secretary of State had certified the paperwork regarding Italy as a "safe third country" to which the child AA should and could be removed and where his asylum claim could be heard. That process was canceled as the result of the child bringing two judicial reviews.[40] Both requests for judicial review were denied (on 4 November 2014 in respect of the first judicial application and on 12 January, 2015 in respect of the second application).[41]

The issues in the case were (1) whether AA, the child refugee claimant, had been unlawfully detained by U.K. immigration authorities for the entire period of his deprivation of liberty; that is unlawfully detained once the initial 24 h in detention had expired and if not then (2) whether AA's detention was unlawful from at least 23 February, 2015 to 1 March, 2015 given that the U.K. Secretary of State had received confirmation 23 February, 2015 of AA's status as chronologically a child (through a written age assessment organized by Wolverhampton City Council) but did not release the child immediately thereafter. Rather on 27 February, 2015 the U.K. Secretary of State made the decision that the child AA should be released from detention but that decision was not put into practice and the child wasn't released until 1 March, 2015.

In the case at bar each side relied on contradictory U.K. Supreme Court judgments that each side held supported their alternate mutually exclusive respective views.

4.3.2 The Arguments of the Parties

The government argued that alleged child status (being a person below age 18 years) can be based on the reasonable belief of an immigration officer and hence this alleged reasonable belief could be the basis for detaining the individual under the relevant statute as an adult. Put differently the U.K. government argued that the statutorily stipulated short-term 24 h maximum detention applicable for an unaccompanied child asylum seeker does *not* operate where the immigration officer *believes* the person in question to be an adult notwithstanding the absence of factual evidence in that regard. On the government's interpretation then the child could be held lawfully for longer than 24 h even though in that period there was no objective evidence that he was, as a factual matter, not a person under the chronological age of 18. In contrast counsel for the child complainant argued such a determination (of childhood status based on chronological age) must be based *at all times* on objective factual evidence as opposed to the "reasonable belief" of the immigration officer as to age without a relevant reliable and valid factual basis. The child claimant

[39] AA vs. [UK] SSHD [2016] EWHC 1453 (Admin) para 7(ii).

[40] AA vs. [UK] SSHD [2016] EWHC 1453 (Admin) para 7(iii).

[41] AA vs. [UK] SSHD [2016] EWHC 1453 (Admin) para 7 (iv).

AA argued then that his detention from 17 February, 2015 to 1 March 2015 was unlawful in that he was in fact an unaccompanied *child* asylum seeker (person under chronological age 18) entitled to the rights set out in the relevant U.K. statute in regards to members of that group (collective) (such rights including then no detention longer than 24 h and the right to have his asylum application judged on its individual merits and in consideration of the fact that he was an 'unaccompanied child refugee asylum seeker'). The child further petitioned the Court that, in the alternative, if the Court should find that he was not unlawfully detained for the *entire* period of his detention then the Court hold that his detention was unlawful from at least the date on which the U.K. Secretary of State obtained the age assessment report from the local city authority confirming, as a factual matter, that AA was chronologically a child to the date of his release:

> In that event, the Claimant would be entitled to damages for unlawful detention from 23 February 2015 until 27 February 2015 as well as from the admitted period of wrongful detention from 27 February 2015 until 1 March 2015.[42]

The child claimant argued also citing UK case law *Khawaja v Secretary of State* [1984] 1AC 74 that the burden was always on the government to show that detention was lawful whereas in this case the detention was not justified factually and therefore not lawful.[43] Counsel for the claimant also relied "on the well-known principle of statutory construction that where an enactment uses a term [i.e. 'child' as in the case at bar], which is one upon whose meaning the courts have previously pronounced, it may be presumed that it was intended to have that meaning in subsequent enactments..."[44] In other words; the term 'child' as used in the statute in question refers to someone who *in fact* is under age 18 years and not to a person who is simply defined as a 'child' based on the alleged reasonable belief of an immigration officer that the individual in question is under age 18 years. Counsel for the claimant noted that while the Immigration Act did use language referring to the immigration officer holding an unaccompanied child in a short term detention facility *on the reasonable belief the child would be held only for 24 hours*; no such reasonable belief reference or standard was set out in the statute in respect of whether the person being detained was a 'child'.

In respect of AA's detention from 23 February, 2015 to 27 February, 2015[45]; the U.K. Secretary of State argued that this was a period during which the Secretary of State office was giving due consideration to the age assessment information received from Wolverhampton City Council. Counsel for the government argued that:

> ...it was lawful to maintain the Claimant's detention from 23 February 2015 to 27 February 2015 because the Secretary of State was entitled to take "*some time*" in which to give the Age Assessment "*careful consideration*" before accepting it as proof that the Claimant was a

---

[42] AA vs. [UK] SSHD [2016] EWHC 1453 (Admin) para 6.

[43] AA vs. [UK] SSHD [2016] EWHC 1453 (Admin) para 14.

[44] AA vs. [UK] SSHD [2016] EWHC 1453 (Admin) para 15.

[45] The U.K. Secretary of State received the age assessment prepared by the local authority social workers early morning February 23, 2015.

child. He [counsel for the government] contends that four days was a reasonable period to perform that task in the circumstances of this case (emphasis added).[46]

Government counsel also maintained that the statutory reference to 'child' in the Immigration Act was ambiguous. The argument was advanced by the government that the immigration officer must first decide whether the asylum seeker should be detained and then whether the person is an unaccompanied child in order to decide in what type of facility -short term detention centre or other detention centre—the person in question should be detained.[47] While the government did not dispute the local authority's age assessment of 16/17 years at the same time counsel for the government highlighted that:

the Interested Party in the Age Assessment concluded only that it was "more likely" that the Claimant is 16/17 years old, but it then qualified its conclusion by stating that "Social workers are mindful that this process is not an exact science and that there can be a five year error either way" [and argued that] "it is necessary to bear in mind that the statute seeks accuracy to the degree of days and hours because the decision required is whether a person is over or under 18 years of age."[48]

It was put to the Court that the immigration officer in the case at bar continued in good faith to hold the alleged reasonable belief from July 2014 until 22 February 2015 that AA was an adult and not a child. The latter due to the child's purported "physical demeanour".[49] The government argued that the statute must mean that it was for the immigration officer to decide based on reasonable belief rather than entirely objective evidence if the person in question was a child given the short time available to make the decision and given that objective age assessment can be a complex process and not lead to a definitive conclusion as to roughly exact age of the asylum seeker.[50] The government argued then that both the determination as to whether the asylum seeker AA was 'unaccompanied' and whether or not he was a 'child' fell to the reasonable belief of the immigration officer.[51] The government referred to the fact that:

the Secretary of State has a policy under which age-disputed individuals are regarded as adults if they meet one of a number of criteria, as the approach of the Home Office is not to treat an individual as an adult where there is any doubt as to whether they are an adult or a child.[52]

The government's criteria set out as policy for an immigration officer to follow in deciding in the first instance whether an asylum seeker is a child was as follows:

---

[46] AA vs. [UK] SSHD [2016] EWHC 1453 (Admin) para 74.

[47] AA vs. [UK] SSHD [2016] EWHC 1453 (Admin) para 19.

[48] AA vs. [UK] SSHD [2016] EWHC 1453 (Admin) para 21.

[49] AA vs. [UK] SSHD [2016] EWHC 1453 (Admin) para 21.

[50] AA vs. [UK] SSHD [2016] EWHC 1453 (Admin) para 21–22.

[51] AA vs. [UK] SSHD [2016] EWHC 1453 (Admin) para 23.

[52] AA vs. [UK] SSHD [2016] EWHC 1453 (Admin) para 30.

> Where there is little or no evidence to support the applicant's claimed age and their claim to be a child is doubted, the following policy should be applied:
>
> The applicant should be treated as an adult if their physical appearance /demeanour very strongly suggests that they are significantly over 18 years of age. Careful consideration must be given to assessing whether an applicant falls into this category as they would be considered under adult processes and could be liable for detention.
>
> Before a decision is taken to assess an applicant as significantly over 18, the assessing officer's countersigning officer (who is at least a Chief Immigration Officer (CIO)/Higher Executive Officer must be consulted as a 'second pair of eyes'. They must make their own assessment of the applicant's age. If the countersigning officer also agrees to assess the applicant as significantly over18, the applicant should be informed that their claimed age is not accepted....Form 1S.97M should be completed and served and signed by the countersigning officer (CIO/HEO grade or above)..."[53]

The Court held and it was not disputed that it had *not* been suggested or established that the Secretary of State complied with the procedure set out in its own policy regarding first instance age assessment by the immigration officer in this case.[54]

The government argued that should the immigration officer have to rely on objective evidence of age assessment (of someone who arrived without a passport or birth certificate or other age relevant document) that officer would be unable to detain an asylum seeker he/she reasonably believed to be an adult. This since the officer would likely be unable to obtain the needed evidence regarding age within the 24 h period that is the maximum detention period for an unaccompanied child. Therefore, on the government's assessment of the issue, interpreting the term 'child' in the immigration statute to mean someone who is *factually* a child would lead to an "absurd and anomalous result."[55]

4.3.3 The Court's Assessment

The Court pointed out that (1) while one paragraph (18B4) of the 1971 Immigration Act stated that there was reliance on the reasonable belief of the immigration officer that in detaining a child the child would be removed within 24 h from detention; another paragraph (18B7) (2) "does not state that a child is a person who the immigration officer reasonably believes to be a child, but merely states that a child is a "person ...who is under 18 year of age".[56] The Court rejected the notion that paragraph 18B7 should be read to say a 'child' is a "person ...who the immigration

---

[53]AA vs. [UK] SSHD [2016] EWHC 1453 (Admin) para 32.

[54]AA vs. [UK] SSHD [2016] EWHC 1453 (Admin) para 33.

[55]AA vs. [UK] SSHD [2016] EWHC 1453 (Admin) para 30–31.

[56]AA vs. [UK] SSHD [2016] EWHC 1453 (Admin) para 38.

officer reasonably believes is under 18 year of age".[57] The Court held rather that the absence of statutory language regarding reasonable belief of the immigration officer in relation to determination of status of the asylum seeker as child indicated that:

> the intention of Parliament was that (in contrast to the matter set out in Paragraph 18B (4)) the issue of whether a person is a "child" in Paragraph 18B (7) would *not* be resolved by the reasonable belief of the immigration officer as to whether the person concerned was a child (emphasis added).[58]

The Court held that interpreting the provision set out in Paragraph 18B (7) in the Immigration Act to mean that 'child' is to be determined on a *factual basis* rather than on the basis of reasonable belief of the immigration officer would not lead to an absurd result "as the provision means that the immigration officers have to be very careful in detaining individuals who claim to be children."[59] The Court further found that the fact that age assessment is not an exact science and there may be difficulties in determining exact age objectively did not detract from the need to make the determination factually rather than based on reasonable belief. The Court cited Baroness Hale in that regard:

> ... There is a right or a wrong answer. It may be difficult to determine what that answer is. The decision-makers may have to do their best on the basis of less than perfect or conclusive evidence. But that is true of many questions of fact which regularly come before the courts. That does not prevent them from being questions for the courts rather than for other kinds of decision makers.[60]

In the case at bar the Court found that the local authorities are obligated to provide for any child in need and that also in non-asylum cases, a decision may have to be made almost immediately as to age of the person in order to properly address the situation (i.e. ensure the child is not homeless). Thus the court did not accept that time constraints in the case at bar required that the Immigration Officer rely in the first instance on his reasonable belief in determining the child AA's age. In both asylum and non-asylum cases then the Court held age must be determined as a factual matter and the authority involved must be cautious not to preclude a child from the special care and protection owed due to extraneous factors such as reasonable but false belief.[61]

The Court rejected the notion that the Immigration Officer's discretion to detain people based on 'reasonable belief' regarding their detention being lawful extended to a determination of age also based on reasonable belief rather than objective fact.[62] The Court, in addition, noted that determining that someone is an "illegal

[57] AA vs. [UK] SSHD [2016] EWHC 1453 (Admin) para 39.

[58] AA vs. [UK] SSHD [2016] EWHC 1453 (Admin) para 40.

[59] AA vs. [UK] SSHD [2016] EWHC 1453 (Admin) para 42.

[60] R(A) v Croydon [2009] 1 WLR 2557 at p.2567. Cited in AA vs. Secretary of State [2016] EWHC 1453 (Admin) para 49.

[61] Compare AA vs. [UK] SSHD [2016] EWHC 1453 (Admin) para 53, 55–56.

[62] AA vs. [UK] SSHD [2016] EWHC 1453 (Admin) para 44.

immigrant" (someone who entered illegally) must also be determined factually and not simply be based on reasonable belief.[63]

4.3.4 Commentary on AA v [UK] SSHD and Wolverhampton City Council (Interested Party) UK High Court of Justice, Queens Bench (Administrative Court)

In the case at bar the attempt of the government *in effect* was to grant Immigration Officers the authority to deny, in the absence of objective fact, and based instead on reasonable belief, that a child (a person who was a child as a matter of actual chronological age below 18 years) was a member of the relevant social group; namely (unaccompanied) children. Certain special rights under the 1971 UK Immigration Act (detention no longer than 24 h) were, as mentioned, set out in respect of the asylum seeking *collective* at issue—unaccompanied asylum seeking children. Thus denying that members of the group were in actual fact members is tantamount to denying, at least to an extent, the collective rights of the group itself (a form of non-recognition of the collective itself through rejecting the membership of children who did belong to the identifiable group ('unaccompanied children'). That there appears to have been an attempt to deny collective rights (the rights of members of the group "unaccompanied children' not to be detained longer than 24 h) is further suggested by the fact that the child AA was detained *even after* the objective age assessment was provided to the Secretary of State. The Secretary of State relied on the following from the Immigration Officer in mischaracterizing AA as an adult: "physical appearance/demeanour[64] very strongly suggests that [he is] significantly over 18 year [sic] of age and no other credible evidence exists to the contrary" [However] "once the Age Assessment was provided to the Secretary of State on 23 February 2015, this criterion no longer applied because there was then "credible evidence" in existence that the Claimant was a child."[65] Yet it was not until 27 February, 2015 that the Secretary of State even took the decision that the child AA should be released (it was only on 27 February, 2015 that a Senior Immigration Officer reviewed the age assessment and determined the child should be released). The latter notwithstanding that there was evidence not in dispute that he was *factually* a child (evidence from a social work report provided by the interested party Wolverhampton City Council). The potential impact of detaining the child AA in the first instance on a non-factual basis and then still even after the Secretary of State had received the age assessment report from the local city authority could have been to set a case precedent had the child not filed a successful court challenge. That case precedent would then impact the handling of other such cases in future and

[63]AA vs. [UK] SSHD [2016] EWHC 1453 (Admin) para 45.
[64]AA vs. [UK] SSHD [2016] EWHC 1453 (Admin) para 73.
[65]AA vs. [UK] SSHD [2016] EWHC 1453 (Admin) para 73.

possibly create deterrence for other unaccompanied children who considered entering the U.K. in an unauthorized manner without proper documents and seeking U.K. asylum. That the child AA was treated harshly in terms of the length of his detention by immigration authorities sends a message to other prospective unaccompanied child asylum seekers that (1) unaccompanied child asylum seekers very often would be deemed in the first instance not to be children based only on the discretionary opinion of the Immigration Officer and would as a result receive no special consideration or protective care and (2) such children would be readily deported if they had not applied for asylum in the State of first entry where the latter was considered safe (for AA that first entry was in Italy). In fact the U.K. Secretary of State, before there had been a hearing on the matter of AA's removal from the U.K., predicted that the child AA likely would be deported to Italy soon and that statement of belief became part of the child's asylum file:

> the evidence in this case does not support the contention of the Secretary of State that she was giving *"careful consideration"* to the Age Assessment between its receipt on 23 February 2015 and the decision to release the Claimant on 27 February 2015 (emphasis in the original).[66]
>
> . . . the detention review conducted by the Secretary of State on 24 February 2015 stated that: "[age assessment] letter received and barrier to removal raised, this will be responded to shortly. Detention to be maintained due to disregard shown for EU immigration laws and [since] risk of absconding is significant. *Removal remains a likely prospect in the near future*".
>
> [Court speaking] It seems clear that a positive decision was made to maintain the Claimant's detention notwithstanding the Age Assessment.[67]

The U.K. Secretary of State maintained the detention of AA for four days *after* receiving the local authority report on the chronological age of AA and before taking a decision to release (detention February 23–27, 2015) and then took another three days to actually effectuate the release (detention from February 27 to March 1, 2015). This despite the fact that:

> the Secretary of State's own published guidance stipulates that "considerable weight" should be given to findings of age by local authorities, and that local authority age assessments will "normally be accepted as decisive evidence" as stated in paragraph 2.2.1 of the Secretary of State's Assessing Age guidance.[68]

The Court in the case at bar concluded that there had been no justification for not releasing the child on February 23, 2015 when the age assessment was received on that date at 10:55 am.[69] The detention of the child in this case, both before and after the local authority age assessment was received, is striking given also Chapter 55 of the Secretary of State's *Enforcement Instructions and Guidance*".

---

[66] AA vs. [UK] SSHD [2016] EWHC 1453 (Admin) para 75.

[67] AA vs. [UK] SSHD [2016] EWHC 1453 (Admin) para 76.

[68] AA vs. [UK] SSHD [2016] EWHC 1453 (Admin) para 79.

[69] AA vs. [UK] SSHD [2016] EWHC 1453 (Admin) para 80.

> "even where one of the statutory powers to detain is available in a particular case, unaccompanied children (that is, persons under the age of 18) must not be detained other than in very exceptional circumstances", "for the shortest possible time" and "must not be held in an immigration removal centre in any circumstances" [70]

In sum then the child AA's membership in the identifiable, discrete and especially vulnerable asylum seeking collective "unaccompanied child refugees" was at first rejected on the basis of an incorrect belief that AA's chronological age was that of an adult. The latter belief was, as discussed, without factual basis but professed by the Immigration Officer and then adopted by the U.K. Secretary of State Office and maintained (1) even after receiving contrary evidence from the local authority and (2) despite the Secretary of State Office policy and guidelines on enforcement stipulating as "normally accepted as decisive evidence"[71] the age assessment provided by a local authority." On the analysis here the case illustrates then the government's intentional or unintentional undercutting of the possibility of *prima facie* recognition of the aforementioned child refugee collective (unaccompanied child refugees) allowing for sidestepping the likelihood of *prima facie* recognition also of individual members of that group as *bona fide* asylum seeking refugees pending further detailed individual assessment. Here there was detailed further age assessment and factual evidence about the situation in Sudan available that would, at a minimum, substantiate AA's individual asylum claim on a *prima facie* basis.

In the next case here discussed (a European Court of Human Rights case), *Abdullahi Elmi and Aweys Abubakar v Malta*,[72] concerning unaccompanied child asylum seekers, there is again an attempt by a government (here Malta) to deny particular child claimants' group membership in the 'social group' 'unaccompanied child asylum seekers'. In the latter case this was accomplished in practice in a variety of ways: (1) by treating the two children in question as 'non-children' even after an age assessment (including medical examination which had confirmed the two to be children in terms of their biological age) and (2) by regarding the two minors (who were teens chronologically) *in practice* as if they were adults not entitled to the special protections and considerations accorded to minors; their deprivation of rights as children being rationalized even after the professional age assessment based on the fact that the minors in question were not *younger children* though still children (persons under age 18 years). Further there was an attempt to discourage other would-be unaccompanied child asylum seekers entering Malta by, in this test case of sorts, detaining the minors for an unreasonable period after they lodged their asylum claim and even after they were determined subsequent to interviews and medical assessments to in fact be children. The European Court of Human Rights in this particular case *Abdullahi Elmi and Aweys Abubakar v Malta*[73] found that the

---

[70] AA vs. [UK] SSHD [2016] EWHC 1453 (Admin) para 82.

[71] AA vs. [UK] SSHD [2016] EWHC 1453 (Admin) para 79.

[72] Abdullahi Elmi and Aweys Abubakar v Malta, European Court of Human Rights Judgment, Application No. 25794/13 and 28151/13), Chamber Judgment 22 November, 2016.

[73] Abdullahi Elmi and Aweys Abubakar v Malta, European Court of Human Rights Judgment, Application No. 25794/13 and 28151/13), Chamber Judgment 22 November, 2016.

government of Malta had *not* acted in "good faith" in detaining the child appellants for what the Court found to be an inordinately long period considering (1) the particular circumstances surrounding their age assessment and how long it should have reasonably taken to arrange for and conduct that age assessment; (2) what should have occurred in terms of terminating the detention once that age assessment ultimately established that they were in fact minors; (3) the lack of procedural safeguards afforded the children during their detention and (4) the inadequate conditions under which the children were detained which conditions did not properly respect their human dignity and, more specifically, also their fundamental human rights as children and in particular child refugee asylum seekers.

4.4 Case 2: Abdullahi Elmi and Aweys Abubakar v Malta (European Court of Human Rights, Chamber Judgment)

Headnotes: 'unaccompanied child refugee asylum seekers' as a vulnerable 'social group', unreasonably long immigration detention of unaccompanied children in a custodial facility and as other than a last resort, unlawful detention of child asylum seekers post both their request for asylum and affirmation of their status as children, procedural safeguards in child refugee asylum cases, unreasonable delay of age assessment, degrading treatment while in immigration detention, untoward delay in recognizing the individual child asylum seeker's membership in the persecuted 'social group' namely 'unaccompanied child refugee asylum seekers', 'pushback' collective refugee migration control measure.

4.4.1 The Facts

The European Court of Human Rights case at bar concerned two children from Somalia (Burhaan Abdullahi Elmi born 1996 and Cabdulaahi Aweys Abubakar-born 1995) who had entered Malta on an irregular basis. The children complained that (1) their detention in a custodial facility (immigration detention) by Malta had been unlawful post their request for asylum and their asserting that they were children (persons under age 18). (The children did *not* complain that their detention from the date of arrival to Malta until their request for asylum was unlawful per Maltese immigration law); (2) that they were afforded no remedy for that unlawful detention by the State of Malta and (3) that the conditions of their detention and its length were a violation of their human rights.

The Court commented that:

> ... the focus of the applicants' complaint concerns the fact that they were detained despite the fact that at the time they had claimed to be minors (and later found to be so). *The Court*

> *reiterates that the necessity of detaining children in an immigration context must be very carefully considered by the national authorities* (emphasis added).[74]

Under Maltese law:

> *when an individual is found to be a minor, the latter is no longer detained, and he or she is placed in a non-custodial residential facility,* ...detention of minors should be no longer than what is absolutely necessary to determine their identification and health status (emphasis added).[75]

Both children were detained at the Safi Barracks Detention Centre, Safi, Malta. Burhaan Abdullahi Elmi had arrived by boat and entered Malta without status on 16 August, 2012. Cabdulaahi Aweys Abubakar also arrived by boat and entered Malta irregularly 31 August, 2012. In both cases the children were registered by immigration police and when they were provided assistance in filling out a preliminary questionnaire (as per the Malta Immigration law and procedure requirements) they requested asylum in Malta. In response to questioning Burhaan informed the immigration officers that he was 16 and that his date of birth was 1996 while Cabdulaahi informed the immigration officers he was 17 and that he had been born in 1995. In both cases the children were given two documents *in English*; one a return decision and the other a removal order. In both cases the children were unable to read the documents as their English competence was either non-existent or inadequate. The Return Decision stated in both cases that each child respectively was a:

> prohibited immigrant by virtue of Article 5 of the Immigration Act (Chapter 217 of the Laws of Malta) because he was in Malta "without means of subsistence and liable to become a charge on public funds" and "without leave granted by the principal Immigration Officer".[76]

The Return document in each case also stated that the child in question had "the possibility to apply for a period of voluntary departure."[77] Further in each case *the removal order stated that consideration for voluntary departure had been rejected* and that both the return decision and removal order could be appealed within three working days before an Immigration Appeal Board.[78] Both children maintained before the ECtHR that they could not understand the documents as the papers were in English while the government submitted to the ECtHR that it was Malta's policy

[74]Abdullahi Elmi and Aweys Abubakar v Malta, European Court of Human Rights Judgment, Application No. 25794/13 and 28151/13, Chamber Judgment 22 November, 2016 at para 144.

[75]Abdullahi Elmi and Aweys Abubakar v Malta, European Court of Human Rights Judgment, Application No. 25794/13 and 28151/13, Chamber Judgment 22 November, 2016 at para 144.

[76]Abdullahi Elmi and Aweys Abubakar v Malta EctHR Application No. 25794/13 and 28151/13, ECtHR Chamber Judgment 22 November, 2016) at para 12.

[77]Abdullahi Elmi and Aweys Abubakar v Malta, ECtHR Application No. 25794/13 and 28151/13, ECtHR Chamber Judgment 22 November, 2016) at paras 7 and 12.

[78]Abdullahi Elmi and Aweys Abubakar v Malta, ECtHR Application No. 25794/13 and 28151/13, ECtHR Chamber Judgment 22 November, 2016) at paras 7 and 12.

and practice that the Immigration Officers explain the situation to the asylum seekers in English and that the "migrants" translate for each other.[79]

Malta further submitted to the ECtHR in the case at bar that persons appearing to be young children are fast tracked through the asylum process while older looking children who may appear to be young adults undergo a lengthier process. The ECtHR in this case noted that:

> An issue may, however, arise, *inter alia,* in respect of a State's good faith, in so far as the determination of age may take an unreasonable length of time - indeed, a lapse of various months may also result in an individual reaching his or her majority pending an official determination.[80]

The Court noted that in 2012 less than 10% of irregular arrivals to Malta claimed to be minors though not all were (correctly or incorrectly) ultimately deemed by Malta to be minors as a matter of fact (i.e. in 2012, 46 out of 75 asylum seekers claiming to be children were found to be children). It must be recognized that age assessment, even that including medical testing, involves a rather significant margin of error that may favor or not favor the case of the particular asylum seeker involved.

4.4.2 The Court's Assessment

The ECtHR in the case at bar held that notwithstanding that age assessment is not exact when based on interviews and/or medical testing and

> that "borderline" cases may require further assessment, the numbers of alleged minors per year put forward by the Government [of Malta] cannot justify a duration of more than seven months to determine the applicants' claims.[81]

The Court rejected the notion that in the case at bar the duration of the claimants' detentions following their claims to asylum were of reasonable duration:

> Indeed, the Government have not explained why it was necessary for the first applicant in the present case to wait for a few weeks for his first age-assessment interview . . . and to wait for around seven months to have a decision following a standard medical test. The Court notes that during this time the first applicant remained in detention, despite having been told orally that he had been found to be a minor six months before. Similarly the Government have not explained why, following his interview, the second applicant had to wait for five months to have the FAV [age assessment test] test and to wait for another two and a half months for such a decision, and therefore for his release under a care order. Indeed, in the present case it transpires that in October 2012 the authorities were already aware that the first applicant was a minor, and yet he remained in detention until a care order was issued on 19 April 2013,

[79]Abdullahi Elmi and Aweys Abubakar v Malta, ECtHR Application No. 25794/13 and 28151/13, ECtHR Chamber Judgment 22 November, 2016) at paras 8 and 13.

[80]Abdullahi Elmi and Aweys Abubakar v Malta, ECtHR Application No. 25794/13 and 28151/13, ECtHR Chamber Judgment 22 November, 2016) at para 144.

[81]Abdullahi Elmi and Aweys Abubakar v Malta, ECtHR Application No. 25794/13 and 28151/13, ECtHR Chamber Judgment 22 November, 2016) at para 145.

while the second applicant remained in detention for at least another month after his age was determined. ***In this connection the Court notes that Government policy clearly states that vulnerable people are exempt from detention*** *and that* ***unaccompanied minors*** *are considered as a vulnerable* ***category*** (emphasis added)[82]

The Court found that the government had *not* acted in good faith in respect of these two child refugee asylum seekers:

It follows that, even accepting that the detention was closely connected to the ground of detention relied on, namely to prevent an unauthorised entry, and in practice to allow for the applicants' asylum claim to be processed with the required prior age assessment, the delays in the present case, particularly those subsequent to the determination of the applicants' age, raise serious doubts as to the authorities' good faith. A situation rendered even more serious by the fact that the applicants lacked any procedural safeguards ... as well as the fact that at no stage did the authorities ascertain whether the placement in immigration detention of the applicants was a measure of last resort for which no alternative was available.[83]

In addition the Court found that the conditions of detention violated Article 3 of the European Convention on Human Rights in that the specific circumstances were degrading. The Court also held that the claimants' age (16 and 17 respectively) and their history as asylum seekers exacerbated their suffering in such unacceptable conditions of immigration detention:

The Court reiterates that the applicants, as asylum-seekers, were particularly vulnerable because of everything they had been through during their migration and the traumatic experiences they were likely to have endured previously ... Moreover, in the present case the applicants, who were sixteen and seventeen years of age respectively, were even more vulnerable than any other adult asylum seeker detained at the time because of their age.[84]

In sum the European Court of Human Rights in *Abdullahi Elmi and Aweys Abubakar v Malta*[85] found a violation of Article 3 of the European Convention on Human Rights[86] in respect of the failure to protect the children against degrading treatment relating to their immigration detention given (a) the conditions in and length of that detention and (b) the suffering caused the child complainants by their lengthy detention and the circumstances of that detention. On the Court's view these unaccompanied children as children, and given their traumatic history, were especially vulnerable and hence the detention in and of itself and the conditions, apart

[82]Abdullahi Elmi and Aweys Abubakar v Malta, ECtHR Application No. 25794/13 and 28151/13, ECtHR Chamber Judgment 22 November, 2016) at para 145.

[83]Abdullahi Elmi and Aweys Abubakar v Malta, ECtHR Application No. 25794/13 and 28151/13, ECtHR Chamber Judgment 22 November, 2016) at para 146.

[84]Abdullahi Elmi and Aweys Abubakar v Malta, ECtHR Application No. 25794/13 and 28151/13, ECtHR Chamber Judgment 22 November, 2016) at para 113.

[85]Abdullahi Elmi and Aweys Abubakar v Malta, ECtHR Application No. 25794/13 and 28151/13, ECtHR Chamber Judgment 22 November, 2016).

[86]European Convention on Human Rights (as amended by the provisions of Protocol No. 14 (CETS no. 194) as from its entry into force on 1 June 2010.) original entry into force of the Convention 21 September 1970. http://www.echr.coe.int/Documents/Convention_ENG.pdf (Accessed 21 October, 2016).

from the length of detention, would have been experienced as profoundly degrading[87] (The Court concluded as follows:"... in the present case...since the applicants were minors who were detained for a period of around eight months, the cumulative effect of the conditions complained of amounted to degrading treatment within the meaning of the Convention").[88] The Court also found that there had been infringement of Article 5(1) of the European Convention on Human Rights[89] regarding the right to liberty and security (after the children in the case at bar were found by the government factually to be children their detention on the facts of this case could not be justified even under Maltese immigration law). However no attempts were made to place the children in a non-custodial age appropriate setting pending the outcome of their asylum applications. The Court in addition held that a violation of Article 5(4) of the Convention had occurred in that the children in practice had no fast and effective remedy to their rights being violated by agents of the Maltese government (immigration authorities) i.e. no effective way to readily access review of their detention by an immigration appeal body or to access the courts for judicial review).

It appears that there was, at the time of this case, a systematic widespread pattern of violation by agents of the State (i.e. immigration police and certain other authorities working for the Maltese government immigration system) of the immigration laws of Malta and of Maltese official immigration policy as well as of international human rights, refugee and child rights law regarding the proper treatment to be accorded unaccompanied child refugee asylum seekers. Instead unaccompanied child refugee asylum seekers arrived irregularly to Malta by boat were treated in a punitive manner via mandatory detention in substandard conditions for untoward lengthy periods. Such punitive measures were in particular (but not exclusively) applied to children who purportedly appeared to be at or above a certain cut off age (12 or 14 years of age) based on their alleged physical appearance etc. and according to the immigration officer's impression of their perhaps being adults rather than children. [90] The types of human rights violations as occurred in the case at bar were thus occurring also in other cases in Malta involving unaccompanied child refugee

---

[87]Abdullahi Elmi and Aweys Abubakar v Malta, ECtHR Application No. 25794/13 and 28151/13, ECtHR Chamber Judgment 22 November, 2016) at para 112:

> The Court has also previously found...in respect of an unaccompanied minor ...in such facilities, that the conditions of his detention were so poor that they undermined the very essence of human dignity and that they could be regarded in themselves, without taking into consideration the length of the detention...as degrading treatment in breach of Article 3 of the Convention.

[88]Abdullahi Elmi and Aweys Abubakar v Malta, ECtHR Application No. 25794/13 and 28151/13, ECtHR Chamber Judgment 22 November, 2016) at para 114.

[89]Council of Europe (2014) Guide on Article 5 of the Convention: Right to Liberty and Security http://www.echr.coe.int/Documents/Guide_Art_5_ENG.pdf Accessed 5 October, 2017.

[90]Human Rights Watch (18 July, 2012) Boat ride to detention: Adults and child migrants to Malta https://www.hrw.org/report/2012/07/18/boat-ride-detention/adult-and-child-migrants-malta Accessed 5 October, 2017.

asylum seekers[91] i.e. inordinate delay of age assessment and frequent ignoring of the findings (where confirmatory regarding child status of the asylum seeker) for as long as possible with the result of keeping the unaccompanied child refugee asylum seekers in immigration detention in substandard conditions without procedural safeguards and for unreasonable lengthy periods (sometimes unlawfully for months even after the child refugees were declared by the government in fact to be children as was the case for the unaccompanied child refugee asylum applicants in the case at bar).[92]

Thus the actual practice of the Maltese government at the time of the case at bar appeared to have been, as a matter of routine, to violate and obstruct the *collective rights* of, among other refugees, unaccompanied child refugee asylum seekers (targeting especially those who were allegedly not obviously, on their appearance, children and who had arrived irregularly by boat). There was then a pattern of violations of international human rights law with respect to the rights of older children (or of children *perceived* to be older) including but not necessarily limited to: (1) their right as children to have their age assessments conducted and asylum applications addressed as a priority with as little delay as possible; (2) their right under European Union regulations as children and as unaccompanied children (who have declared themselves to be children)[93], an especially vulnerable group, in non-exceptional cases to be exempt from detention (thus not to be detained in immigration detention or any other pending the professional age assessment or post that assessment or pending the remaining asylum process but rather to be placed in a timely fashion in a child friendly non-custodial setting) and (3) their right not to be exposed to degrading or otherwise substandard conditions in any placement. Hence individual child refugee asylum applications in the aforementioned cases were *not* dealt with, at least for prolonged periods, entirely based on the merits of the applications, if at all, but rather based in large part or in whole on a socio-political agenda. That agenda was it would appear (1) to discourage then currently arrived

[91]Note that *accompanied* child refugees arrived to Malta by boat were typically placed in immigration detention facilities with other family members who had irregularly entered with them but then quickly moved to open facilities whereas unaccompanied children spent months in immigration detention typically in overcrowded substandard conditions (see Human Rights Watch (18 July, 2012) Boat ride to detention: Adults and child migrants to Malta https://www.hrw.org/report/2012/07/18/boat-ride-detention/adult-and-child-migrants-malta Accessed 5 October, 2017.

[92]"Asylum seekers who arrive by boat are detained for up to 12 months, and migrants who do not apply for asylum, or whose asylum claims are rejected, can be detained for up to 18 months... In Malta, the detention policy operates in an automated, indiscriminate, and blanket manner in violation of international law": Cited from Human Rights Watch (18 July, 2012) Boat ride to detention: Adults and child migrants to Malta (Summary) https://www.hrw.org/report/2012/07/18/boat-ride-detention/adult-and-child-migrants-malta Accessed 5 October, 2017.

[93]Under the immigration law in Malta at the time; it was lawful, notwithstanding the complainants professing to be children and theirs being borderline cases on appearances (they were not obviously adults), to detain the children until the age determination was completed and their child status affirmed factually (See Abdullahi Elmi and Aweys Abubakar v Malta, ECtHR Application No. 25794/13 and 28151/13, ECtHR Chamber Judgment 22 November, 2016) at para 141).

unaccompanied child refugee asylum seekers (among others) arrived by boat from pursuing their applications for asylum in Malta and (2) to deter future members of the 'social group' 'unaccompanied child refugees asylum seekers' (among others) from coming to Malta by boat and entering without authorization or valid entry documentation in search of refuge. While Malta was coping with a huge influx of refugee asylum seekers[94] the aforementioned tactics involving grievous violations of international human rights and refugee law amongst other violations cannot be legally or ethically justified on that basis or any basis.

It was noted in the concurring opinion of Judge Pinto De Albuquerque in the case at bar that detention is often used as a mechanism to obstruct asylum seekers who have already crossed irregularly into the country and at the same time also would-be asylum seekers:

> detention is frequently applied as part of a policy to deter future asylum-seekers or to dissuade those who have commenced their claims from pursuing them. Sometimes it is even used as a punitive measure for irregular entry or presence in the country, lack of documentation or failure to comply with administrative requirements or other restrictions related to residency in the host country. Access to legal advice is virtually impossible, decisively affecting the asylum-seeker's ability to present his or her case. Possibilities of judicial review are in practical terms very limited, if available at all. *This scenario alone results in en masse and needless detention* (emphasis added).[95]

En masse (collective) immigration detention (sometimes for indefinite periods) of refugee and non-refugee migrants often without legal assistance to the detained is thus used by some States to delay or sometimes even block legitimate claims to refugee asylum being fairly and genuinely considered individually based on the merits of each particular case. Detention in such a circumstance is a denial of collective refugee rights (as well as of individual such rights) where many if not most or all of the detained group meet the criteria for refugee (under the Refugee Convention together with the accompanying Protocol).[96] In addition such automatic mass immigration detention is a violation of international law in respect of the right to protection against arbitrary detention as set out, for instance, in Article 9 of the International Covenant on Civil and Political Rights.[97] It would appear (based on NGO reports such as that mentioned here by Human Rights Watch) that many if not most of those children arrived to Malta irregularly by boat and being held for long

[94]Human Rights Watch (18 July, 2012) Boat ride to detention: Adults and child migrants to Malta https://www.hrw.org/report/2012/07/18/boat-ride-detention/adult-and-child-migrants-malta Accessed 5 October, 2017.

[95]Abdullahi Elmi and Aweys Abubakar v Malta, Application No. 25794/13 and 28151/13, ECtHR Chamber Judgment, 22 November, 2016, Concurring opinion of Jude Pinto De Albuquerque at para 3.

[96]The treatment accorded by Malta to Convention refugee asylum seekers would also have violated the rights of other asylum seekers, including children, who were persons in need of international protection but may have not fit the definition of Convention refugee per the criteria set out in the Refugee Convention.

[97]International Covenant on Civil and Political Rights. Entered into force 33 March, 1976 http://www.ohchr.org/EN/ProfessionalInterest/Pages/CCPR.aspx Accessed 5 October, 2017.

periods in immigration detention in Malta at the time of the case at bar in fact would have met the criteria for *prima facie* refugee at the outset. However no such *prima facie bona fide* refugee status was granted collectively or individually and the children were instead greatly delayed or, in effect, in some cases, completely obstructed due to lengthy immigration detention and its psychological and other impacts from obtaining refugee asylum in Malta.

The length of immigration detention in the case at bar[98] and the degrading conditions of detention for the child complainants (and for so many other children similarly situated in immigration detention in Malta at the time) thus constituted both a discriminatory and punitive measure. Here the State 'collective pushback migration control measures' included *en masse* lengthy detention in degrading conditions applied by Malta against, among others, 'unaccompanied child refugee asylum seekers' irregularly entered into the State territory (or intercepted en route via the Mediterranean). Such collective measures violate the international customary norm regarding the high international obligation to afford protection to children and to particularly vulnerable child groups[99]; especially unaccompanied children or those separated from family.[100] The failure to provide that protection in a timely fashion, if at all, is also inconsistent with the fact that *bona fide* refugees per the Refugee Convention, notwithstanding whether they have formally yet been assigned that legal status, *are* refugees.[101] As such they have a right to seek asylum[102] and have their request considered fairly and humanely without facing State punitive and

[98]Recall that under immigration law in Malta at the time; detention of child asylum seekers irregularly entered was permissible until the children's status as children was timely established as a precursor to asylum processing. However the Court found in the case at bar that there had been delays and other factors surrounding the detention that indicated bad faith on the government's part.

[99]This obligation, for instance, is codified in the 8 June, 1977 Additional Protocol I and Additional Protocol II to the 12 August, 1949 Geneva Conventions which arguably have become customary law (respectively at Protocol I Article 77-Protection of Children and Protocol II Article 4(3)-Fundamental Guarantees: "Children shall be provided with the care and aid they require...") (See International Committee of the Red Cross Commentary on the Additional Protocols of 8 June, 1977 http://www.loc.gov/rr/frd/Military_Law/pdf/Commentary_GC_Protocols.pdf Accessed 5 October, 2017) Note that this international high and special obligation to protect children is found in a host of international human rights treaties and other law (i.e. child law: Convention on the Rights of the Child) and not only in humanitarian law and has, it is here contended, become customary law if not also a *jus cogens* norm.

[100]See Article 22(2) of the Convention on the Rights of the Child entered into force 2 September, 1990 http://www.ohchr.org/EN/ProfessionalInterest/Pages/CRC.aspx (accessed 30 June, 2017).

[101]UNHCR Handbook and Guidelines on Procedures and Criteria for Determining Refugee Status under the 1951 Convention and the 1967 Protocol Relating to the Status of Refugees (December, 2011 ed.) at para 28.

[102]Likewise persons entitled to international protection under other international complementary legal regulatory schemes who do not fit the Refugee Convention eligibility criteria have the right under international law to seek asylum without facing punitive collective measures for doing so or for having entered the country irregularly (the collective punitive measures adversely affect individual asylum rights).

arbitrary detention measures or other collective refugee migration control measures that effectively deny their individual right to seek asylum:

> Although States have the right to control the entry to and stay of persons on their territory, this right is limited by human rights, namely by the right to be accorded refugee status when the required international- law conditions obtain. . .*This is valid not only with regard to recognised refugees, regardless of whether individual or group recognition took place, but also to asylum-seekers*. Recognised refugees and registered asylum-seekers are lawfully within the territory of the entry State, under international refugee law. ***Indeed, those who submit an application for refugee status are already lawfully present in the national territory***. *States should not indefinitely deny refugees their international-law rights simply by refusing or delaying to verify their status. This results from the declaratory nature of the refugee status determination* (emphasis added).[103]

In the case at bar Malta wished to remove the child complainants to Italy as a safe third country and country of first entry to the EU rather than to the home country where they likely would face persecution. Recall, however, that under European regulations unaccompanied minors (including child refugees seeking asylum) are not in any case to be detained and there can be no legal justification for the same also where removal is anticipated.[104] As noted in Abdullahi Elmi and Aweys Abubakar v Malta:

> Any form of detention is ill-suited to the vulnerability of children, be it before or after the asylum application assessment decision has been taken. *Unaccompanied or separated children must never be detained.* Accompanied children and their primary caregivers must not be detained unless there is an absolute need for the latter's detention and where keeping the children with them is considered to be in the children's best interests (emphasis added).[105]

Judge Pinto De Albuquerque noted that "the number of refugees, asylum-seekers, rejected asylum-seekers, stateless persons. . . [and certain other categories of persons irregularly in a European State] jailed is at unprecedented levels in Europe."[106]

[103] Abdullahi Elmi and Aweys Abubakar v Malta, Application No. 25794/13 and 28151/13, ECtHR Chamber Judgment, 22 November, 2016, Concurring opinion of Jude Pinto De Albuquerque at para 6.

[104] There may be exceptional cases where in the child's own best interests and for his /her safety he/she is placed for no longer than necessary in a child friendly setting that is secure and can provide the proper level of individual attention and protective and other care (i.e. mental heath services etc.) needed. However detention of a child in an immigration detention facility or other secure custodial facility pending age determination and/or simply and solely to ensure that enforcement of a removal order can be effected cannot be properly legally rationalized under refugee or child rights international law.

[105] Abdullahi Elmi and Aweys Abubakar v Malta, Application No. 25794/13 and 28151/13, ECtHR Chamber Judgment 22 November, 2016) Concurring opinion of Jude Pinto De Albuquerque at para 14.

[106] Abdullahi Elmi and Aweys Abubakar v Malta, Application No. 25794/13 and 28151/13, ECtHR Chamber Judgment 22 November, 2016) Concurring opinion of Jude Pinto De Albuquerque at para 3.

> Asylum-seekers are detained for indefinite or very prolonged periods of time, placed at best in mid-security, special detention centres, at worst in police stations and common prison facilities, but in any event treated as if they were convicted criminals. Some States resort to double-speak such as labelling migration detention centres as "foreigners' admission and accommodation centres", "transit centres" or "guest houses" and detention as "retention"... Detaining someone when there is no prospect of removal to the country of origin is not unusual.[107]

Many States are now engaged in practices directed to undermining and circumventing what it means to be a refugee asylum seeker in order to evade State human rights obligations to that population. It is essential to recall however that:

> A person is a refugee within the meaning of the 1951 Convention as soon as he fulfils the criteria contained in the definition. This would necessarily occur prior to the time at which his refugee status is formally determined. Recognition of his refugee status does not therefore make him a refugee but declares him to be one. ***He does not become a refugee because of recognition, but is recognized because he is a refugee*** (emphasis added).[108]

> Determination of refugee status is a process which takes place in two stages. Firstly, it is necessary to ascertain the relevant facts of the case. Secondly, the definitions in the 1951 Convention and the 1967 Protocol have to be applied to the facts thus ascertained.[109]

One of the collective refugee migration control tactics (applied also to unaccompanied child refugee asylum seekers) in the State repertoire of legally insupportable such strategies, has been, in many instances, not to determine the facts of individual cases or correctly apply the 1951 Refugee Convention/1967 Protocol refugee definitions and criteria (or that of other relevant international protection legal schemes) to those facts in a timely fashion if at all (undue delay being an aspect of the State refugee migration control tactic of choice in the case at bar). Such undue delay in determining the asylum status of unaccompanied child refugees was found essentially to be the pattern and practice in Malta as illustrated by the facts in *Abdullahi Elmi and Aweys Abubakar v Malta*[110] in the relevant time period of that case and as revealed, for instance, in the Human Rights Watch Report *Boat Ride to Detention: Adult and Child Migrants in Malta.*[111] The aforementioned 2012 Human Rights

---

[107] Abdullahi Elmi and Aweys Abubakar v Malta, Application No. 25794/13 and 28151/13, ECtHR Chamber Judgment 22 November, 2016) Concurring opinion of Jude Pinto De Albuquerque at para 4.

[108] UNHCR Handbook and Guidelines on Procedures and Criteria for Determining Refugee Status under the 1951 Convention and the 1967 Protocol Relating to the Status of Refugees (December, 2011 ed.) at para 28.

[109] UNHCR Handbook and Guidelines on Procedures and Criteria for Determining Refugee Status under the 1951 Convention and the 1967 Protocol Relating to the Status of Refugees (December, 2011 ed.) at para 29.

[110] Abdullahi Elmi and Aweys Abubakar v Malta, Application No. 25794/13 and 28151/13, ECtHR Chamber Judgment 22 November, 2016).

[111] Human Rights Watch (2012) Boat Ride to Detention: Adult and Child Migrants in Malta https://www.hrw.org/report/2012/07/18/boat-ride-detention/adult-and-child-migrants-malta (Accessed 5 October, 2017).

Watch Report concerning Malta's treatment of asylum seekers generally also specifically addressed the manner in which Malta handled cases of unaccompanied child asylum seekers. Human Rights Watch reported that:

> Malta detains all age-disputed cases pending age determination, and applies a very low *threshold for disputing the age of children.* As a result, children may be detained for weeks or months, despite alternative available facilities. During detention, children are detained with adults, without any accommodation for their young age, and with no access to school. *Once determined to be children—and released to other accommodation—children do not receive adequate legal representation.* ***Under international and European standards, unaccompanied children should never be detained for reasons related to irregular entry, and pending age determination the person claiming to be a child should be treated as such until the determination is complete*** *. . .Malta detains all unaccompanied children whose status as children is in question, pending age determination* (emphasis added).[112]

Malta's violation of the collective and individual rights of unaccompanied child refugee asylum seekers was evidenced by the treatment (including the detention particulars) of the complainants in Abdullahi Elmi and Aweys Abubakar v Malta.[113] These children were automatically detained both before and after the age assessments (that is after confirmations of their child status) were completed. Thus for the period post age assessment; the individualized status of Abdullahi Elmi and Aweys Abubakar[114] as (1) registered asylum seekers (at that point ruled lawfully, as a result, in the country) and as (2) persons found factually to be children did *not* assist them in effectively and efficiently obtaining asylum or being released from their immigration detention in substandard conditions and with adults. This, it would appear, as these children were members of the collective ('unaccompanied child asylum seekers') which the State of Malta sought to dissuade from irregularly entering Malta by boat and to deter from seeking and obtaining asylum in Malta.

The question could reasonably be raised as to whether or not Malta, like many other States, often uses age assessment as a pretext for untoward blanket treatment involving, for instance (1) mandatory immigration detention and undue delay in deciding on the legal status of unaccompanied minors seeking refugee asylum as well as (2) rejection commonly of the children's asylum claims relating to membership in the persecuted social group 'unaccompanied child refugees' (deserving of special protections) by way of denial of the applicants' 'child status'(based on unreliable non-exact and/or scientifically invalid age assessment methods). This in the hopes of also stemming the flow of this specific refugee group/class in part perhaps due to a fear that extending asylum to these unaccompanied children as a humanitarian gesture to a particularly vulnerable group may lead to their applying to

---

[112]Human Rights Watch (2012) Boat Ride to Detention: Adult and Child Migrants in Malta at p. 37 https://www.hrw.org/report/2012/07/18/boat-ride-detention/adult-and-child-migrants-malta Accessed 5 October, 2017.

[113]Abdullahi Elmi and Aweys Abubakar v Malta, Application No. 25794/13 and 28151/13, ECtHR Chamber Judgment 22 November, 2016).

[114]Abdullahi Elmi and Aweys Abubakar v Malta, Application No. 25794/13 and 28151/13, ECtHR Chamber Judgment 22 November, 2016).

be reunited in the asylum State with parents and other close family not yet in that territory.[115]

Thus young children around 12–14, as well as those older but under 18, were having their professed age disputed by the State of Malta and being subjected to formal interviews and frequently medical testing as well while they waited many months for an official age determination process to be completed:

> Malta's trigger for questioning the age individuals claim to be, and thus detaining them, is low: interviewees reported seeing children as young as 12 detained while undergoing age determination procedures.... In practice... the cut-off for those who are "visibly" children is around 12 to 14 years old, with children who appear older presumed to be adults—and detained—until an age determination is carried out.[116]

According to the 2012 Human Rights Watch report often those who professed to be children and may or may not 'visibly' have appeared to be children were not timely provided by the State of Malta with information as to how to legally establish their age and hence their detention for that reason was greatly unduly prolonged.[117] The considerable time that may elapse before medical testing is even done to establish chronological age may add months to the final age estimate made regarding the particular child.[118] Prolonged detention of asylum seeking children and other asylum seekers produces adverse symptoms and it "exacerbates pre-existing symptoms, including mental trauma sustained while fleeing torture or persecution"[119] The children in Malta were often held with adults and at risk of being the victims of violence while in detention and for this and other reasons such detention rose to the level of degrading treatment especially given children's vulnerability.[120] The age determination process in Malta seems to have been a major stumbling block and often an insurmountable hurdle for large numbers of the collective 'unaccompanied

---

[115] Human Rights Watch (2012) Boat Ride to Detention: Adult and Child Migrants in Malta (Summary): "While the number of migrants arriving in Malta is low in absolute terms, Malta now has the highest number of asylum seekers relative to the national population of any country in the industrialized world. Malta, a country of only 400,000 people, received 20.1 asylum seekers per 1,000 inhabitants in the years 2007–2011, whereas France, the EU member state receiving the largest number of asylum seekers in absolute terms in 2011, received about 3 per 1,000."

[116] Human Rights Watch (2012) Boat Ride to Detention: Adult and Child Migrants in Malta at p. 39 https://www.hrw.org/report/2012/07/18/boat-ride-detention/adult-and-child-migrants-malta Accessed 5 October, 2017.

[117] Human Rights Watch (2012) Boat Ride to Detention: Adult and Child Migrants in Malta at p. 40 https://www.hrw.org/report/2012/07/18/boat-ride-detention/adult-and-child-migrants-malta Accessed 5 October, 2017.

[118] Human Rights Watch (2012) Boat Ride to Detention: Adult and Child Migrants in Malta at p. 44 https://www.hrw.org/report/2012/07/18/boat-ride-detention/adult-and-child-migrants-malta Accessed 5 October, 2017.

[119] Human Rights Watch (2012) Boat Ride to Detention: Adult and Child Migrants in Malta at p. 35 (referring to research published in the medical journal Lancet: Keller et al. (2003), pp. 1721–1723.

[120] Human Rights Watch (2012) Boat Ride to Detention: Adult and Child Migrants in Malta at pp. 40–42 https://www.hrw.org/report/2012/07/18/boat-ride-detention/adult-and-child-migrants-malta Accessed 5 October, 2017.

minors' rather than being a pathway to a greater likelihood of the grant of asylum on humanitarian grounds:

> Children lack adequate information about the age determination process (including whether documents are accepted and whether there is an appeal). Some migrants who request an age determination procedure are seemingly ignored: interviewees reported telling authorities they were minors but never receiving age determination. Other children never request an age determination because they lack information on the procedure.[121]

> There is no appeal of the age determination process within AWAS (and while an appeal to the Immigration Appeals Board is possible, it is rarely done), nor is there any clear guidance on whether documents are accepted[122]

> Unaccompanied migrant children in Malta receive little or no legal representation, either in requesting asylum or in challenging detention in age-disputed cases.[123]

Human Rights Watch reported in 2012 that the Maltese "Refugee Commissioner has urged his staff to view children's cases in light of child-specific forms of persecution and appropriate credibility standards."[124] This admonition re the need for child sensitive practices was well warranted given that unaccompanied child asylum seekers arriving in Malta in the time period covered by the Human Rights Watch 2012 report were not uncommonly at high risk as a class of persecution in the form of denial of adequate humanitarian assistance and support due to as mentioned (1) flawed age determinations and/or undue delays in determining age and (2) reliance on detention of children throughout the age determination process and even in some instances into the asylum processing period and even after the child may have been determined to factually be a minor. This though unaccompanied child asylum seekers, according to official Maltese policy, once determined to be children are to be assigned a guardian (who most often is not a lawyer) to safeguard the child's best interests.[125] Human Rights Watch pointed out:

> provision of legal representation to unaccompanied migrant children is . . .necessary to protect the interests of this vulnerable group.[126]

---

[121] Human Rights Watch (2012) Boat Ride to Detention: Adult and Child Migrants in Malta at p. 45 https://www.hrw.org/report/2012/07/18/boat-ride-detention/adult-and-child-migrants-malta Accessed 5 October, 2017.

[122] Human Rights Watch (2012) Boat Ride to Detention: Adult and Child Migrants in Malta at p. 46 https://www.hrw.org/report/2012/07/18/boat-ride-detention/adult-and-child-migrants-malta Accessed 5 October, 2017.

[123] Human Rights Watch (2012) Boat Ride to Detention: Adult and Child Migrants in Malta at p. 46.

[124] Human Rights Watch (2012) Boat Ride to Detention: Adult and Child Migrants in Malta at p. 47 https://www.hrw.org/report/2012/07/18/boat-ride-detention/adult-and-child-migrants-malta Accessed 5 October, 2017.

[125] Human Rights Watch (2012) Boat Ride to Detention: Adult and Child Migrants in Malta at p. 47 https://www.hrw.org/report/2012/07/18/boat-ride-detention/adult-and-child-migrants-malta Accessed 5 October, 2017.

[126] Human Rights Watch (2012) Boat Ride to Detention: Adult and Child Migrants in Malta at p. 48 https://www.hrw.org/report/2012/07/18/boat-ride-detention/adult-and-child-migrants-malta Accessed 5 October, 2017.

The pattern of failing to afford unaccompanied minors seeking asylum legal representation is a recurring pattern also in other States eager to stem the flow of unaccompanied child refugee asylum seekers among others (i.e. the United States).[127] The failure to provide access to legal representation for unaccompanied child asylum seekers especially when the children are in detention violated Malta's obligations under the Convention on the Rights of the Child:

> **Article 37**
> d) Every child deprived of his or her liberty shall have the right to prompt access to legal and other appropriate assistance, as well as the right to challenge the legality of the deprivation of his or her liberty before a court or other competent, independent and impartial authority, and to a prompt decision on any such action.[128]

In fact detention for so-called 'unlawful entry' in search of asylum is contrary to the stipulation of the Refugee Convention where the asylum seeker enters directly from the country in which they are persecuted which is most often interpreted to mean the homeland but may not be restricted to the same.[129] On the analysis here it is clear that 'unaccompanied child refugee asylum seekers' are often persecuted in transit countries such that so-called 'safe third countries' have not necessarily been experienced as such (as in many cases the children have suffered inhuman and/or degrading treatment in the transit State and arbitrary detention as can occur also in the prospective asylum State). The blanket detention of unaccompanied minors who have professed to be minors or visibly are minors is, in addition, contrary to Article 22 of the Convention on the Rights of the Child (CRC) ratified by Malta 30 September, 1990[130]:

> **Article 22**
> 1. States Parties shall take appropriate measures to ensure that a child who is seeking refugee status or who is considered a refugee in accordance with applicable international or domestic law and procedures shall, whether unaccompanied or accompanied by his or her parents or by any other person, receive appropriate protection and humanitarian assistance in the enjoyment of applicable rights set

---

[127] J.E. F.M. V. Lynch United States Federal Court of Appeals for the Ninth District (Decision Filed 20 September, 2016).

[128] Convention on the Rights of the Child, entry into force 2 September 1990.

[129] Article 31 Refugee Convention: "The Contracting States shall not impose penalties, on account of their illegal entry or presence, on refugees who, coming directly from a territory where their life or freedom was threatened in the sense of article 1, enter or are present in their territory without authorization, provided they present themselves without delay to the authorities and show good cause for their illegal entry or presence."

[130] United Nations Treaty Collection Ratifications of the CRC.

forth in the present Convention and in other international human rights or humanitarian instruments to which the said States are Parties.[131]

Human Rights Watch comments:

Maltese laws should allow detention of migrants only in exceptional circumstances, with individualized determinations, and access to procedures to challenge detention.[132]

Clearly individualized assessment of unaccompanied child asylum seekers[133] was, at the time of the case at bar, effectively blocked in Malta, in the first instance, by denial of collective refugee asylum rights through the imposition of blanket detention of all such children (often for unduly long periods supposedly justified by systematic delays in conducting the age determinations needed for asylum processing and with detentions that often continued even after the individual was assessed to be a child and ought to have been released per Maltese immigration law).

4.4.3 Current Situation in Malta, and New EU Agreements Criticized as Violating the Principle of Non-Refoulement

Maltese Interior Minister Carmelo Abela reported at a conference (the 'Lost in Migration' Conference sponsored by Missing Children Europe)[134] that Malta no longer detains unaccompanied child refugees asylum seekers on arrival.[135] Terre des Hommes, however, an international child rights NGO reported in March, 2017 that:

The same day Mr Abela declared how Malta was willing to do more to protect child refugees, national media reported how the current Maltese Council of the EU Presidency was exploring ways of returning migrants and refugees who attempted to enter Europe back to Libya... Malta's claim to have stopped detaining child refugees also does not hold up to scrutiny. UNHCR Malta have stated that a newly created 'initial reception centre' is detaining children for up to 14 days for health screening and to make assessments of their

[131]Convention on the Rights of the Child, entry into force 2 September 1990.

[132]Human Rights Watch (2012) Boat Ride to Detention: Adult and Child Migrants in Malta at p. 49.

[133]Average detention of children interviewed in the Human Right s Watch Report Human Rights Watch (2012) Boat Ride to Detention: Adult and Child Migrants in Malta was 3.4 months.

[134]This was a conference intended to produce recommendations regarding how EU countries (also in collaboration with other countries) could work to prevent children from disappearing when they journey to Europe or within Europe once arrived (if they arrive) in search of asylum.

[135]Terre des Hommes (1 March, 2017) Malta's two-faced treatment of child refugees and migrants http://destination-unknown.org/maltas-two-faced-treatment-of-child-refugees-and-migrants / Accessed 8 October, 2017.

age. The centre was supposed to only detain adults, but is now housing both families and unaccompanied minors too.[136]

UNHCR's progress report on Malta in mid -2016[137] stated that 2015 changes to legislation in Malta prohibited detention of child asylum seekers irregularly arrived except as a last resort and then only with legal grounds and for the shortest time feasible in the circumstance. Notwithstanding the new Maltese legislative prohibition on detention of child asylum seekers irregularly arrived (save in exceptional circumstances), however, Malta set up initial reception centres (IRCs) "where asylum-seekers [are] confined, screened medically, and assessed for release to the community or issuance of a detention order."[138]The UNHCR considers any such Initial Reception Centre as "a place of detention and, thus, has questioned its legality under Maltese law, especially when it comes to children."[139] (One of the IRCs was designated for children and families). The law in Malta permits detaining unaccompanied and separated children as well as families with children up to seven days in an IRC which is a closed facility.[140] The legislative changes also provide for the opportunity of asylum seekers to challenge their detention and afford them free legal assistance and mandatory review of the detention order.[141] UNHCR expressed the following concerns:

> While the revised legislation no longer supports the automatic and mandatory detention of asylum-seekers who have entered Malta in an irregular manner, UNHCR remains concerned with the interpretation of the legal grounds for detention, lack of clarity on the applicability of ATDs [alternatives to detention re placement], and the need to establish safeguards to ensure that detention is always used in proportionality to a legitimate purpose. *Some of the guidelines for immigration authorities contained in the new policy document are not fully in line with well-established international human rights and refugee law standards, and could potentially lead to situations of arbitrary and unlawful detention*(emphasis added).[142]

---

[136]Terre des Hommes (1 March, 2017) Malta's two-faced treatment of child refugees and migrants http://destination-unknown.org/maltas-two-faced-treatment-of-child-refugees-and-migrants/ Accessed 8 October, 2017.

[137]UNHCR Global Strategy: Beyond Detention: Progress under the Global Strategy 2014-2019, mid 2016 (Malta) http://www.unhcr.org/en-us/protection/detention/57b5839b7/malta-progress-report.html Accessed 8 October, 2017.

[138]UNHCR Global Strategy: Beyond Detention: Progress under the Global Strategy 2014–2019, mid 2016 (Malta) at p. 1 http://www.unhcr.org/en-us/protection/detention/57b5839b7/malta-progress-report.html Accessed 8 October, 2017.

[139]UNHCR Global Strategy: Beyond Detention: Progress under the Global Strategy 2014–2019, mid 2016 (Malta) at pp. 1–2 http://www.unhcr.org/en-us/protection/detention/57b5839b7/malta-progress-report.html Accessed 8 October, 2017.

[140]UNHCR Global Strategy: Beyond Detention: Progress under the Global Strategy 2014–2019, mid 2016 (Malta) at p. 1. http://www.unhcr.org/en-us/protection/detention/57b5839b7/malta-progress-report.html Accessed 8 October, 2017.

[141]UNHCR Global Strategy: Beyond Detention: Progress under the Global Strategy 2014–2019, mid 2016 (Malta) at p. 1 http://www.unhcr.org/en-us/protection/detention/57b5839b7/malta-progress-report.html.

[142]UNHCR Global Strategy: Beyond Detention: Progress under the Global Strategy 2014–2019, mid 2016 (Malta) at p. 4 http://www.unhcr.org/en-us/protection/detention/57b5839b7/malta-progress-report.html Accessed 8 October, 2017.

Note that by 2014 irregular boat arrivals to Malta had stopped. There has been a reported increase; however, of regularly arrived asylum seekers to Malta and the latter are detained in the first instance at least in IRCs until a determination is made regarding whether they will be released to the community or further detained in another facility rather than the IRC.[143]

As Human Rights Watch explains:

> The central Mediterranean migration route—typically from Libya to Malta or Italy—is a major entrance point to the EU.[144]

The EU has recently endorsed the closing of borders and Italy has made an agreement to support Libya to block the flow of migrants (through Libya across the Mediterranean) to the EU:

> *ASGI (Association for Juridical Studies on Immigration) asks the Italian government to fully implement the Geneva Convention (and notably the non-refoulement principle)*, the Italian Constitution and, more generally, to fulfill the duty to receive those fleeing wars, persecutions and fundamental rights violations, by revoking the memorandum it just signed with Libya and with other undemocratic African governments, and by suspending financial and military support to third countries governments (including Sudan, Libya, Niger and Nigeria), tasked with violently blocking the refugee flows.
>
> It is necessary to reverse European policies by mainstreaming a political agenda making the right to asylum effective and truly accessible, starting from an effective and broad European resettlement plan for refugees[145] stranded in third countries that cannot adequately ensure their safety (emphasis added).[146]

In essence the EU has begun outsourcing 'collective refugee migration control measures' intended to block refugee asylum seekers from exercising their basic

---

[143]UNHCR Global Strategy: Beyond Detention Progress under the Global Strategy 2014–2019, mid 2016 (Malta) at p. 4 http://www.unhcr.org/en-us/protection/detention/57b5839b7/malta-progress-report.html Accessed 8 October, 2017.

[144]Human Rights Watch (2012) Boat Ride to Detention: Adult and Child Migrants in Malta (Summary) https://www.hrw.org/report/2012/07/18/boat-ride-detention/adult-and-child-migrants-malta Accessed 5 October, 2017.

[145]UNHCR The UN Refugee Agency FAQ about refugee resettlement (February, 2017): "Resettlement under the auspices of the United Nations High Commissioner for Refugees (UNHCR) involves the selection and transfer of refugees from a State in which they have sought protection to a third State that has agreed to admit them - as refugees - with permanent residence status. The status provided by the resettlement State ensures protection against refoulement and provides a resettled refugee and his/her family or dependents with access to civil, political, economic, social and cultural rights similar to those enjoyed by nationals. Resettlement also carries with it the opportunity to eventually become a naturalized citizen of the resettlement country." (at p. 1) 7 http://www.unhcr.org/en-us/protection/resettlement/4ac0873d6/frequently-asked-questions-resettlement.html Accessed 8 October, 2017.

[146]Association for Juridical Studies on Immigration (*Associzione per gli Studi Giurdici sull'Immigrazione*, ASGI), Press Release (6 February 2017) the EU and Italy de facto violate the principle of non-refoulement http://www.statewatch.org/news/2017/feb/it-libya-deal-asgi-pr.htm Accessed 10 October, 2017.

human rights to seek asylum.[147] This under the pretence that these refugee asylum seekers will be blocked in a humane way (setting aside for the moment that the blocking is itself inhumane) and that their indeterminate future (perhaps in lengthy or even indefinite formal detention, or languishing in an overcrowded refugee camp likely posing, in a variety of ways, its own significant dangers to health and safety etc.) somehow counts as meeting their fundamental human right to substantive international protection that ensures respect for their human dignity and their access to basic human rights entitlements.

4.4.4 Further Comment: Collective Refugee Control Measures in Selected Western European States

The negating, in practice, by some States of the status of individual refugee asylum seeker is often linked to denial, in a myriad of ways, of collective refugee rights in international law. For instance; Denmark adopted legislation stipulating, among other things, that authorities could search the asylum seeking refugees' person and belongings and confiscate cash and valuables (though sentimental items such as wedding rings were later exempted after international protest) up to a specified limit to help cover the cost of providing them basic necessities, and delay the wait time for family reunion for recognized refugee asylum seekers from one year to three.[148]

In respect of the delay regarding family reunion the Danish Refugee Council stated that:

> This is "against the right to family life as stated in the European Convention on Human Rights and... inhumane, because the amendments to the rules for family reunification will have huge consequences for refugees coming to Denmark"[149]

Switzerland also has adopted a similar law arguably denigrating the human dignity of *registered* refugee asylum seekers.[150] In such instances the asylum seeker is deprived of basic human rights accorded to the non-refugee with legal status simply due to his/her membership in a persecuted social group (refugee asylum

---

[147]Recall Article 3 (1) of the UN Declaration on Territorial Asylum unanimously adopted by the General Assembly in 1967 [res. 2312 (XXII)].

"No person referred to in Article 1, paragraph 1, [persons seeking protection from persecution] shall be subjected to measures such as rejection at the frontier or, if he has already entered the territory in which he seeks asylum, expulsion or compulsory return to any State where he may be subjected to persecution." EU policy regarding the pushback of asylum seekers by Libya would appear to return refugee asylum seekers to third States where protection from persecution cannot be guaranteed (see UNHCR Note on Non-Refoulement (November, 1997) available at: http://www.refworld.org/docid/438c6d972.html Accessed 8 October 2017.

[148]BBC News Denmark's 'Migrants Confiscation Law' Yields Little Cash 4 November 2016.

[149]Danish Refugee Council cited in BBC News Denmark's 'Migrants Confiscation Law' Yields Little Cash 4 November 2016.

[150]BBC News Migrant crisis: Switzerland defends asset seizure law 15 January, 2016.

seekers) The denial of the collective rights of refugee asylum seekers i.e. codified in the aforementioned Danish and Swedish immigration/asylum law then, in practice, results in the breach of particular basic individual refugee asylum seeker human rights. Judge Pinto De Albuquerque has commented on the plight of refugee asylum seekers in Europe as follows:

> Most worryingly, a practice of commodification and dehumanisation of . . .asylum-seekers in particular is present in some countries. States are either indifferent to or even condone the serious deleterious effects of such a policy on the health or well-being of migrants, causing long-lasting, psychological damage, among other things, especially in the case of children.[151]

The dehumanization of individual refugee asylum seekers (including unaccompanied child refugee asylum seekers) then is often accomplished through a denial of collective refugee rights. The latter is, furthermore, frequently operationalized via, in effect, *blanket* refugee policy and practice approaches without effective particularized thorough assessments of individual refugee asylum cases. These refugee migration control tactics are often unjustifiably rationalized based on nondemocratic domestic immigration statutes and governmental implementation guidelines for the handling of refugee asylum seekers arrived near or at the border without authorization and without proper entry documents or irregularly entered. In the next chapter we will consider constructive refoulement by the U.S. of unaccompanied child refugee asylum seekers from Central America and Mexico as a blanket strategy essentially applied as a collective migration control measure.

Literature, Materials and Cases

Literature

Aleinikoff TA (2003) Protected characteristics and social perceptions: an analysis of the meaning of 'membership of a particular social group'. p 264. Available http://www.refworld.org/docid/470a33b30.html. Accessed 7 Oct 2017

Allain J (2001) The jus cogens nature of non-refoulement. Int J Refug Law 13(4):533–558

Grover S (2014) The Torture of children during armed conflicts: the ICC failure to prosecute and the negation of children's human dignity. Springer, Berlin

Keller AS et al (2003) Mental health of detained asylum seekers. Lancet 362(9397):1721–1723. https://www.hrw.org/report/2012/07/18/boat-ride-detention/adult-and-child-migrants-malta. Accessed 5 Oct 2017

[151] Abdullahi Elmi and Aweys Abubakar v Malta (ECtHR Chamber Judgment 22 November, 2016) Concurring opinion of Jude Pinto De Albuquerque at para 5.

Materials

Association for Juridical Studies on Immigration (*Associzione per gli Studi Giurdici sull'Immigrazione*, ASGI). Press release (6 February 2017) the EU and Italy de facto violate the principle of non-refoulement http://www.statewatch.org/news/2017/feb/it-libya-deal-asgi-pr.htm Accessed 10 October, 2017

BBC News Denmark's 'Migrants Confiscation Law'Yield Little Cash 4 November 2016. http://www.bbc.com/news/world-europe-37871792 (Accessed 3 February, 2017)

BBC News Migrant crisis: Switzerland defends asset seizure law 15 January, 2016. http://www.bbc.com/news/world-europe-35323315 (Accessed 3 February, 2017)

1951 Convention and 1967 Protocol relating to the Status of Refugees. http://www.unhcr.org/en-us/3b66c2aa10 (accessed 30 June, 2017)

Council of Europe (2014) Guide on Article 5 of the Convention: Right to Liberty and Security http://www.echr.coe.int/Documents/Guide_Art_5_ENG.pdf Accessed 5 October, 2017

European Convention on Human Rights (as amended by the provisions of Protocol No. 14 (CETS no. 194) as from its entry into force on 1 June 2010.) original entry into force of the Convention 21 September 1970. http://www.echr.coe.int/Documents/Convention_ENG.pdf (Accessed 21 October, 2016)

Human Rights Watch (2012) Boat Ride to Detention: Adult and Child Migrants in Malta https://www.hrw.org/report/2012/07/18/boat-ride-detention/adult-and-child-migrants-malta (Accessed 5 October, 2017)

International Committee of the Red Cross Commentary on the Additional Protocols of 8 June, 1977. http://www.loc.gov/rr/frd/Military_Law/pdf/Commentary_GC_Protocols.pdf Accessed 5 October, 2017

Terre des Hommes (1 March, 2017) Malta's two-faced treatment of child refugees and migrants http://destination-unknown.org/maltas-two-faced-treatment-of-child-refugees-and-migrants/ Accessed 8 October, 2017

UNHCR (United Nations High Commissioner on Refugees) Global Strategy: Beyond Detention: Progress under the Global Strategy 2014-2019, mid 2016 (Malta) http://www.unhcr.org/en-us/protection/detention/57b5839b7/malta-progress-report.html Accessed 8 October, 2017

UNHCR (2008) Guidelines on Determining the Best Interests of the Child http://www.unhcr.org/4566b16b2.pdf Accessed 7 October, 2017

UNHCR (United Nations High Commissioner on Refugees) (22 December, 2009) Guidelines on international protection: Child Asylum Claims under Articles 1(A)2 and 1(F) of the 1951 Convention and/or 1967 Protocol relating to the Status of Refugees at para 48 http://www.unhcr.org/afr/publications/legal/50ae46309/guidelines-international-protection-8-child-asylum-c Accessed 7 October, 2017

UNHCR (United Nations High Commissioner on Refugees) Handbook and Guidelines on International protection No. 12 (Issued 2 December, 2016) HCR/GIP/16/12 02 at p. 4 Available at https://reliefweb.int/report/world/guidelines-international-protection-no-12 Accessed 4 October, 2017

UNHCR (United Nations High Commissioner on Refugees) Handbook and Guidelines on Procedures and Criteria for Determining Refugee Status under the 1951 Convention and the 1967 Protocol Relating to the Status of Refugees (re-issued December, 2011 ed.) HCR/1P/4/ENG/REV. 3 http://www.refworld.org/docid/4f33c8d92.html (Accessed 4 October, 2017)

UNHCR (United Nations High Commissioner on Refugees) Note on Non-Refoulement (November, 1997) available at: http://www.refworld.org/docid/438c6d972.html Accessed 8 October 2017

UNHCR (United Nations High Commissioner on Refugees) Refugee Children: Guidelines on Protection and Care (preface) (1988) http://www.unhcr.org/protect/PROTECTION/3b84c6c67.pdf (Accessed 4 October, 2017)

UNHCR The UN, Refugee Agency: FAQ about refugee resettlement (February, 2017) http://www.unhcr.org/en-us/protection/resettlement/4ac0873d6/frequently-asked-questions-resettlement.html Accessed 8 October, 2017

United Nations Treaty Collection.: Ratification of the Convention on the Rights of the Child https://treaties.un.org/Pages/ViewDetails.aspx?src=IND&mtdsg_no=IV-11&chapter=4&clang=_en (Accessed 15 February, 2017)

Cases

AA v [UK] Secretary of State for the Home Department, High Court of Justice, Queens Bench (Administrative Court), Strand, London (Case No: CO/920/2015) [2016] EWHC 1453 (Admin) (Decision date:20 June, 2016) http://www.asylumlawdatabase.eu/en/case-law/uk-queen-application-aa-v-secretary-state-home-department-interested-party-wolverhampton Accessed 1 February, 2018

Abdullahi Elmi and Aweys Abubakar v Malta, (Application No. 25794/13 and 28151/13) European Court of Human Rights Chamber Judgment 22 November, 2016

Andrews *v*. Law Society of British Columbia [1989] 1 SCR 143

Chan v Canada (Minister of Employment and Immigration) [1995] 3 S.C.R. (Dissenting Opinion La Forest, L'Heureux-Dube and Gothier, JJ

R(A) v Croydon [2009] 1 WLR 2557

United States v Aguilar 883 F.2d 662 (U.S. Court of Appeals Ninth Circuit) Decided March 30, 1989. As amended on Denial of Rehearing and Rehearing En Banc April 14, 1989 http://openjurist.org/883/f2d/662/united-states-v-aguilar (accessed 25 June, 2017)

Chapter 5
Child Refugees and Recent U.S. Migration Control Strategies

5.1 Unaccompanied Child Refugee Asylum Seekers from Central America and Mexico

5.1.1 Child Victims of Political or Gang Violence as Convention Refugees

Next we will consider 'constructive refoulement'[1] (or arguably refoulement proper in the ordinary sense) by the United States and Mexico of unaccompanied child refugee asylum seekers from Central America in violation of the Refugee Convention non-refoulement principle. It is here argued that a strategy of, in effect, virtual blanket return of an identifiable class of persons-here unaccompanied minors of Central American national origin (whether the children had already entered the U.S. and then were removed, or were at the Mexican-U.S. border and turned back or whether instead blocked by extraterritorial measures) violates Mexico's and the United States' special protection obligations in regards to 'unaccompanied child refugee asylum seekers' and in regards to the non-refoulement obligation more generally. This is the case as these children for the most part, if not in every case, face political and other violence (i.e. gang violence) in their home country.[2] The UNHCR has held also gang violence adequate to recognize these children as refugees under the Refugee Convention:

---

[1]Amnesty International Public Statement (24 July, 2015) Index: ASA 23/2157/2015 Cambodia and the question of voluntariness: "International law prohibits "constructive" refoulement, which occurs when states use indirect means to carry out refoulement… it follows directly from the principle of non-refoulement: the involuntary return of refugees would in practice amount to refoulement" at p. 1 https://www.amnesty.org/download/Documents/ASA2321572015ENGLISH.pdf Accessed 14 October, 2017.

[2]In *Henriquez-Rivas v. Holder*, 707 F.3d 1081 (9th Circ. 2013) (en banc) a child from El Slavador was granted asylum in the U.S. after testifying in the prosecution of gang members who had murdered her father.

© Springer International Publishing AG, part of Springer Nature 2018

S. C. Grover, *Child Refugee Asylum as a Basic Human Right*,
https://doi.org/10.1007/978-3-319-78013-9_5

> At this particular time, UNHCR is aware of and has worked to understand the increasing numbers of unaccompanied and separated children arriving in the United States from Central America. Recognizing that many of these children are in need of international protection, *UNHCR has taken the view that the refugee definition, found in Article 1 of the 1951 Convention relating to the Status of Refugees and Article 1 of the 1967 Protocol relating to the Status of Refugees, should be read to encompass claims from Central American children fleeing gang recruitment and/or gang related harms* (emphasis added).[3]

These children are too often being 'returned' to the home State without having had the opportunity with adequate support to effectively make an asylum claim and/or have it considered fairly and impartially on its individual merits with due consideration of child-specific forms of persecution.

> Globally, the protection of children is a core priority for UNHCR. The international community has long recognized both the right of children to seek asylum and their inherent vulnerability. *Children also face specific forms of persecution that may give rise to a claim for refugee status* (emphasis added).[4]

The UNHCR designates unaccompanied child refugees as a particularly vulnerable group in need of asylum protection and resettlement[5] as they fall into several refugee high risk/vulnerability categories.[6] The vulnerability criteria used by the UNHCR are as follows: 'Legal and/or Physical Protection Needs', 'Survivors of Torture and/or Violence', 'Medical Needs', 'Women and Girls at Risk', 'Family Reunification', 'Children and Adolescents at Risk', and 'Lack of Foreseeable Alternative Durable Solutions'. Unaccompanied children fleeing persecution in Central America and in Mexico do fall into several of the UNHCR refugee vulnerability categories including but not limited to being 'a child or adolescent at risk' and being 'survivors of violence'.

The U.S and Mexico are amongst the State Parties to the Refugee Convention and its 1967 Protocol and hence support the UNHCR overseeing international refugee protection. These States, as a corollary, then must also accept, as per the implications

---

[3]United Nations High Commissioner on Refugees (November, 2016) UNHCR (Asylum Lawyers' Project) UNHCR's Views on Child Asylum Claims: Using international law to support claims from Central American children seeking protection in the US at p. 1 http://www.unhcr.org/582226064.pdf Accessed 10 October, 2017.

[4]Hansford, B and Dobbs, L for UNHCR 'UNHCR calls on the Americas to keep children on the run safe from violence' (12 March, 2014) http://www.unhcr.org/en-us/news/latest/2014/3/53206a3d9/unhcr-calls-americas-keep-children-run-safe-violence.html (accessed 25 June, 2017).

Child specific forms of persecution are varied and include but are not limited to child soldiering, child trafficking, female genital mutilation, child slave labor, gang recruitment and targeting for gang violence etc.

[5]Resettlement in a third country is one possible durable solution if the asylum country itself, while providing temporary protection, has not agreed to recognize the child as a refugee who will be integrated fully into the community and eventually have permanent residence status on some legal basis.

[6]UNHCR Resettlements Submission Categories http://www.unhcr.org/558bff849.pdf Accessed 10 October, 2017 (see also UNHCR The UN, Refugee Agency: FAQ about refugee resettlement (February, 2017) at p. 4 http://www.unhcr.org/en-us/protection/resettlement/4ac0873d6/frequently-asked-questions-resettlement.html Accessed 8 October, 2017.

of the Refugee Convention setting out the UNHCR's special role in international refugee protection, the UNHCR's designation of categories of especially vulnerable refugees i.e. 'children and adolescents at risk'. This UNHCR high vulnerability classification applicable to unaccompanied child refugees then, on the analysis here, highlights the State's pressing obligation regarding the protection of members of that particular refugee asylum seeking group and in terms of the State ensuring that refoulement by any direct or indirect means does not occur under its authority.

The UNHCR has grave concerns for unaccompanied children from Central America seeking safe haven (refuge) in Mexico or in the United States, the risks they undertake in making the journey and the probability of refoulement by some means. The UNHCR sought in 2014 to have Mexico and the United States consider as refugee asylum seekers unaccompanied children from Central America[7] fleeing political violence as well as criminal gang violence in Central America. In regard to unaccompanied child asylum seekers from Central America as Convention refugees consider that:

> *Any of the Convention grounds may be applicable to children fleeing areas affected by gangs. For example, child asylum-seekers who resist gang recruitment or oppose gang practices may be seen as articulating a political opinion, or their resistance may be a manifestation of religious conviction.* Thus, persecution in such settings might effectively be linked to religion or political opinion, actual or imputed. A large number of these claims fall under the "*particular social group*" ground… (emphasis added)[8]
>
> In UNHCR's view, children fleeing harms related to gangs may base their claims on membership in a particular social group, either through the "protected or immutable characteristic" or the "social perception" standard[9]. …Although gang-related violence may be widespread and affect large segments of society, distinct groups have been specifically targeted because of certain shared characteristics such as their youth, gender, marginalization in society, lack of protection or other factors that make them more vulnerable[10]

[7] Lee, E. Y. H. (Immigration Reporter at Think Progress) UN officials seek refugee label for kids coming into America alone, 8 June, 2014 https://thinkprogress.org/u-n-officials-seek-refugee-label-for-kids-coming-into-america-alone-277764f84b7d Accessed 25 June, 2017.

[8] United Nations High Commissioner on Refugees (November, 2016) UNHCR (Asylum Lawyers' Project) UNHCR's Views on Child Asylum Claims: Using international law to support claims from Central American children seeking protection in the US at p. 7 http://www.unhcr.org/582226064.pdf Accessed 10 October, 2017.

[9] United Nations High Commissioner on Refugees (November, 2016) UNHCR (Asylum Lawyers' Project) UNHCR's Views on Child Asylum Claims: Using international law to support claims from Central American children seeking protection in the US at p. 7 http://www.unhcr.org/582226064.pdf Accessed 10 October, 2017.

[10] United Nations High Commissioner on Refugees (November, 2016) UNHCR (Asylum Lawyers' Project) UNHCR's Views on Child Asylum Claims: Using international law to support claims from Central American children seeking protection in the US at p. 8 http://www.unhcr.org/582226064.pdf Accessed 10 October, 2017.

> *Accordingly, youth who are targeted for recruitment may be set apart in society and recognized as a particular social group because of their age, vulnerability, social background or class* (emphasis added)[11]

It would appear, however, that often the independent right of 'unaccompanied child refugees' to asylum is not recognized (either collectively based on recognition of a *prima facie* Convention refugee 'particular social group' nor in respect of acknowledgement of the actual *bona fide* refugee status of individual child group members where the latter should apply per the Refugee Convention eligibility criteria). This is especially the case; it would appear, when the child refugees are fleeing political or gang violence. The reason for this reluctance in recognizing as refugees unaccompanied children fleeing political and/or gang violence is in part perhaps due to the fact that children are erroneously often viewed as excluded as specific particularized targets of political persecution or gang violence. This even though children may in fact be so targeted precisely because they are vulnerable as children. As the current author has discussed previously; children are often a prized target for those using violence to seek a political or socio-political objective. This given the terror that ensues when children are the intended victims of extreme violence[12] as is evidenced for instance in the NGO-suspected Assad regime's precise targeting also of children with chemical weapons and by other means; children whose parents may or may not have been part of the civilian opposition to the regime.[13]

In addition children may be at risk of targeted violence in instances also due to their own resistance, where it occurs, to involvement in gang or in politically motivated State or non-State violence or in opposition to authoritarian rule. In regards to the latter it is apparent that youth and even young children under 12 are not then necessarily always apolitical. As discussed in the UNHCR Asylum Lawyers' Project, a child, for instance, who resists gang recruitment or is an informant on the gang or witness in a prosecution of gang members can be considered to be expressing a political opinion.[14] At the same time; it should be recognized that there is no precise delimitation in UNHCR guidelines as to what constitutes 'persecution' generally. Hence children

[11]United Nations High Commissioner on Refugees (November, 2016) UNHCR (Asylum Lawyers' Project) UNHCR's Views on Child Asylum Claims: Using international law to support claims from Central American children seeking protection in the US at p. 9 http://www.unhcr.org/582226064.pdf Accessed 10 October, 2017.

[12]Grover (2014).

[13]Grover (2015), pp. 1112–1128. See also Amnesty International Report 2017/2018: The State of the World's Human Rights (Violations by Syrian Forces and Allies...) at p. 351.

[14]United Nations High Commissioner on Refugees (November, 2016) UNHCR (Asylum Lawyers' Project) UNHCR's Views on Child Asylum Claims: Using international law to support claims from Central American children seeking protection in the US at p. 7 http://www.unhcr.org/582226064.pdf Accessed 10 October, 2017.

targeted for violence other than gang violence or political violence and for reasons other than to send a terror message to the political opposition may potentially also qualify as victims of persecution[15] depending on the particular fact pattern:

> There is no universally accepted definition of "persecution", and various attempts to formulate such a definition have met with little success. From Article 33 of the 1951 Convention, it may be inferred that a *threat to life or freedom* on account of race, religion, nationality, political opinion or membership of a particular social group is always persecution. *Other serious violations of human rights – for the same reasons – would also constitute persecution* (emphasis added).
>
> Whether other prejudicial actions or threats would amount to persecution will depend on the circumstances of each case...
>
> In addition, an applicant may have been subjected to various measures not in themselves amounting to persecution..., in some cases combined with other adverse factors (e.g. general atmosphere of insecurity in the country of origin). In such situations, the various elements involved may, if taken together, produce an effect on the mind of the applicant that can reasonably justify a claim to well-founded fear of persecution on "cumulative grounds[16]

It would appear that unaccompanied children fleeing extreme poverty, gang and political violence in their home State located in Central America (and in some instances also child abuse) may well and properly meet the criterion of the Refugee Convention of being persecuted (i.e. as the result of the cumulative effect of a variety of adverse factors and/or being targeted for political or gang violence).[17] They may have been so targeted for victimization precisely because they belong to a specified social group one, for instance, defined by young age and or gender. Unlike a purely economic migrant[18] who leaves his/her home country voluntarily with the prime objective of a better economic personal situation; these child refugees (very often unaccompanied) from Central America and Mexico are generally in such extreme fear for their safety and often their lives should they remain in their home country that they feel they must flee to survive. Though they know they might be abducted along the

[15]For instance children may be considered as persecuted in Refugee Convention terms where they are targeted as children for certain traditional practices that may be deemed to be violent and/or an infringement on the security of the person that violates the basic human dignity of the child and his/her right to be protected from violence and sexual exploitation (*bacha bazi* in Afghanistan where the boys may, in many instances, be sexually violated by adult males).

[16]UNHCR Handbook of Procedures and Criteria for Determining Refugee Status under the 1951 Convention and 1967 Protocol Relating to the Status of Refugees paras 51–53 (reedited January, 1992).

[17]See also Inter-American Commission on Human Rights (11 November, 2015): Violence, children and organized crime Available at http://www.oas.org/en/iachr/reports/pdfs/violencechildren2016.pdf Accessed 24 October, 2017.

[18]See UNHCR Handbook of Procedures and Criteria for Determining Refugee Status under the 1951 Convention and 1967 Protocol Relating to the Status of Refugees paras 51–53 (reedited January, 1992) at para 62.

way in their search for refugee asylum and/or attacked sexually or otherwise on that difficult journey, they also know that the risks of victimization by violence is an almost certainty should they stay in the home country.

In the next section we consider the commonplace violations of the principles of due process that occur in many States in respect of considering unaccompanied child refugee requests for asylum and/or regularized legal status. We will focus, in particular, on the frequently occurring and widespread lack of legal assistance/support afforded unaccompanied child refugee asylum seekers (which often occurs at every stage from initial formal asylum request to proceedings including any immigration/asylum tribunal appeal or other court proceedings i.e. regarding removal (deportation) orders. In this regard we will consider an illustrative leading American case *J.E. F.M. v. Lynch* (United States Federal Court of Appeals for the Ninth District (Decision 20 September, 2016)).[19] That case involved a class action suit regarding the fact that most unaccompanied child refugee asylum seekers in the United States must face federal immigration hearings alone without a legal representative to argue their refugee asylum case in court this thus infringing the children's due process right and significantly diminishing the possibility that the child asylum seekers will defeat their deportation order.[20] It should be understood, however, as mentioned, that the lack of legal support occurs for unaccompanied child refugees in many States and in many forms. In the UK, for instance, significant barriers exist for some unaccompanied child refugees in obtaining the legal aid necessary to hire counsel expert in the refugee field who could assist them in potentially regularizing their status.[21]

---

[19]J.E. F.M. v. Lynch United States Federal Court of Appeals for the Ninth District No. 15-35738 and 15-35739 (Decision 20 September, 2016) https://cdn.ca9.uscourts.gov/datastore/opinions/2016/09/20/15-35738.pdf Accessed 10 October, 2017.

[20]Kids in Need of Defense (KIND) (an NGO founded by Angelina Jolie and Microsoft Corporation to assist unaccompanied children) https://supportkind.org/wp-content/uploads/2017/06/General-KIND-Fact-sheet_June-2017.pdf 12 October, 2017.

[21]Connolly, H, Crellin, R, and Parhar, R (Research Report, August 2017) An update to 'Cut Off From Justice': The impact of excluding migrant and separated children from legal aid (University of Bedfordshire and The Children's Society) Available at https://www.basw.co.uk/resource/?id=6736 Accessed 12 October, 2017 (Note that under the UK Legal Aid, Punishment and Sentencing of Offenders Act 2012 (LASPO) that entered into force in 2013; children requesting asylum or who have been trafficked would be eligible for legal aid but children who have been granted temporary leave to stay in the UK would *not* be eligible for legal aid (that is they would be ineligible for funding for legal assistance in attempting to regularize their legal status so that they can stay indefinitely in the UK)).

5.1.2 Denial of Legal Assistance to Child Refugee Asylum Seekers (a Violation of CRC Article 12)

The UNHCR's view of child *bona fide* refugee asylum seekers is simultaneously that they are (1) highly vulnerable children[22] in urgent need of international protection[23] (especially when they are unaccompanied)[24] but also (2) children with their own agency who must be supported (i.e. through legal representation acting on their behalf etc.) in exercising their basic human right in this context to *active participation* in their refugee asylum process.[25]

> 8.3 Not being legally independent, an asylum-seeking child should be represented by an adult who is familiar with the child's background and who would prow his/her interests. *Access should-also be given to a qualified legal representative.* This principle should apply to all children, including those between sixteen and eighteen, even where application for refugee status is processed under the normal procedures for adults.[26]

Appropriate legal standards in State processing of child refugee asylum applications, according to the UNHCR, thus must include, among other things, due consideration of and respect for child participation rights (as per Article 12 of the *Convention on the Rights of the Child* (CRC)) as well as for the other applicable child rights articulated in the CRC.[27] Note further that the *Convention on the Rights*

---

[22]The Vulnerability Screening Tool: Identifying and Addressing Vulnerability: A Tool for Migration and Asylum Systems at p. 1 http://www.refworld.org/pdfid/57f21f6b4.pdf Accessed 10 October, 2017.

[23]UNHCR Conclusion on Children at Risk (2007): Conclusion on Children at Risk (2007), No. 107 (LVIII) Executive Committee 56th session. Contained in United Nations General Assembly document A/AC.96/1048 http://www.unhcr.org/en-us/excom/exconc/4717625c2/conclusion-children-risk.html Accessed 30 June, 2017.

[24]UNHCR (2009) Guidelines on International Protection: Child Asylum Claims under Articles 1 (A)2 and 1(F) of the 1951 Convention and/or 1967 Protocol relating to the Status of Refugees http://www.unhcr.org/afr/publications/legal/50ae46309/guidelines-international-protection-8-child-asylum-claims-under-articles.html Accessed 10 October, 2017.

[25]UNHCR (2012) A Framework for the Protection of Children at p. 22 Children http://www.unhcr.org/en-us/protection/children/50f6cf0b9/framework-protection-children.html Accessed 10 October, 2017.

[26]UN High Commissioner for Refugees (UNHCR), Guidelines on Policies and Procedures in Dealing with Unaccompanied Children Seeking Asylum, February 1997, available at: http://www.refworld.org/docid/3ae6b3360.html Accessed 11 October 2017.

[27]Convention on the Rights of the Child, entered into force 2 September, 1990, http://www.ohchr.org/EN/ProfessionalInterest/Pages/CRC.aspx Accessed 30 June, 2017.

Article 12:

> 1. States Parties shall assure to the child who is capable of forming his or her own views the right to express those views freely in all matters affecting the child, the views of the child being given due weight in accordance with the age and maturity of the child.
>
> 2. For this purpose, the child shall in particular be provided the opportunity to be heard in any judicial and administrative proceedings affecting the child, either directly, or through a representative or an appropriate body, in a manner consistent with the procedural rules of national law.

of the Child at Article 22 stipulates that all applicable CRC rights are to be afforded child refugees whether they are accompanied or unaccompanied.[28] However, States Parties to the 1951 Refugee Convention and its 1967 Protocol have commonly denied unaccompanied child asylum seekers, through various direct and indirect means, their right to active informed participation in their own refugee asylum process or in any other applicable international protection scheme.[29] The unaccompanied child's lack of meaningful participation in refugee asylum proceedings is also perhaps reflective of a certain pre-existing bias in regards to asylum claims brought by these children as children:

> Although the definition of a refugee contained in Article 1(A)2 of the 1951 Convention relating to the Status of Refugees and its 1967 Protocol (hereafter "1951 Convention" and "1967 Protocol") applies to all individuals regardless of their age, it has traditionally been interpreted in light of adult experiences. *This has meant that many refugee claims made by children have been assessed incorrectly or overlooked altogether* (emphasis added).[30]

---

[28]Convention on the Rights of the Child, entered into force 2 September, 1990, http://www.ohchr.org/EN/ProfessionalInterest/Pages/CRC.aspx Accessed 12 October, 2017.

Article 22:

> 1. States Parties shall take appropriate measures to ensure that a child who is seeking refugee status or who is considered a refugee in accordance with applicable international or domestic law and procedures shall, *whether unaccompanied or accompanied* by his or her parents or by any other person, receive appropriate protection and humanitarian assistance in the enjoyment of applicable rights set forth in the present Convention and in other international human rights or humanitarian instruments to which the said States are Parties.
>
> 2. For this purpose, States Parties shall provide, as they consider appropriate, co-operation in any efforts by the United Nations and other competent intergovernmental organizations or non-governmental organizations co-operating with the United Nations to protect and assist such a child and to trace the parents or other members of the family of any refugee child in order to obtain information necessary for reunification with his or her family. In cases where no parents or other members of the family can be found, the child shall be accorded the same protection as any other child permanently or temporarily deprived of his or her family environment for any reason, as set forth in the present Convention (emphasis added). http://www.ohchr.org/EN/ProfessionalInterest/Pages/CRC.aspx Accessed 30 June, 2017.

[29]In the two cases discussed previously in chapter four; child asylum seekers effectively had no chance to be heard i.e. in Case 1:*AA v [UK] Secretary of State for the Home Department* High Court of Justice, Queens Bench (Administrative Court), Case No: CO/920/2015 [2016] EWHC 1453 (Admin) the child refugee was by virtue of an immigration officer's belief or impression detained and then kept in detention even after child status was established by objective evidence (the Court held that the UK Home Secretary did not do a careful review which would at that point have properly allowed for release of the child from detention) while in Case 2: *Abdullahi Elmi and Aweys Abubakar v Malta, (*Application No. 25794/13 and 28151/13) the European Court of Human Rights Chamber Judgment 22 November, 2016; the two child refugee asylum seekers were subjected to mandatory detention which did not end even after it was determined they were children and they had no effective opportunity to have their detention order reviewed by an immigration appeal board.

[30]UNHCR Guidelines on International Protection: Child Asylum Claims under Articles 1(A)2 and 1(F) of the 1951 Convention and/or 1967 Protocol relating to the Status of Refugees, 22 December 2009 at p. 3, point 1 http://www.refworld.org/pdfid/4b2f4f6d2.pdf Accessed 7 October, 2017.

The violation of child refugee asylum rights then is in contravention, for instance, to selected principles set out by the Executive Committee of the UNHCR in its 2007 Conclusion respecting State obligations in the treatment to be accorded children at high risk including child refugee asylum seekers:

> The (UNHCR) Executive Committee
>
> *Recognizes* that strategies and actions under this operational guidance should be underpinned by the following principles and approaches, amongst others:
>
> States, UNHCR, and other relevant agencies and partners shall assure to the child who is capable of forming his or her own views the right to express those views freely in all matters affecting the child, the views of the child being *given due weight* in accordance with the age and maturity of the child, and that mechanisms exist to inform children and adults alike of children's rights and options...
>
> *A rights-based approach, which recognizes children as active subjects of rights...*
>
> *Facilitate access to administrative or judicial procedures of States that are in accordance with their international obligations* ...(emphasis added)[31]

Rather child refugee asylum seekers are often, by State design, but passive 'participants' in the asylum process without adequate counselling and little if any legal support provided by the prospective asylum State.[32] Without legal support it is unlikely that for most unaccompanied child asylum seekers their voices are properly heard and their evidence correctly weighted at immigration proceedings including deportation hearings. The latter issue is addressed in the class action case *J.E. F.M. v. Lynch*, United States Federal Court of Appeals for the Ninth District (Decision 20 September, 2016) discussed next.[33] The case concerns the thousands of children arrived irregularly to the United States, mostly from Central America and Mexico, who often must appear at immigration deportation hearings without legal representation given the limited such support the U.S. government provides to these children.

[31]UNHCR (United Nations High Commissioner on Refugees) Conclusion on Children at Risk (2007), No. 107 (LVIII) Executive Committee 56th session. Contained in United Nations General Assembly document A/AC.96/1048 http://www.unhcr.org/en-us/excom/exconc/4717625c2/conclusion-children-risk.html Accessed 30 June, 2017.

[32]Note that "children may have independent claims to refugee status" (i.e. based on child-specific persecution etc.) apart from the claims-meritorious or not-of persons accompanying them (See United Nations High Commissioner on Refugees (November, 2016) (UNHCR Asylum Lawyers' Project) UNHCR's Views on Child Asylum Claims: Using international law to support claims from Central American children seeking protection in the US at p. 2 http://www.unhcr.org/582226064.pdf Accessed 10 October, 2017).

[33]J.E. F.M. v. Lynch, United States Federal Court of Appeals for the Ninth District (Decision 20 September, 2016) https://cdn.ca9.uscourts.gov/datastore/opinions/2016/09/20/15-35738.pdf Accessed 10 October, 2017.

5.1.3 Case 1: J.E. F.M. v. Lynch (U.S. Attorney General) et al., *United States Federal Court of Appeals for the Ninth District*

5.1.3.1 The Facts

A group of indigent children aged 3–17 were in U.S. deportation proceedings; some in the early stages of the process; some at more advanced stages. The children, in addition, had significant English language barriers and/or faced other challenges in bringing 'right-to-counsel' claims and defending against the U.S. government's intention to deport them. The children brought a class action in U.S. District Federal Court and then in the Federal Court of Appeals against the U.S. Attorney General and various other relevant government officials regarding the claimants' (and other similarly situated children's) lack of access to *pro bono* legal assistance funded by the U.S. government. The children argued that the procedures set out under U.S. immigration statutory procedures (Petition for Review; known as the 'PFR process') regarding making out a 'right-to-counsel' claim infringed the *U.S. Immigration and Nationality Act* and blocked them from receiving "a full and fair opportunity to identify defenses or seek relief for which they qualify".[34]

> The complex PFR Process requires a relevant minor without counsel to: (i) appear before immigration judges without lawyers; (ii) petition an immigration judge for an attorney; (iii) appeal the denial of such petition to the Board of Immigration Appeals; and (iv) file a petition for review of a final removal order with a *federal* ***appellate*** *court* in order to make a right-to-counsel claim (emphasis added).[35]

The children petitioned the District Federal Court to rule that indigent children in their position, facing deportation and unable to obtain *pro bono* counsel on their own, be permitted by law to make out their claim of 'right-to-to counsel' directly in the District Federal Court thus *bypassing* the hurdle of the complex aforementioned statutory process before an immigration judge and the Board of Immigration Appeals and, if unsuccessful, then having to await a final removal order before having access only to a Federal Court of Appeals to advance an appeal (regarding the defeated right-to-counsel claim and an appeal of the deportation final removal order; both orders having been issued in the prior immigration proceedings outside the federal court system). The child petitioners were ultimately unsuccessful at the U.S. Federal Court of Appeals in their petition for indigent children to be able to have direct access to the lower federal courts regarding right to court-appointed counsel claims for indigent children involved in deportation proceedings.

---

[34]J.E. F.M. v. Lynch (US Attorney General) et al., United States Federal Court of Appeals for the Ninth District (Decision 20 September, 2016), Case Summary (Children's Rights International Network) https://www.crin.org/en/library/legal-database/je-fm-v-lynch Accessed 1 February, 2018.

[35]J.E. F.M. v. Lynch, (US Attorney General) et al., United States Federal Court of Appeals for the Ninth District (Decision 20 September, 2016) Case Summary (Children's Rights International Network) https://www.crin.org/en/library/legal-database/je-fm-v-lynch Accessed 1 February, 2018.

5.1.3.2 The Federal Court of Appeals' Assessment (Appeal from the U.S. Federal District Court for the Western District of Washington)

The Federal Court of Appeals in *J.E. F.M. v. Lynch (US Attorney General) et al.* addressed the key questions below as follows:

Substantive Question: Do Indigent Children Have a Right to Counsel in Immigration Proceedings Under the U.S. INA Act (Immigration and Naturalization Act)?[36]

This case involved a class action suit brought by a group of indigent minors in the U.S. courts "alleging that they have due process and statutory rights to appointed counsel at [U.S.] government expense in immigration proceedings."[37] The children thus were *in part* advancing due process constitutional claims. The Federal Court of Appeals for the Ninth District upheld the decision of the District Court to dismiss the minor's class action lawsuit in which the children claimed (in part) a constitutional right to court-appointed counsel at government expense for their immigration hearings. The Federal Court of Appeals dismissal relied upon alleged jurisdictional grounds and left the merits of the children's case undecided.[38]

The Court of Appeal held that the children's claim for appointed counsel arose directly out of the removal proceedings and therefore was covered by a particular statute.[39] Further the Appeal Court held that the particular statute in question (the INA (U.S. Immigration and Naturalization Act) requires exhaustion of the immigration procedure and allowed for petition for review only by a Federal Court of Appeals and then if and only when a final deportation (removal) order had been issued at the end of the completed immigration proceedings. There was also under the statute, according to the Federal Court of Appeals, no recourse to a District Federal Court; that is judicial review was available only through the appeals court (Federal Appeal Court system). The Federal Court of Appeals thus was to be the

[36]All references (in the context of this case) to 'the statute' (or statute as amended) refer to the U.S. Immigration and Naturalization Act and the process it sets out for review of deportation orders including the Act's stipulations regarding the exclusive jurisdiction (once the immigration proceedings have been exhausted) of the Federal Courts of Appeals to consider judicial review of a final deportation order.

[37]J.E. F.M. v. Lynch (US Attorney General) et al., United States Federal Court of Appeals for the Ninth District (Decision 20 September, 2016) at p. 3 (Summary) https://cdn.ca9.uscourts.gov/datastore/opinions/2016/09/20/15-35738.pdf Accessed 10 October, 2017.

[38]J.E. F.M. v. Lynch (US Attorney General) et al., United States Federal Court of Appeals for the Ninth District (Decision 20 September, 2016) at p. 6: Opinion: "We underscore that we address only the jurisdictional issue, not the merits of the claims." https://cdn.ca9.uscourts.gov/datastore/opinions/2016/09/20/15-35738.pdf Accessed 10 October, 2017.

[39]8 U.S.C. §§ 1252(b)(9) and 1252(a)(5).

final arbiter of all factual and legal questions "including interpretation and application of constitutional and statutory provisions, arising from any action taken or proceeding brought to remove an alien from the United States"[40] The children in the case at bar did not in fact challenge the INA statute as applied in all cases but rather its alleged unconstitutional interpretation and application in the case of unrepresented indigent minors:

> The minors do not seriously dispute that the plain text of § 1252(b)(9) prohibits them from filing a complaint in federal district court. Instead, they attempt to get around the statute by claiming that they have been (or will be) denied meaningful judicial review in light of their juvenile status. In other words, they argue that § 1252(b)(9), as applied in this context, creates a Catch-22 that effectively bars all judicial review of their claims.[41]

Jurisdictional Question: Does a U.S. District Court Have Jurisdiction to Hear Right-to-Counsel Constitutional Claims Brought by Indigent Minors Denied Legal Assistance in Immigration Proceedings?

In the case at bar the Federal Court of Appeals *reversed* the District Court finding that the issue of whether the children (indigent unaccompanied minors) were constitutionally entitled to court-appointed counsel in their immigration proceedings was a matter collateral to the removal proceedings and therefore fell under the review jurisdiction of the District Court:

> the [District] court explained that the due process claims challenged a procedure or policy collateral to the substance of removal proceedings and, in light of the fact that "an immigration judge is unlikely to conduct the requisite [due process] balancing, the administrative record would be insufficient to provide a basis for meaningful judicial review."[42]

The District Federal Court set out that the contrary view (which it had *not* adopted) as being that it had no jurisdiction (over the children's due process right-to-counsel claims) as being grounded on the following *untenable* presumptions; namely that: (1) there was no need to balance the children's constitutional right to due process versus State interests which may be in conflict with that right and (2) the court need not concern itself with the risk of an inadequate judicial record for review (due to the children not having had legal representation during the removal

---

[40] J.E. F.M. v. Lynch (US Attorney General) et al., United States Federal Court of Appeals for the Ninth District (Decision 20 September, 2016) at p. 10 https://cdn.ca9.uscourts.gov/datastore/opinions/2016/09/20/15-35738.pdf Accessed 10 October, 2017.

[41] J.E. F.M. v. Lynch (US Attorney General) et al., United States Federal Court of Appeals for the Ninth District (Decision 20 September, 2016) at p. 18 https://cdn.ca9.uscourts.gov/datastore/opinions/2016/09/20/15-35738.pdf Accessed 10 October, 2017.

[42] J.E. F.M. v. Lynch (US Attorney General) et al., United States Federal Court of Appeals for the Ninth District (Decision 20 September, 2016) at p. 9 https://cdn.ca9.uscourts.gov/datastore/opinions/2016/09/20/15-35738.pdf Accessed 10 October, 2017.

proceedings) as any such concerns were unwarranted.[43] In essence such a contrary view negates the fact that foreign aliens irregularly in the United States-whether undocumented immigrants or refugees-have a constitutional right to due process in immigration proceedings. The government filed an interlocutory appeal to the District Federal Court's decision to assume jurisdiction over the case

The Federal Court of Appeals rejected the notion that the District Federal Court had jurisdiction to consider the right-to-counsel constitutional claims of indigent children who had received a final removal order. Notwithstanding the foregoing, however, *in obiter*, the Federal Court of Appeals in the case at bar maintained that it was up to the legislature to address a lacunae in the law since it was undoubtedly the case (also in the Federal Court of Appeal's opinion) that without a lawyer the children's right to due process was not adequately protected in the immigration proceedings.

5.1.3.3 The Position of the Child Appellees

The appellees in the case were children aged 3–17 years old placed in administrative proceedings regarding deportation (or as the court refers to it "removal proceedings"). It should be noted that the Federal Court of Appeals referred to the indigent child appellants as "indigent minor immigrants" though a segment of these were asylum seekers.[44] The American Civil Liberties Union reports that "A federal court in Seattle certified a class of asylum-seeking children in the Ninth Circuit, bringing thousands more children into the case."[45] Many of the child claimants are refugees "fleeing persecution in Guatemala, Honduras and El Salvador."[46]

The child appellees in the case at bar, at the time, were at various stages of the removal process individually "some . . .waiting to have their first removal hearing,[47] some . . .already had a hearing, and some . . .[were] ordered removed in absentia."[48]

---

[43]J.E. F.M. v. Lynch (US Attorney General) et al., United States Federal Court of Appeals for the Ninth District (Decision 20 September, 2016) at p. 9 https://cdn.ca9.uscourts.gov/datastore/opinions/2016/09/20/15-35738.pdf Accessed 10 October, 2017.

[44]As mentioned in this work previously, on the view here, asylum seekers are ***not*** illegal (unlawful) or irregular or undocumented immigrants but rather persons who can potentially assert a proper claim for asylum as a refugee and who have not then performed an illegal act in crossing a border without proper documents to seek asylum.

[45]American Civil Liberties Union; Young, Scared, Alone and In Court: J.E. F.M. v. Lynch, Update June 24, 2016.

[46]New York Times Editorial Board: Migrant children deserve a voice in court (March 8, 2016).

[47]The District Court had dismissed the claims of the children who had not yet had an immigration hearing holding that their right-to-counsel claim was not yet ripe suggesting their removal proceedings might never be held which at best seems an unlikely best case scenario for these children who were under immigration scrutiny (see J.E. F.M. v. Lynch et al. at p. 8).

[48]J.E. F.M. v. Lynch (US Attorney General) et al., United States Federal Court of Appeals for the Ninth District (Decision 20 September, 2016) at p. 6 https://cdn.ca9.uscourts.gov/datastore/opinions/2016/09/20/15-35738.pdf Accessed 10 October, 2017 (Some of the children do not show up for the deportation hearing no doubt not understanding the process or what is required or out of fear given that they are unrepresented and alone).

Each of the children had attempted to retain a *pro bono* lawyer as none could afford counsel and all had failed in their attempts to retain *pro bono* counsel. "The children, suing on behalf of themselves and a class, claim a due process and statutory right to appointed counsel at government expense in immigration proceedings."[49] The children argued that without legal representation in these complex immigration proceedings "[they and] thousands of children [are] deprived of a full and fair opportunity to identify defenses or seek relief for which they qualify"[50] and hence they were being denied their constitutional right to due process.

The child complainants further maintained that they as unrepresented minors were not equipped to raise right-to-counsel arguments through a petition for judicial review to the Federal Court of Appeals (per the process laid out by statute which stipulates that petition for judicial review to the Federal Court of Appeals can occur only after the Immigration Appeals Board, an administrative body, declines to dismiss the deportation order). The children held that these statutory requirements should not apply to indigent children facing immigration proceedings (i.e. deportation proceedings) without legal representation since the statute created insurmountable impediments to their ability to timely file a right-to-counsel legal challenge and ensure due process in their immigration hearings.

5.1.3.4 Commentary on *J.E. F.M. v. Lynch (U.S. Attorney General) et al.*, United States Federal Court of Appeals for the Ninth District

The Federal Court of Appeals set as the central question to be answered "Does a district court have jurisdiction over a claim that indigent minor immigrants without counsel have a right to government-appointed counsel in removal proceedings?".[51] The Federal Court of Appeals articulated the children's argument thus:

> The argument goes as follows: Minors who obtain counsel in their immigration proceedings will be unable to raise right-to-counsel claims because they have no such claim. As a practical matter, children who lack counsel will be unable to reach federal court to raise a right-to-counsel claim because they are subject to the same exhaustion requirements and filing deadlines that apply to adults. Even if an unrepresented child were able to navigate the PFR [Petition for Review] process, the child would still be deprived of meaningful judicial review, because the record on appeal would be insufficient to sustain review. *Because, according to the minors, their right-to-counsel claims will never see the light of day through the PFR process, the panel should construe § 1252(b)(9) [of the statute in question] as not*

[49] J.E. F.M. v. Lynch (US Attorney General) et al., United States Federal Court of Appeals for the Ninth District (Decision 20 September, 2016) at p. 7 https://cdn.ca9.uscourts.gov/datastore/opinions/2016/09/20/15-35738.pdf Accessed 10 October, 2017.

[50] J.E. F.M. v. Lynch (US Attorney General) et al., United States Federal Court of Appeals for the Ninth District (Decision 20 September, 2016) at p. 7 https://cdn.ca9.uscourts.gov/datastore/opinions/2016/09/20/15-35738.pdf Accessed 10 October, 2017.

[51] J.E. F.M. v. Lynch (US Attorney General) et al., United States Federal Court of Appeals for the Ninth District (Decision 20 September, 2016) at p. 6 https://cdn.ca9.uscourts.gov/datastore/opinions/2016/09/20/15-35738.pdf Accessed 10 October, 2017.

> *covering these claims* [such that indigent migrant children should be able to raise claims in District Court regarding their right to court-appointed counsel in immigration proceedings] (emphasis added).[52]

The Federal Court of Appeals in the case at bar in effect (on the view here) held that despite the risks to the constitutional rights of due process also owed to a certain class of non-citizens (namely indigent minors irregularly in the country (the U.S.) and without legal representation in removal proceedings) the statutory scheme blocking meaningful exercise of those rights supersedes and controls:

> We would be naive if we did not acknowledge that having an unrepresented minor in immigration proceedings poses an extremely difficult situation.[53]

> Congress has clearly provided that all claims—whether statutory or constitutional—that "aris[e] from" immigration removal proceedings can only be brought through the petition for review process in the federal courts of appeals. 8 U.S.C. §§ 1252(a)(5) & (b)(9).[54]

> *Despite the gravity of their claims, the minors cannot bypass the immigration courts and proceed directly to district court. Instead, they must exhaust the administrative process before they can access the federal courts* (emphasis added).[55]

Thus the Federal Court of Appeals held that the statute at issue must be read to apply also to unaccompanied indigent minors. This then such that any claim of a right of these children to have court-appointed counsel in immigration hearings must await a final deportation order.[56] Only then can the claim by each individual child complainant of the right-to-counsel be made and only to a Federal Court of Appeals such that the legal supportability of the final deportation order can be reviewed in light of the child not having had legal representation in the deportation proceedings. The unaccompanied indigent children, the Federal Court of Appeals ruled, are statute barred from seeking the right to court-appointed counsel through the District Federal Court and prior to issuance of a final deportation order. Respectfully, let us

[52]J.E. F.M. v. Lynch (US Attorney General) et al., United States Federal Court of Appeals for the Ninth District (Decision 20 September, 2016) at pp. 18–19 https://cdn.ca9.uscourts.gov/datastore/opinions/2016/09/20/15-35738.pdf Accessed 10 October, 2017.

[53]J.E. F.M. v. Lynch (US Attorney General) et al., United States Federal Court of Appeals for the Ninth District (Decision 20 September, 2016) at p. 21 https://cdn.ca9.uscourts.gov/datastore/opinions/2016/09/20/15-35738.pdf Accessed 10 October, 2017.

[54]J.E. F.M. v. Lynch (US Attorney General) et al., United States Federal Court of Appeals for the Ninth District (Decision 20 September, 2016) at p. 6 https://cdn.ca9.uscourts.gov/datastore/opinions/2016/09/20/15-35738.pdf Accessed 10 October, 2017.

[55]J.E. F.M. v. Lynch (US Attorney General) et al., United States Federal Court of Appeals for the Ninth District (Decision 20 September, 2016) at p. 6 https://cdn.ca9.uscourts.gov/datastore/opinions/2016/09/20/15-35738.pdf Accessed 10 October, 2017.

[56]Recall that neither the immigration judge nor the Board of Immigration Appeal was authorized under the statute at issue to appoint counsel for an unaccompanied indigent child in deportation proceedings (see J.E. F.M. v. Lynch United States Federal Court of Appeals for the Ninth District (Decision 20 September, 2016) at p. 25 https://cdn.ca9.uscourts.gov/datastore/opinions/2016/09/20/15-35738.pdf Accessed 10 October, 2017).

consider then whether the Federal Court of Appeals' reasoning in the case at bar is open to any legally viable substantive critique.

It is, as we have previously here discussed, rather commonplace across at least some jurisdictions internationally that individual child refugee asylum cases (amongst other refugee asylum cases) are mishandled by a State through the denial of collective refugee rights. These human rights violations (and infringements of UNHCR Guidelines on implementation of the Refugee Convention[57]) often occur through State initiatives of various sorts, including legislative, that unjustly target and/or greatly adversely impact the refugee collective. For instance, in the class action case at bar *J.E. F.M. v. Lynch*[58]; a U.S. Federal Court of Appeals addressed alleged denial of due process to (1) indigent unaccompanied refugee children seeking asylum who arrived irregularly to or near the U.S. border or irregularly entered into U.S. territory and (2) to other unaccompanied children who arrived at or near the U.S. border irregularly or who entered the U.S. without proper entry documents. This alleged State violation of due process (according to the child complainants' view with which the current author concurs, and which appears consistent with the UNHCR requirement[59] of effective access to legal representation for the unaccompanied child asylum seeker) arises as the consequence of the failure of the U.S. federal government to provide such children, in the vast majority of cases, as a due process entitlement, court-appointed counsel at government expense in deportation proceedings.

The Federal Court of Appeals held on the preliminary jurisdictional issue that the child complainants must first, as per U.S. immigration law, bring any civil rights claim to the Board of Immigration Appeals. Only when the latter avenue is exhausted can the child complainants, the Federal Court of Appeals held, request a remedy from the Federal Court of Appeals i.e. seek judicial review of an unfavourable Board of Immigration Appeals decision on the issue of providing, at no cost to the child, a court-appointed counsel to the indigent unaccompanied child (such as the 'unaccompanied child refugee asylum seeker'). Thus the Federal Court of Appeals issued no ruling in this case on the actual merits of the constitutional due process and statutory arguments advanced by the child appellants. Reactions from the children's ACLU (America Civil Liberties Union) lead counsel and from counsel

[57]See for example UN High Commissioner for Refugees (UNHCR), Guidelines on Policies and Procedures in Dealing with Unaccompanied Children Seeking Asylum, February 1997, available at: http://www.refworld.org/docid/3ae6b3360.html Accessed 11 October 2017.

[58]J.E. F.M. v. Lynch (US Attorney General) et al., United States Federal Court of Appeals for the Ninth District (Decision 20 September, 2016) https://cdn.ca9.uscourts.gov/datastore/opinions/2016/09/20/15-35738.pdf Accessed 10 October, 2017.

[59]UN High Commissioner for Refugees (UNHCR), Guidelines on Policies and Procedures in Dealing with Unaccompanied Children Seeking Asylum, February 1997, point 4.2 at p. 5 and point 8.3 at p. 12 available at: http://www.refworld.org/docid/3ae6b3360.html Accessed 11 October 2017.

for the U.S. government on the Federal Court of Appeals deciding it had, at the time of *J.E. F.M. v. Lynch*[60] (for the aforementioned reason) no jurisdiction to rule on the merits, were respectively as follows:

> Advocates for the children argue that this poses a Catch-22 in that no child without an attorney can be expected to navigate such a complicated appeals process. The system becomes punitive, they say, and effectively denies due process, requiring the courts to intervene.... "The 9th Circuit today held that the courthouse doors are effectively closed to thousands of children whose only opportunity to seek appointed counsel in their immigration proceedings is through this case," said Ahilan Arulanantham, who has been the ACLU's lead counsel on the case. "The court issued that ruling even as it simultaneously recognized that virtually all children cannot represent themselves in immigration proceedings."[61]

> "Whatever Congress provides them, is their due process," a Justice attorney [attorney for the government] told the court bluntly in one exchange when the case was argued in July.[62]

In considering *J.E. F.M. v. Lynch*[63] it is to be recalled that the United States ratified the Protocol relating to the Status of Refugees[64] on 1 November, 1968 through accession. Thus on this basis also[65] the U.S. is obligated, among other things, to provide to the child, as it is to the adult asylum seeker, fair and impartial hearings of their refugee asylum requests and ensure that they, as yet undeclared refugees, are not penalized for irregular entry to the U.S. in search of asylum:

> *Grounded in Article 14 of the Universal Declaration of human rights 1948*, which recognizes the right of persons to seek asylum from persecution in other countries, *the United Nations Convention relating to the Status of Refugees, adopted in 1951, is the centrepiece of international refugee protection today*. The Convention entered into force on 22 April 1954, and it has been subject to only one amendment in the form of a 1967 Protocol, which removed the geographic and temporal limits of the 1951 Convention (emphasis added).[66]

On this author's view it can reasonably be argued that a deportation proceeding without legal representation for an indigent unaccompanied child refugee asylum

---

[60] J.E. F.M. v. Lynch (US Attorney General) et al., United States Federal Court of Appeals for the Ninth District (Decision 20 September, 2016) https://cdn.ca9.uscourts.gov/datastore/opinions/2016/09/20/15-35738.pdf Accessed 10 October, 2017.

[61] Rogers, D (Politico) (20 September, 2016) Child migrants lose major case in federal court http://www.politico.com/story/2016/09/child-migrants-immigration-228432.

[62] Rogers, D (Politico) (20 September, 2016) http://www.politico.com/story/2016/09/child-migrants-immigration-228432.

[63] J.E. F.M. v. Lynch (US Attorney General) et al., United States Federal Court of Appeals for the Ninth District (Decision 20 September, 2016) https://cdn.ca9.uscourts.gov/datastore/opinions/2016/09/20/15-35738.pdf Accessed 10 October, 2017.

[64] Protocol relating to the Status of Refugees entry into force 4 October, 1967 extended the protection of the *Convention relating to the Status of Refugees* done at Geneva on 28 July 1951 also to persons who became refugees after 1 January 1951.

[65] The right to seek asylum including refugee asylum is arguably part of customary law and hence such requests must be handled humanely and justly by all States.

[66] UNHCR Protocol relating to the Status of Refugees entry into force 4 October, 1967 http://www.ohchr.org/Documents/ProfessionalInterest/protocolrefugees.pdf (Accessed 7 November, 2016).

seeker is indirectly most often tantamount to punishment for the child's breaking of the immigration rules. This is the case in that where unaccompanied children are unrepresented at deportation hearings they are many times more likely than children with legal counsel to be deported by the U.S. This fact (regarding the differential rates of deportation for represented versus unrepresented unaccompanied child asylum seekers) suggests that often times, notwithstanding whether any of these children without legal representation are in fact *bona fide* refugees, they will *not* be able to defeat the removal order.[67] Since in the U.S. very few indigent unaccompanied children are provided- at no cost to the child- court-appointed legal counsel for deportation hearings; this contributes to a large number of adverse immigration decisions for the children (that is deportation orders upheld). There is thus inevitably a message sent as a result that the government presumably considers will deter other unaccompanied children arriving to the U.S. without authorization in search of asylum.

On the analysis here, respectfully, the Federal Court of Appeals in the case at bar, *in effect*, appears to have taken the same erroneous view as counsel for the government; namely that purportedly due process is 'whatever Congress (the body that makes the laws) says it is'.[68] That proposition, aside from being (on the view here) illogically circular, is also legally insupportable (as properly argued by the child appellants) when the State, as here, is poised to take adverse action against which the targets have valid legal defences (for instance under domestic and international human rights and refugee law) that they cannot raise or cannot effectively raise due to age-related incapacity. Were it indeed the situation as asserted by the government in *J.E. F.M. v. Lynch*[69] that in blanket fashion (1) 'due process in the United States is whatever the U.S. Congress holds it to be' and (2) that such is the case even where what the U.S. Congress holds due process to be denies procedural and substantive fair process to a particular identifiable class of persons on U.S. territory; then U.S. constitutional protections would be, in certain instances at least, potentially nothing more than empty promises. In sum the U.S. Congress, on the view here, is *not* empowered to neutralize certain basic bedrock U.S. constitutional protections for any persons within U.S. territory and/or persons in some significant way under U.S. jurisdictional control. That is; the U.S. Congress, operating as it does in a democratic State, is not empowered through 'designer' statutes to negate protections that are in fact consistent with, for instance, international human rights and refugee law and, in some cases, also with customary and *jus cogens* norms and domestic refugee statutes (i.e. the right to fair consideration of requests for international protection). Yet the outcome at the Federal Court of

[67]Kids in Need of Defense (KIND) (founded by Angelina Jolie and Microsoft Corporation to assist unaccompanied children wherever they are) https://supportkind.org/wp-content/uploads/2017/06/General-KIND-Fact-sheet_June-2017.pdf Accessed 12 October, 2017.

[68]Rogers, D (Politico) (20 September, 2016) http://www.politico.com/story/2016/09/child-migrants-immigration-228432.

[69]J.E. F.M. v. Lynch (US Attorney General) et al., United States Federal Court of Appeals for the Ninth District (Decision 20 September, 2016) https://cdn.ca9.uscourts.gov/datastore/opinions/2016/09/20/15-35738.pdf Accessed 10 October, 2017.

Appeals in the case at bar, for all practical purposes, on the analysis here (1) nullified the unaccompanied child appellees' (and the class of similarly situated children's) right to due process in their immigration deportation proceedings (by *in effect* negating their chance to have court-appointed counsel during that process)[70] and (2) hence, in most instances, negated the chance also for the unaccompanied children receiving international protection even where their refugee asylum claims were *bona fide*.[71]

> …tens of thousands of children will remain unrepresented. A meritorious application for asylum, refuge, withholding of removal or other relief may fall through the cracks, despite the best efforts of immigration agencies and the best interests of the child.[72]

Where unaccompanied children were not afforded due process at their immigration deportation hearings resultant from: (1) the lack of court-appointed counsel to act on the children's behalf and in their legal interest and (2) given the children's inability on their own to effectively advance their refugee asylum cases; bona *fide* child refugee asylum seekers 'returned' can be said (on the view here), as a result, to have been the victims of 'constructive refoulement':

> In determining the question of "voluntariness," the UNHCR explains that one must scrutinize objectively the refugees' situation and that "one of the most important elements in the verification of voluntariness is the legal status of the refugees in the country of asylum."[73]

Here the children were denied refugee legal status and deported arguably *without a fair hearing* and hence their removal from the U.S. meets the criteria (it is here contended) for, at a minimum, 'constructive refoulement'. Note that for unaccompanied children who arrived irregularly to the U.S. and whose legal cases in

[70]Neither the immigration judge nor the Board of Immigration Appeals was empowered to order court-appointed counsel for the indigent unaccompanied minors in their removal proceedings (and judicial review by the Federal Court of Appeals was only possible after a final deportation order) (See J.E. F.M. v. Lynch (U.S. Attorney General) United States Federal Court of Appeals for the Ninth District (Decision 20 September, 2016) at p. 24 https://cdn.ca9.uscourts.gov/datastore/opinions/2016/09/20/15-35738.pdf Accessed 10 October, 2017.

[71]Large numbers of the child appellees in the case were child refugee asylum seekers and likely genuinely in need of international protection from persecution rather than being purely 'economic migrants' given UNHCR data on the profile of Central American and Mexican unaccompanied children arriving irregularly near or at the U.S. border or entering the U.S. without authorization or proper entry documents: See UNHCR Washington (2014) Children on the Run: Unaccompanied children leaving Central America and Mexico and the need for international protection Available at https://resourcecentre.savethechildren.net/library/children-run-unaccompanied-children-leaving-central-america-and-mexico-and-need Accessed 13 October, 2017.

[72]J.E. F.M. v. Lynch (US Attorney General) et al., United States Federal Court of Appeals for the Ninth District (Decision 20 September, 2016) at p. 30 https://cdn.ca9.uscourts.gov/datastore/opinions/2016/09/20/15-35738.pdf Accessed 10 October, 2017.

[73]Amnesty International Public Statement (24 July, 2015) Index: ASA 23/2157/2015 Cambodia and the question of voluntariness at p. 1 https://www.amnesty.org/download/Documents/ASA2321572015ENGLISH.pdf Accessed 14 October, 2017.

immigration court started in 2017, three out of four do *not* have legal representation hence greatly reducing their chances of obtaining refugee asylum.[74]

It is here further argued that the U.S. federal statute that barred the unaccompanied indigent children in the case at bar accessing the District Federal Court (to make a right-to-counsel/due process claim) imposed an 'unreasonable' and therefore unconstitutional limit on the children's right to equal protection under the law. The latter in part requires due process and effective access to the courts (the unrepresented children were, as previously discussed, required by statute to wait for the final deportation order and then file any rights claim only to the Federal Court of Appeals). The bar on the child petitioners accessing the District Federal Court *in effect* expedited their removal proceedings. On the respectful view here; the process described reflects a lack of sufficient regard for the fundamental human rights of these unaccompanied child refugees and for the State's constitutional and international legal obligations to the children. This bar on accessing the lower federal court occurred then in the context of impending deportation proceedings without the children having had legal representation. The right to effective access to the courts; due process and equal protection of the law are all U.S. constitutional protections that also apply without unreasonable limitation to foreign nationals whether in the U.S. lawfully or unlawfully.[75]

The unaccompanied indigent children in the case at bar had argued that they were entitled to a timely opportunity to voice their concerns in District Court rather than having to wait for a final removal (deportation) order to be issued and then making an essentially after-the-fact appeal to the Federal Court of Appeals for judicial review (based on the children's lack of legal representation in the immigration removal proceedings). Being able to assert in District Federal Court their right-to-counsel in immigration deportation proceedings would have inured to the children's great benefit in possibly giving them access to court-appointed counsel and a fair chance to avoid deportation where their cases were meritorious. Further; being provided court-appointed counsel on order of the District Federal Court would avoid the very real possibility (a possibility acknowledged by the Federal Court of Appeals in the case at bar) of there being an incomplete and perhaps therefore misleading judicial record arising from the immigration proceedings should some of the children seek, on any permissible ground, review by the Federal Court of Appeals of a deportation decision (though it was exceedingly unlikely that any of the unaccompanied children would have been able to reach the Federal Court of Appeals without legal assistance/representation).

The federal statutory scheme relating to immigration that the U.S. Congress has enacted (which *blocks* unaccompanied indigent minors, among others, from seeking

[74]Trac Immigration Research Centre (affiliated with the Newhouse School of Public Communications and the Whitman School of Management, University of Syracuse) (Report 28 September, 2017) Children: Amid a Growing Court Backlog Many Still Unrepresented http://trac.syr.edu/immigration/reports/482/ Accessed 15 October, 2017.

[75]Cole (2003), pp. 367–388 at p. 370: "The Court [U.S. Supreme Court] has repeatedly stated that 'the "Due Process Clause applies to all 'persons' within the United States, including aliens, whether their presence here is lawful, unlawful, temporary, or permanent."'

judicial review (i.e. relating to the denial of right-to-counsel) *prior* to the issuance of a final deportation order) results in denial of certain of the fundamental rights of indigent unaccompanied child refugee asylum seekers as an identifiable category or class of persons. The unaccompanied indigent children are denied, as discussed, access to a U.S. District Federal Court to timely challenge the refusal by the immigration court and Board of Immigration Appeals to provide court-appointed counsel to represent them in their deportation proceedings. The children are denied then in parallel an individual assessment of their circumstance which would in most cases support the need for honouring their right-to-counsel (through court-appointed lawyers) as essential to their ability to access due process in the immigration deportation proceedings.

This statutory scheme as amended was devised in respect of the aspect here discussed; it would appear, to serve the State interest in expediency in removing, in effect, *en masse* very large numbers of unaccompanied minors irregularly arrived to the U.S. (including child refugee asylum seekers).[76] This to some extent virtual 'collective expulsion' occurs then after having afforded the unaccompanied children (including child refugee asylum seekers) but rather superficial limited legal proceedings arguably not sufficient to meet the constitutional requirements for due process (or in some instances no immigration court hearings regarding deportation).[77]

> Given the onslaught of cases involving unaccompanied minors, there is only so much even the most dedicated and judicious immigration judges (and, on appeal, members of the Board of Immigration Appeals) can do. . .Immigration judges are constrained by "extremely limited time and resources." ... Indeed, those judges may sometimes hear as many as 50 to 70 petitions in a three-to four hour period,. . .leaving scant time to delve deeply into the particular circumstances of a child's case.[78]

---

[76]J.E. F.M. v. Lynch (US Attorney General) et al., United States Federal Court of Appeals for the Ninth District (Decision 20 September, 2016) at p. 15 https://cdn.ca9.uscourts.gov/datastore/opinions/2016/09/20/15-35738.pdf Accessed 10 October, 2017.

[77]The policy at the time of the case at bar was as follows: "Under expedited removal, unless they establish a credible fear of persecution or torture, foreign nationals arriving in the United States from Mexico without proper documentation can be returned to their countries of origin, *without immigration court removal hearings*. . . It is well documented that officials fail to adequately screen asylum seekers for fear of return before ordering them deported—violating the non-refoulement principle of Article 33 of the Refugee Convention." [President Trump's new executive orders direct] "DHS [U.S. Department of Homeland Security] to ensure that applicants for admission arriving on land from Mexico and Canada are returned to those countries to await their removal proceeding in the United States. . .Sending asylum seekers back to Mexico for any length of time would violate U.S. domestic and international obligations [of non-refoulement]. . . If the United States sends asylum seekers back to Mexico pending a formal removal proceeding, there is a significant likelihood that Mexico would send those asylum seekers back to their countries of origin. Reports show that Mexico has increasingly been deporting asylum seekers to their countries of origin without providing them an opportunity to present their claims to protection." (See Harvard Law School: Harvard Immigration and Refugee Clinical Program: The impact of President Trump's Executive Orders on asylum seekers at p. 7.

[78]J.E. F.M. v. Lynch (US Attorney General) et al., United States Federal Court of Appeals for the Ninth District (Decision 20 September, 2016) at p. 29 https://cdn.ca9.uscourts.gov/datastore/opinions/2016/09/20/15-35738.pdf Accessed 10 October, 2017.

On the respectful view here, this U.S. federal immigration statutory scheme then, in practice, and as reflected in the case at bar, has been taken to override certain key human rights considerations. The statutory scheme was apparently crafted, as amended, to produce results that would send a strong message of deterrence to other unaccompanied children similarly situated lest they too contemplated irregular arrival or entry to the U.S. (including thus also potential unaccompanied child refugee asylum seekers):

> Consolidation of the review process for immigration orders of removal began in 1961, when Congress amended the INA [Immigration and Naturalization Act] to channel immigrants' challenges to their removal proceedings to the courts of appeals via the PFR [Petition for Review]... The change was intended to "create a single, separate, statutory form of judicial review of administrative orders for the [removal] of aliens from the United States" and ***to shorten the time frame for judicial review of deportation orders by "eliminat[ing]... a suit in a District Court*** (emphasis added).[79]

> *review of a **final removal order** is the only mechanism for reviewing any issue raised in a removal proceeding*," and ...the statute was "*intended to preclude all district court review of any issue raised in a removal proceeding.*" (emphasis added)[80]

The judicial review scheme at issue in *J.E. F.M. v. Lynch*, on the analysis here, thus denies the *'collective rights'* of a highly vulnerable class or category of foreign nationals; namely unaccompanied indigent children irregularly arrived to the U.S.: (1) in respect of unaccompanied indigent minors being unable in practice to effectively exercise their right-to-counsel (resulting in a denial also of the individual human rights of members of the class i.e. their right to due process) and (2) in creating a risk of 'refoulement' (for the collective within the larger collective of unaccompanied minors at issue—the smaller collective being comprised of child refugee asylum seekers with a credible well-founded fear of persecution in the homeland or in a proposed third alleged safe country). The Federal Court of Appeals in the case at bar conceded that in fact the government's intent in amending the statute at issue in the case at bar was to speed up the removal process (where allegedly legally supportable). However, the impact was not just a speeding up of the deportation proceedings but, it is here contended, impeding of the exercise of the *collective human rights* of certain categories of non-citizens (i.e. the effect of the statute was to block exercise of certain of the constitutional rights (right to due process) required to be afforded to unaccompanied children once arrived irregularly to the U.S.). Rather than ruling that the unaccompanied indigent children *as a class* could raise their constitutional and statutory claim of right-to-counsel (as a right of

[79]J.E. F.M. v. Lynch (US Attorney General) et al., United States Federal Court of Appeals for the Ninth District (Decision 20 September, 2016) at p. 15 https://cdn.ca9.uscourts.gov/datastore/opinions/2016/09/20/15-35738.pdf Accessed 10 October, 2017.

[80]J.E. F.M. v. Lynch (US Attorney General) et al., United States Federal Court of Appeals for the Ninth District (Decision 20 September, 2016) at p. 16 https://cdn.ca9.uscourts.gov/datastore/opinions/2016/09/20/15-35738.pdf Accessed 10 October, 2017.

due process)[81] in Federal District Court (*prior to* the issuance of a final deportation order); the Federal Court of Appeals held that the children were statute barred from accessing the Federal District Court individually or as a class to raise a right-to-counsel claim relating to immigration deportation proceedings. This as the statute, according to the Federal Court of Appeals (in contrast to the view of the Federal District Court in the case at bar) removed jurisdiction from the Federal District Court to hear such a claim arising from an immigration removal proceeding:

> *We recognize that a class remedy arguably might be more efficient than requiring each applicant to file a PFR* [Petition for Review -filed to the Federal Court of Appeals-regarding a final deportation order], but that is not a ground for ignoring the *jurisdictional statute*.... (emphasis added).[82]

On the view of the current author; no statute in a democratic State can be held to be constitutional and, at the same time, be understood to effectively block a constitutional right such as the right to due process (as this author contends was the impact of the statute at issue in the case at bar). Due process is, it is here contended, defined by fundamental principles of fairness and not by arbitrary legislative dictate with political objectives.[83] On the analysis of the current author, had the Federal Court of Appeals ruled in the children's favour in the case at bar (held that the unaccompanied indigent children had a proper cause of action in Federal District Court to raise right-to-counsel claims prior to a final deportation order being issued in the immigration proceedings) the Federal District Court would *not* have been overstepping its jurisdiction.[84]

---

[81]Note that Eric Holder who was the U.S. Attorney General in 2014 took the position that "these children may not have a Constitutional right to a lawyer" though he maintained there were "policy reasons" and also "a moral obligation" to provide counsel to unaccompanied indigent children in immigration deportation proceedings J.E. F.M. v. Lynch (US Attorney General) et al., United States Federal Court of Appeals for the Ninth District (Decision 20 September, 2016) at p. 29 https://cdn.ca9.uscourts.gov/datastore/opinions/2016/09/20/15-35738.pdf Accessed 10 October, 2017. On the view of the current author there is a constitutional right to a lawyer for these unaccompanied children in such circumstances as one necessary precondition for due process.

[82]J.E. F.M. v. Lynch (US Attorney General) et al., United States Federal Court of Appeals for the Ninth District (Decision 20 September, 2016) at p. 24 https://cdn.ca9.uscourts.gov/datastore/opinions/2016/09/20/15-35738.pdf Accessed 10 October, 2017.

[83]It is telling that the unaccompanied children's claim to right-to-counsel in this case was characterized as a political matter rather than being viewed strictly through a constitutional lens: "...the Executive and Congress have the power to address this crisis *without judicial intervention*...solving the representation problem is a highly controversial *political* matter..." (emphasis added) (See J.E. F.M. v. Lynch (US Attorney General) et al., United States Federal Court of Appeals for the Ninth District (Decision 20 September, 2016) at p. 4 https://cdn.ca9.uscourts.gov/datastore/opinions/2016/09/20/15-35738.pdf Accessed 10 October, 2017. In the case at bar, on the view here, it would appear that substantive (constitutional issues) could not properly be divorced from purely statutory jurisdictional questions despite the Federal Court of Appeals attempting that tack.

[84]One of the Justices in the case at bar held that the Federal Court of Appeals had no option but to rule as it did since the justices "...must heed the Supreme Court's admonition that "[f]ederal courts are courts of limited jurisdiction. They possess only that power authorized by Constitution and statute, which is not to be expanded by judicial decree." However, on the analysis here, the

The constitutional obligation to provide the unaccompanied indigent children due process through appointment of counsel, if honoured, would have slowed the removal process or perhaps even halted deportation in the vast majority of cases involving unaccompanied minors from Central America and Mexico irregularly arrived to the U.S. (as the individual children's lawyers would have argued their client's case thoroughly, presented in-depth evidence regarding the child having suffered child-specific forms of persecution, in some cases the child being motivated both by economic considerations and a credible fear of persecution in the home country etc.). The effect of the statute at issue then was in part to block challenges to U.S. immigration policy and practices that impacted *collectives* such as the collective discussed here (unaccompanied children, including child refugee asylum seekers, arriving to the U.S. irregularly). As a result; certain aspects of U.S. immigration polices and practices were upheld notwithstanding that these aspects adversely and arguably (on the respectful view here) unfairly, unconstitutionally and *in blanket fashion*, impacted a certain class or category of non-U.S. citizens currently under U.S. jurisdiction; namely unaccompanied indigent children who had arrived without authorization near or at the border with the U.S. or entered the U.S. across the border irregularly:

> In 1991, in McNary v. Haitian Refugee Center, the Court [U.S. Supreme Court] offered a blueprint for how Congress could draft a jurisdiction-channeling statute that would cover not only individual challenges to agency decisions, but also broader challenges to agency policies and practices.[85]
>
> In *McNary*, the Court did everything but write the future statute[86] [referring to the statute at issue in J.E. F.M. v. Lynch[87] which blocked right-to counsel claims until a final deportation

constitution requires that statutes alleged inconsistent with the Constitution must be read to be consistent or else struck (in part or in whole as pertinent). Here the unaccompanied minors requested that the statute be read to exempt them from the bar against accessing the Federal District Court to make rights-to-counsel claims such that they could be represented by court appointed counsel in their deportation proceedings (See J.E. F.M. v. Lynch (US Attorney General) et al., United States Federal Court of Appeals for the Ninth District (Decision 20 September, 2016) at p. 26 https://cdn.ca9.uscourts.gov/datastore/opinions/2016/09/20/15-35738.pdf Accessed 10 October, 2017.

[85]J.E. F.M. v. Lynch (US Attorney General) et al., United States Federal Court of Appeals for the Ninth District (Decision 20 September, 2016) at p. 16 https://cdn.ca9.uscourts.gov/datastore/opinions/2016/09/20/15-35738.pdf Accessed 10 October, 2017.

In *McNary* the appellees were successful in their assertion that the District Court had jurisdiction to hear their case under the relevant statute at the time.

[86]J.E. F.M. v. Lynch (US Attorney General) et al., United States Federal Court of Appeals for the Ninth District (Decision 20 September, 2016) at p. 17 https://cdn.ca9.uscourts.gov/datastore/opinions/2016/09/20/15-35738.pdf Accessed 10 October, 2017.

In *MacNary* the U.S. Supreme Court held that the statute at that time did not address the constitutional issues the agricultural workers in the case (the appellees) were raising and that they thus had the right to access judicial review in the District Court.

[87]J.E. F.M. v. Lynch (US Attorney General) et al., United States Federal Court of Appeals for the Ninth District (Decision 20 September, 2016) https://cdn.ca9.uscourts.gov/datastore/opinions/2016/09/20/15-35738.pdf Accessed 10 October, 2017.

order was issued and which statute allowed judicial review only by the Federal Court of Appeals]

Remarkably the U.S. Supreme Court in *McNary*[88] offered guidance (perhaps in some sense unwittingly) to the legislature respecting an alleged legally supportable statutory scheme that effectively, for all practical purposes, blocks judicial review for many thousands of unaccompanied indigent minors (and perhaps also other categories of non-citizens) undergoing removal through the U.S. immigration system. This as their cases (given their having no legal representation) generally never reach the Federal Court of Appeals for judicial review (i.e. petition to the Federal Court of Appeals for certiorari of a final deportation order for lack of due process (arising from lack of court appointed counsel) in the deportation immigration proceedings).

While the Federal Court of Appeals in the case at bar acknowledged the special vulnerabilities of unaccompanied minors without legal representation who are in immigration removal proceedings; the Court highlighted, it is here contended, a purported set of existing safeguards (described in the excerpt from the Court's majority opinion below) that fall far short of what would be required to ensure that the children's *constitutional right* to due process was adequately protected:

> Unrepresented minors receive additional special protections in removal proceedings. Unless the child is accompanied by "an attorney or legal representative, a near relative, legal guardian, or friend," the immigration judge cannot accept the child's admission of removability... Immigration judges also must ensure that any waiver of the right to counsel is knowing and voluntary; on review, we can "indulge every reasonable presumption against waiver,"[89]
>
> when the petitioner is a minor, we factor "the minor's age, intelligence, education, information, and understanding and ability to comprehend" into our analysis.[90]
>
> in 2014, the Office of the Chief Immigration Judge provided guidelines for "The Friend of the Court Model for Unaccompanied Minors in Immigration Proceedings." *Although the friend of the court does not act as a representative*, the friend's assistance role can be critical in monitoring the proceedings (emphasis added)[91]

Thus, on the view here, the Federal Court of Appeals in the case at bar failed in particular to address (1) the special obligation of the U.S. government under customary law and treaty law (i.e. the Refugee Convention) as well as U.S. refugee statutory law *to ensure* that international protection is afforded also to *bona fide* unaccompanied

---

[88]McNary v. Haitian Refugee Center, Inc., 498 U.S. 479 (1991).

[89]J.E. F.M. v. Lynch (US Attorney General) et al., United States Federal Court of Appeals for the Ninth District (Decision 20 September, 2016) at pp. 21–22 https://cdn.ca9.uscourts.gov/datastore/opinions/2016/09/20/15-35738.pdf Accessed 10 October, 2017.

[90]J.E. F.M. v. Lynch (US Attorney General) et al., United States Federal Court of Appeals for the Ninth District (Decision 20 September, 2016) at p. 22 https://cdn.ca9.uscourts.gov/datastore/opinions/2016/09/20/15-35738.pdf Accessed 10 October, 2017.

[91]J.E. F.M. v. Lynch (US Attorney General) et al., United States Federal Court of Appeals for the Ninth District (Decision 20 September, 2016) at p. 22 https://cdn.ca9.uscourts.gov/datastore/opinions/2016/09/20/15-35738.pdf Accessed 10 October, 2017.

child refugees fleeing persecution and (2) the obligation of a constitutional democratic State such as the U.S. to ensure constitutional protections such as due process in judicial proceedings are effectively afforded *at every stage* also to highly vulnerable groups including unaccompanied (or accompanied) indigent minors who are foreign nationals on U.S. soil.

On the view here the Federal Court of Appeals in *J.E. F.M. v. Lynch* sidestepped the fundamental question at issue: the INA statutory denial *in practice* of the collective constitutional rights of a certain category of non-citizen (denial of indigent minors' right-to-counsel (due process) in immigration removal proceedings). This it did by endorsing the jurisdictional statutory scheme that, in the normal course in most cases of unaccompanied indigent children, would *not* in practice have given this category of persons (1) access to the Federal Court of Appeals in their deportation case or (2) provided an adequate judicial record on which to petition the appeals court for judicial review based on a constitutional claim. Rather than rectify this block to a *collective* fundamental constitutional right to due process for unaccompanied indigent minors involved in removal proceedings in the U.S. (i.e. by providing a remedy in the form of an exemption to application of the statute which barred court-appointed lawyers for these unaccompanied indigent minors); the Federal Court of Appeals in the case at bar stressed that per the statute *each member* of *the class* would have to (1) *individually* make out their right-to-counsel claim by first exhausting the immigration proceedings in their case until a final deportation order was issued (while not having access to a District Federal Court to challenge the law denying them the opportunity to have a court appointed counsel in the immigration deportation proceedings) and then (2) assume the burden, again without assistance of counsel, to advance the constitutional claim to right-to-counsel in deportation hearings for unaccompanied indigent children (constitutional challenge re lack of due process) before a Federal Court of Appeals:

> *We recognize that a class remedy arguably might be more efficient than requiring each applicant to file a PFR* Petition for Review, but that is not a ground for ignoring the jurisdictional statute (emphasis added).[92]

The INA[93] statute provisions at issue, given the Federal Court of Appeals ruling in the case at bar on interpretation and application, effectively blocks collective constitutional challenge and greatly diminishes the chance of a successful right-to-counsel constitutional claim by an individual unaccompanied child in the Federal Court of Appeals (given the likelihood—due to the child having been unrepresented in the deportation proceedings in immigration court—of a limited judicial record that speaks to the unaccompanied child's legal interests and establishes his/her credible fear of persecution-assuming that, for example, an indigent minor appellee seeking asylum even managed to petition the Federal Court of Appeals for judicial review

[92]J.E. F.M. v. Lynch (US Attorney General) et al., United States Federal Court of Appeals for the Ninth District (Decision 20 September, 2016) at p. 25 https://cdn.ca9.uscourts.gov/datastore/opinions/2016/09/20/15-35738.pdf Accessed 10 October, 2017.

[93]INA refers to the US Immigration Naturalization Act.

(for the most part an unlikely eventuality). Note that were an individual unaccompanied child successful *on a constitutional claim* that unaccompanied indigent minors cannot be properly barred from being afforded court-appointed counsel under the INA statute; this would have established the collective rights of the group and rendered the statute of no force and effect insofar as non-payment of counsel for members of this group is concerned:

> *should a court determine that the statute barring payment for counsel does not mean what it says—a position taken by the minors*—that statute would be "infirm across the circuit and in every case"...[94]

Further, it can be argued that the unaccompanied indigent minors in the case at bar were not taking the position that "the statute barring payment for counsel does not mean what it says"[95] (a position the Federal Court of Appeals attributes to the minors in the case at bar). Rather their position was that (1) the statute was premised on the notion that persons *in practice* and not just in theory would have effective access to judicial review at the Federal Court of Appeals level which in actuality was not the case for indigent children in their circumstance and that (2) therefore their group should be exempted from the bar against payment for counsel (bar against court-appointed counsel at government expense). Indeed at certain points in the opinion the Federal Court of Appeals in the case at bar appeared to acknowledge the likelihood of the unaccompanied indigent children being without legal representation given the statutory bar on court-appointed counsel in immigration proceedings:

> ***We also recognize that there are limited—and already more than stretched—pro bono resources available to help unaccompanied minors navigate the removal process.*** *But these considerations cannot overcome a clear statutory prescription against district court review.* Relief is through review in the court of appeals or executive *or congressional action* (emphasis added)[96]

Since such individual or group right-to-counsel cases involving indigent minors (most often unaccompanied minors) were likely never to arrive on appeal in a U.S. Federal Courts of Appeals; there would be little possibility of an individual remedy nor recognition of the systematic denial of the children's collective constitutional rights (to due process and freedom of expression). It appears the effect, if arguably not also the objective, of the PFR (Petition for Review) immigration statutory scheme was not simply to expedite deportations but to reduce the

---

[94]J.E. F.M. v. Lynch (US Attorney General) et al., United States Federal Court of Appeals for the Ninth District (Decision 20 September, 2016) at p. 25 https://cdn.ca9.uscourts.gov/datastore/opinions/2016/09/20/15-35738.pdf Accessed 10 October, 2017.

[95]J.E. F.M. v. Lynch (US Attorney General) et al., United States Federal Court of Appeals for the Ninth District (Decision 20 September, 2016) at p. 25 https://cdn.ca9.uscourts.gov/datastore/opinions/2016/09/20/15-35738.pdf Accessed 10 October, 2017.

[96]J.E. F.M. v. Lynch (US Attorney General) et al., United States Federal Court of Appeals for the Ninth District (Decision 20 September, 2016) at p. 25 https://cdn.ca9.uscourts.gov/datastore/opinions/2016/09/20/15-35738.pdf Accessed 10 October, 2017.

likelihood of a successful challenge of a removal order (the latter challenge requiring legal representation for indigent minors).

The Federal Court of Appeals in the case at bar challenged the argument of the unaccompanied indigent child appellees that it was in practice impossible for indigent children in their position to get the right-to-counsel claim before a Federal Court of Appeals:

> At argument, counsel for the children claimed that it was essentially impossible to get the right-to-counsel claim before a federal court. This assertion is belied by the fact that the minors' counsel [in another case] has previously raised a right-to-counsel claim through the PFR process See Guzman-Heredia v. Gonzales, No. 04-72769 (9th Cir.).[97]

Whether or not the indigent minors in the present case *in practice* would be able under the current U.S. immigration and naturalization system to advance a claim concerning their right-to-counsel before a Federal Court of Appeals goes to the core of the case. The Federal Court of Appeals in the case at bar held that such would be the case and pointed to *Guzman-Heredia v. Gonzales* as evidence.

> In Guzman-Heredia, the petitioner was a fourteen-year-old boy who was placed in removal proceedings. He explained to the immigration judge "that he had been unable to find an attorney to represent him and requested that the Immigration Judge appoint an attorney for him." The judge denied the request, stating that he could not "give people a free lawyer." The immigration judge then ordered the petitioner removed, and the Board of Immigration Appeals affirmed. ***At this stage, the petitioner obtained pro bono counsel, who argued in a PFR [Petition for Review] that***:
>
> Petitioner's Fifth Amendment right to due process was violated when the Immigration Judge refused to appoint an attorney to represent him in removal proceedings. Because Petitioner is an unaccompanied child of 14 years of age, he is of limited cognitive abilities and lacks understanding of legal process. Due to the seriousness of the proceedings against him and the importance of the interest at stake, namely immigration proceedings in which the government seeks to remove Petitioner from his family, home and school in the United States, the Constitution compels that Petitioner have been afforded the protection of appointed counsel at public expense. Although the case ultimately settled, *Guzman-Heredia* lays rest to the contention that right-to-counsel claims will never surface through the PFR process. . .(emphasis added).[98]

Yet it is noteworthy that the child in *Guzman-Heredia* was exceptional in that he raised the right-to-counsel issue on his own before an immigration judge and then had the good luck to be able to retain a *pro bono* counsel just when the *final* removal (deportation) order had been affirmed by the Board of Immigration Appeals. Many, if not most, unaccompanied indigent minors, many of whom do not speak English well if at all, would not have the notion to ask for counsel in the midst of complex legal proceedings taken by the government against them. Further the likelihood of an

---

[97] J.E. F.M. v. Lynch (US Attorney General) et al., United States Federal Court of Appeals for the Ninth District (Decision 20 September, 2016) at p. 22 https://cdn.ca9.uscourts.gov/datastore/opinions/2016/09/20/15-35738.pdf Accessed 10 October, 2017.

[98] J.E. F.M. v. Lynch (US Attorney General) et al., United States Federal Court of Appeals for the Ninth District (Decision 20 September, 2016) at pp. 22–23 https://cdn.ca9.uscourts.gov/datastore/opinions/2016/09/20/15-35738.pdf Accessed 10 October, 2017.

indigent unaccompanied child denied court-appointed counsel being able to retain *pro bono* counsel in time to appeal the final removal order in federal court would also be slim as the Federal Court of Appeals in *J.E. F.M. v. Lynch* in effect acknowledged: "We also recognize that there are limited—and already more than stretched—pro bono resources available to help unaccompanied minors navigate the removal process."[99] Hence it seems an overreach, to say the least, that an unusual case such as *Guzman-Heredia* negates the children's proposition in *J.E. F.M. v. Lynch* that, in the usual course, unaccompanied indigent minors' due process claims involving right-to-counsel will never see "the light of day" in a Federal Court of Appeals; the latter being the only avenue for judicial review of a final deportation order.[100]

Despite dismissing, in the case at bar, the unaccompanied children's constitutional claim (one advanced as a class), the Federal Court of Appeals appeared to acknowledge and encourage the possibility and feasibility of test cases; each with their own specific rich factual context. This arguably can be read as the Court's acknowledgement *in effect* that the right-to-counsel collective constitutional claim of unaccompanied indigent minors is yet not a settled matter notwithstanding the ruling in *J.E. F.M. v. Lynch*:

> The reality is that current counsel for the minors are in a unique position to bring multiple test cases on the counsel issue. The claim in this suit is that indigent minors are entitled to government-provided counsel as a matter of constitutional and statutory right. For accompanied minors, a parent could make the claim or, for unaccompanied minors, a next friend could help them do so. Even better, the IJ [Immigration Judge] and the government could acknowledge that absent a knowing and voluntary waiver, a minor proceeding without counsel has de facto requested a right to court-appointed counsel.[101]

The implicit encouragement regarding advancing test cases and cooperation between the government and counsel for the appellees was evident also in the following footnote in the case at bar:

> Following discussion at oral argument, to facilitate a test case, through December 2016 the government is providing the children's counsel with notice of any minor without counsel that the government is aware of ordered removed by an immigration judge following a merits hearing. To take the government at its word that it is willing to cooperate with counsel, the government should continue such notice.[102]

---

[99]J.E. F.M. v. Lynch (US Attorney General) et al., United States Federal Court of Appeals for the Ninth District (Decision 20 September, 2016) at p. 25 https://cdn.ca9.uscourts.gov/datastore/opinions/2016/09/20/15-35738.pdf Accessed 10 October, 2017.

[100]Recall that the unaccompanied indigent minors in *J.E. F.M. v. Lynch* (US Attorney General) et al., United States Federal Court of Appeals for the Ninth District (Decision 20 September, 2016) argued they should have the right to petition for court-appointed counsel at the District Court level rather than having to wait until the immigration proceedings in their case were exhausted and a final deportation order issued.

[101]J.E. F.M. v. Lynch (US Attorney General) et al., United States Federal Court of Appeals for the Ninth District (Decision 20 September, 2016) at pp. 23–24 https://cdn.ca9.uscourts.gov/datastore/opinions/2016/09/20/15-35738.pdf Accessed 10 October, 2017.

[102]J.E. F.M. v. Lynch (US Attorney General) et al., United States Federal Court of Appeals for the Ninth District (Decision 20 September, 2016) at pp. 23–24 https://cdn.ca9.uscourts.gov/datastore/opinions/2016/09/20/15-35738.pdf Accessed 10 October, 2017.

It is necessary in considering the *J.E. F.M. v. Lynch* case[103] to point out that unaccompanied child refugee asylum seekers are particularly vulnerable to the possibility of 'refoulement'. Hence they are in urgent need of legal representation in deportation proceedings. That is; such children, even when *bona fide* refugees in need of asylum, may frequently ultimately be returned to an unsafe homeland (or place of habitual residence) or an unsafe third country in contravention of the Refugee Convention non-refoulement provision. The latter is often precisely due to the disadvantages confronting child refugees in advancing their refugee asylum case. These challenges are commonly linked to their young age and often unaccompanied status in combination with erroneous State assessments of the risks of return:

> Children may not be able to articulate their claims to refugee status in the same way as adults and, therefore, *may require special assistance to do so* (emphasis added)[104]

> I agree with my colleagues that a child (or for that matter, an adult) is unlikely to be able to protect all his rights in a deportation proceeding unless he has a lawyer.[105]

Assistance in communicating the specifics of their refugee asylum case to the frontline immigration border agent and in immigration court (if the latter is accessed) through legal representation is most often not forthcoming and, as a result for this reason and others, unaccompanied child asylum seekers, for instance in the United States, are often predictably unfairly deemed to have failed to have made their case for refugee asylum. They then often face speedy deportation with no or a very limited immigration proceeding (i.e. a single hearing) without legal representation.[106]

> Unprecedented numbers of children have come alone to the U.S. in the last three years seeking protection ("Over 200,000 unaccompanied children have arrived in the United States since 2014") Many have survived severe abuse, including sexual and physical violence, trafficking, and persecution. These children have no one to protect them in their home countries and see no choice but to flee, or die.

[103] J.E. F.M. v. Lynch (US Attorney General) et al., United States Federal Court of Appeals for the Ninth District (Decision 20 September, 2016) https://cdn.ca9.uscourts.gov/datastore/opinions/2016/09/20/15-35738.pdf Accessed 10 October, 2017.

[104] UNHCR (2009) Guidelines on International Protection: Child Asylum Claims under Articles 1 (A)2 and 1(F) of the 1951 Convention and/or 1967 Protocol relating to the Status of Refugees point 2 at p. 3.

[105] J.E. F.M. v. Lynch (US Attorney General) et al., United States Federal Court of Appeals for the Ninth District (Decision 20 September, 2016) at p. 31 https://cdn.ca9.uscourts.gov/datastore/opinions/2016/09/20/15-35738.pdf Accessed 10 October, 2017.

[106] Eagly, I, Esq. and Shafer, S Esq. (Special Report 28 September, 2016) American Immigration Counsel, 'Access to Counsel in Immigration Court': "It has long been the case that immigrants have a right to counsel in immigration court, but that expense has generally been borne by the noncitizen. Because deportation is classified as a civil rather than a criminal sanction, immigrants facing removal are not afforded the constitutional protections under the Sixth Amendment that are provided to criminal defendants." https://www.americanimmigrationcouncil.org/research/access-counsel-immigration-court Accessed 12 October, 2017.

Over 60 % of children arriving in the U.S. have noone to represent them in immigration court. Children without representation are five times more likely to be deported back to danger (emphasis added).[107]

The impact of such, in effect, 'pushback strategies' inconsistent with international refugee law (and arguably also with U.S. domestic refugee law which incorporates non-refoulement as a core principle) in regards, for example, to unaccompanied Mexican and Central American children arriving at the U.S. border irregularly is commented on by the NGO Lutheran Immigration and Refugee Service as follows:

> . . .unaccompanied alien children . . .come fleeing violence or persecution and embark on an often dangerous journey from their home countries to seek protection in the United States. Historically, these children have mostly come from Mexico and Central America—in particular, El Salvador, Honduras and Guatemala. The demographics of children seeking refuge from Central America is changing- the average age is dropping and the percentage of girls is rising.
>
> ***DHS [United States Department of Homeland Security] has failed to . . fulfill their legal obligations of screening***[108] ***and non-refoulement of Mexican children who arrive alone and instead return roughly 95% of all Mexican children*** *(*emphasis added*).*[109]

Note that a UNHCR Washington 2014 interview study with 400 child asylum seeker interviewees from Mexico, Honduras, Guatemala and El Salvador investigating why these children fled to the United States found that a majority were in need of international protection::

> 58% of those interviewed were forcibly displaced because they suffered or faced harms that indicated a potential or actual need for international protection. Two common sources of harm that the interviewees cited were: violence by organized armed criminal actors and violence in the home (abuse from a caretaker). The children from Mexico cited a third concern: recruitment into and exploitation by the criminal element for human smuggling, i.e. facilitating others in crossing the US border illegally.[110]

Notwithstanding findings such as presented in the aforementioned 2014 UNHCR Washington report *Children on the Run: Unaccompanied children leaving Central*

---

[107]Kids in Need of Defense (KIND) (an NGO founded by Angelina Jolie and Microsoft Corporation to assist unaccompanied children https://supportkind.org/wp-content/uploads/2017/06/General-KIND-Fact-sheet_June-2017.pdf 12 October, 2017.

[108]Referring here to lack of adequate 'screening' of children as possible victims of trafficking crimes and/or as children seeking refugee asylum which under the U.S. domestic statute specifically the 'Trafficking Victims Protection Reauthorization Act' (2008)' would bar refoulement and necessitate an immigration hearing.

[109]Lutheran Immigration and Refugee Service (2014) Unaccompanied migrant children: U.S. law and policy backgrounder 'Protecting the best interests of all children' http://lirs.org/wp-content/uploads/2014/07/UAC-Law-and-Policy-FINAL.pdf Accessed 12 October, 2017.

[110]UNHCR Washington (2014) Children on the Run: Unaccompanied children leaving Central America and Mexico and the need for international protection Available at https://resourcecentre.savethechildren.net/library/children-run-unaccompanied-children-leaving-central-america-and-mexico-and-need Accessed 13 October, 2017.

America and Mexico and the need for international protection[111]; U.S. President Trump, in a memorandum of October, 2017 to his Department of Homeland Security, articulated his administration's new aggressive 'pushback' migration control objectives and policy. The latter were to be applied also to accompanied and unaccompanied child asylum seekers arriving without proper entry papers or authorization at the U.S. border or irregularly entered across the border. President Trump's migration control policy/strategy, on the respectful view here, is likely to significantly jeopardize further the security and asylum rights of unaccompanied child refugee asylum seekers arriving irregularly (without proper authorization and entry documents) to the U.S.

President Trump's early October 2017 memorandum did not stipulate, it would appear, that substantive and procedural safeguards consistent with international refugee, and human rights law (including child rights law) must be *strictly adhered to* in implementation of any then current or future U.S. law and policy (revised under President Trump) affecting child refugee asylum seekers who arrive at the U.S.-Mexico border or otherwise enter irregularly (i.e. adherence to the principle of 'non-refoulement'). The aforementioned President Trump memorandum to the Department of U.S. Homeland Security in part stated:

> ENSURE PROMPT REMOVAL OF MINORS & RELATIVES CROSSING BORDER ILLEGALY: Ensure the swift return of Unaccompanied Alien Children (UAC) and family units by amending current laws that require authorities to release them en masse into the United States.[112]

In August 2017 the Trump administration ended a program (initiated by former President Obama) that allowed minors from Central America arrived at the U.S.-Mexico border irregularly and (1) who did *not* allegedly meet the criteria of 'refugee' but (2) who did have a parent with legal status in the U.S. to enter on a 2 year parole that was renewable:

> *It was a safety net for children who were in danger but whose parts of their stories might not match a certain class under refugee status,* said J. Kevin Appleby, a senior director at the Center for Migration Studies (emphasis added).[113]

[111]UNHCR Washington (2014) Children on the Run: Unaccompanied children leaving Central America and Mexico and the need for international protection Available at https://resourcecentre.savethechildren.net/library/children-run-unaccompanied-children-leaving-central-america-and-mexico-and-need Accessed 13 October, 2017.

[112]American Immigration Lawyers Association 'Whitehouse releases details on Border security principles and policies, President Trump Memorandum to the U.S. Department of Homeland Security 'Secure the Border by Deterring and Swiftly removing Illegal Entrants' (9 October, 2017) Available at http://www.aila.org/infonet/wh-details-border-security-principles-and-policies Accessed 10 October, 2017.

[113]Nakamura, David (2017) Trump administration ends Obama-era protection program for Central American minors Washington Post, August 16, 2017.

Instead the children would now have to seek entry in their own right under other U.S. immigration schemes that are not specifically directed to easing the plight of unaccompanied or separated minors from Central America irregularly arrived at the U.S. border and seeking protection in the U.S. from violence in their home country and who have a parent in the U.S, with legal status. Unaccompanied or separated children under international human rights law are to be given priority in international protection as is family reunification. On the view here, hence, it is difficult to rationalize the termination of the CAM parolee program based on refugee law informed by human rights international obligations. Rather the Trump perspective in crafting homeland security policy and practice guidelines in part appears, on the view here, to be focused on the anticipated better deterrence of future unaccompanied or separated children from Central America or Mexico, including *bona fide* child refugee asylum seekers, arriving to the U.S.-Mexico border without permission or proper entry documents.[114]

Clearly, as indicated for instance by the 2014 UNHCR study 'Children on the Run',[115] there are an inordinately high number of unaccompanied child *bona fide* refugees from Central America and Mexico arriving at the U.S. border in search of asylum and risking their safety and often their lives in making this journey. Denial of child asylum seekers' right to due process (i.e. lack of access to legal counsel), and the U.S. government's use, where it occurs, of migration control tactics inconsistent with international human rights norms[116] in regards to children who are genuinely in need of international protection results, it is here contended, in erosion of the

[114]Nakamura, D Washington Post (16 August, 2017) Trump administration ends Obama-era protection program for Central American minors https://www.washingtonpost.com/politics/trump-administration-ends-obama-era-protection-program-for-central-american-minors/2017/08/16/8101507e-82b6-11e7-ab27-1a21a8e006ab_story.html?utm_term=.e5367d0aea9f Accessed 20 October, 2017.

[115]UNHCR Washington (2014) Children on the Run: Unaccompanied children leaving Central America and Mexico and the need for international protection Available at https://resourcecentre.savethechildren.net/library/children-run-unaccompanied-children-leaving-central-america-and-mexico-and-need Accessed 13 October, 2017.

[116]These migration control tactics inconsistent with international human rights and humanitarian law norms have included, for instance, expedited return-removal without an immigration hearing (as is permitted under U.S. law when the child comes from a country contiguous to the U.S. such as Mexico and has arrived irregularly at or near the U.S. border (as opposed to having entered the U.S. interior) and the frontline border agent of the Department of Homeland Security having concluded that the child allegedly does *not* have a valid asylum request and allegedly is not the victim of trafficking (see American Immigration Council (2015) *A Guide to children arriving at the border: Laws, policies and responses* https://www.americanimmigrationcouncil.org/research/guide-children-arriving-border-laws-policies-and-responses Accessed 13 October, 2017). The tactics also include, for instance, failure to consider 'child-specific' forms of persecution (i.e. the child having been targeted for gang violence in the home country precisely due to his/her vulnerability as a child) as 'persecution' in Refugee Convention terms. The latter then may lead to refoulement based on this erroneous assessment of whether there was a history of persecution suffered by the child and/or there is real threat of persecution in the home country

democratic rule of law and democratic core values. Respectfully, the latter, it can reasonably be argued, is the actual threat to the U.S. national interest.

Of course there is a necessity for the international community to assist in improving the security and economic status of the countries from which these unaccompanied children fled if there is to be a durable solution; especially given the enormity of the current international refugee crisis (which includes also child refugees). However, in the interim, there is a high international obligation of States, in cooperation with each other, also to provide meaningful protection to child refugee asylum seekers that respects their rights as legal persons and also as children with certain specific developmental needs and vulnerabilities. In the majority of the unaccompanied child refugee cases this may mean providing asylum with a pathway to regularized status as a permanent resident or citizen or at least leave to stay indefinitely as a protected person. Instead what is occurring all too commonly is that States are cooperating in refoulement efforts targeting, among others, unaccompanied and separated child refugees who in the majority of cases are *bona fide* Convention refugees or otherwise children in need of and eligible for international protection.

5.2 Some Historical Background Regarding the Treatment Accorded by the U.S. to Refugee Asylum Seekers from Central America: *United States v Aguilar*

Let us consider some of the history of U.S. refoulement of refugees from Central America and then compare the historical situation to that of today specifically in respect of unaccompanied child refugees from Central America.

That Central America has a long history of political violence is well recognized. In *United States v Aguilar*; religious and other members of the old[117] sanctuary movement were found to have smuggled, transported and harboured "illegal aliens" from Central America.[118] One of the arguments the defendants advanced in their defence was that these aliens were in fact *bona fide* Convention refugees persecuted in their home State due to their political opinion and hence not 'illegal aliens'. The defendants argued, in addition in part, that they had counselled these refugees not to officially claim refugee asylum with U.S. Immigration and Naturalization officials in that systematically the "INS improperly failed to approve the meritorious political asylum applications of aliens who applied at official ports of entry"[119] Thus the defendants maintained that 'necessity' was a defence in this circumstance as

[117] United States v Aguilar 883 F.2d 662 (U.S. Court of Appeals Ninth Circuit) Decided March 30, 1989. As amended on Denial of Rehearing and Rehearing En Banc April 14, 1989 at para 2.

[118] United States v Aguilar 883 F.2d 662 (U.S. Court of Appeals Ninth Circuit) Decided March 30, 1989. As amended on Denial of Rehearing and Rehearing En Banc April 14, 1989.

[119] United States v Aguilar 883 F.2d 662 (U.S. Court of Appeals Ninth Circuit) Decided March 30, 1989. As amended on Denial of Rehearing and Rehearing En Banc April 14, 1989 para 3.

defendants' actions were consistent with the 'non-refoulement principle' embodied in the US Refugee Act of 1980 that incorporated principles of the Refugee Convention. As INS, they held, would have returned these refugees to likely torture and death in their home State in Central America, the defendants had no choice but to arrange for the refugees' sanctuary in the U.S.; bringing them into the country and dispersing them to safe living arrangements across the country. In fact at the time INS was indeed improperly and routinely rejecting valid political asylum claims:

> After the passage of the [U.S.] Refugee Act in the 1980s, thousands of refugees came to the United States from El Salvador and Guatemala to apply for political asylum, fleeing violence and political oppression. In Guatemala, a civil war resulted in the death of 50,000 people and the disappearance of 100,000 more. In El Salvador, the military executed over 10,000 people. Though the refugees from Central America met the statutory requirements for asylum, their applications were routinely denied. While 5,500 Salvadorians applied for asylum, only two were approved. From the passage of the Refugee Act in 1980 to 1986, only three percent of Central American refugees seeking political asylum were approved. For some refugees, the denial of political asylum was a death sentence. A study by the American Civil Liberties Union found that 130 of the Salvadorians who were denied political asylum and deported to El Salvador were tortured, killed, or disappeared.[120]

The Ninth Circuit however found that the defendants had acted with the criminal intent to conceal these foreign nationals (refugees) from INS detection and that harbouring so-called illegal aliens *with such an intent* did create criminal liability under the relevant statute. Eight of the defendants were ultimately convicted for various offences under the statute[121]

> Despite the prosecution of its members, the Sanctuary Movement achieved success during the 1990s as the United States made changes to immigration policies; particularly the grant of special refugee status to Guatemalan and Salvadoran refugees[122]

One such initiative regarding special consideration of refugee asylum seekers from Central America (though farther removed in time from the experience of the *United States v Aguilar* case but perhaps inspired in part by the facts revealed in that case regarding the U.S. handling at the time of refugees from Central America and the refugees' dire plight) is the 'United States In-Country Refugee Processing for Minors in Honduras, El Salvador and Guatemala (Central American Minors—CAM)' which we discuss next.

[120]Maun (2011), p. 451.

[121]Maun (2011), p. 453.

[122]Maun (2011), p. 454.

5.3 The United States' 'In-Country' Refugee Processing for Minors in Honduras, El Salvador and Guatemala (Central American Minors—CAM)

The United States' In-Country Refugee Processing for Minors in Honduras, El Salvador and Guatemala (Central American Minors—CAM) program was launched in 2014 with the objective of "provid[ing] certain qualified children in El Salvador, Guatemala and Honduras a safe, legal, and orderly alternative to the dangerous journey that some children are currently undertaking to the United States."[123] The program allowed children who were minors; and while still in their home country of Honduras, El Salvador or Guatemala, and who had a qualifying parent legally in the United States, to be considered for refugee resettlement in the United States if they (these children) met the eligibility requirements including refugee status. Other such children who met all eligibility requirements except the refugee requirement could be considered also to come to the United States but under a "parole provision":

> The program was conceived in 2014 as a way to allow legal residents of the U.S. to bring their children to them and away from violence and dangerous situations in their home countries, and in certain specific cases, the child's parent and legal spouse of the U.S. resident was also considered along with them. That served as an alternative for parents who might otherwise turn to smugglers to bring their children to the U.S. illegally.[124]

> The CAM program began accepting applications from qualifying parents in the U.S. for their children on December 1, 2014. *Only certain parents who are legally present in the U.S. are eligible to be qualifying parents and file for their children.* Each qualified child must be unmarried, under the age of 21, *and residing in El Salvador, Guatemala or Honduras. In certain cases, the in-country parent*[125] *of the qualifying child may also qualify for access if the in-country parent is the legal spouse of the qualifying parent in the U.S.* (emphasis added).[126]

The Central American Minors In-Country Refugee program listed the following as the program eligibility criteria regarding the Central American child refugees, which if met, rendered them 'qualifying children' under the program:

---

[123]Department of (U.S.) Homeland Security In-Country Refugee/Parole Processing for Minors in Honduras, El Salvador and Guatemala (Central American Minors—CAM) https://www.uscis.gov/CAM Accessed 20 October, 2017.

[124]Kopan, Tal DHS [United States Department of Homeland Security] ends program for Central American minors (16 August, 2017) http://www.cnn.com/2017/08/16/politics/trump-ending-central-american-minors-program/index.html.

[125]That is the parent in Honduras, El Salvador and Guatemala.

[126]Department of (U.S.) Homeland Security In-Country Refugee/Parole Processing for Minors in Honduras, El Salvador and Guatemala (Central American Minors—CAM) pre expansion of eligibility criteria guidelines https://www.uscis.gov/CAM Accessed 20 October, 2017.

Eligibility

Qualifying Child

The qualifying child in El Salvador, Guatemala or Honduras must be:

The child (e.g. genetic, step or legally adopted) of the qualifying parent);

Unmarried;

Under the age of 21;

A national of El Salvador, Guatemala, or Honduras; and

Residing in his or her country of nationality (emphasis added).[127]

In 2016 the program expanded to permit the following also to make applications to the CAM program:

(1) The children, regardless of age or marital status, of a U.S.-based lawfully present parent;

(2) The in-country biological parent of a qualifying child that is not legally married to the U. S.-based lawfully present parent; and

(3) The caregiver of a qualifying child who is related to either the U.S.-based lawfully present parent or the qualifying child.[128]

Under the CAM in-country refugee program, if the child while still in the Central American country applies for asylum to the U.S. as a refugee along with a parent also still in that Central American Country; each must establish independent refugee status:

> Both the qualifying child and any in-country parent of the qualifying child must each establish independent refugee claims to be granted refugee status[129]

The qualification for an in-country unaccompanied or accompanied minor child *applying as a refugee* under CAM is somewhat of a contradiction in terms in that in order that the child can be permitted to establish a so-called 'independent refugee claim' *under the program*; he/she must establish the existence of a *bona fide* relationship *with a parent legally present in the US*. Thus the child is not in fact

[127]Department of (U.S.) Homeland Security In-Country Refugee/Parole Processing for Minors in Honduras, El Salvador and Guatemala (Central American Minors—CAM) https://www.uscis.gov/CAM Accessed 20 October, 2017.

[128]U.S. Department of State: Expansion of the CAM Program In-Country Refugee Processing for Minors in Honduras, El Salvador and Guatemala (January 20, 2017) https://www.state.gov/j/prm/releases/factsheets/2017/266363.htm Accessed 20 October, 2017.

[129]Department of (U.S.) Homeland Security In-Country Refugee/Parole Processing for Minors in Honduras, El Salvador and Guatemala (Central American Minors—CAM) https://www.uscis.gov/CAM Accessed 20 October, 2017.

fully considered for refugee asylum in his or her own right under this program[130] which is in that way contrary to the rights-based approach to international child protection promoted by the UNHCR guidelines. Those UNHCR guidelines do not precondition a child's consideration for refugee asylum upon their having a close relative in the prospective asylum country (though for the UNHCR family reunification may be one factor leading to prioritizing a case amongst many factors to be considered).[131]

Arguably the CAM in-country refugee program is, to some extent, discriminatory on the basis of social status in disadvantaging unaccompanied children who have lost both parents (orphaned children) or who have no close family tie in the U.S. While family reunification is a priority under international refugee and child rights law; it should not exclude special consideration for those unaccompanied child refugees who may be especially high need in terms of the urgency of a grant of asylum (i.e. children at imminent or other foreseeable concrete high risk of their well-being and safety due to: i.e. their youth political activism, LGBTQ status, being an ex child soldier, children previously subjected to torture by agents of their government and currently also targeted etc., children with urgent humanitarian need but for whom family reunification is not possible for whatever reason). In fact recall that under the United States resettlement program family reunification is just one of the priority categories; the priority one category being those refugee asylum seekers who had been designated by the UNHCR for resettlement in the U.S. and the priority two category being those refugee asylum seekers who were at special heightened risk and vulnerability.[132]

Children from the so-called Northern Triangle of Central America (El Salvador, Honduras and Guatemala) are at high risk of injury or death. It was estimated that in 2015–2016, for instance, 33,000 people had been murdered "due to rampant violence in the region"[133] Insisting as a screen for acceptance into the CAM program on

[130]United States Citizenship and Immigration Services Update on Central American Minors Program (CAM) November 15, 2017: "On Nov. 9, 2017, the Department of State stopped accepting new applications for the Central American Minors (CAM) refugee program. USCIS [United States Citizenship and Immigration Services] will stop interviewing CAM cases on Jan. 31, 2018. After that date, individuals with pending applications who have not been interviewed will receive a notice with further instructions. The CAM program was established in 2014 to provide certain minors in El Salvador, Guatemala, and Honduras the opportunity to be considered, while still in their home country, for refugee resettlement in the United States. Individuals who were determined to be ineligible for refugee status were then considered by USCIS for the possibility of entering the United States under parole. The parole portion of the CAM program was terminated in August 2017. (emphasis added)" https://www.uscis.gov/CAM.

[131]UNHCR Conclusion on Children at Risk (2007) at p. 4 No. 107 (LVIII) Executive Committee 56th session. Contained in United Nations General Assembly document A/AC.96/1048 http://www.unhcr.org/en-us/excom/exconc/4717625c2/conclusion-children-risk.html (accessed 30 June, 2017).

[132]The United States Refugee Admissions Program (USRAP) Consultation & Worldwide Processing Priorities (US Citizenship and Immigration webpage).

[133]The Guardian (Nina Lakhani in Mexico City reporting) Thousands of young Central Americans at risk as refugee ban halts key program, 2 February, 2017.

a family tie regarding a parent in the US legally (a genetic, step or other legal parent of the child) seems inconsistent with the humanitarian objectives of the U.S. refugee resettlement initiative more generally:

> The United States actively supports efforts to provide protection, assistance, and durable solutions to these refugees, as these measures fulfill our humanitarian interests and further our foreign policy and national security interests.[134]

> The United States and UNHCR recognize that resettlement in third countries is a vital tool for providing refugees protection and/or durable solutions in some particularly difficult cases. For some refugees, resettlement is the best, and perhaps the only, alternative.[135]

> Resettlement in a third country is a durable solution for refugees who are among the most vulnerable in the world...[136]

Note that the US refugee/admission resettlement program[137] also sometimes permits referrals of individuals and identifiable refugee groups (by the UNHCR and other approved NGOs and U.S. agencies) while the highly vulnerable refugee individual is still *in-country* (in their home State); the referral being based on high humanitarian concern and protection need.[138] Unlike the CAM program directed specifically to minors from Central America with a parent legally present in the U.S.; the aforementioned cases of 'in-country' referral under the U.S. resettlement program (aside from CAM) are not automatically excluded from the program if they have no family ties in the U.S.

The U.S. refugee resettlement program more generally and CAM in particular have a tradition of in a sense bringing the U.S. frontier to the refugee. The latter is reflected by, in part, in some instances, allowing consideration of 'in-country refugees' (where the refugee has not yet crossed out of the State territory where they are experiencing persecution). This 'in-country' consideration occurs especially

---

[134]U.S Department of State, U.S Department of Homeland Security, U.S. Department of Health and Human Services. Proposed Refugee Admissions for 2014 submitted on behalf of the U.S. President to the Committees on the Judiciary, United States Senate and United States House of Representatives at p. 1.

[135]U.S Department of State, U.S Department of Homeland Security, U.S. Department of Health and Human Services. Proposed Refugee Admissions for 2014 submitted on behalf of the U.S. President to the Committees on the Judiciary, United States Senate and United States House of Representatives at p. 2.

[136]U.S Department of State, U.S Department of Homeland Security, U.S. Department of Health and Human Services. Proposed Refugee Admissions for 2014 submitted on behalf of the U.S. President to the Committees on the Judiciary, United States Senate and United States House of Representatives at p. 2.

[137]Under new immigration guidelines; President Trump has drastically cut the number of refugees to be permitted for resettlement in the U.S. in the coming year which cap will stand unless successfully defeated in the courts.

[138]U.S Department of State, U.S Department of Homeland Security, U.S. Department of Health and Human Services. Proposed Refugee Admissions for 2014 submitted on behalf of the U.S. President to the Committees on the Judiciary, United States Senate and United States House of Representatives at pp. 7–8.

where the individual refugee or refugee collective is in very high need of protection or in the case of CAM a vulnerable refugee child can be reunited through the program with a parent who is in the U.S. legally. This humanitarian spirit that traditionally pervaded the U.S. refugee admission/resettlement program and the consequent bringing of the U.S. frontier (jurisdiction) to the refugee prospective asylee is also reflected in the fact that in respect of the U.S. refugee admission/ resettlement/program:

> Interviews of refugees by American officials from the Department of Homeland Security's U.S. Citizenship and Immigration Services (USCIS) *are often conducted in remote locations and are geared toward populations in greatest need of third country resettlement opportunities* (emphasis added).[139]

At the same time; recent deterrence efforts (under the Trump and the Obama administrations) aimed at dissuading refugees from Central America and elsewhere (including, among others, unaccompanied minors and families with children) from traveling to the U.S. border irregularly in search of asylum have often been, as here discussed, unforgiving and commonly applied without the necessary standards fully consistent with due process and humane treatment. The latter is inconsistent thus with the requirements of international human rights and refugee law.

5.4 U.S. Border Control: On Whether There Is U.S. 'Outsourcing' of 'Refoulement' of Unaccompanied Minors from Central America and Mexico

Some legal scholars have accused the U.S. of "outsourcing refoulement" to Mexico in respect of refugees from Central America including unaccompanied and separated minors.[140] Korthius discusses the U.S. funding of programs by Mexico to deport undocumented economic migrants *as well as refugees*; the latter with a legitimate well grounded fear of persecution who arrived at the Mexican border from Central America (specifically from El Salvador, Guatemala, and Honduras) including those whose ultimate goal had been to seek refuge (officially or unofficially) in the U.S. as Convention refugees. The program in Mexico, partially funded by the U.S., and involving also deportation of Central American unaccompanied child refugees,

---

[139] U.S Department of State, U.S Department of Homeland Security, U.S. Department of Health and Human Services. Proposed Refugee Admissions for 2014 submitted on behalf of the U.S. President to the Committees on the Judiciary, United States Senate and United States House of Representatives at p. 3.

[140] Korthuis (2016).

among others, is called *Program Frontera Sur*[141] Korthius holds that *Program Frontera Sur* "is designed to turn around Central Americans in their tracks" and that hence the significant U.S. financial contributions to the program, for instance, "tie the United States to what occurs at the Guatemalan border."[142] Korthius alleges that the U.S. is exporting refoulement to Mexico but that having Mexico 'do U.S. bidding' in this regard (to mitigate the problem of the large numbers of unaccompanied child refugees and others from Central America arriving at the U.S. southern border) does not preclude U.S. culpability in that alleged refoulement through an agent (constructive refoulement). This since: "the United Nations High Commissioner on Refugees, the Inter-American Commission on Refugees and the European Union, have all determined that Article 33 [of the Refugee Convention re the principle of non-refoulement] places the same legal obligations on the way that states handle refugees even where the state is acting outside its formal territory" (the U.S. employs in part extraterritorial means thus to block Central American refugees from U.S. ports of entry through its financial and political support of Mexico's alleged refoulement practices).[143] Consider on the latter point also the conclusions of L Naar who points out that were extraterritorial application of non-refoulement obligations not recognized; in practice the principle in large part would *in effect* be nullified:

> states may blatantly breach their non-refoulement obligation or craftily conceive of ways to circumvent their obligations... If the principle of non-refoulement were to be strictly interpreted to apply only at the border and within a state's territory, states could assume extremely wide latitude in preventing asylum seekers from ever being protected by the principle (emphasis added).[144]

A few further remarks before we consider the Korthius claim of refoulement of Central Americans, in particular unaccompanied or separated children in need of international protection in light of findings by Human Rights Watch.

President Trump is not the first U.S. President supporting Mexico-U.S. joint efforts through territorial and extraterritorial means to stem the tide of unaccompanied and separated child refugees arriving at their respective borders. President Obama[145] it is noteworthy stated:

---

[141] A study by the United Nations High Commissioner on Refugees (UNHCR) involved the UNHCR interviewing 404 unaccompanied children between the ages of 12 and 17 who had arrived at the U.S. border (often through Mexico) from Central America and others from Mexico as their place of origin during or after October 2011 and found that "58 % ...of [the] children interviewed were forcibly displaced because they suffered or faced harms that indicated a potential or actual need for international protection" Cited in Korthuis (2016) (primary source: UNHCR Children on the Run (2014)).

[142] Korthuis (2016).

[143] Korthuis (2016).

[144] Naar, L February 9, 2016) The extraterritoriality of the principle of non-refoulement: A critique of the Sale case and Roma case (London School of Economics blog) http://blogs.lse.ac.uk/humanrights/2016/02/09/the-extraterritoriality-of-the-principle-of-non-refoulement-a-critique-of-the-sale-case-and-roma-case/ (Accessed 24 February, 2017).

[145] Recall that there was no movement toward the U.S. ratifying the Convention on the Rights of the Child under Obama and that Article 22 of the CRC addresses the rights of refugee children

> I very much appreciate Mexico's efforts in addressing the unaccompanied children who we saw spiking during the summer. In part because of strong efforts by Mexico, including at its southern border, we've seen those numbers reduced back to much more manageable levels But one of the things that we both agreed on is our continued need to work with Central American governments so that we can address some of the social and economic challenges there that led to that spike in unaccompanied children.
>
> *...but we're also going to be much more aggressive at the border in ensuring that people come through the system legally.* And the Mexican government has been very helpful in how we can process and message that effectively both inside of the United States and in Mexico (emphasis added).[146]

Note that former U.S. President Obama's statement "...we're also going to be much *more aggressive at the border* in ensuring that people come through the system legally..." (emphasis added)[147] belies the fact that (1) refugee asylum seekers arriving irregularly near or at a land border or other port of entry are permitted to do so under international refugee and humanitarian law and are to receive no penalty for the same and (2) refoulement in response simply to irregular arrival and especially without proper individual assessment of the refugee asylum case is what is unlawful in a substantive way under U.S. refugee statutory law as well as under international human rights and refugee law.

Unaccompanied and accompanied children face very clear grave dangers in the perilous arduous journey from their homeland to the Mexican-U.S. border (abduction, traffickers etc.). Refoulement by whatever means (direct or indirect constructive refoulement) to the home country or to another insecure jurisdiction where these children face violence and persecution is inexcusable in law grounded on democratic principles. Rather an orderly refugee strategy in coordination with other States and the UNHCR and *consistent with Refugee Convention treaty obligations*—including non-refoulement—is what the situation demands if the States involved are to respond in a civilized manner with due regard to the international rule of humanitarian and human rights law and its underlying values as pertains to refugees especially child refugees (see the UNHCR report 'Children on the Run' in respect of unaccompanied and separated children from Central America and Mexico and recommendations regarding how best States may meet these children's international protection needs).[148]

---

including unaccompanied such children to "receive appropriate protection and humanitarian assistance in the enjoyment of applicable rights set forth in the present Convention [CRC] and in other international human rights or humanitarian instruments to which the said States are Parties."

[146]Cited in Korthuis (2016) (primary source: Remarks by President Obama, 6 January, 2015 following bilateral meeting with President Penieto of Mexico).

[147]Cited in Korthuis (2016) (primary source: Remarks by President Obama, 6 January, 2015 following bilateral meeting with President Penieto of Mexico).

[148]UNHCR (2014) Children on the Run: Unaccompanied children leaving Central America and Mexico and the need for international protection at pp. 54–55 Available at http://www.unhcr.org/en-us/about-us/background/56fc266f4/children-on-the-run-full-report.html Accessed 20 October, 2017.

Unaccompanied and separated children from Central America seeking refugee asylum are amongst 'mixed migrants' (i.e. Convention refugees as well as those perhaps who are economic migrants in the main) arriving at the Mexican southern border and the US-Mexican border.[149] The mixed migrant aspect must not be used, however, to deflect from the fact that a significant proportion of this unaccompanied or separated child population group (among others) arriving at the Mexican border are *prima facie* refugees according to Convention criteria or entitled to international protection on other grounds and as discussed may be fleeing poverty as well as targeted persecution.[150]

> *Tens of thousands of children travel from Central America to Mexico each year, most from El Salvador, Guatemala, and Honduras.... as many as half are fleeing threats to their lives and safety, meaning that they have plausible claims to international protection, the United Nations High Commissioner for Refugees (UNHCR) has estimated.*
>
> By law, Mexico offers protection to refugees as well as to others who would face risks to their lives or safety if returned to their countries of origin. Mexican government data suggest, however, that *less than 1 percent of children who are apprehended by Mexican immigration authorities are recognized as refugees or receive other formal protection in Mexico* ...Human Rights Watch conducted multiple research missions in 2015 to examine how Mexico is applying its own and international law in its treatment of Central American migrants, particularly children.
>
> [Human Rights Watch] found wide discrepancies between Mexico's law and the way it is enforced. Children who may have claims for refugee recognition confront multiple obstacles in applying for refugee recognition from the moment they are taken into custody by INM. *As one UNHCR official told us, "the biggest problem in Mexico is not the [asylum] procedure itself, but access to the procedure* (emphasis added)[151]

Human Rights Watch in its study 'Closed doors: Mexico's Failure to Protect Central American Refugee and Migrant Children'[152] found that amongst the barriers to unaccompanied and separated child refugees (and other children with international protection needs) receiving international protection consistent with international treaty obligations were the following (here paraphrased):

- INM agents (immigration agents of Instituto Nacional de Migración), commonly fail to inform unaccompanied or separated children they may seek refugee

[149]UNHCR Children on the Run (2014) at p. 3 Available at http://www.unhcr.org/en-us/about-us/background/56fc266f4/children-on-the-run-full-report.html Accessed 20 October, 2017.

[150]UNHCR Children on the Run (2014) at p. 42 Available at http://www.unhcr.org/en-us/about-us/background/56fc266f4/children-on-the-run-full-report.html Accessed 20 October, 2017.

[151]Human Rights Watch (2016). Closed doors: Mexico's Failure to Protect Central American Refugee and Migrant Children (31 March, 2016) https://www.hrw.org/report/2016/03/31/closed-doors/mexicos-failure-protect-central-american-refugee-and-migrant-children Accessed 20 October, 2017.

[152]Human Rights Watch (2016). Closed doors: Mexico's Failure to Protect Central American Refugee and Migrant Children (31 March, 2016) https://www.hrw.org/report/2016/03/31/closed-doors/mexicos-failure-protect-central-american-refugee-and-migrant-children Accessed 20 October, 2017.

recognition and generally do not inform them a humanitarian visa would be possible if they are successful in obtaining recognition as a refugee;
- INM agents generally do not do proper screening/interviewing of the unaccompanied or separated children to determine whether they may have a valid refugee claim;
- Generally the unaccompanied or separated child who does apply for refugee asylum does not have legal representation or assistance except in those less common instances where a certain NGO offers legal services to the child as part of the NGO normal protocol in such cases;
- Detention of the unaccompanied or separated child migrants commonly occurs and most often in "prison-like conditions" (In Mexico "Over 35,000 children were held in immigration detention centers in 2015 more than half of that total were unaccompanied").[153] This is the case though Mexican law requires children be transferred to child protection facilities (which should be child friendly shelters) where there is a concern/consideration for their safety. Under Mexican law; children who apply for refugee status or who obtain a humanitarian visa are generally not to be detained pending the final determination of their status unless special circumstances warrant[154]:

> Detention—never appropriate for children—is particularly problematic for those who want to apply for refugee recognition. Children report being told by INM agents that merely applying for recognition will result in protracted detention, either in INM-run facilities or in the virtual detention of DIF [child protection] shelters, while their applications are considered. We heard from children . . .who decided not to apply or who withdrew applications because they did not want to remain locked up. Some children remained in immigration detention centers for a month or more, and those who exercise their right to appeal adverse decisions on their applications for refugee recognition might be held in immigration detention centers for six months or more.[155]

Human Rights Watch concluded that Mexico is effectively engaged in 'constructive refoulement' given the barriers that are systematically put in place by Mexican immigration officials to prevent unaccompanied and separated children from Central America from accessing refugee asylum procedures and due process in that regard:

> These obstacles are serious barriers for children who have claims for refugee recognition. Where the indirect pressure on individuals is so intense that it leads them to believe that they have no access to the asylum process and no practical option but to return to countries where

[153] Human Rights Watch (2016). Closed doors: Mexico's Failure to Protect Central American Refugee and Migrant Children (31 March, 2016) at p. 5 https://www.hrw.org/report/2016/03/31/closed-doors/mexicos-failure-protect-central-american-refugee-and-migrant-children Accessed 20 October, 2017.

[154] Human Rights Watch (2016). Closed doors: Mexico's Failure to Protect Central American Refugee and Migrant Children (31 March, 2016) at pp. 4–5 https://www.hrw.org/report/2016/03/31/closed-doors/mexicos-failure-protect-central-american-refugee-and-migrant-children Accessed 20 October, 2017.

[155] Human Rights Watch (2016). Closed doors: Mexico's Failure to Protect Central American Refugee and Migrant Children (31 March, 2016) at p. 5 https://www.hrw.org/report/2016/03/31/closed-doors/mexicos-failure-protect-central-american-refugee-and-migrant-children Accessed 20 October, 2017.

> they face serious risk of persecution or threats to their lives and safety, these factors in combination may constitute constructive refoulement, in violation of international law.[156]

Insofar as the U.S. is helping to fund such NGO alleged unacceptable refugee migration control tactics by Mexico which violate international refugee and human rights law, the U.S. is arguably complicit in Mexico's alleged 'constructive refoulement' of these unaccompanied and separated child refugee asylum seekers and others.[157]

5.5 The 'Bona Fide Relationship to the U.S.' Rule in U.S. Refugee Policy

As here discussed; under the CAM program (concerning child refugees from Central America) the child's right to asylum as a refugee in the U.S. is tied to having a parent legally present in the U.S. (a parent with U.S. legal status of some sort but not necessarily U.S. citizenship).[158] This aspect is, in some respects, reminiscent of the rule formulated by the Supreme Court of the United States (USSC) in its preliminary judgment in the Trump travel ban case *United States v International Refugee Assistance Project et al.*[159] This in that USSC rule sets out that *refugees*, as certain other foreign nationals, would be allowed entry (exemption from the Trump travel ban) if they had *bona fide* pre-existing ties to the U.S. with a person or entity in the U.S. that had U.S. recognized legal status. That Trump Executive Order travel ban, the USSC ruled, was to be implemented in accord with the aforementioned stipulation formulated by the USSC *per curium* in the case.,[160] More specifically, the

---

[156]Human Rights Watch (2016). Closed doors: Mexico's Failure to Protect Central American Refugee and Migrant Children (31 March, 2016) https://www.hrw.org/report/2016/03/31/closed-doors/mexicos-failure-protect-central-american-refugee-and-migrant-children Accessed 20 October, 2017.

[157]"...when a control procedure takes place in the territory of a third state and the ... State involved does not exert effective control over the persons concerned, the examination of the asylum claims may take place in that third state only if there are guarantees that the non-refoulement principle and other protection standards will be fully ensured." See Vandvik (2008).

[158]The child's right to asylum under CAM then is not assessed with respect to the child's possible independent right to refugee asylum as an autonomous person in his/her own right on a basis separate and apart from the issue of family reunification.

[159]Supreme Court of the United States Donald J. Trump, President of the United States et al v International Refugee Assistance Project et al. 582 U. S. ____ (2017) (26 June, 2017).

[160]It is as yet an unanswered question whether the USSC rule in the Trump travel ban case will be let stand and whether it conforms to the 1980 U.S. Refugee Act and other relevant U.S. statutory law (the immigration and naturalization statute). The USSC rule referred to here is that a foreign national who is a refugee must have a *bona fide* tie to a U.S. entity or person before (1) he/she can be considered for the U.S. admission/resettlement program and if successful in that program and in the U.S. vetting system gain entry to the U.S. or before (2) he/she can enter the U.S. on his/her own without proper documents and then apply for U.S. refugee asylum or do so at a land or water port of entry to the U.S. with any chance of success in obtaining asylum.

Supreme Court of the United States set out a rule[161] that (1) foreign nationals who were outside the U.S. at the time the revised Trump travel ban (Executive Order (EO2)) went into partial force[162] and (2) who did not yet have authorized entry/travel documents to the U.S. by the specified date (that is the date of the *partial* lifting of a nation-wide injunction on President Trump's travel ban)[163]; would be subject to the travel ban only if they did not have a *bona fide* relationship to a person[164] or entity with legal status in the US. Thus those foreign nationals to whom the travel ban applied and who were seeking entry to the U.S. would have to be able to make a credible claim of a *bona fide* relationship to a person (legally present in the U.S.) or

---

[161]See Supreme Court of the United States, Donald J. Trump, President of the United States v International Refugee Assistance Project et al. 582 U. S. ____ (2017).

[162]On January 27, 2017 American President Donald Trump issued Executive Order 13769, "Protecting the Nation from Foreign Terrorist Entry into the United States.". That order, on the respectful view here, epitomizes the denial of collective refugee asylum rights leading to a denial of such rights on the individual level. In part the Executive Order (1) banned for a period of 90 days entry into the United States of persons from seven designated countries; Iraq, Iran, Libya, Somalia, Sudan, Syria, and Yemen who did not have their entry documents by a specified date in the Executive Order; (2) suspended the United States' Refugee Admissions/Resettlement Program barring all refugees entry for 120 days (with waivers potentially available on a case-by-case basis as per specified grounds) with a direction that once the Refugee resettlement program was resumed that the Secretary of State was to prioritize refugees claiming religious persecution where the religion of the asylum seeker was a minority religion in the country of national origin, and (3) denied entry to the United States of Syrian refugees indefinitely. A second Executive Order issued March 6, 2017 modified the travel ban by, among other things, omitting Iraq as one of the countries of origin from which foreign nationals would be barred under the aforementioned conditions (leaving now Iran, Libya, Somalia, Sudan, Syria, and Yemen as the countries covered by the 90 day suspension), removing the indefinite bar against Syrian refugees being included in the U.S. resettlement program and instead including them also in a 120 day suspension of the U.S. resettlement program and removing a preference in resettlement (once the program resumed) for persons of a minority religion in their homeland. The third iteration of the Trump travel ban included also the following additional countries (Chad, North Korea and Venezuela) however Chad has now been dropped from the list as targeted for the suspension of travel from those states to the U.S. by foreign nationals who did not have entry papers by the specified date (with certain exceptions and particular country-specific application as articulated). Travel ban 3.0 is titled "Presidential Proclamation Enhancing Vetting Capabilities and Processes for Detecting Attempted Entry into the United States by Terrorists or Other Public-Safety Threats." and pertains then to suspension (with no expiry date specified) now of travel to the United States from Iran, Libya, North Korea, Syria, Venezuela, Somalia and Yemen by foreign nationals who did not have the required papers permitting entry to the U.S. by the designated date (the refugee resettlement program was reactivated with additional vetting October 24, 2017). See Fact Sheet on the Trump Travel Ban 3.0 released September 24, 2017 and updated April 10, 2018 https://www.dhs.gov/news/2017/09/24/fact-sheet-president-s-proclamation-enhancing-vetting-capabilities-and-processes.

The Proclamation is dated September 24, 2017 and scheduled to take effect 18 October, 2017.

[163]Persons with a visa who would otherwise have been excluded under the travel ban did *not* have their visas revoked and previously arranged visa application appointments were not cancelled by U.S. immigration authorities (Jarrett, L and Labott, E CNN Travel ban 2.0 in effect, court challenges begin, 30 June, 2017).

[164]The U.S. government, hours before implementation of the Executive Order, set out and released to the public a list of categories of persons with whom, if the foreign national had a bona fide familial relationship, the government would as a consequence allow entry to the foreign national who posed no security or other known risk to the U.S. The list included "a parent, spouse, fiancée, child, adult son, or daughter, son-in-law, daughter-in-law or sibling in the U.S. " (Jarrett, L and Labott, E CNN Travel ban 2.0 in effect, court challenges begin, 30 June, 2017).

entity (a legitimate entity) in the U.S. to be exempt from the travel ban (or they might be exempt instead based on some applicable specific case waiver as the Trump travel ban Executive Order allowed for case-by-case exceptional waivers). In sum then if it were deemed that the foreign national's exclusion from entry to the U.S. would create an unacceptable hardship on a person or entity in the U.S. (with legal status in the United States) given that the foreign national seeking entry had a *bona fide* tie[165] to that person or entity in the U.S.; then the foreign national under the USSC rule would have to be allowed entry notwithstanding the Trump travel ban.

It is to be recalled that Trump's first Executive Order travel ban that was in part to suspend the U.S. admission/resettlement refugee program for 120 days was briefly implemented prior to the imposition of a nationwide injunction by the lower courts. As a result, prior to the nationwide injunction on application of the travel ban, the CAM in-country refugee program was suspended for children from Honduras, El Salvador and Guatemala. (Recall that it has been reported that in 2015 and 2014 at least 60,000 children had left El Salvador alone or dropped out of school there due to the violence (the latter according to Ministry of Education statistics)).[166] Due to the refugee ban imposed temporarily by President Trump under the First Executive Order (later stayed by the courts) it was estimated that "as many as 9000 youngsters whose CAM applications [were] ... under consideration, or who [had been] accepted but were waiting for permission to travel to the U.S. ...[found] themselves in legal limbo"[167] while the executive order travel ban was in effect. However, under a rule formulated by the USSC in *Donald J. Trump, President of the United States v International Refugee Assistance Project et al.*,[168] children who have a *bona fide* relationship with a person in the U.S. (which would in fact be the case for children accepted for resettlement to the U.S. under the CAM in-country refugee program)[169] would be deemed to be exempted from the travel ban. However later developments have involved a staged termination of the CAM program.[170] In addition, the U.S. Supreme Court later abandoned its bona fide relationship rule in the Trump travel ban case for the time being until the case is heard on the merits by the High Court.[171]

---

[165]If the tie between the foreign national and the U.S. person or legal entity was created for the purpose of avoiding the travel ban it was not to be considered a *bona fide* tie and would not exempt the foreign national from the Trump travel ban.

[166]The Guardian (Nina Lakhani in Mexico City reporting) Thousands of young Central Americans at risk as refugee ban halts key program, 2 February, 2017.

[167]The Guardian (Nina Lakhani in Mexico City reporting) Thousands of young Central Americans at risk as refugee ban halts key program, 2 February, 2017.

[168]Supreme Court of the United States, Donald J. Trump, President of the United States v International Refugee Assistance Project et al. 582 U. S. ____ (2017) (26 June, 2017).

[169]Refugee children, under the United States' CAM program, must have a parent legally present in the US. to be eligible to participate in that resettlement program which is based on family reunification.

[170]See FN130 supra.

[171]Donald J. Trump, President of the United States, et al., Applicants v. Hawaii, et al. (Opinion of December 4, 2017).

Note, however, that the Trump Executive Order, as implemented following the USSC June, 2017 decision in *Donald J. Trump, President of the United States v International Refugee Assistance Project et al.*, appeared to violate, in some respects, the Supreme Court rule as set out in the case (i.e. the rule regarding entry permissible to the refugee also where there is a *bona fide* relationship of the refugee with a U.S. person or entity with legal status in the U.S.). According to the USSC rule; a *bona fide* relationship or tie between, for instance, the vetted refugee child and any close family member lawfully in the U.S. i.e. parents, grandparents and certain other close family members such as aunts or uncles would be sufficient to meet the criteria for entry. However post the USSC ruling in the *International Refugee Assistance Project* case,[172] many close family ties were *not* listed in the government (Trump) guidelines as 'approved persons' regarding establishing a *bona fide* relationship with a person legally present in the U.S.[173] The USSC rule (formulated in the *International Refugee Assistance Project* case)[174] would also arguably include as a *bona fide* relationship or tie between the refugee child and a U.S. entity; a tie between the refugee child and a US. government recognized refugee resettlement program or organization (and also where the child has no family ties in the U.S.). The latter as long as the U.S. NGO had not reached out to initiate contact and had not formed that relationship with the refugee child for the very purpose of the refugee child meeting the *bona fide* relationship with a U.S. entity requirement for entry.[175]

> As for entities, the relationship must be formal, documented, and formed in the ordinary course, rather than for the purpose of evading EO–2.
>
> Not so [re having a bona fide relationship to a U.S. entity is] someone who enters into a relationship simply to avoid §2(c): For example, a nonprofit group devoted to immigration issues may not contact foreign nationals from the designated countries, add them to client lists, and then secure their entry by claiming injury from their exclusion[176] (portion in square brackets added for clarity)

Later litigation regarding various iterations of the Trump Executive Order travel ban (1) established a broader category of family members who could be included as establishing that the foreign nationals (including refugees) had a *bona fide* tie to a person with legal status in the U.S. and the government did not appeal on that issue of the broader family category but (2) to date whether a tie between a vetted refugee abroad and a U.S. refugee resettlement agency is sufficient to establish a *bona fide* tie

---

[172]Supreme Court of the United States, Donald J. Trump, President of the United States v International Refugee Assistance Project et al. 582 U. S. ____ (2017) (26 June, 2017).

[173]Margulies, P The EO stay "The government doubles down on excluding grandparents and refugees (4 July, 2017).

[174]Supreme Court of the United States, Donald J. Trump, President of the United States v International Refugee Assistance Project et al. 582 U. S. ____ (2017) (26 June, 2017).

[175]The USSC rule regarding a bona fide relationship with a U.S. entity stipulated that the tie to the legal entity in the U.S. must have been formed in the ordinary course and not to evade the Trump travel ban.

[176]Supreme Court of the United States, Donald J. Trump, President of the United States v International Refugee Assistance Project et al. 582 U. S. ____ (2017) at p. 12.

to a U.S. legal entity has not been finally settled (it has not been ruled on as to the merits) by the United States Supreme Court. However a recent lower court decision has held that (1) a *bona fide* tie between a specific refugee or refugee family abroad and a U.S. resettlement agency is established through the assurance the resettlement agency has given to the U.S. Department of State to provide basic services when that vetted particular refugee or refugee family arrives in the U.S. and (2) this tie will exempt that refugee or refugee family from the Trump travel ban and regardless the cap specified in the Trump travel ban on the numbers of refugees to be permitted entry for a certain period under the U.S. resettlement program.[177]

5.5.1 Re-Considering the Legal Viability of the USSC 'Bona Fide Relationship to the U.S.' Rule as Applied to Refugees

It is (on the view here) not at all clear on what legal basis (i.e. considering UNHCR guidelines and that the U.S. has incorporated the Refugee Convention definition of refugee into U.S. statutory law)[178] it can be held (as the USSC did in *Donald J. Trump, President of the United States v International Refugee Assistance Project et al.*[179]) that a refugee abroad to whom the Trump travel ban would have applied must have a *bona fide* relationship with a person or entity in the U.S. (with legal status in the U.S.) prior to entry to be exempted from the Trump travel ban. The refugee's right to non-refoulement cannot be, it is here argued, conditioned on the refugee having a *bona fide* tie to the U.S. Thus, on the view here, in any case where the U.S., by direct or indirect means, exercises jurisdiction in such a manner so as to cause or be complicit in the refoulement of a refugee (whether the refugee is abroad or arrived irregularly at a U.S. border); this would be a profound violation of international humanitarian and human rights law *not* at all excusable based on the refugee's lack of a *bona fide* tie to a person or entity in the U.S. with legal status in the U.S. Yet such may very well be the implication should the *bona fide* rule be considered a prerequisite for refugee resettlement or asylum seeking entry to the U.S. post the pending (at the time of writing) USSC ruling on the merits of the

[177]United States Court of Appeal for the Ninth Circuit, State of Hawaii; Ishmail Elshikh v Donald J Trump et al (7 September, 2017) at p. 34 http://cdn.ca9.uscourts.gov/datastore/general/2017/09/07/17-16426%20Opinion%20Filed.pdf Accessed 17 October, 2017.

[178]The U.S. Refugee Act adopts the definition of refugee found in the Refugee Convention as "a person who is unable or unwilling to return to his or her home country because of a 'well-founded fear of persecution' due to race, membership in a particular social group, political opinion, religion, or national origin" American Immigration Council, An overview of U.S. Refugee Law and Policy (November 18, 2015). Note that while the U.S. is not a party to the Refugee Convention it is a party to the 1967 Protocol to the Convention (having acceded in 1968 to the 1967 Protocol) and is legally bound by articles 2 to 34 of the Convention (see McCuiston 2014, p. 532).

[179]Supreme Court of the United States, Donald J. Trump, President of the United States v International Refugee Assistance Project et al. 582 U. S. ____ (2017).

Trump travel ban. Unaccompanied children, for instance, in desperate need of humanitarian assistance who do not have family ties in the U.S. may not be considered *in the first instance* for the U.S. resettlement program especially once the year cap for refugee resettlement numbers specified by the Trump administration is reached (a cap that is half what the cap has been under the previous administration). These children then if considered qualified by the UNHCR for resettlement in the U.S. (on humanitarian grounds consistent with the Refugee Convention) but for their lack of ties to the U.S. can, on the view here, be considered to have suffered a form of constructive refoulement if excluded only on the basis of lack of family pre-existing ties to the U.S. Such unaccompanied children, among others, may as a consequence be even more likely left languishing in substandard refugee camps out of their homeland. The latter given the low numbers of refugees accepted for resettlement overall in comparison to the need and the significant contribution the U.S. has made to resettlement to the U.S. (working with the UNHCR) in the past compared to most other countries.

Refugee asylum seekers who have arrived to the U.S. irregularly without any recognized status—many or most of whom have no ties to a person legally in the U.S. or to a U.S. authorized entity—are not, *under the Refugee Convention*, 'excludable' (from entry and consideration of an asylum request) due only to the possible lack of *bona fide* ties to the U.S. In the case of refugees abroad selected for refugee resettlement through the U.S. Refugee Admission Resettlement program (as will be discussed here shortly), on the view here, there is a *bona fide* relationship in any case with a U.S. entity (the U.S. resettlement agency).

It would appear that, in some sense at least, the *bona fide* relationship rule set out by the United States Supreme Court in the Trump travel ban litigation[180] is a new iteration, *in a somewhat different form*, of the notion of "excludable aliens" deprived of certain necessary procedural safeguards in consideration of their case. In this instance these alleged 'excludable aliens' are refugees abroad who did not have their entry papers by a certain stipulated date and are automatically deemed excludable (per the categorical specifications of the Trump travel ban that relate to refugee status and/or country of origin) if they do not have a *bona fide* tie to a person or entity in the U.S. with legal status in the U.S.[181] In previous times; the 'excludable alien' category was a declining of U.S. jurisdiction to consider the refugee asylum claim (where such an asylum request was made) due to the foreign national allegedly not having actually entered U.S. territory but rather irregularly arriving at or near a U.S. port of entry/border and asking for asylum.[182] In neither of the aforementioned instances is the basis for exclusion consistent with the Refugee Convention or another internationally accepted international refugee scheme.

[180]Boston College Third World Journal *The Disproportionate Effect of the Entry Fiction on Excludable Aliens*, 9 B.C. Third World L.J. 271 (1989), (Accessed 4 June, 2017).

[181]The targeted countries of origin in the Trump travel ban has changed from only selected specified Muslim-majority countries to now including in the third iteration of the travel ban also two non-Muslim majority countries (Venezuela and North Korea).

[182]See Coffey, K (2000) The due process right to seek asylum in the United States: The immigration dilemma and constitutional controversy, Yale Law and Policy Review, 19(2), 303–339 at p. 309.

5.5.2 *The Refugee's 'Bona Fide Relationship with a U.S. Legal Entity': U.S. Resettlement of Refugees and the Trump Travel Ban*

Those refugees abroad designated for resettlement in the U.S. by the IRC (International Rescue Committee) abroad, the UNHCR or other NGO are thoroughly vetted by U.S. authorities abroad before issuance of their entry papers to the U.S. The IRC has 29 centres in the U.S. amongst its centres globally. The U.S. IRC centers link with other NGO's locally in the U.S. to arrange for essential services to new refugee arrivals. Yet in June, 2017 the IRC commented as follows on the Trump travel ban implementation guidelines then in place:

> Out of 2,500 people IRC was scheduled to resettle, roughly 1,950 would not meet the arbitrary definitions imposed by the administration– either because they do not possess U.S. ties [as per the Trump guidelines] or because they do not meet a near-nuclear family definition.[183]

Where a refugee is sponsored by a U.S. resettlement agency (as is required under the U.S. admission/resettlement program to allow the refugee entry to the U.S. under that program), the agency provides assurances to the U.S. government (the Department of State) that it will provide basic services to the refugee upon the arrival of that particular refugee to the U.S. The U.S. government then reimburses the U.S. resettlement agency for those services. However the Trump administration has argued in the travel ban litigation that a tie of a refugee to a U.S. resettlement agency does *not* meet the requirement for an exemption to the travel ban (as set out in the USSC *bona fide* relationship to a U.S. legal entity exemption criterion). The government argued that no tie to a legal entity exists in such a case in that the US entity (the U.S. resettlement agency) does not have direct, personal contact with the individual refugee before that refugee's entry into the U.S. However, it must be recalled that in fact prospective refugees do have contact with U.S. officials before entry is granted and the cases are prioritized on the basis of the urgency of the humanitarian considerations in the particular cases:

> The United States Citizenship and Immigration Services ("USCIS") is responsible for interviewing refugee applicants and adjudicating applications for refugee status. USCIS defines three "processing priorities," which enable a refugee applicant the opportunity to interview with a USCIS officer.[184]

---

[183]David Miliband (2017). IRC responds to administration's arbitrary and cruel travel ban guidelines. Press release 29 June, 2017, David Miliband President and CEO of the International Rescue Committee (IRC) Note that the family category was later broadened.

[184]Hawaii et al (Plaintiffs-Appellees) v Trump, President of the United States et al (Defendants-Appellants) United Sates Court of Appeals for the Ninth Circuit Brief of the Amicus Curiae Human Rights First (Formerly known as The Lawyers Committee for Human Rights) in Support of Appellees at p. 6, August 3, 2017.

Thus although the U.S. resettlement agency does not have direct personal contact with the refugee prior to entry of the refugee to the U.S.; the United States Citizenship and Immigration Services does have such contact. In a sense arguably the federal government acts as an agent for the refugee in that it is the federal government that assigns *particular* refugees and refugee families who have been vetted and approved for entry to the U.S. to certain U.S. resettlement agencies. The resettlement agencies then rely on a network of non-profit partners in various communities across the U.S. whom they work with and to whom they contract out to provide services to these designated refugees approved for entry. In addition, in some cases, the resettlement agency (i.e. USCRI; the United States Committee for Refugees and Immigrants) works directly with refugees they have been assigned once the refugees are arrived in the U.S. in providing services through its own field offices in the U.S.:

> USCRI does not independently solicit refugees to sponsor for resettlement in the United States. The State Department requires the resettlement volags [non-profit volunteer agencies dedicated to providing refugee services], including USCRI, to provide it with a "formal assurance" that it will sponsor a refugee candidate (or refugee family) that has been referred to it.[185]

> This assurance is a written guarantee that various basic services will be provided to the refugee and any accompanying family members who have been pre-cleared for resettlement. Before issuing a formal assurance of services, USCRI examines the refugee's file and considers a number of factors. . .and approaches one of its partner agencies with a request that it accept the refugee. When a partner agency agrees to accept a candidate for resettlement, USCRI submits a formal Assurance Form to the State Department.[186]

If for some reason a particular U.S. refugee resettlement agency is unable to provide the services as had been planned; the U.S. federal government under the refugee resettlement program would make alternate arrangements with another such U.S. agency and assign the identified specific refugees to the substitute resettlement agency. It is the case that a "resettlement agency has no authority or claim with respect to any particular alien abroad for whom it has provided an assurance"[187](for instance there is no basis for a U.S. resettlement agency to bring a lawsuit for not being able to provide services to a particular refugee or refugee collective).

---

[185]Hawaii et al (Plaintiffs-Appellees) v Trump, President of the United States et al (Defendants-Appellants) United Sates Court of Appeals for the Ninth Circuit, On Appeal from the U.S. District Court for the District of Hawaii, No. 1:17-cv-00050-DKW-KSC (Derrick K. Watson, J.) Brief of the Amicus Curiae Brief of Committee for Refugees and Immigrants, August 9, 2017 at p. 11.

[186]Hawaii et al (Plaintiffs-Appellees) v Trump, President of the United States et al (Defendants-Appellants) United Sates Court of Appeals for the Ninth Circuit, On Appeal from the U.S. District Court for the District of Hawaii, No. 1:17-cv-00050-DKW-KSC (Derrick K. Watson, J.) Brief of the Amicus Curiae Brief of Committee for Refugees and Immigrants, August 9, 2017 at p. 11.

[187]Hawaii et al (Plaintiffs-Appellees) v Trump, President of the United States et al (Defendants-Appellants) United Sates Court of Appeals for the Ninth Circuit Brief of the Amicus Curiae Human Rights First (Formerly known as The Lawyers Committee for Human Rights) in Support of Appellees at p. 8, August 3, 2017.

However, the fact that an assurance (to provide basic services) has been given to the Department of State by a U.S. resettlement agency means *specific identified refugees*[188] were accepted for the U.S. refugee admissions and resettlement program by U.S. Immigration Services and referred by the U.S. State Department to a particular U.S. resettlement agency. Further; while the U.S. resettlement agency has had no direct contact with the refugee prior to his/her arrival in the U.S., the resettlement agency (such as Committee for Refugees and Immigrants and its partner agencies) is quite familiar with the particular refugee's individual biography and family situation and the agency has made preparations to ensure the refugee's essential needs as well as any special needs are met upon arrival in the U.S. and for a period thereafter (i.e. for those who have been the victims of torture, those who may be LGBTQ, unaccompanied children etc. there are significant additional vulnerabilities and additional supports are typically required and will be provided by the resettlement agency). This also demonstrates that there is a *bona fide* ***case-specific*** *tie* between the U.S. resettlement agency and a particular refugee or refugee family. The latter thus, in the view of the litigation party opposing the Trump travel ban, meets the Supreme Court definition of a refugee having a *bona fide* relationship with a U.S. entity (here the U.S. resettlement agency).[189] In addition, that *bona fide* tie was created through federal government initiatives and referrals and not resettlement agency independent efforts (thus it *cannot* be said that any U.S. resettlement agency had created a relationship with a refugee or refugee family to avoid the Trump travel ban):

> Although representatives of USCRI or one of its partner agencies only meet the refugee and her family in person when they arrive, the refugees are, in a very real sense, already well-known to them. *USCRI receives a dossier [from the Department of State] on the refugee and all family members travelling with her, typically months before she is cleared to fly to the United States* (emphasis added)[190]

> "[The resettlement agency] must invest extensively in its relationship with the named refugee well before she arrives. the agency must provide "*[p]re-arrival services*" for the refugee,

[188]The refugee considered for resettlement to the U.S. in most cases is first referred by the UNHCR, a U.S. Embassy or designated NGO for resettlement to the U.S. There are some categories of prospective refugees to the U.S., however, such as Iraqis who assisted the U.S. military who can apply to the U.S. refugee admission program directly under a special federal government programme rather that having to go through the U.N. referral system See Hawaii et al (Plaintiffs-Appellees) v Trump, President of the United States et al (Defendants-Appellants) United Sates Court of Appeals for the Ninth Circuit Brief of the Amicus Curiae Human Rights First (Formerly known as The Lawyers Committee for Human Rights) in Support of Appellees at p. 7, August 3, 2017.

[189]The State of Hawaii also argued that a refugee abroad who had a tie to a U.S. legal assistance program should be considered to have met the criterion for an exemption of the Trump travel ban in their case.

[190]Hawaii et al (Plaintiffs-Appellees) v Trump, President of the United States et al (Defendants-Appellants) United Sates Court of Appeals for the Ninth Circuit, On Appeal from the U.S. District Court for the District of Hawaii, No. 1:17-cv-00050-DKW-KSC (Derrick K. Watson, J.) Brief of the Amicus Curiae Brief of Committee for Refugees and Immigrants, August 9, 2017 at p. 20.

> including "[a]ssum[ing] responsibility for sponsorship, plan[ning] for the provision" of "health services," and making arrangements for children who must be placed in foster care (emphasis added).[191]

It is here argued that once the refugee has had contact with U.S. Citizenship and Immigration Services and has been accepted for admission to the U.S., the U.S. has established jurisdiction over the refugee and a *bona fide* relationship between the U.S. and the refugee has been established. The current author would contend further, as did 'Human Rights First', that the assurance letter from a refugee resettlement program provided to the Department of State is part and parcel of the *bona fide* relationship that has been established between a U.S. legal entity and the particular refugee(s) from abroad who has been cleared for admission to the United States:

> the government makes the related argument that the issuance of a formal assurance does not create a relationship "that is independent of the refugee admission process itself." ... Here, too, no such requirement appears in the Supreme Court's June 26 Opinion. What is more, the government's distinction makes no sense. *It is the refugee admission and assurance process that is under scrutiny, and it is that process, as noted, that cements the bona fides of the relationship between the refugee and USCRI* [the U.S. Committee for Refugees and Immigrants is a U.S. non-profit refugee resettlement agency] (emphasis added)[192]

The State of Hawaii argued these points in a motion to the District Court of the Ninth Circuit and then on appeal to the Appeals Court of the Ninth Circuit (relating to that same motion) asking for clarification on the scope of the injunction that still applied to the Trump travel ban but exempted (among certain others) refugees abroad who had a *bona fide* relationship (tie) to a U.S. entity with legal status in the U.S.[193] The District Court of Hawaii declined to clarify the USSC '*bona fide*

---

[191]Similarly the State of Hawaii argued that the U.S. government, in contravention of the USSC 'bona fide relationship rule', was still unlawfully excluding refugees abroad from entry to the U.S. who had a bona fide relationship to a U.S. entity: "The Supreme Court's guidance with respect to refugee admissions is straightforward: The *injunction continues to apply* where a U.S. entity "has a bona fide relationship with a particular" refugee such that the entity "can legitimately claim concrete hardship if that person is excluded. The Government has nonetheless issued guidance stating that "a formal assurance for a refugee seeking admission is not sufficient in and of itself to establish a qualifying relationship for that refugee" Emergency Motion to Clarify Scope of Emergency Injunction, State of Hawaii et al v Donald J Trump, President of the United States and others, Court of Appeals for the Ninth District 7 July, 2017 at p. 16.

[192]Hawaii et al (Plaintiffs-Appellees) v Trump, President of the United States et al (Defendants-Appellants) United Sates Court of Appeals for the Ninth Circuit, On Appeal from the U.S. District Court for the District of Hawaii, No. 1:17-cv-00050-DKW-KSC (Derrick K. Watson, J.) Brief of the Amicus Curiae Brief of Committee for Refugees and Immigrants, August 9, 2017 at p. 19.

[193]United States District Court of the District of Hawaii, State of Hawaii and Ismail Elshikh v Donald J. Trump in his official capacity as President of the United States, John F. Kelly in his official capacity as Secretary of Homeland Security and Rex Tillerson in his official capacity as Secretary of State; United States of America: Emergency Motion to Clarify the Scope of Preliminary Injunction Washington, D.C 29 June, 2017 (hereafter State of Hawaii and Ismail Elshikh v Donald J. Trump et al, emergency motion) The District Court dismissed the motion and held that the scope of the injunction on the Trump second travel ban should be clarified by the United States Supreme Court as it was that Court that had formulated the rule on the scope of the injunction and to

relationship with the U.S. rule’ regarding which foreign nationals including refugees abroad had a right of entry (were exempted from the Trump travel ban) holding it had no jurisdiction to offer clarification of a United States Supreme Court ruling and found such clarification could only be provided by the Supreme Court itself.[194] The Ninth Circuit Court of Appeals upheld the District Court’s declining to provide clarification on which groups of foreign nationals could be barred from entry to the U.S. on an alleged ***no*** *bona fide* relationship with the U.S. basis and dismissed the plaintiffs’ appeal (plaintiffs including the State of Hawaii).[195] The Court of Appeals held that the State of Hawaii had incorrectly put its question to the District Court but could go back to the District Court and complain that the federal government had misapplied and misinterpreted the USSC interim direction regarding bona fide relationship with the U.S. as a basis for entry of foreign nationals including refugees abroad accepted through the resettlement program.

In the interim; the U.S. federal government appealed to both the Ninth Circuit and to the Supreme Court maintaining that its *restrictive interpretation* of the United States Supreme Court preliminary injunction was valid. The government argued thus that the government was correct in its *refusal* to consider the relationship between (1) a specific refugee abroad and (2) a U.S. resettlement agency (that had issued a formal assurance to the U.S. Department of State in respect of that refugee to provide basic services once the refugee arrived in the U.S.) as a pre-existing *bona fide* relationship with a legal U.S. entity (which *bona fide* tie to the U.S. where its exists exempts that refugee from the Trump travel ban)).The Trump administration, as discussed, considered that refugees abroad for whom formal assurance had been given to the Department of State by a U.S. resettlement agency did *not* fall into a category entitled to an exemption from the Trump travel ban on that basis if they met (on the government’s view) the criteria for exclusion under the travel ban.

> As the government explained... the fact that a U.S.-based resettlement organization has provided an assurance to the Department of State for an individual refugee does not in itself satisfy the requirement that the refugee *himself* has a “bona fide relationship” with the U.S. organization that is “formal, documented, and formed in the ordinary course. *The only “formal” and “documented” relationship is between the resettlement organization and the*

what extent and in what respects the Trump travel ban (Executive Order 2) could be implemented. The State of Hawaii then appealed to the Appeals Court of the Ninth Circuit to clarify the rule fashioned by the Supreme Court of the United States regarding to what extent the Trump travel ban applied and to what extent it was enjoined (State of Hawaii v Donald J Trump, Appeals Court of the Ninth Circuit No. 17-16366.

[194]Hawaii et al v Trump et al In the United States District Court for the District of Hawaii Order Denying Plaintiffs’ Emergency Motion to Clarify Scope of Preliminary Injunction Civil No. 17-00050 DKW-KSC; July 6, 2017.

[195]Hawaii et al v Trump et al United States Court of Appeals for the Ninth District D.C. (Denial of appeal of the district court’s July 6, 2017 denial of Plaintiffs’ “Emergency Motion to Clarify Scope of Preliminary Injunction) No. 1:17-cv-00050-DKW-KSC July 7, 2017.

> *Department of State, not the alien*. . ..the refugee will eventually benefit from that relationship, but no individual alien is party to the agreement and there is generally no contact between the refugee and the resettlement agency prior to arrival (emphasis added).[196]

> Resettlement agencies, which claim a relationship through an assurance only with the government to carry out the government's program, have no relationship at all with the alien, much less a "formal" one[197]

On July 19, 2017 the United Sates Supreme Court responded to the federal government's appeal and issued an order without reasons.[198] That order *denied* the government's request seeking clarification of the USSC June 26, 2017 ruling[199] setting out the *bona fide* relationship to the U.S. rule in the case. The United States Supreme Court in the same order, however, stayed the preliminary injunction that the District Court of Hawaii had set in place regarding refugees abroad for whom an assurance letter from a U.S. refugee resettlement agency had already been filed with the U.S. Department of State. Thus the latter refugees were *not* permitted at that point in the litigation to enter the U.S. pending a decision on that issue from the Ninth Circuit Court of Appeals. The Ninth Circuit Court of Appeals ruled that refugees on whose behalf formal assurance letters had been issued to the U.S. Department of State (refugees therefore who had been accepted for resettlement through the U.S. admissions/resettlement program) would be allowed to enter the U.S. on the ground they in fact did have a *bona fide* relationship with a lawful U.S. entity as required by the rule articulated by the USSC for exemption to the Trump travel ban.[200] The Ninth Circuit found that:

> Resettlement agencies will face concrete harms and burdens if refugees with formal assurances are not admitted. In the same way that the Court considered the harms of the U.S. citizen who wants to be reunited with his mother-in-law and the permanent resident

[196]State of Hawaii et al (Plaintiffs-Appellees) v Donald J Trump President of the U.S. et al (Defendants-Appellants) In the United States Court of Appeals for the Ninth District On Appeal from the United States District Court for the District of Hawaii, Reply Brief for the Appellants August 9, 2017 at pp. 4–5.

[197]State of Hawaii et al (Plaintiffs-Appellees) v Donald J Trump President of the U.S. et al (Defendants-Appellants) In the United States Court of Appeals for the Ninth District On Appeal from the United States District Court for the District of Hawaii, Reply Brief for the Appellants, August 9, 2017 at p. 6.

[198]Trump, President of the U.S. et al v Hawaii et al Order List 582 U.S.__2017 (16-1540, 16A1191) Wednesday, July 19, 2017 Available for down load under miscellaneous order 07/19/17 https://www.supremecourt.gov/orders/ordersofthecourt/16 (Accessed 19 August, 2017).

[199]Donald J. Trump, President of the United States et al v International Refugee Assistance Project et al, Supreme Court of the United States, On Application for a Stay and Petition for Writ of Certiorari to the United States Court of Appeals for the Ninth District 582 U. S. ____ (2017) Opinion Per Curiam of June 26, 2017.

[200]Zapotosky, M (7 September, 2017) (The Washington Post) Grandparents, refugees with formal assurances can enter under Trump travel ban, appeal court rules https://www.washingtonpost.com/world/national-security/grandparents-refugees-with-formal-assurances-can-enter-under-trumps-travel-ban-appeals-court-rules/2017/09/07/d0763ca8-9415-11e7-8754-d478688d23b4_story.html?utm_term=.2b867e415c17 Accessed 17 October, 2017.

> who wants to be reunited with his wife, the employer that hired an employee, the university that admitted a student, and the American audience that invited a lecturer, the district court correctly considered the resettlement agency that has given a formal assurance for specific refugees...[201]

The USSC had left standing the District Court of Hawaii's expanded list of close family members (the addition of fiancée, grandparents, grandchildren, brothers-in-law, sisters-in-law, aunts, uncles, nieces, nephews or cousins)[202] of persons legally present in and living in the United States. A *bona fide* relationship between these aforementioned family members with a person in the U.S. (where that person had legal status in the U.S.) then would also allow for an exemption to the travel ban for these vetted family members (of foreign nationality; refugee or non-refugee) to come to the U.S. and be reunited with their family.

The issue of just what constitutes a *bona fide* relationship between a foreign national (i.e. a refugee still abroad or arrived at a U.S. port of entry) with a person (who has legal status in the U.S.) or a lawful entity in the U.S. is to be clarified when the Trump travel ban case is decided on the merits by the United States Supreme Court (i.e. the USSC will rule on the constitutional issues that arise from the Trump travel ban and address just what is the scope of the U.S. President's authority in restricting, on ostensibly national security grounds, entry to the U.S. to certain identifiable categories of persons). The travel ban is now in its third iteration and the case concerning the second Trump travel ban has been ruled moot.

It is to be noted also that in its latest preliminary ruling (as of the time of this writing) the Supreme Court of the United States (USSC) has allowed *the third iteration* of the Trump travel ban to be fully implemented *for the time being*. The latest U.S. Supreme Court ruling (with no reasons given) allows *no exemptions* based on a *bona fide* relationship to an approved person or entity with legal status in the U.S. for those who did not have the required entry documents by the required effective date specified by the government.[203] This latest USSC ruling will stand pending the consolidated Trump travel ban case arriving at the High Court to be heard on the merits and the USSC issuing its opinion on the travel ban (in its third iteration) in terms of what constitutional and/or statutory limits, if any, it exceeds and what exemptions, if any, are to be provided in the application of the third version of the travel ban. In the meantime the Ninth Circuit Court of Appeals has issued an

[201]United States Court of Appeal for the Ninth Circuit, State of Hawaii; Ishmail Elshikh v Donald J Trump et al (7 September, 2017) at p. 34 http://cdn.ca9.uscourts.gov/datastore/general/2017/09/07/17-16426%20Opinion%20Filed.pdf Accessed 17 October, 2017.

[202]Hawaii argued that some if not all of these family relations are considered close family ties in Hawaii but were *excluded* by the U.S. federal government as 'approved' family ties for the purpose of exemption from the Trump travel ban. Further Hawaii argued that the Supreme Court in the case at bar had made it clear that under its order immediate family (familial bona fide relationships) were not limited to the relationships set out in the Immigration Nationality Act but rather extended to the relationships that the Trump implementations guidelines excluded.

[203]Donald J. Trump, President of the United States, et al., Applicants v. Hawaii, et al. (Opinion of December 4, 2017).

opinion regarding the third iteration of the Trump travel ban that would "give relief only to those with a credible bona fide relationship with the United States"[204]; a decision that the Ninth Circuit has stayed pending the Supreme Court of the United States reviewing the case on its merits.

5.5.3 Concluding Remarks

It must be kept foremost in mind that refugees considered for any country's resettlement program are amongst the most vulnerable of an already highly vulnerable group. Yet the Trump travel ban was in part highly focused on suspension of the U.S. resettlement program and on drastically cutting the numbers allowed for refugee resettlement to the U.S. per year if and when the program resumed (which it did in October, 2017 with additional severe hurdles for refugees to overcome). Included amongst the prospective U.S. resettlement collective (i.e. those considered by UNHCR as suitable candidates to be resettled in the U.S.) are also accompanied and unaccompanied child refugees; some with additional special vulnerabilities (being disabled, having suffered extreme violence etc.):

> The refugees who are part of USCRI's [the NGO 'US Committee for Refugees and Immigrants'] resettlement process are some of the most vulnerable members of already marginalized populations throughout the world. They are primarily female heads of households, disabled individuals, ***children***, individuals who identify as homosexual, bi-sexual, or transsexual, victims of torture, the elderly, and refugees seeking to join family members who left the country before them (emphasis added).[205]

> Only a few countries take part in the United Nations High Commissioner on Refugees ("UNHCR") resettlement program, with the United States being the world's top resettlement country. In 2013, 2014, and 2015, the United States offered 70,000 refugees resettlement. *In 2016, the United States resettled 84,995 refugees.* ***Seventy-two percent of the individuals who were resettled [to the U.S.] during that period were women and children***(emphasis added).[206]

On the view here, the Trump travel ban in certain of its versions represented (with limited case-by-case exemptions on humanitarian grounds or exemptions based on a

---

[204]Hawaii et al (Plaintiffs-Appellees) v Trump, President of the United States et al (Defendants-Appellants) United Sates Court of Appeals for the Ninth Circuit. Per Curiam Opinion, 22 December, 2017 at pp. 70–71.

[205]Hawaii et al (Plaintiffs-Appellees) v Trump, President of the United States et al (Defendants-Appellants) United Sates Court of Appeals for the Ninth Circuit, On Appeal from the U.S. District Court for the District of Hawaii, No. 1:17-cv-00050-DKW-KSC (Derrick K. Watson, J.) Brief of the Amicus Curiae Brief of Committee for Refugees and Immigrants, August 9, 2017 at p. 5.

[206]Hawaii et al (Plaintiffs-Appellees) v Trump, President of the United States et al (Defendants-Appellants) United Sates Court of Appeals for the Ninth Circuit, On Appeal from the U.S. District Court for the District of Hawaii, No. 1:17-cv-00050-DKW-KSC (Derrick K. Watson, J.) Brief of the Amicus Curiae Brief of Committee for Refugees and Immigrants, August 9, 2017 at p. 9.

pre-existing *bona fide* tie to a U.S. person or entity with legal status in the U.S.[207]) a *blanket denial* for a limited period (that potentially could be renewed) of (1) entry of refugees abroad who would normally have qualified for the US resettlement program[208] and (2) foreign nationals fitting certain *categorical descriptors* (regarding national origin). This is the case even though (1) the refugee while abroad traditionally has been *individually* thoroughly vetted by U.S. authorities as part of the U.S. resettlement program process; and (2) according to many highly experienced security experts the risks of foreign nationals to the security interests of the U.S. homeland cannot be linked to country of origin of the foreign national in a reliable blanket fashion and thus individualized threat assessment is required:

> As a national security measure, this Ban is unnecessary. National security-based immigration restrictions have consistently been tailored to respond to: (1) specific, credible threats *based on individualized information*, (2) the best available intelligence, and (3) thorough interagency legal and policy review. . ..[209]

> Defendants have provided no evidence or specific information that nationals of the banned countries pose a credible threat to the safety of Americans if they are allowed to enter the United States *after individualized screenings*, or of the alleged harm that would occur in the absence of the ban (emphasis added).[210]

The Trump travel ban 3.0 combined with additional applicable Executive Orders represents, on the view here, an extraterritorial collective migration control measure that greatly adversely impacts refugees including children and unaccompanied children who are in great humanitarian need (as well as other foreign nationals as described) and is not

---

[207]The USSC rule articulated that the refugee needs to be able to make a "credible claim" regarding the *bona fide* relationship between the refugee and a person or entity in the US (with lawful status in the US) as the test for an exemption to application of the travel ban in their case See State of Hawaii; Ishmail Elshikh v Donald J Trump et al (7 September, 2017) United States Court of Appeal for the Ninth Circuit at p. 7 Citing the USSC on this point http://cdn.ca9.uscourts.gov/datastore/general/2017/09/07/17-16426%20Opinion%20Filed.pdf Accessed 17 October, 2017.

[208]Various European States also have been reluctant to do their fair share in resettlement of refugees fleeing current conflicts such as that in Syria. This serves to undermine the Refugee Convention and the international rule of law by, in effect, eroding respect for international human rights norms through the abysmal treatment these European States have too often afforded these refugees. See Carrera, S and Guid, E (27 January, 2017) for CEPS (Centre for European Policy Studies) Offshore processing of asylum applications. Out of sight, out of mind? https://www.ceps.eu/publications/offshore-processing-asylum-applications-out-sight-out-mind Accessed 20 October, 2017. As mentioned; the U.S. refugee resettlement program was reactivated in October 2017 with new additional vetting and other restrictive stipulations.

[209]State of Hawaii, Ismail Elshikh, John Does 1&2 and Muslim Association of Hawaii, Inc. v Donald J Trump in his official capacity as President et al. In the U.S. District Court for the District of Hawaii, 'Joint Declaration of Former National Security Officials' (15 October, 2017) p. 6 Available at https://www.hoganlovells.com/publications/documents-in-state-of-hawaii-et-al-v-trump-a-challenge-to-president-trumps-march-6-2017-travel-ban Accessed 19 October, 2017.

[210]State of Hawaii, Ismail Elshikh, John Does 1&2 and Muslim Association of Hawaii, Inc. v Donald J Trump in his official capacity as President et al. In the U.S. District Court for the District of Hawaii, 'Joint Declaration of Former National Security Officials' (15 October, 2017) pp. 7–8 Available at https://www.hoganlovells.com/publications/documents-in-state-of-hawaii-et-al-v-trump-a-challenge-to-president-trumps-march-6-2017-travel-ban Accessed 19 October, 2017.

consistent with the requirements of the Refugee Convention. The Trump travel ban, in combination with the U.S. current border control policy and practices described here previously[211] constitute, it is here contended, a significant challenge to the internationally recognized individual and collective right to seek asylum and, in particular, refugee asylum. That right of seeking refugee asylum and of non-refoulement belonging also to i.e. 'unaccompanied child refugees' (a highly vulnerable child refugee identifiable (Convention) 'social group') though most compelling is not, in practice, always respected and honoured. Under collective migration control measures such as the Trump travel ban and border control policy; the status of 'unaccompanied child refugee asylum seeker' seems rather to place the child's right to seek and be fairly and individually considered for refugee asylum or resettlement in jeopardy. The latter then occurring as opposed to leading U.S. immigration authorities to routinely prioritize for consideration the unaccompanied child refugee's claim to international protection.

Note that ironically and tragically the Trump travel ban may in fact increase anti-American extremism and further therefore increase security risk to the U.S. homeland. This is the view outlined by a number of U.S. former security experts.[212] Being involved in global conflicts and then not adequately sharing the burden in international protection of refugees (including of accompanied and unaccompanied children) furthermore would send a counterproductive message that undermines the U.S. as a champion of human rights; one of the markers for a robust democracy and serves to erode international trust. The same is true for all other democratic States that have employed blanket refugee migration control measures through direct and indirect means.[213]

It is inconsistent with international refugee law and the U.S. Refugee Act, it is here argued, that a *bona fide* relationship with a person or entity in the U.S. (with legal status in the U.S.) should be considered as the precondition for entry to the U.S. *as a refugee*. This is reflected, for instance, in that the Refugee Convention (incorporated by statute also into U.S. law) stipulates that refugees are not to be

[211]The reference here is to unaccompanied child refugees from Central America and Mexico arrived irregularly—that is without authorization—to the US southern border in search of asylum.

[212]In the U.S. District Court for the District of Hawaii, State of Hawaii, Ismail Elshikh, John Does 1&2 and Muslim Association of Hawaii, Inc. v Donald J Trump in his official capacity as President et al 'Joint Declaration of Former National Security Officials' (15 October, 2017) pp. 9–10 Available at https://www.hoganlovells.com/publications/documents-in-state-of-hawaii-et-al-v-trump-a-challenge-to-president-trumps-march-6-2017-travel-ban Accessed 19 October, 2017.

[213]Australia has gone so far as to outsource its extraterritorial blanket refugee control measures. This by taking by force refugees attempting to arrive to Australia by boat to remote offshore locations such as Nauru where Australia funds a so-called refugee processing centre. See Amnesty International (2016) *Island of despair: Australia's 'processing' of refugees on Nauru* "Although asylum-seekers and refugees on Nauru are not technically detained, because they are able to move around the island, they are nonetheless in a detention-like environment. Nauru is to all intents and purposes an open-air prison that people cannot leave, even when they have been officially recognized as refugees." At p. 4 Available at https://www.amnesty.org/en/documents/asa12/4934/2016/en/ Accessed 20 October, 2017.

penalized for entry or arriving at the border irregularly even where they do not have valid entry documents (Article 31). This illustrates that the Refugee Convention does *not* contemplate that a pre-existing *bona fide* relationship or tie to the prospective country of asylum through ties to a person or entity with legal status in that country must obtain in order (1) to allow for entry of a refugee without penalty and (2) for lack of prejudice in considering a refugee asylum claim from a person without such a pre-existing *bona fide* tie to the country in which he/she seeks asylum. A person with a family tie to a person in the U.S. or arguably to an entity in the U.S. (such as a refugee resettlement program) is likely to have or in principle be qualified to receive the proper entry documents. However, Refugee Convention Article 31 contemplates that a refugee would still have the right to seek asylum and have his or her asylum claim considered even if he or she arrived to or entered the prospective asylum State without valid paperwork and without any proper State authorization.

The refugee is often regarded as the quintessentially 'other' with most often no *bona fide* ties to a person or entity with legal status in the prospective country of asylum. However, with the extension of jurisdiction of the prospective asylum country beyond its borders via extraterritorial refugee migration control measures; various refugee individuals and collectives can no longer be discounted as 'the other' over whom the particular State in question has no direct pressing international protection obligation. Extraterritorial extension of jurisdiction can also occur in a positive manner through programs, for instance, such as the U.S admissions/resettlement program working with the UNHCR (the representatives of the U.S. government abroad, as part of the resettlement process, meet the refugee where the refugee is located outside the U.S. to consider that individual from a highly vulnerable refugee collective for possible refugee resettlement in the U.S.). The Refugee Convention articulates that States Parties to the Convention will support the UNHCR's international protection efforts which, in part, involve resettlement of UNHCR or other recognized NGO designated highly vulnerable refugees (Refugee Convention Article 35). UNHCR guidelines for resettlement of Convention refugees do not contemplate excluding high protection need refugees based on lack of a *bona fide* relationship of the refugee to the prospective asylum country (i.e. a tie between the refugee and an approved person or entity in the U.S.)[214] Yet under the USSC order in *Donald J. Trump, President of the United States v International Refugee Assistance Project et al.*[215]; consular officers could deny a refugee asylum seeker entry (i.e. deny a visa or other entry document to the U.S.) if the official were unclear as to whether the refugee seeking entry to the U.S. had a *bona fide* relationship or tie with a U.S. person or entity in the U.S. (was unsure if the refugee to whom the Trump travel ban would normally apply had or had not made a credible claim of a *bona fide* tie to the U.S.). It is here

---

[214]The Trump guidelines exclude the resettlement program and local U.S. sponsors as 'approved' U.S. entities for the purpose of establishing a bona fide tie to a U.S. entity and exemption as a refugee from the Trump travel ban.

[215]Donald J. Trump, President of the United States v International Refugee Assistance Project et al 582 U. S. ____ (2017).

argued that extraterritorial migration control measures such as the Trump travel ban also move the frontier abroad and extends the prospective asylum State's jurisdiction over the *particular refugees* impacted beyond its mainland territory. There is then no escaping State responsibility and accountability for the impact, positive or negative or in-between, upon desperate refugee asylum seekers over whose lives the State has exerted direct influence through its migration control polices and practices.

The Supreme Court of the United States held that the Trump travel ban could be enforced against foreign nationals including refugees with no *bona fide* tie to the U.S. as this would allegedly create no undue hardship for any American person or entity in the U.S. (with legal status in the U.S.). The current author would respectfully argue, in opposition to the USSC holding,[216] however, that denying entry visas or other U.S. authorized travel documents to vetted refugees abroad based only on the Trump travel ban narrowed in scope by the rule formulated by the USSC (that is these refugees barred for the period of implementation of the travel ban only if they have no *bona fide* relationship with a U.S. person or entity[217]) does in fact burden all Americans. This in that the blocking of refugee admission for *bona fide* refugees who have no pre-entry ties to a person legally present in the U.S. or to an entity in the U.S. serves to contribute, by adding to the refugees left in limbo, to the erosion of international peace and security and humanitarian norms in which all Americans, as all peoples, have a vital interest.

States, in the normal course, seek to regulate the flow of refugee (and non-refugee) migrants to their borders. However, respectfully, it is on the view here not consistent with international refugee or human rights treaty obligations to formulate and rely on a rule[218] that blocks asylum seekers (or recognized refugees, some of whom may even have been approved for resettlement in a particular State) from abroad reaching a port of entry of a certain State in search of refugee asylum or to be resettled there (i.e. where they had been approved to resettle in that State or were in the process of obtaining that approval). In the Trump travel ban case, the block to arrival at a U.S. port of entry (with certain exemptions in exceptional cases and in regards to certain programs such as the CAM program discussed previously) arises due to the refugee in the affected cases having no *bona fide* pre-existing tie to a person or entity in the U.S. with legal status in the U.S. (the prospective resettlement or asylum State) such that the refugee's exclusion would create hardship for the person or entity in question. The *bona fide* relationship rule, on the respectful view here, undermines the very right (under international refugee and human rights law as well as customary law) (1) to seek and be fairly considered for international protection as a refugee (if not already so recognized as a refugee and

[216]Referring to the Preliminary ruling in Donald J. Trump, President of the United States v International Refugee Assistance Project et al 582 U. S. ____ (2017) regarding which foreign nationals could be barred from entry to the U.S. based on the Trump travel ban.

[217]Where the refugee has ties to a US refugee resettlement program this arguably would be a bona fide relationship to the U.S.

[218]Donald J. Trump, President of the United States v International Refugee Assistance Project et al 582 U. S. ____ (2017).

approved, for instance, for resettlement to that State) and (2) to move freely to the location necessary in the attempt to access that protection.

In sum it seems clear that the US. Government under the Trump administration (as well as the USSC) are not considering that the U.S. *exercising jurisdiction* over a refugee abroad *itself* creates a *bona fide* tie between the U.S. and that individual whether or not the refugee is successful in being selected for resettlement[219] or asylum[220] in the U.S. The latter tie then is based on U.S. jurisdictional control which in turn gives rise to accountability for that particular refugee or refugee family or larger refugee collective. Hence an extraterritorial measure that blocks an individual refugee or a particular identifiable refugee collective (whose individual members can be identified) from consideration for resettlement to the U.S. or asylum in the U.S. creates a jurisdictionally based *bona fide* relationship with the particular identified refugee(s) impacted. This then results in creating the very State positive obligations to provide international protection to Convention refugees (or bona fide refugees meeting the eligibility criteria in other international protection schemes) that the State had earnestly sought to avoid through its border push back as well as extraterritorial migration control measures.

Literature, Materials and Cases

Literature

Cole D (2003) Are foreign nationals entitled to the same constitutional rights as citizens? Thomas Jefferson Law Rev 25:367–388

Grover S (2014) The torture of children during armed conflicts: the ICC failure to prosecute and the negation of children's human dignity. Springer, Berlin

Grover S (2015) R2P and the Syrian crisis: when semantics becomes a matter of life or death. Int J Hum Rights 19(8):1112–1128

Korthuis A (2016) Outsourcing refoulement: the United States and the Central American Refugee Crisis. Yale J Int Law. http://www.yjil.yale.edu/outsourcing-refoulement-the-united-states-and-the-central-american-refugee-crisis/. Accessed 15 July 2017

Maun K (2011) Sanctuary from de facto deportation: the new sanctuary movement and de facto deportation claims for children challenging illegal immigrant parents' removal orders. Richmond Public Interest Law Rev 15(2):448–474

[219]Jurisdiction is exercised by the U.S. in the U.S. resettlement screening process through US consular or other authorities interviewing the refugee and his or her family abroad, refugee assistance personnel in certain instances interviewing the refugee abroad as well as may occur with the International Rescue Committee for instance which also has U.S. based branches, various US government agencies doing investigations into private matters pertaining to that refugee asylum seeker's background and security and other status etc.

[220]The use of extraterritorial means to block refugee arrival at the border or any port of entry in search of asylum itself is an exercise of jurisdiction over the refugee asylum seekers impacted.

McCuiston H (2014) "Membership in a Particular Social Group": why United States courts should adopt the disjunctive approach of the United Nations High Commissioner for Refugees. St. John's Law Rev 88(2):531–560

Vandvik B (2008) Extraterritorial border controls and responsibility to protect: a view from ECRE (European Council on Refugees and Exiles). Amsterdam Law Forum. http://amsterdamlawforum.org/article/view/38/40. Accessed 20 Oct 2017

Materials

American Civil Liberties Union; Young, Scared, Alone and In Court: J.E. F.M. v. Lynch Update June 24, 2016 https://www.aclu.org/cases/jefm-v-lynch (Accessed 7 November, 2016)

American Immigration Council (2015) A Guide to children arriving at the border: Laws, policies and responses (26 June, 2015) https://www.americanimmigrationcouncil.org/research/guide-children-arriving-border-laws-policies-and-responses Accessed 13 October, 2017

American Immigration Council (2015) An overview of U.S. Refugee Law and Policy (November 18, 2015) https://www.americanimmigrationcouncil.org/research/overview-us-refugee-law-and-policy (accessed 14 July, 2017)

American Immigration Lawyers Association 'Whitehouse releases details on Border security principles and policies, President Trump Memorandum to the U.S. Department of Homeland Security 'Secure the Border by Deterring and Swiftly removing Illegal Entrants' (9 October, 2017) Available at http://www.aila.org/infonet/wh-details-border-security-principles-and-policies Accessed 13 October, 2017

Amnesty International (2016) Island of despair: Australia's 'processing' of refugees on Nauru Available at https://www.amnesty.org/en/documents/asa12/4934/2016/en/ Accessed 20 October, 2017

Amnesty International Public Statement (24 July, 2015) (Index: ASA 23/2157/2015) Cambodia and the question of voluntariness https://www.amnesty.org/download/Documents/ASA2321572015ENGLISH.pd Accessed 14 October, 2017

Amnesty International Report (2017/2018) The state of the world's human rights. https://www.amnesty-international.be/sites/default/files/bijlagen/air201718-english_2018-02-12_12-36-44.pdf. Accessed 17 April, 2018

Boston College Third World Journal *The Disproportionate Effect of the Entry Fiction on Excludable Aliens*, 9 B.C. Third World L.J. 271 (1989), http://lawdigitalcommons.bc.edu/twlj/vol9/iss2/4 (accessed 4 June, 2017)

Carrera, S and Guid, E (27 January, 2017) for CEPS (Centre for European Policy Studies) Offshore processing of asylum applications. Out of sight, out of mind? https://www.ceps.eu/publications/offshore-processing-asylum-applications-out-sight-out-mind Accessed 20 October, 2017

Coffey K (2000) The due process right to seek asylum in the United States: The immigration dilemma and constitutional controversy. Yale Law and Policy Review 19(2):303–339

Connolly, H, Crellin, R, and Parhar, R (Research Report, August 2017) An update to 'Cut Off From Justice': The impact of excluding migrant and separated children from legal aid (University of Bedfordhire and The Children's Society) Available at https://www.basw.co.uk/resource/?id=6736 Accessed 12 October, 2017

1951 Convention and 1967 Protocol relating to the Status of Refugees http://www.unhcr.org/en-us/3b66c2aa10 Accessed 30 June, 2017

Convention on the Rights of the Child, entered into force 2 September, 1990. http://www.ohchr.org/EN/ProfessionalInterest/Pages/CRC.aspx Accessed 30 June, 2017

Department of (U.S.) Homeland Security In-Country Refugee/Parole Processing for Minors in Honduras, El Salvador and Guatemala (Central American Minors—CAM) https://www.uscis.gov/CAM Accessed 25 June, 2017

Eagly, I, Esq. and Shafer, S Esq. (Special Report 28 September, 2016) American Immigration Counsel, 'Access to Counsel in Immigration Court' https://www.americanimmigrationcouncil.org/research/access-counsel-immigration-court Accessed 12 October, 2017

Fact Sheet on the Trump Travel Ban 3.0 released September 24, 2017 and updated April 10, 2018. https://www.dhs.gov/news/2017/09/24/fact-sheet-president-s-proclamation-enhancing-vetting-capabilities-and-processes

Hansford, B and Dobbs, L for UNHCR 'UNHCR calls on the Americas to keep children on the run safe from violence' (12 March, 2014) http://www.unhcr.org/en-us/news/latest/2014/3/53206a3d9/unhcr-calls-americas-keep-children-run-safe-violence.html (accessed 25 June, 2017)

Harvard Law School: Harvard Immigration and Refugee Clinical Program: The impact of President Trump's Executive Orders on asylum seekers Available at https://today.law.harvard.edu/harvard-releases-first-report-effect-trumps-executive-orders-asylum-seekers/ Accessed 15 October, 2017

Human Rights Watch (2016) Closed doors: Mexico's Failure to Protect Central American Refugee and Migrant Children (31 March, 2016) https://www.hrw.org/report/2016/03/31/closed-doors/mexicos-failure-protect-central-american-refugee-and-migrant-children (accessed 17 July, 2017)

Human Rights Watch (2012) Boat Ride to Detention: Adult and Child Migrants in Malta https://www.hrw.org/report/2012/07/18/boat-ride-detention/adult-and-child-migrants-malta (Accessed 5 October, 2017)

Inter-American Commission on Human Rights (11 November, 2015): Violence, children and organized crime Available at http://www.oas.org/en/iachr/reports/pdfs/violencechildren2016.pdf Accessed 24 October, 2017

Jarrett, L and Labott, E (for CNN Politics) Travel ban 2.0 in effect, court challenges begin, 30 June, 2017 http://www.cnn.com/2017/06/29/politics/revised-travel-ban-thursday/index.html (accessed 30 June, 2017)

Kids in Need of Defense (KIND) (founded by Angelina Jolie and Microsoft Corporation to assist unaccompanied children wherever they are) https://supportkind.org/wp-content/uploads/2017/06/General-KIND-Fact-sheet_June-2017.pdf 12 October, 2017

Kopan, Tal DHS [United States Department of Homeland Security] ends program for Central American minors (16 August, 2017) http://www.cnn.com/2017/08/16/politics/trump-ending-central-american-minors-program/index.html

Lutheran Immigration and Refugee Service (2014) Unaccompanied migrant children: U.S. law and policy backgrounder 'Protecting the best interests of all children' http://lirs.org/wp-content/uploads/2014/07/UAC-Law-and-Policy-FINAL.pdf Accessed 12 October, 2017

Miliband, D (2017) IRC responds to administration's arbitrary and cruel travel ban guidelines. Press release 29 June, 2017, David Miliband President and CEO of the International Rescue Committee (IRC) https://www.rescue.org/press-release/irc-responds-administrations-arbitrary-and-cruel-travel-ban-guidelines (accessed 14 July, 2017)

Naar, L (February 9, 2016) The extraterritoriality of the principle of non-refoulement: A critique of the Sale case and Roma case (London School of Economics blog) http://blogs.lse.ac.uk/humanrights/2016/02/09/the-extraterritoriality-of-the-principle-of-non-refoulement-a-critique-of-the-sale-case-and-roma-case/ (Accessed 24 February, 2017)

Nakamura, D (2017) Washington Post (16 August, 2017) Trump administration ends Obama-era protection program for Central American minors https://www.washingtonpost.com/politics/trump-administration-ends-obama-era-protection-program-for-central-american-minors/2017/08/16/8101507e-82b6-11e7-ab27-1a21a8e006ab_story.html?utm_term=.e5367d0aea9f Accessed 20 October, 2017

New York Times Editorial Board: Migrant children deserve a voice in court (March 8, 2016) http://www.nytimes.com/2016/03/08/opinion/migrant-children-deserve-a-voice-in-court.html?_r=2 (Accessed 7 November, 2016)

President Obama, Remarks 6 January, 2015 following bilateral talks with President Penieto of Mexico, https://obamawhitehouse.archives.gov/the-press-office/2015/01/06/remarks-president-obama-and-president-pe-nieto-after-bilateral-meeting (accessed 15 July, 2017)

Trac Immigration Research Centre (affiliated with the Newhouse School of Public Communications and the Whitman School of Management, University of Syracuse) (Report 28 September, 2017) Children: Amid a Growing Court Backlog Many Still Unrepresented http://trac.syr.edu/immigration/reports/482/ Accessed 15 October, 2017

United States Citizenship and Immigration Services Update on Central American Minors (CAM) Program (November 15, 2017) https://www.uscis.gov/CAM

UNHCR (2012) A Framework for the Protection of Children http://www.unhcr.org/en-us/protection/children/50f6cf0b9/framework-protection-children.html Accessed 10 October, 2017

UNHCR (United Nations High Commissioner on Refugees) (2014) Children on the run:Unaccompanied children leaving Central America and Mexico and in need of international protection http://www.unhcr.org/en-us/about-us/background/56fc266f4/children-on-the-run-full-report.html Accessed 20 October, 2017

UN High Commissioner for Refugees (UNHCR), Guidelines on Policies and Procedures in Dealing with Unaccompanied Children Seeking Asylum, February 1997, available at: http://www.refworld.org/docid/3ae6b3360.html Accessed 11 October 2017

UNHCR Guidelines on International Protection: Child Asylum Claims under Articles 1(A)2 and 1 (F) of the 1951 Convention and/or 1967 Protocol relating to the Status of Refugees, 22 December 2009 at p. 3, point 1 http://www.refworld.org/pdfid/4b2f4f6d2.pdf Accessed 7 October, 2017

UNHCR (United Nations High Commissioner on Refugees) HCR/1P/4/ENG/REV. 3 Handbook and Guidelines on Procedures and Criteria for Determining Refugee Status under the 1951 Convention and the 1967 Protocol Relating to the Status of Refugees (re-issued December, 2011 ed.) http://www.refworld.org/docid/4f33c8d92.html (Accessed 4 October, 2017)

UNHCR Protocol relating to the Status of Refugees entry into force 4 October, 1967 http://www.ohchr.org/Documents/ProfessionalInterest/protocolrefugees.pdf (Accessed 7 November, 2016)

UNHCR Resettlements Submission Categories (n.d.) http://www.unhcr.org/558bff849.pdf Accessed 10 October, 2017

United Nations High Commissioner on Refugees (November, 2016) (UNHCR Asylum Lawyers' Project) UNHCR's Views on Child Asylum Claims: Using international law to support claims from Central American children seeking protection in the US http://www.unhcr.org/582226064.pdf Accessed 10 October, 2017

UNHCR The UN Refugee Agency: FAQ about refugee resettlement (February, 2017) http://www.unhcr.org/en-us/protection/resettlement/4ac0873d6/frequently-asked-questions-resettlement.html Accessed 8 October, 2017

UNHCR Washington (2014) Children on the Run: Unaccompanied children leaving Central America and Mexico and the need for international protection Available at https://resourcecentre.savethechildren.net/library/children-run-unaccompanied-children-leaving-central-america-and-mexico-and-need Accessed 13 October, 2017

United States Refugee Admissions Program (USRAP) Consultation & Worldwide Processing Priorities (Homeland Security). https://www.uscis.gov/humanitarian/refugees-asylum/refugees/united-states-refugee-admissions-program-usrap-consultation-worldwide-processing-priorities (Accessed 23 February, 2017)

U.S Department of State, U.S Department of Homeland Security, U.S. Department of Health and Human Services. Proposed Refugee Admissions for 2014 submitted on behalf of the U.S. President to the Committees on the Judiciary, United States Senate and United States House of Representatives https://www.state.gov/documents/organization/219137.pdf

U.S. Department of State: Expansion of the CAM Program In-Country Refugee Processing for Minors in Honduras, El Salvador and Guatemala (January 20, 2017) https://www.state.gov/j/prm/releases/factsheets/2017/266363.htm Accessed 20 October, 2017

Zapotosky, M (7 September, 2017) (The Washington Post) Grandparents, refugees with formal assurances can enter under Trump travel ban, appeal court rules https://www.washingtonpost.com/world/national-security/grandparents-refugees-with-formal-assurances-can-enter-under-trumps-travel-ban-appeals-court-rules/2017/09/07/d0763ca8-9415-11e7-8754-d478688d23b4_story.html?utm_term=.2b867e415c17 Accessed 17 October, 2017

Cases

AA v [UK] Secretary of State for the Home Department High Court of Justice, Queens Bench (Administrative Court) (Case No: CO/920/2015) [2016] EWHC 1453 (Admin)

Abdullahi Elmi and Aweys Abubakar v Malta, (Application No. 25794/13 and 28151/13) European Court of Human Rights Chamber Judgment 22 November, 2016

Donald J. Trump, President of the United States v International Refugee Assistance Project et al. 582 U. S. ____ (2017) (Supreme Court of the United States, Opinion of June 26, 2017))

Guzman-Heredia v. Gonzales, No. 04-72769 (9th Cir.) Cited in J.E. F.M. v. Lynch United States Federal Court of Appeals for the Ninth District No. 15-35738 and 15-35739 (Decision 20 September, 2016) https://cdn.ca9.uscourts.gov/datastore/opinions/2016/09/20/15-35738.pdf Accessed 10 October, 2017

Henriquez-Rivas v. Holder, 707 F.3d 1081 (9th Circ. 2013) (en banc)

J.E. F.M. v. Lynch (U.S. Attorney General) United States Federal Court of Appeals for the Ninth District No. 15-35738 and 15-35739 (Decision 20 September, 2016) https://cdn.ca9.uscourts.gov/datastore/opinions/2016/09/20/15-35738.pdf Accessed 10 October, 2017

McNary v. Haitian Refugee Center, Inc., 498 U.S. 479 (1991)

State of Hawaii, Ismail Elshikh, John Does 1&2 and Muslim Association of Hawaii, Inc. v Donald J Trump in his official capacity as President et al. In the U.S. District Court for the District of Hawaii, 'Joint Declaration of Former National Security Officials' (15 October, 2017) Available at https://www.hoganlovells.com/publications/documents-in-state-of-hawaii-et-al-v-trump-a-challenge-to-president-trumps-march-6-2017-travel-ban Accessed 19 October, 2017

State of Hawaii; Ishmail Elshikh v Donald J Trump et al (7 September, 2017) United States Court of Appeal for the Ninth Circuit http://cdn.ca9.uscourts.gov/datastore/general/2017/09/07/17-16426%20Opinion%20Filed.pdf Accessed 17 October, 2017

United States v Aguilar 883 F.2d 662 (U.S. Court of Appeals Ninth Circuit) Decided March 30, 1989. As amended on Denial of Rehearing and Rehearing En Banc April 14, 1989 http://openjurist.org/883/f2d/662/united-states-v-aguilar (accessed 25 June, 2017)

Chapter 6
In Defence of Non-Refoulement

6.1 Introduction

The misleading and overbroad notion is widespread that there is no right of asylum of the individual set out in the Refugee Convention but rather that the right of asylum is instead purely a State discretionary prerogative. That over-simplistic perspective further seems to be premised on an erroneous view of the refugee asylum seeker[1] as 'the other' in the sense also of being a person beyond the sovereign protective jurisdiction of *any* State but for the *discretionary* decision of a particular State to exercise its authority and control over the asylum seeker and possibly grant asylum. Yet, as the analysis here (it is contended) illustrates in respectful opposition to the holding of the European Court of Justice Grand Chamber in *X and X v. Belgium*[2]; the asylum seeker is *not* beyond the protective aspect of democratically based national or regional law. Under law that is grounded in democratic values, which law is inevitably and inextricably bound with respect for fundamental human rights, an absence of a positive 'duty to protect' (purportedly flowing from, for instance, the *ostensible* declining by a prospective asylum State of jurisdiction over an asylum request) is, on the view here, but a 'legal fiction' where refoulement would be the practical effect. It is, however, a legal fiction that when adopted and applied to actual decision-making generally has tragic consequences for refugees seeking and in dire need of asylum.

There is no possible legally supportable bar, it is here argued, under international, regional or national law which is founded on democratic human rights principles to

[1]The reference here is to the asylum seeker fleeing persecution who may or may not be stateless and who may or may not as yet be a declared refugee (an officially recognized refugee under the Refugee Convention or a person recognized as in need of international protection under some complementary international protection framework).

[2]European Court of Justice (Grand Chamber Judgment) Reference for a Preliminary Ruling (7 March, 2017) (Case No. C-638-16) X and X v. Belgium Available at http://curia.europa.eu Accessed 22 October, 2017.

© Springer International Publishing AG, part of Springer Nature 2018
S. C. Grover, *Child Refugee Asylum as a Basic Human Right*,
https://doi.org/10.1007/978-3-319-78013-9_6

the asylum seeker accessing *a particular* territory to seek asylum where that is the only practical option. Nor is there any possibility of the State under any democratically grounded legal framework to effect an actual declining of jurisdiction to consider the asylum application of a *prima facie* declared or undeclared refugee where shunting the application to a third country would constitute an abuse of the asylum seeker's basic human rights. Nor is there a legally supportable possibility for the prospective asylum State to absolve itself of the non-refoulement obligation by violating the principle either directly or through extra-territorial or any other indirect measures.

It is here contended that the right to international protection is a basic human right of the individual-that is of the *bona fide* (declared or undeclared) refugee asylum seeker fleeing persecution—as is also affirmed in the Refugee Convention. Thus while no *particular* State itself is required to provide a "durable solution" to the *bona fide* refugee's search for international protection,[3] at the same time, no State is free from accountability nor immune from the non-refoulement obligation in the interim when the asylum seeker makes the request to *that* State for protection:

> The principle of non-refoulement as provided for in Article 33(1) of the 1951 Convention does not, as such, entail a right of the individual to be granted asylum ***in a particular State.*** *It does mean, however, that where States are not prepared to grant asylum* to persons who are seeking international protection on their territory, *they must adopt a course that does not result in their removal, directly or indirectly, to a place where their lives or freedom would be in danger on account of their race, religion, nationality, membership of a particular social group or political opinion* (emphasis added).[4]

> As a general rule, in order to give effect to their obligations under the 1951 Convention and/or 1967 Protocol, ***States will be required to grant individuals seeking international protection access to the territory and to fair and efficient asylum procedures*** (emphasis added).[5]

Non-refoulement (from which there can be no derogation by the particular State to which a direct asylum request is made nor by any other State serving as a proxy to the first to accomplish refoulement) thus *in effect* morphs into (1) the right of the individual to asylum in the interim in humane conditions and (2) in principle at least; the right to a more durable protection solution (to be provided by a willing State) tabled but as an imperative. Hence the asylum seeker's basic human rights are the 'red line' between on the one hand a prospective asylum State's 'margin of appreciation', if any and in any respect, in regards to an asylum request on the particular fact pattern and on the other its humanitarian obligation under democratically based

---

[3]Compare Gowlland-Debbas (1994), p. 3.

[4]United Nations High Commissioner on Refugees (UNHCR) Advisory Opinion on the Extraterritorial Application of Non-Refoulement Obligations under the 1951 Convention relating to the Status of Refugees and its 1967 Protocol (26 January, 2007) at point 8, p. 3.

[5]United Nations High Commissioner on Refugees (UNHCR) Advisory Opinion on the Extraterritorial Application of Non-Refoulement Obligations under the 1951 Convention relating to the Status of Refugees and its 1967 Protocol (26 January, 2007 point 8).

law (at the international, national and/or regional level) to *ensure* non-refoulement does not occur by any means:

> . . .the principle of non-refoulement applies not only to recognized refugees, but also to those who have not had their status formally declared. ***The principle of non-refoulement is of particular relevance to asylum-seekers***. As such persons may be refugees, it is an established principle of international refugee law that they should not be returned or expelled pending a final determination of their status (emphasis added).[6]

It is here contended that the State exercises its authority and control over an asylum seeker and is making jurisdictional decisions both when it (1) declines to consider the asylum application on some ground (attempting thus to decline jurisdiction) or accepts jurisdiction and denies the request for asylum as not meeting eligibility requirements and (2) when it does the converse and accepts the request as *bona fide*. In both instances the State has, in large part, effective control over the asylum seeker's fate (given the State's handling of the asylum request) in terms of the potential created, if any, for continuation of significant risk to the refugee's life, liberty and/ or 'security of the person' more broadly:

> ***In determining whether a State's human rights obligations with respect to a particular person are engaged, the decisive criterion is*** not whether that person is on the State's national territory, or within a territory which is *de jure* under the sovereign control of the State, but rather ***whether or not he or she is subject to that State's effective authority and control*** (emphasis added).[7]

The current author thus holds that State 'pushback' and extraterritorial refugee migration control measures[8] (such as the denial of humanitarian visas) cannot eliminate the State's jurisdiction over those asylum seekers blocked by these means (blocked in terms of their search for international protection) nor remove the obligations that flow from such jurisdiction under both international refugee and human rights law where there is a risk of refoulement. In the case to be discussed next; the attempt is (on the analysis s here) by Belgium to use the European regional level Visa Code to attempt *in effect to 'decline jurisdiction' in enforcing non-refoulement* when an asylum request is made at Belgium's embassy located

---

[6]United Nations High Commissioner on Refugees (UNHCR) Advisory Opinion on the Extraterritorial Application of Non-Refoulement Obligations under the 1951 Convention relating to the Status of Refugees and its 1967 Protocol (26 January, 2007 point 6).

[7]UNHCR Advisory Opinion on the Extraterritorial Application of Non-Refoulement Obligations under the 1951 Convention relating to the Status of Refugees and its 1967 Protocol, point 35 at p. 16.

[8]Pushback measures can involve refoulement of asylum seekers irregularly arrived near or at the border or of those who have irregularly entered the State interior territory i.e. often through expedited removal without a hearing or fast tracked removal with a hearing without the full procedural safeguards of due process to an unsafe homeland or third country etc. The Trump travel ban (ostensibly temporary) previously here discussed is a blanket extraterritorial control measure targeting refugees who had not yet received final entry and travel papers through the US resettlement program by a set date and banning also entry by certain foreign nationals abroad more generally based on specific nationality. The decision regarding entry under the Trump travel is thus not based on the merits or demerits of individual applications for entry documents.

outside the main (homeland) territory of Belgium in a third country. As will be discussed; this author contends that since there is no derogation of the non-refoulement principle (which principle is widely agreed by legal scholars and practitioners of international law to be part of customary and *jus cogens* law as well as certain treaty law); it is, as a necessary corollary, *ultra vires* of the exercise of State sovereignty for the State to decline to substantively and fairly consider asylum requests to determine the *bona fides* of the asylum claim where doing so may result in refoulement. The latter applies, it is here contended, whether the asylum request was made to the State through access to the State's embassy located in a third country or at the border of the prospective asylum State or after entering into that State's territory proper. Hence, on the analysis here, the prospective asylum State cannot in practice lawfully decline its jurisdiction over the refugee asylum seeker (a third part national) who is metaphorically 'knocking at the door' while standing on that State's homeland main territory or while he/she is standing on that State's circumscribed territory at an embassy located within a third country.[9] This author's view then differs from that of Gowlland-Debbas' perspective reflected below (for instance as to the last line of the excerpt). The current author holds that once jurisdiction is exercised through, for instance, denial of a humanitarian visa to a third-country national seeking asylum; non-refoulement obligations flow and there is therefore no possibility of declining jurisdiction over and accountability for the asylum seeker's fate:

> It is indeed ironical at a time when it has become fashionable to speak of the withering away or erosion of State sovereignty that we are witnessing a reinforcement of that last bastion of State sovereignty which is the right to decide who to admit and who to expel. This is reflected in the way States are establishing defence of their borders in areas outside or increasingly remote from these borders - for instance through interdiction at sea, control at foreign airport departure points by means of visa requirements and sanctions on carriers, and the creation of international airport zones - ***in other words asserting jurisdiction in order to deny jurisdiction and the obligations which flow from*** **it** (emphasis added)[10]

Let us then turn now to consideration of *X and X v Belgium*[11] as a recent illustration (on the view here) of a European State attempting to legally justify shirking its obligations under the Refugee Convention to allow asylum seekers to seek asylum including its obligation to not engage in refoulement in any form.

[9]Should a State allow humanitarian visas to be issued to asylum seekers through its embassy located in a third country (outside its own territory and also outside the asylum seeker's home State) that would *not* constitute extraterritorial processing of an asylum application. This since the embassy located in that third State is as an embassy the designated territory of the State granting that asylum and not that of the third State hosting the embassy.

[10]See Gowlland-Debbas (1994), pp. 3–4.

[11]*X and X v. Belgium* European Court of Justice (Grand Chamber Judgment) Reference for a Preliminary Ruling (7 March, 2017) (Case No. C-638-16).

6.2 Case 1: Reconsidering the Judgment in X and X *v.* Belgium (European Court of Justice, Grand Chamber Judgment)

6.2.1 The Facts

Asylum seekers commonly have no legal way to enter European territory to lodge an asylum request and hence desperate "protection seekers are left with very few choices but to embark upon dangerous, irregular and undignified journeys entailing high human risks and costs."[12] This as EU member States will consider an asylum request only once the asylum seeker "arrives on the territory of a Member State, including at the border or in the transit zones of that Member State."[13] Humanitarian visas, in contrast, would allow the asylum seekers to access the prospective European asylum country through its diplomatic missions located outside the State's territory proper and where the third country national may have access. If the prospective State issues the humanitarian visa the asylum seeker can travel safely and legally to that State's main territory and apply for asylum.[14] The latter was the objective of the complainants in the following case.

This case concerns a married couple and their three young children as asylum seekers. The family was living in Aleppo Syria. On October 12, 2016 the family attended at the Belgium embassy in Beirut Lebanon and requested humanitarian visas for the family members and returned to Syria the next day. The request for the humanitarian visas was made on the basis of Article 25(1)(a) of the European Visa Code which allows in exceptional cases a visa with limited territorial validity (one that expires after a certain short period) to be issued where "the Member State concerned *considers* it necessary on *humanitarian grounds*, for reasons of national interest or *because of international obligations* to derogate from the principle that the entry conditions ...by Regulation ...of the European Parliament and of the Council 15 March 2016 establishing a Community Code on the rules governing movement of persons across borders must be fulfilled. ..." (emphasis added).[15] The parents communicated to the embassy representatives of the State (Belgium) that their intention was to travel to Belgium on the humanitarian visas and there to file a request for asylum and for a residence permit. They provided at least three bases for a well-grounded fear of persecution should they be forced to stay in Syria: they were Orthodox Christians and faced the risk of religious persecution; the husband had been tortured by terrorists in Aleppo and then released after payment of a ransom, and the situation in Aleppo from a human rights and humanitarian perspective was

[12]Jensen (2014), p. 4.

[13]Jensen (2014), p. 3.

[14]Jensen (2014).

[15]European Visa Code Article 25(1) Cited in *X and X v. Belgium* European Court of Justice (Grand Chamber Judgment) Reference for a Preliminary Ruling (7 March, 2017) (Case No. C-638-16).

fast deteriorating further. Belgium's immigration office communicated its denial of the humanitarian visa requests on 25 October, 2016. Belgium's decision was, according to Belgium, *purportedly* properly supported on three grounds: the family would be travelling on a limited duration visa of 90 days but actually intended to stay in Belgium over the 90 days (given the intention to apply for asylum and a residence permit once arrived in Belgium); the EU member States are *allegedly* not obligated under Article 3 of the European Convention on Human Rights (the prohibition against torture, inhuman or degrading treatment or punishment) to admit persons who are 'victims of a catastrophic situation" and diplomatic posts are allegedly not an authority of the State to which a foreign national could properly submit an application for asylum. While the Belgian government acknowledged that the applicants for asylum in this case were in a situation of need for humanitarian assistance, the government nevertheless denied the humanitarian visas holding Belgium had no obligation to issue the visa under Article 3 of the ECHR or Article 33 of the Refugee Convention. The Applicants argued in the referring court proceedings that their situation triggered the Article 18 right to asylum provision in the European Charter. Further they maintained that (1) only if they were granted humanitarian visas (and hence the opportunity to travel to Belgium and there apply for asylum and a residence permit) would they not become victims of torture and/or inhuman or degrading treatment or punishment in Syria and that (2) denial of the humanitarian visas for the family would be a violation of Article 3 of the European Convention on Human Rights and Article 4 of the European Charter.

6.2.2 Commentary on X and X v. *Belgium (European Court of Justice, Grand Chamber Judgment)*

Belgium held that neither the prohibition against torture, inhuman or degrading treatment or punishment (Article 3 ECHR) nor the Geneva Convention prohibition of refoulement (Article 33) obligated the State to admit these third-country nationals as asylum seekers to its territory. Belgium maintained that its non-refoulement obligation is met if it does not deport asylum seekers from its territory to meet a fate of persecution. Even setting aside that an embassy of the Belgian State is Belgian territory; the Belgian government position is in any case contrary to UNHCR guidance and interpretation of Article 33 of the Refugee Convention. Belgium, contrary to the UNHCR guidelines regarding interpretation and application of the Refugee Convention Article 33, did not accept the notion in the case at bar that refoulement occurs and is barred whether carried out through deportation from the State territory to an unsafe homeland or unsafe third country State or return is effected through extraterritorial or other means:

> 26. ***The obligation set out in Article 33(1) of the 1951 Convention is subject to a geographic restriction only with regard to the country where a refugee may not be sent to, not the place where he or she is sent from The extraterritorial applicability of the non-refoulement obligation under Article 33(1) is clear*** from the text of the provision itself,

> which states a simple prohibition: "No Contracting State shall expel or return ("refouler") a refugee in any manner whatsoever to the frontiers of territories where his [or her] life or freedom would be threatened..." (emphasis added).[16]
>
> 27... *The ordinary meaning of the terms "return" and "refouler" does* ***not*** *support an interpretation which would restrict its scope to conduct within the territory of the State concerned,* nor is there any indication that these terms were understood by the drafters of the 1951 Convention to be limited in this way (emphasis added).[17]
>
> 29. Furthermore, any interpretation which construes the scope of Article 33(1) of the 1951 Convention as not extending to measures whereby a State, acting outside its territory, returns or otherwise transfers refugees to a country where they are at risk of persecution would be fundamentally ***inconsistent*** with the humanitarian object and purpose of the 1951 Convention and its 1967 Protocol (emphasis added).[18]

On the view here the denial of the humanitarian visas to this Syrian family constituted refoulement in that Belgium had assumed jurisdiction (notwithstanding that the humanitarian visas were ultimately denied) by addressing/processing the visa request. The referring Court had in fact posed the question to the European Court of Justice also of "whether the implementation of the [EU] visa policy may be regarded as the exercise of jurisdiction in that sense". The referring Court opined that if Belgium *had* assumed jurisdiction by implementation of the EU common Visa Code; the asylum seekers in the case at bar could rely on Article 3 of the European Convention on Human Rights (the prohibition against torture and inhuman or degrading treatment or punishment) as establishing a right of entry as a preventative measure and as a corollary also then there would be application to the case of Article 33 of the Geneva Convention regarding non-refoulement.

The referring Court opined that Article 25 of the EU Visa Code rendered it compulsory that a humanitarian visa be issued when the State "***considers*** it necessary because of ...international obligations." The referring court requested, however, clarification from the ECJ (European Court of Justice) as to whether there is in fact any State discretion regarding issuing or not issuing humanitarian visas given that the exceptions to the EU Visa Code territorial entry requirements can be made (according to the text of the Code) based on whether or not the State "considers" international legal obligations to exist relating to the facts of a specific case which allow for an exception in that case to the normal application of the Visa Code. The wording of Article 25 of the Code then was somewhat ambiguous in the view of the

---

[16]See United Nations High Commissioner on Refugees (UNHCR) Advisory Opinion on the Extraterritorial Application of Non-Refoulement Obligations under the 1951 Convention relating to the Status of Refugees and its 1967 Protocol (26 January, 2007) at point 26, p. 12.

[17]See United Nations High Commissioner on Refugees (UNHCR) Advisory Opinion on the Extraterritorial Application of Non-Refoulement Obligations under the 1951 Convention relating to the Status of Refugees and its 1967 Protocol (26 January, 2007) at point 27, p. 13.

[18]See United Nations High Commissioner on Refugees (UNHCR) Advisory Opinion on the Extraterritorial Application of Non-Refoulement Obligations under the 1951 Convention relating to the Status of Refugees and its 1967 Protocol (26 January, 2007) at point 29, p. 14.

referring court on the issue of State discretion, if any, in the issuing of the humanitarian visas.

The European Court of Justice (ECJ) engaged in its analysis of the issues in the case at bar (on the respectful view here) largely in some tautological circular reasoning with little if any support in international human rights or refugee law. The ECJ held that since Article 1 of the Visa Code set out the objectives of the uniform EU Visa Code as being that of allowing for transit through or intended stay on the territory of an EU State member of a duration of not more than a 90 or 180 day period; the limited territorial visa applications of the Syrian asylum seekers in the case at bar fell outside the scope of the Visa Code "in particular with respect to Article 25(1)(a)" of the Code and *notwithstanding* that the applications were "formally submitted on the basis of Article 25 of the code" (Article 25 permitting exceptions to be made re EU entry requirements and allowing for visas to be issued for instance on humanitarian grounds and/or to meet international obligations). The current author holds, however, that Article 1 of the EU Visa Code must be read in the context of the entire Code including Article 25. This since if Article 25 were not to be regarded as a qualifier in interpretation of Article 1, Article 25 would have no purpose and effect and would not have been included in the Visa Code in the first instance. Further the text of Article 25 directly speaks to the view advanced here that humanitarian considerations and international obligations require in *bona fide* cases "derogation" from the normal entry requirements to be met under the Code before a limited term territorial visa can be issued. Further this author holds that humanitarian considerations and international human rights obligations arising either exist as an objective factual matter or they do not. The EU State member cannot then, on the respectful view here, evade those obligations where they exist (arising from the factual circumstances of the humanitarian visa applicant) through an alleged right of *discretionary application* of Article 25 of the Code rationalized on the basis of whether the State member "considers" there is an international obligation in a particular case that compels issuance of a humanitarian visa.

Let us consider also the EU directive re issuance of humanitarian limited term territorial visas. That directive stipulates that 'derogations' from entry requirements on, for instance, humanitarian grounds or the need to fulfill international obligations does *not* obtain in cases where the application for territorial asylum/humanitarian visas was made to representatives of the member State (i.e. at an embassy of the Member State which embassy or consular office is located in a third country). That directive, on the analysis here, represents a vehicle for denial of the right to seek asylum and, depending on the facts of the case, a potential mechanism also of refoulement in violation of international human rights[19] and refugee law. The

---

[19]See Suresh *v.* Canada (Minister of Citizenship and Immigration), [2002] 1 S.C.R. 3, 2002 SCC 1. This Supreme Court of Canada ruling affirms that refoulement (deportation where the individual could face torture and/or inhuman or degrading treatment or punishment is a violation also of the ICCPR "Deportation to torture is prohibited by both the *International Covenant on Civil and Political Rights* [ICCPR] and the *Convention against Torture and other Cruel, Inhuman or Degrading Treatment or Punishment*... International law generally rejects deportation to torture, even where national security interests are at stake."

directive itself, on the respectful view here, thus cannot be considered lawful given EU obligations under refugee treaty law and international and national human rights law.

It is here contended, in addition, that Belgium could not lawfully decline its non-refoulement obligations as it arguably did in the case at bar as those obligations are part of customary and *jus cogens* law from which there is no permissible derogation. The applications for the humanitarian visas then in this case at bar were *not* just a matter of application of Belgium national law not informed by international human rights and refugee law or so informed in extent or at all on a discretionary basis by Belgium (as the European Court of Justice seems to imply[20]). This as both the EU Visa Code and Belgium national law cannot (on the view here) be properly interpreted and applied in a manner that it is inconsistent with *jus cogens* law (such as the non-refoulement principle of the relevant Geneva Convention which embodies respect for the fundamental human rights of asylum applicants):

> 34. . . .*Article 33(1), which embodies the humanitarian essence of the 1951 Convention and safeguards fundamental rights of refugees, must be interpreted in a manner which is consistent with developments in international human rights law.* An analysis of the scope ratione loci of States' non-refoulement obligations under international human rights law is particularly pertinent to the question of the extraterritorial applicability of the prohibition on returning a refugee to a danger of persecution under international refugee instruments (emphasis added).[21]

Hence, on the analysis here, the fact that the EU had not set out measures or procedures covering issuance of *long-term visa* and residence permits to third-country nationals does *not* establish that there was no obligation to issue a *limited territorial stay* visa in the case at bar given the non-refoulement duty implicated in the case. The European Court of Justice (ECJ) appeared to fear that ruling in favour of the applicants in this case at bar would "be tantamount to allowing third-country nationals to lodge applications for visas on the basis of the Visa Code in order to *obtain international protection in the Member State of their choice* which would undermine the general structure of the system established"(emphasis added).[22] However, *in effect*, the ECJ ruling held as lawful under the EU Visa Code the denial to third-country nationals of humanitarian visas generally (with this case of Belgium

[20] *X and X v. Belgium* European Court of Justice (Grand Chamber Judgment) Reference for a Preliminary Ruling (7 March, 2017) (Case No. C-638-16) Available at http://curia.europa.eu Accessed 22 October, 2017:

> . . .since . . .no measure has been adopted, to date, by the EU legislature . . .with regard to the conditions governing the issue by Member States of long-term visas and residence permits to third- country nationals on humanitarian grounds, the applications at issue in the main proceedings fall solely within the scope of national law

[21] See United Nations High Commissioner on Refugees (UNHCR) Advisory Opinion on the Extraterritorial Application of Non-Refoulement Obligations under the 1951 Convention relating to the Status of Refugees and its 1967 Protocol (26 January, 2007) point 34, at p. 16.

[22] *X and X v. Belgium* European Court of Justice (Grand Chamber Judgment) Reference for a Preliminary Ruling (7 March, 2017) (Case No. C-638-16).

being but a test case) and not in regard to any particular territory as a prospective asylum territory. The ECJ, for instance, did *not* suggest that Belgium had an obligation (given the non-refoulement issue in the case) to make arrangements with another EU State to issue humanitarian visas to the family of asylum seekers in the case at bar (since Belgium was unwilling to issue the visas) thus permitting access to *that* State's territory in anticipation of an asylum claim being filed by the visa holders once they reached that alternate EU State. On the view here the reality is that it is not an issue of the third-country nationals seeking to obtain a humanitarian visa from the country of their choice through an embassy located outside that EU Member State territory proper. Rather the issue is that no EU member State is prepared to issue such humanitarian visas, it would appear, outside its territory proper. If it were the case that some EU countries did issue humanitarian visas then the application for the visa could be *transferred* to one of those (which might be, for instance, the safe country of first entry)[23] where and if the latter is held to be the responsible State member for the case. Hence, with respect, it would appear to be somewhat irrelevant and misleading that the ECJ raised the spectre of asylum seekers being purportedly able to select the EU member of their choice in issuance of a humanitarian visa should third-country nationals be able to obtain such visas through embassies or consular offices located outside the territory proper of an EU Member.

Respectfully, on the view here, the central issue, in the final analysis, is whether the EU member States have a *mandatory* obligation to issue humanitarian visas where there is a risk of refoulement. On this author's analysis; the ECJ through its restrictive interpretation of the common EU Visa Code, an interpretation that arguably was not adequately informed by international refugee and human rights law, preserved the EU State members' alleged discretion in the issuing of humanitarian visas. This even where the State member appeared, *in effect*, to accept that the denial of the visas in the case in question would result in constructive refoulement (i.e. here Belgium acknowledged the humanitarian crisis in Syria at the time the asylum applicants in the case at bar requested humanitarian visas via the Belgian embassy in Beirut). The ECJ held essentially that it was led to its conclusions since the purpose of the short term visas requested in the case at bar was to provide the applicants the opportunity to file asylum applications in Belgium once they arrived on that territory having travelled there on humanitarian visas. The ECJ opined that were the ECJ to have ruled other than it did, in the view of the ECJ, this "would mean that Member States *are required*, on the basis of the Visa Code, de facto to allow third-country nationals to submit applications for international protection to the representations of Member States that are within the territory of a third

[23]For instance see European Court of Justice (Grand Chamber) (26 July, 2017) Referral for a Preliminary Ruling Case Khadija Jafari and Zainab Jafari v Bundesamt für Fremdenwesen und Asyl. Case No. C-646/16 "Determination of the Member State responsible for examining an application for international protection lodged in one of the Member States by a third-country national" http://www.refworld.org/cases,ECJ,598dc9d14.html Accessed 24 October, 2017.

country"(emphasis added).[24] The ECJ thus appears to have worked backwards from the objective of removing any such obligation rather than considering whether that result (allowing third-country nationals access to humanitarian visas through accessible means (filing a humanitarian visa request to representations of the prospective asylum State located in a third country) was supportable under the EU Visa Code properly informed by EU Member international law obligations.

The ECJ held that the matter fell under national law and not under the Visa Code as, according to the ECJ, issuing a short-term visa under the facts of the case was beyond the scope of the EU Visa Code. Presumably the ECJ opined that the national law could provide the discretion to issue third country nationals humanitarian visas under circumstances such as described in the case at bar while the EU Visa Code could not permit the issuing of the visas in the context described. However, note that Article 25 of the EU Visa Code refers also to issuing humanitarian visas based on national interest. It is here maintained that it is in every EU member's national interest to uphold basic international law principles such as non-refoulement and which in this case, on the facts, it is here argued, required the issuing of humanitarian visas.

While the ECJ held that Belgium was wrong to refer to the visas requested as short-term visas, the current author holds they were short-term visas. Once the asylum seekers had filed their asylum applications *in Belgium*; only then would their legal status *at that point* be changed to persons being officially and formally considered for asylum with leave to stay pending the outcome of that consideration and of the request for a residence permit. On the view here, there is nothing in the EU Visa Code consistent with international human rights and refugee law that does or could explicitly bar issuance of a short-term visa on the basis of blocking the search for asylum but there is a bar to denial of a humanitarian visa for the purpose *in effect* of refoulement.

It is to be noted also that in this case at bar and other such cases; children are often amongst the asylum seekers as part of a family travelling together or as unaccompanied or separated children in search of asylum.[25] To deny humanitarian visas to the children (along with their parents) in circumstances analogous to those in *X and X v Belgium*[26] is to consign generations to oppression and suppression for the foreseeable future and for a time of indeterminate end in most instances. For democratic States to contribute to creating 'lost generations' through various

---

[24]European Court of Justice (Grand Chamber Judgment) Reference for a Preliminary Ruling (7 March, 2017) (Case No. C-638-16) X and X v. Belgium Available at http://curia.europa.eu Accessed 22 October, 2017.

[25]Germany has admitted over one million asylum seekers since 2015 including over 65,000 unaccompanied minors See Reuters 19 October, 2017 'Refugees in Germany: Fewer family reunifications than expected. says study' http://www.dw.com/en/refugees-in-germany-fewer-family-reunifications-than-expected-says-study/a-41043907.

[26]European Court of Justice (Grand Chamber Judgment) Reference for a Preliminary Ruling (7 March, 2017) (Case No. C-638-16) X and X v. Belgium Available at http://curia.europa.eu Accessed 22 October, 2017.

modes of refoulement masquerading as something else; and as purportedly consistent with international rule of law based on democratic values is to add exponentially to the global refugee crisis tragedy and to weaken the international legal framework overall. We are all accountable to the extent that we do not challenge[27] State refoulement in whatever form and context it occurs and for diminishing our own humanity in the process.

Literature, Materials and Cases

Literature

Gowlland-Debbas V (ed) (1994) The problem of refugees in the light of contemporary international law issues. Papers presented at the Colloquium organized by the Graduate Institute of International Studies in collaboration with the Office of the United Nations High Commissioner for Refugees, Geneva, 26–27 May, 1994. p 3. http://www.unhcr.org/4ca348026.pdf. Accessed 22 Oct 2017

Jensen UI (2014) Humanitarian Visas: option or obligation? EEPS Paper No. 68. Available https://www.ceps.eu/publications/humanitarian-visas-option-or-obligation. Accessed 22 Oct 2017

Materials

Communiqué (14 February, 2017) titled 'The Situation in Nauru and Manus Island:Liability for crimes against humanity in the detention of refugees and asylum seekers' submitted by Stanford University's International Human Rights and Conflict Resolution Clinic to the ICC Prosecutor Available at https://law.stanford.edu/publications/communique-to-the-office-of-the-prosecutor-of-the-international-criminal-court-under-article-15-of-the-rome-statute-the-situation-in-nauru-and-manus-island-liability-for-crimes-against-humanity/ Accessed 24 October, 2017

United Nations High Commissioner on Refugees (UNHCR) Advisory Opinion on the Extraterritorial Application of Non-Refoulement Obligations under the 1951 Convention relating to the Status of Refugees and its 1967 Protocol (26 January, 2007) http://www.unhcr.org/4d9486929.pdf Accessed 22 October, 2017)

[27] See for instance the Communiqué (14 February, 2017) titled 'The Situation in Nauru and Manus Island:Liability for crimes against humanity in the detention of refugees and asylum seekers' submitted by Stanford University's International Human Rights and Conflict Resolution Clinic to the ICC Prosecutor Available at https://law.stanford.edu/publications/communique-to-the-office-of-the-prosecutor-of-the-international-criminal-court-under-article-15-of-the-rome-statute-the-situation-in-nauru-and-manus-island-liability-for-crimes-against-humanity/ Accessed 24 October, 2017.

Cases

European Court of Justice (Grand Chamber) (26 July, 2017) Referral for a Preliminary Ruling Case Khadija Jafari and Zainab Jafari v Bundesamt für Fremdenwesen und Asyl. Case No. C-646/16 "Determination of the Member State responsible for examining an application for international protection lodged in one of the Member States by a third-country national" http://www.refworld.org/cases,ECJ,598dc9d14.html Accessed 24 October, 2017

European Court of Justice (Grand Chamber Judgment) Reference for a Preliminary Ruling (7 March, 2017) (Case No. C-638-16) *X and X v. Belgium* Available at http://curia.europa.eu Accessed 22 October, 2017

Suresh *v*. Canada (Minister of Citizenship and Immigration), [2002] 1 S.C.R. 3, 2002 SCC 1

Index

© Springer International Publishing AG, part of Springer Nature 2018

S. C. Grover, *Child Refugee Asylum as a Basic Human Right*,
https://doi.org/10.1007/978-3-319-78013-9

D

The manufacturer's authorised representative in the EU is Springer Nature Customer Service Centre GmbH, Europaplatz 3, 69115 Heidelberg, Germany. If you have any concerns regarding our products, please contact ProductSafety@springernature.com

Printed and bound by CPI Group (UK) Ltd, Croydon, CR0 4YY

30/09/2026

02225195-0016